The Keys
to the Kingdom

JEFF SHEAR

The Keys to the Kingdom

The FS-X Deal and the Selling of America's Future to Japan

DOUBLEDAY

New York   London   Toronto   Sydney   Auckland

PUBLISHED BY DOUBLEDAY
a division of Bantam Doubleday Dell Publishing Group, Inc.
1540 Broadway, New York, New York 10036

DOUBLEDAY and the portrayal of an anchor with a dolphin are
trademarks of Doubleday, a division of Bantam Doubleday Dell
Publishing Group, Inc.

Library of Congress Cataloging-in-Publication Data
Shear, Jeff.
The keys to the kingdom: the FS-X deal and the selling of
America's future to Japan/Jeff Shear.
p.   cm.
1. Technology transfer—Government policy—United States. 2. FS-X
(Jet fighter plane) 3. Aircraft industry—United States—
Technological innovations. 4. Aircraft industry—Japan. 5. United
States—Foreign economic relations—Japan. 6. Japan—Foreign
economic relations—United States. I. Title.
HC110.T4S53   1994
338.9'173052—dc20   93-47228
CIP

ISBN 0-385-47353-2

To my wife, Bonnie, and my daughter, Zoë

Contents

Prologue: February 24, 1989   ix
Introduction   xiii

Book One   THE DEAL

1   Rebuilding the Future: 1980   3
2   Zero-Sum Game   11
3   Congress Stirs   18
4   The Little State Department in the Pentagon   28
5   American Desires   37
6   An Airport Theory of Nations   48
7   The Sound of One Shoe Dropping   57
8   A D-Day in December   67
9   Sounding the Alarm   76
10   Dondi at the Boei-cho   87
11   The Silence of the Subs   95
12   June 1987: The Power Play   104
13   A Beauty Contest   113
14   Kurihara's Choice   123

Book Two   THE FIGHT

15   Mutiny in a Hot Tub   135
16   A Coup for Congress   143
17   The Sound of One Hand Washing the Other   151
18   The Grandfather Clause   160

19   The Baker Gambit   171
20   A Shot Across the Bow   181
21   The President's Best Friend   193
22   Japanic   203
23   A Consumer Revolt   211
24   Dirty Dancing   220
25   Air Force Won   229
26   The Mountain and the Mouse   240
27   The Center Holds   250
28   Power Shift   261
29   A Single Vote   270
30   The Test of Time   278

Notes   287
Index   309

Prologue:
February 24, 1989

IN THE DARK DEEP MOAT that guarded the sacred grounds of the Imperial Palace, the overfed carp swam aimlessly, like torpedoes that have missed their mark. Cold pellets of rain raked the waters of the swarthy channel, and the wet black boulders of the steep palace walls loomed forbiddingly against the silent throng below. The Emperor of Japan was dead. His mourners, nearly 300,000 strong, stood in a somber mass in the icy rain.

At the state ceremonies held at the 148-acre Shinjuku Gyoen Imperial Gardens, an unprecedented 10,000 official mourners from 164 nations were present. "Never before in the 20th century," wrote *Time* magazine, "had such a large and distinguished assemblage of dignitaries convened for a funeral." Chief among these luminaries was the American President, George Bush, a man who had almost died fighting the Imperial forces of Hirohito forty-four years earlier.

Hirohito's death coincided with a momentous shift in Japanese-American cooperation. The roles that had defined the relationship between the United States and Japan since August 1945—conqueror and vanquished, protector and ward, patron and loyal ally—were no longer clearly delineated, irrevocably altered by the emergence of Japan as an economic superpower. Indeed, the President had not come to Tokyo merely to attend the funeral of the Emperor; he had business to discuss, a deal that had negotiators on both sides wondering whether Japan was America's strongest ally or its most formidable competitor. Bush's presence signaled the passing not only of a man but of an era.

Taken from his seventeen-year-old mother when he was three months old, the late Emperor had been allowed no friends and no games when growing up. His marriage was arranged. His own children were reared in separate residences. None could look directly upon him. Raised to be a god, he died as a mortal at age eighty-seven, from a stomach cancer that his doctors never revealed to him.

When the fifty-one pallbearers hoisted Hirohito's 1.5-ton coffin and palanquin toward its final resting place, Japanese mourners lowered their umbrellas out of respect, baring their bowed heads to the pelting storm. As the funeral cortege inched slowly forward, flutes were heard, filling the sodden air with a gentle dirge of lamentation. Shinto priests made their offerings: silk brocade, rice, twenty quail, three lotus roots, bream, and other sacramental objects. Hirohito's reign had been named Showa, meaning "enlightened peace." Now the Emperor Showa was buried with his sword, ceremonial shoes, spectacles, and several of the books he had written on marine biology; the god's mortal pursuit was jellyfish.

Hirohito was said to have been the 124th Emperor in an unbroken 2,600-year-old dynastic line. Almost a fifth of the Japanese people still regarded the Emperor as their deity.

The Emperor Showa's successor, Crown Prince Akihito, was a different kind of man, a modern Japanese. One waggish Japan scholar called him "the first salaryman Emperor," a businessman of a god. Unlike any of his predecessors, he began his education under an American tutor, a Quaker woman named Elizabeth Vining, who taught him: "Think for yourself, live like a regular person." Akihito grew up and married a commoner, for love. He sent his eldest son, the crown prince, to study at Oxford, where the young man kept a pinup of Brooke Shields in his apartment.

Akihito's ascension to the Chrysanthemum Throne ushered in a new era, Heisei, meaning "achievement of peace." And in peace the whole world had come to Tokyo. By itself, this fact was millennial. As the year 2000 approached, the Japanese sense of national identity was changing; the viewpoint of a small inward-looking island nation was giving way to the vision of one of the most powerful players in the global marketplace. The second-largest economy on the planet stood on the verge of assuming responsibility for its economic miracle: providing for its own security, taking a leadership role in international affairs, joining in a common defense against tyranny. As a practical matter, there was an honored permanent seat on the United Nations Security Council to be considered.

For the United States, this was also a period of great transition. The forty-five-year period of relentless hostility toward the Soviet bloc was drawing to a close, and with the Cold War's demise the certitudes of American confidence and supremacy were crumbling. Increasingly, the men and women paid to think about threats to American well-being studied not the military might of the Soviet Union but the economic might of Japan, Inc. Yet George Bush—scion of a wealthy and powerful New England family, World War II hero, Ivy League graduate, Texas wildcatter, CIA Director, Vice President under Ronald Reagan, the fiercest Cold Warrior of them all—was a man much more of Hirohito's world than of Akihito's. Their Japan was America's protégé, its disciple in Democracy, its student in Capitalism.

A symbol of the new era for both countries had already begun to emerge from the drawing boards of one of the nation's oldest and greatest corporations, Mitsubishi Heavy Industries. Here, taking shape, was a plane some in Japan referred to as the Heisei Zero, linking the name of the new imperium with the memory of the legendary Showa fighter of World War II. This plane was to be a symbol of Japan's leadership in the world of technology. The wings were to be made of plastic—carbon composites actually, the stuff used to make tennis rackets light and strong. Pilots would fly it like a Nintendo toy, manipulating a joystick connected to a computer program that activated its control surfaces—elevators, ailerons, rudders. According to Japanese analysts, this allowed the plane to practically turn flat, almost like a compass needle. The Japanese called it the FS-X, for Fighter Support Experimental.

The tailpipe of a fighter plane is its Achilles' heel. Its kill spot. "Check six," fighter pilots signal each other over their radios: Make sure the enemy isn't in the six o'clock position, on your tail. This is where the FS-X, the Japanese claimed, would prove its advantage. The plane would be able to virtually wheel on its foe, like a tank turret, protecting its rear and firing its weapons head-on. On a bombing run, it would be able to hop left or right to get a better line on its target. The Heisei fighter was to be the embodiment of the new Japan: state of the art; the highest in high technology; the best in the world.

And therein lies the tale.

The FS-X was the other reason George Bush had traveled to Tokyo. A faction within his administration was worried about the plane, not because it was a weapon of war, but because it represented Japan's economic power and purpose. Already, hearings were underway in the House over the warplane, and in the Senate Jesse Helms was sniffing around for political truffles. The fighting within the President's own cabinet over the jet was so sharp it had erupted into the press.

The people who opposed the FS-X feared the plane's development would allow Japan to consolidate its dream of becoming a world power in commercial aviation, America's single most lucrative export industry. Japanese bureaucrats had carefully planned assaults on a variety of industries before: steel, autos, consumer electronics, computer chips. Large segments of the American economy had been overrun. Now the Japanese had their sights set on the largest prize of all: aerospace.

This was one great irony of the FS-X: in the end, the plane was a weapon that finally had nothing to do with the tools of war. Instead, it became a symbol of power in the twenty-first century, the Heisei era: technological supremacy, market dominance, trade balances. The debate over the aircraft, both in Japan and in America, marked the moment when the power of political ideologies was usurped by the power of national economies.

But there was a further irony. For all the claims the Japanese made about the miracles of technology the FS-X would embody, they remained just that: claims. American planes already flying were generations ahead of any other nation's product, and the technology that made their superiority possible was secret, known only to American corporations and American military officials.

Until we decided to give it to the Japanese.

Introduction

"Every company employing a staff of designers and engineers knows that under the present system any worthy model it has created may be torn from its creator and turned over to an underselling, pirating competitor to manufacture . . . And when its product is taken away by the very government it has tried so hard to serve . . . it is spirit killing, discouraging beyond words, unethical and unfair."

—MAJOR REUBEN HOLLIS FLEET, founder of Consolidated Aircraft, complaining to the army in a 1925 letter about the absurdity of their request to make his aircraft designs available to other U.S. companies for the sake of the competitive bidding process.

JAPAN'S EMERGENCE as an ambitious and determined player in international aviation could not have come at a worse time for the United States. Aviation represents a powerful financial counterweight for the faltering economy of fin de siècle America, hauling after it dozens of vital trades, in fields as diverse as paints, hotels, instruments, and business services. Japanese aspirations have serious implications for America's balance of trade, because aviation products are this nation's largest export. In 1991, the industry piled up a colossal surplus in overseas sales totaling more than $35 billion, which nearly backfilled the monstrous $45 billion rut created by autos. Overseas sales promised more growth. Along the Pacific Rim, in such countries as Australia, Japan, Hong Kong, and Taiwan, the United States enjoyed an $8.4 billion trade surplus in aerospace. The International Civil Aviation Organization, a United Nation-sponsored aviation safety agency, forecast that over the decade of the 1990s the region will have the highest travel growth of any comparable market. Congress estimated that every dollar earned by airplane builders generated another $2.30 in economic output. For every $1 billion of aircraft produced, nearly 35,000 jobs were created. In 1988, U.S. aircraft manufacturers rang up a hefty $60.9 billion in sales and employed 698,700 people.

Yet aviation is also a high-risk enterprise. The $180 billion invested in aircraft in the forty years following World War II produced a gaping $40 billion loss. Twenty-two aircraft companies dotted the landscape in 1945. Five remain. In all that time, twenty-nine jet transports were launched, but, omi-nously, only three of them ever flew from the red side of the ledger to the black. All of those were built by one company, Boeing.

Even Boeing has been hurting in the recent economic downturn. In 1990, its share of the market for new orders dropped to 45 percent, below the 50 percent threshold for the first time in more than twenty-five years. In Seattle, where the company has its headquarters, 19,000 layoffs were planned by mid-1994, with 11,000 more throughout the company. Production of commercial jets was slashed 35 percent. The state of Washington grimly predicted an economic tidal wave that would wash away $500 million in state revenues.

Making matters worse, aviation is a cyclical industry, and the defense dol-lars that kept it flying through hard times were running into headwinds. With the fall of the Soviet Union, military sales turned in full retreat. Southern California, the heartland of the aerospace industry, stood to lose up to 368,000 aerospace jobs by 1995.

Further exacerbating the problem, this downward swing comes at a time when serious competition has developed in Europe. Airbus Industries, a con-sortium created by the British, French, German, and Spanish governments, plans to capture a full third of the market by the mid-1990s. The impact on a company like McDonnell Douglas was plain; since the advent of Airbus, its share of the market dove by half, from 30 percent to 15. In 1992, the com-pany had more cancellations than orders.

Now, at a time when the U.S. aerospace industry faces severe and debilitat-ing contraction, Japan's is expanding. This is where the FS-X threatens to have its greatest impact. Japanese aircraft analysts were predicting that sales of aircraft components will increase by 400 percent from 1987 levels by the end of the century. Though the U.S. aviation industry is far larger than Japan's, the gap is narrowing. In 1983, Japanese aircraft parts and compo-nents output was about $1/30$ that of the United States. Two years later, it was $1/20$. In 1992, it was $1/15$. The ten-year, $10 billion FS-X program threatened to go a long way toward closing that gap entirely.

As the well-regarded international technology consulting firm of Booz, Allen & Hamilton put it: "We believe that Japanese growth will far surpass that of the rest of the aerospace industry, even beyond the aggressive projections currently being made by the Japanese government . . . American aerospace firms must avoid the 'it will never happen here' attitude that contributed to the downfall of U.S. companies in the steel, consumer electronics, automobile, shipbuilding, and semiconductor industries."

In the 1980s, America's trade deficit with Japan rose to a stunning $358.8 billion. Now, in the 1990s, the Clinton administration must confront this costly and damaging legacy. Though Japan experiences serious political and economic turmoil at home, its remedy has been to thrust its exports even more forcefully into the international marketplace. Indeed, at no time in history has the United States faced larger deficits with its Pacific partner, and at no time has the threat of an open trade war loomed larger.

Though the temptation to balance the lopsided scales of commerce by punishing Tokyo grows in proportion to our frustration at its closed markets, the story of the FS-X reminds us that we must look to ourselves to stanch these excesses. For here, in this story of the FS-X, we learn that the Japan problem is really an American problem, a Washington problem. Here, step by unassuming step, is the story of how we built up the competition.

I was drawn to the FS-X story because it spoke directly to these crucial trends. The events described in this book raise many disturbing questions about the increasingly stormy U.S.-Japan rivalry. The FS-X stirred up doubts about the crucial security relationship; the importance of maintaining Japan as a bulwark against Communism and all the sacrifices that entailed. Closely related was the rancorous trade relationship. The FS-X was at the heart of what was referred to by the Reagan administration as the trade-defense link. Technology intermingled in all this and loomed large as the chief locus for this conflict. As the 1980s made plain, America was not embarked on a post-industrial age, but an era in which the industrial arts determined the direction of national prosperity. The FS-X framed the debate over industrial policy.

The big surprise for me as I delved into the broad FS-X dispute was the narrowness of U.S. policy toward Japan. In fact, what policy the United States did have was limited to preserving the relationship for the sake of containing Communism. Indeed, one important reason the United States encountered problems with Japan is that this hidebound anti-Communist vision did not keep pace with the realities of Japanese ascendancy.

In the absence of a well-designed and dynamic policy process, what emerged was the importance of individual players. Policy was upstaged by personality. This, of course, is more true of most issues than is widely acknowledged. In the case of the FS-X, these personalities worked closely together through the Pentagon's chain of command, which had the effect of magnifying their influence.

In large part, this was why I chose to approach the FS-X deal as a narrative, for this was a story about people. As a result, in the course of researching this book, I relied heavily and predominantly upon interviews. I spoke to more than 150 people, between August 1991 and June 1993. I had interviews with virtually all the principals in both governments, including former Secretary of Defense Caspar Weinberger, former Commerce Secretary Robert A. Mosbacher, former Prime Minister Yasuhiro Nakasone, and former defense chiefs Koichi Kato and Yuko Kurihara. The interviews took place in Washington, D.C., Boston, Virginia, Memphis, Fort Worth, Pomona, Tokyo, and Nagoya. I spent the summer of 1992 in Japan researching the story.

As a matter of technique, I limited my use of quotation marks in the narrative. I largely paraphrased discussions, believing that impressions tend to dominate and bend individual recollections, and while the gist of what transpires is accurate and has been corroborated, actual quotes are difficult to reproduce. Where I did use quotes, I felt complete confidence in the dialogue and believed the quotations helped to create the most accurate expression of events as they transpired. Where I recount what certain individuals were thinking at particular moments, I relied upon their responses to my interview questions.

Many of the government documents I had access to came from sources on the House and Senate staffs who made their private files available to me. In some cases, I had access to logbooks and journals as well as private notes. For analysis, I relied on the Congressional Research Service, the General Accounting Office, the Office of Technology Assessment, and the MIT-Japan Program.

I had access to English-language versions of the Japanese press through the Dialog Information Service. Whenever possible, I used the Central Intelligence Agency's Foreign Broadcast Information Service to keep track of the translated versions of the daily Japanese press as the FS-X story developed. At the International House in Tokyo, I had access to the American Embassy's daily translations.

Nearly two dozen Freedom of Information Act requests were filed, as were several appeals. Most often, however, I found that Confidential and Secret information cast a fairly wide and often unfair cloak over the story. Japan requires secrecy in some cases where the United States is completely open, further limiting access to certain key documents. I never saw, for example, the Memorandum of Understanding reached by the two governments over the FS-X, although I interviewed about them widely.

I concentrated my research at the staff level throughout, in both the United States and Japan, in the belief that it is here that the actual workings of international relations are revealed.

My deepest thanks in all this goes to my wife, Bonnie Cutler, who supported this work financially, emotionally, and intellectually. No partner could have given more, more selflessly. Another deep debt of gratitude goes to my editor at Doubleday, Bill Thomas, who championed this book and stuck by it, demonstrating to me the real meaning of editorship. Also, much credit goes to my agent and shepherd, Rafe Sagalyn, on whose keen sensibilities I relied with complete confidence.

Numerous people were generous with their time and effort in helping me with my research; chief among them were Gregg Rubinstein, Jim Auer, Kevin Kearns, Clyde Prestowitz, Ron Morse, Edward McGaffigan, Jr., Charles Smith, Chalmers Johnson, Tsunehiko Yui, Hiroshi Ishikawa, Kazuko Koizumi, Ryuichi and Kei Teshima, Seiki Nishihiro, Michael Green, Richard Samuels, Joel Johnson, Steven Scholssstein, Arthur Alexander, Cecil Ueyhara, Peter Ennis, Masaru Honda, Shiuichi Wada, William Heinrich, Tomohisa Sakanaka, James Mihori, Susan Tolchin, Richard Van Atta, Yoshi Komori, Mikio Haruna, Michael Chinworth, Glen Fukushima, Ruben Johnson, and Linda Spenser. I would also like to thank the staff of International House in Tokyo for their courteous and unflaggingly efficient help. Finally, a bow to my patient amanuensis, Jessica Collins.

BOOK ONE

The Deal

1

Rebuilding the Future: 1980

"Nothing is clear about the twenty-first century except that it will be dominated by technology."
—Interview with RYOZO TSUTSUI, father of the FS-X

JAPAN'S LABORATORY THREE was an unknown quantity to American defense wizards, and they largely dismissed it as a charming shop for tinkerers. Their impressions were not entirely misplaced. Obscure, situated outside of Tokyo, underfinanced, nested away in bureaucracy, the lab was a diminutive subdivision of the Japan Defense Agency's Technical Research and Development Institute, the nation's only R&D center for advanced military technology. Known as the Department of Air Systems Development, Laboratory Three had a surprisingly and surpassingly ambitious mission, which was to conquer Japan's high frontier for the twenty-first century: aerospace aviation.

Situated in ancient Tachikawa, a bustling blue-collar suburb at the very western edge of Tokyo's teeming metropolitan sprawl, Laboratory Three was an hour's ride from Shinjuku, the closest of the city's main commuter stations. Though rarely visible except on the clearest days, the 6,000-foot Chichibu Mountains loomed westward. Here, where rice paddies mingled in the urban hustle, emerald bamboo grew tall and thick, resembling willows bowing in the wind.

During World War II, Tachikawa had been the site of the Imperial Army's center for research and development activities, but was occupied by U.S. forces after the war. The town later developed into a symbol of Japan's efforts to free itself from American involvement in its national affairs.

In the first brutal years after the war, prostitution boomed in the area, shaming and angering the morally conservative and largely provincial local population. A theatrical dramatization of the community's unease with America called *The Tachikawa Base: Ten Solid Years of Rape* made its way to the Tokyo stage in April 1960. The thinly disguised allegory decried the corruption Japan suffered as a result of the American occupation. Framed in a flashback, the heavy-handed drama depicts the story of a young, struggling Japanese who murders his sweetheart after she is raped by Yankee fliers based in Tachikawa. The sullied and innocent sweetheart of the play must die because she has been violated by Americans who mistook her for a common whore, and worse, infected her with the American disease, VD.

The Japanese public has never felt easeful about the American military presence in Japan, and U.S. policy has been to grudgingly relinquish bases when possible or necessary. In 1977, when the United States finally returned the base to its original owners, the Self-Defense Forces gave part of the reclaimed compound over to a community park and used the rest as a military reserve.

Laboratory Three was built less than a mile away from Tachikawa Air Base. Housed in a faceless compound of low buildings, the facility looked more like a public high school campus built in the 1950s than a center for advanced research. This nondescript atmosphere echoed the other labs that collectively constituted the Technical Research and Development Institute, where the three military services—army, navy, and air force—pooled their R&D.

The main administrative building was a treetop height three-story rectangle lying on its side. Built of light tan brick with large institutional-size plate-glass windows, four panes by two, it gave off an air of neglect. Rows of buzzing fluorescent lamps lit the dingy high-ceilinged interior, which appeared overcast even on blue-sky days.

Compared with the Pentagon's own bureaucratic General Issue standards of drabness, Laboratory Three looked bleak. Small and apparently unimportant, it scrimped along on published budgets it shared with the other labs, totaling about $518 million per year (compared with the Pentagon's $35 to $40 billion in annual R&D spending). The air conditioning, for example, wasn't switched on until the logy air was gray with humidity and temperatures topped 85, and then only in the weeks of summer after mid-July. This shabbiness, however, was misleading. While Japanese bureaucrats take pride in living on the cheap, these frugal premises represented more the austerity of the institution than its thrift, though it was surely thrifty.

What motivated this stingy attention to bare amenities was an adherence to an ancient philosophy that said a good military toughens itself through asceticism. In the cult of the Bushido, the rules guiding Japan's warrior class, the ideal of strict personal discipline honed the blade of the fighting spirit, keeping it keen. Behind the misleading facade conferred by obscurity and frugality, Laboratory Three's aerospace engineers labored in the mission of recovering their nation's air heritage, which had been obliterated by World War II.

Japan once boasted by far the best fighter aircraft in the skies. Known as the Zero, it flew faster and outmaneuvered anything the United States put aloft in the first year of the war. It figured prominently among the planes that staged the greatest and most daring air-sea strike in combat history. Pearl Harbor brought on the icy realization, in the marble and oak corridors of the Old Executive Office Building adjacent to the White House, that Japan had demonstrated military capabilities far beyond those of the U.S. Navy, much of which was then yet smoldering under the oily waves of Diamond Head.

Forty years later, Japan's war-torn air force had been rebuilt with planes manufactured from American designs. These were the workhorse weevil-nosed F-4s from the Vietnam era, and the more modern and menacing cape-winged F-15s, reputedly the most advanced interceptor in the world. Both planes were the creations of the McDonnell Douglas Corporation, which at first sold Japan the finished planes, and then under Pentagon auspices allowed Japan to build them under license at Mitsubishi Heavy Industries' Nagoya plant.

In all these years, Laboratory Three had been able to call only one plane its own, the supersonic F-1, introduced into service in 1977. Even then, the design derived from a European model dubbed the Jaguar. No one considered the F-1 a success story. Developed as an all-weather fighter, the earnest and laboring F-1 was restricted to daylight missions for safety and operational reasons. It was a clumsy aircraft by frontline standards. In fact, the plane was little more than a homemade trainer with strapped-on guns, missiles, and radar. Only about 80 planes were finally built, its production run cut short.

Laboratory Three was dedicated to resurrecting the humbled tradition of the Zero. More important, Laboratory Three aimed to revivify Japan's once great aviation industry. In 1970 and again in 1980, the prestigious and powerful Ministry of International Trade and Industry singled out aerospace for national attention and government support. This was significant because in the postwar era it was MITI that organized and supported Japan's meteoric rise to manufacturing excellence—first in textiles, then steel, machinery, autos, electronics.

MITI now foresaw the same possibilities for aerospace. Fully 85 percent of Japan's aircraft business came through the storefront of defense, and MITI had little trouble recognizing that building a commercial industry would have to begin there, in the defense sector. Thus MITI began playing the role of ministerial mentor to the Japan Defense Agency, its aspiring and useful protégé. The top JDA man who purchased weaponry for the military was always seconded and rotated from MITI.

Laboratory Three was high up on the senior ministry's wish list. Aerospace had been anointed; it had been assigned a place in the nation's industrial future. In 1970, it gained equal status with Japan's prestigious nuclear power industry and world-class information industry. By the 1980s government subsidies for jet engine development matched those for computer research. This was a powerful message to Japan's industrial centers. Pride, honor, "face" were now at stake, and Laboratory Three was where the Japanese put their reputations on the line.

The significance of military aircraft went far beyond mere warfare. Creating a modern supersonic fighter was a badge of industrial and technological know-how. It stood as the ultimate achievement in the ancient art of weaponry, unexcelled in all history for its complexity and power. A single F-16, which happened to be the lightest fighter-bomber in the U.S. arsenal, could deliver enough nuclear weapons to devastate large sections of the East Coast from New York to Washington, including its biggest cities. And that would be the *least* sophisticated use for the aircraft.

By producing a jet fighter, a nation joins a rare private club whose call is all but irresistible. "You aren't a man until you've designed your own new aircraft," as an American observer of Japan's aircraft program put it.

"It's a very expensive and exclusive club," said Richard Samuels, who studied Japan's defense industry at the Massachusetts Institute of Technology.

Nations will pay almost anything to join. France, for instance, with an economy a third the size of Japan, plunged forward with its Mirage fighter, and then beyond with the $6 billion Refale program. The British, with an economy almost 25 percent smaller than France's, built the Harrier, a plane that could take off and land vertically. The Europeans formed a consortium to develop the next-generation aircraft, dubbed the EFA, for European Fighter Aircraft (a program that was finally scrapped over costs in the summer of 1992, when an overburdened Germany backed out of the taxing and overly complex endeavor).

Beyond the image, aerospace was coveted for its economic ripple effects, washing cold currency over a wide range of critical and capital-intensive industries: computer chips and screens and terminals; new materials, both metal and plastic, and those in the exotic ranges in between. Aviation provided good jobs that paid high wages and required an adroit and educated workforce. The military jet was both the linchpin and the missing link for two great industries: aerospace and transportation.

Herein lay Japan's strategy. With the advent of a jet fleet, first financed through weaponry, and then, as technological and economic advantages developed, through government-subsidized commercial investments, Japan hoped to gain purchase on yet another crucial multinational export sector, as well as the routes of global transport. Aerospace represented to Japan the final great building block in the foundation of a modern industrial economy, toward which it strove as a nation. Ultimately, then, the FS-X plan was as much an economic package as it was a defense program.

The best aeronautical minds in the nation were drawn to Laboratory Three, and the best among them, their anointed leader, was the lank, boyish fifty-two-year-old Ryozo Tsutsui. Charming, resolute, sometimes shy, he was tall and had a wide mouth and an elastic, expressive face. He made a point of his urbanity, wearing fashionable suits and exhibiting his connoisseurship of French wines. He spoke English fluently, with occasional lapses, as well as French and German. He was a man in the mold of his institute—a research entrepreneur out to resurrect Japan as an aerospace power.

Tsutsui was a man of passion, that least obvious but most pervasive of Japanese traits. Laboratory Three was "the most important and intimate institute for me," he said. Tsutsui was an engineer who believed that science held the solution to the practical matter of national security and the relative pleasures of personal prosperity. "Nothing is clear about the twenty-first century except that it will be dominated by technology," he liked to say, and he thoroughly believed it. That was his faith; aerospace was his high frontier.

This meshed neatly with the aims of his defense agency. Since 1952, when the American occupation ended, Japan had been moving steadily and methodically in the direction of building its own arms industry. This did not represent the aim of returning Japan to the disastrous militarism that ran amok in the first half of this century. The modern Japanese military was genuinely and utterly circumscribed by the nation's so-called peace constitution, which says unambiguously in Article Nine: ". . . the Japanese people forever renounce war as a sovereign right of the nation and the threat or use of forces as a means of settling international disputes." Those were powerful words: "forever," "renounce," "sovereign," and "war."

Rather, the drive for independence on the part of the modern Japanese military rested on the more prosaic and fundamental notion of defensive security. The Japanese understood it among themselves as a "defensive defense." Reliance on foreign-made hardware violated the first principle of national security, which was to reduce lines of supply. In time of need, Japan could not be assured that another nation would provide the arms and equipment it required. Foreign dependence begat foreign interference and influence, as Japan well knew.

Defense meant business. It provided the economies of scale that civilian industry could leverage into new and costly products—aviation, for example. In the to-and-fro of business cycles, military requirements were steady and reliable, programmatic. There was also the simple fact that every great nation in the modern world had its own air force. Economically at least, Japan is far larger than France or Britain. Why shouldn't it produce its own aircraft just as they do?

After years of painstakingly co-producing some nineteen U.S. military aircraft, Japan had nearly all the experience it needed to plunge into a venture all its own. One thing remained for Laboratory Three to acquire, Tsutsui knew, and that was design experience. Though the nation built 70 percent of the F-15 at home, the reality was that the plane was still based on American blueprints. Japan had hitched its star to the U.S. Air Force, and Tsutsui thought it was time for the ride to end. So did those around him, right up through the highest levels of Japan's ministries. To have a truly autonomous, homegrown aircraft industry, Japan had to design the planes it built.

As a practical matter, Tsutsui also saw Japan running up against the limits of U.S. defense cooperation. Beginning in 1978, when the defense agency began acquiring and building the F-15 on its own, the United States increasingly began withholding more and more sensitive technology. Certain crucial sections of the aircraft were not available for commercial license. Radar altimeters, onboard computers, weapons tracking and firing systems all came in sealed black boxes, representing 40 percent of the plane's most advanced technology. (The boxes were actually black.) Tsutsui chafed at these constraints.

Japan watchers in the Defense Department grew increasingly conscious of Tsutsui. Unlike many Japanese in official positions, particularly those in the military, Tsutsui was not a good companion. Whereas the defense agency deferred for the most part to U.S. planners, Tsutsui could be blunt, standoffish. Some accused him of arrogance. The more generous detected resentment.

The speculation was that Tsutsui held a grudge as a result of his treatment during the U.S. occupation of Japan immediately after World War II. A student at a prestigious military high school during the conflict, he was barred by the MacArthur regime from entering Tokyo University. There was a ceiling on the number of graduates from academies like his that were allowed into the universities in the early years of the occupation. In a culture where classmates and seniority are so important, such a long delay might have been disastrous. For certain, it made his career far more difficult, though no less distinguished.

Tsutsui was relentless in his efforts to demolish the reputation of superiority boasted by U.S. hardware. The quality of U.S. parts was another of his gripes. When a misplaced tool was discovered riveted inside a wing manufactured in St. Louis, Tsutsui required all imported U.S. wings to be hoisted aloft and rattled around to make certain nothing was left loose that might tear it off in flight. Such histrionics, by themselves, succeeded in turning quality into an American tar baby. Stories began to circulate of cigarette butts left in black boxes, of aircraft wings that leaked hydraulic fluid. So bad was it, the Japanese aircraft technicians complained, that an umbrella was necessary when walking beneath an American-made F-15. Even U.S. defense officials associated with Japan began repeating such tales.

More than anything, Tsutsui's beef with his American partners reflected the arrogance of an engineer on the brink of realizing his highest aspirations. In fact, his actions and his opinions completely ignored the prodigious technological achievement embodied in the F-15 and sometimes descended into caviling attacks over perceived differences in manufacturing quality.

Yet this was not naiveté or ingratitude on the part of Tsutsui. This was a tactic. By rhetorically dismissing U.S. expertise, Tsutsui built the case for an all-Japan fighter. Japan had outgrown U.S. help, he said, though the evidence showed Japan to be deeply dependent on U.S. know-how. Indeed, even as Tsutsui criticized his American partners, he and his designers scoured the U.S. defense industry for licensing opportunities for the FS-X, the code name for Japan's proposed new fighter.

Tsutsui planned this new fighter around three technologies, none of which was exclusive to Japan, but all of which had revolutionary potential. The first technology involved a plastic from Toray Industries, the world's largest manufacturer of such materials. The composite was not only lighter and stronger than metal but could be elaborately molded. Composites were fabrics, woven of metals, plastics, or carbon, that were then glued together under pressure and baked in furnaces, a process known as curing. The new Toray process was still experimental but very promising. Tsutsui hoped to use it for the wings of the new plane, which would cut weight by fully 25 percent. This was a huge saving that would improve the plane's performance, allowing it to fly farther on less power with lower maintenance.

Another technology, which Tsutsui knew was under development by the United States, was an active phased array radar. Instead of the traditional dish radar which scanned the skies by rotating, an active phased array scanned the sky by moving or alternating its beams through thousands of individual miniaturized radar modules. The virtue of the electronic scan was speed. Whereas mechanical radars moved physically through space, the modules allowed instant scanning, triangulation, and comparison. These tiny individual radar modules, each the size of a ballpoint pen, provided a constant view of dozens of targets at a time, detecting enemy ships while searching for enemy planes.

Finally, there were the canards, the winglets beneath the pilot's canopy. Connected to a computer, the canards would allow the jet to perform extraordinary maneuvers: climbing without raising its nose, hopping from side to side to line up on a bombing target, controlling its angle of attack against a foe.

Tsutsui, the planner, even had a timetable for the domestic development of the FS-X. As he saw it, the F-1 program was scheduled to run down at the end of the 1980s, and the Air Self-Defense Forces would need a replacement. By necessity, a program had to be put in place soon if Japan was realistic about developing a plane of its own to replace the F-1s. All the work of the last decade had been aimed at this moment, this new generation of aircraft.

So far along was he that word of this new aircraft began seeping into the Japanese press in September 1980. Japan's leading financial daily, the *Nihon Keizai Shimbun*, described the plane as "Japan's next mainstay support fighter . . . expected to be put into service in the late 1980s."

There were obstacles, of course, and formidable ones. How the United States would react, for one. But Tsutsui was undaunted. This was an opportunity that arose once in a career. He had a chance to revive the air force of Japan as great institution, the symbol of Japan's status as a modern society. He was determined. And Ryozo Tsutsui's patient labors would soon be rewarded, or so it seemed.

2

Zero-Sum Game

"Perhaps it is not in good taste for me to say this, but if, as some people believe, Japanese people excel only in imitating and making small gadgets, then the Zero did not exist. The Zero was of Japanese blood, and its design reflects our philosophy of independent thinking. We were trying to surpass the rest of the world's technology, not just catch up to it. That was the goal of the Zero I designed."
—JIRO HORIKOSHI, *Eagles of Mitsubishi*

TSUTSUI'S CHIEF BACKERS in the push for the domestic development program that was the FS-X was the Mitsubishi group, a corporate entity that was known for its unbending nationalism. That was a signal asset for the engineer from the obscure but ambitious defense lab. Whereas guns and missiles were the plague of Japan's peace constitution, the great Mitsubishi corporation was a government darling. What the politicians and ministers might disallow for the defense agency, they would encourage for Mitsubishi.

The FS-X was a longtime preoccupation for both, and for both it represented a coming of age. For Mitsubishi, producing a leading-edge fighter heralded its maturity in aviation. There was no task in commercial or defense aviation that it would not be able to handle. For Tsutsui, the plane stood as more than a climaxing personal achievement, a life's work, although it was that. It symbolized an endeavor that would bring Japan back to the forefront of national power. This nationalism was as ingrained in Tsutsui as it was in Mitsubishi. In fact, nationalism was at the center of the story of Mitsubishi and reveals the deep roots of cooperation between Japanese industry and government.

In many ways, the rise of Mitsubishi coincided with the emergence of modern Japan. Founded in the 1870s, the company got its start in the rush toward industrialization known as the Meiji Restoration, which began in 1868. In the sweep of just two decades, Japan overthrew a feudal government in favor of a central government, trading rulers for managers and castles for corporations.

The "gentlemen of Mitsubishi," as the leaders of the diversified industrial firm were known, hitched the company's fortunes to the national interest. Mitsubishi became a *seisho* company, a "political merchant," bartering its aggressive loyalty and ready capital for government favor. In this, the budding conglomerate was an archetype for the military-industrial complex that grew up in Germany and the United States at the same time.

Founder Yataro Iwasaki exhorted his managers along these lines in a letter dated April 1878 concerning the Mitsubishi mission: "Our company's success or failure is not a private matter for our company only. I believe that it is a serious matter of public interest. . . . Hence, the spirit of contributing to the company's prosperity is the same as the spirit of contributing to the national interest. . . . Who has ever been able to achieve a great work without this spirit?"

The company made its mark in the shipping business, where it practiced the ways of the political merchant in order to win government contracts. Beginning in 1871, when pirates plagued shipping in Taiwanese waters and the government needed transports to mount an expeditionary force, Mitsubishi volunteered its steamers. Yataro Iwasaki promised the government that "I will do my utmost and never spare myself. I will aim at making eleven successes out of eleven hundred failures and never stop advancing through hundreds and thousands of hardships until I die." He then put the company's entire fleet at Tokyo's disposal. Industry became government and government became industry. When the expeditionary forces returned triumphant, Mitsubishi was awarded the use of thirteen of the Meiji's most modern steamers, which tipped the competitive balance in Japan's shipping industry in favor of Iwasaki's audaciously ambitious company.

At the time, the archrival of the Mitsubishi shipping juggernaut was the American-owned Pacific Mail Steamship Company. It had enjoyed a growing and profitable cargo route along the Japanese coast for most of the decade. The company was among the first businesses to expand into Japan in the wake of Commodore Perry's trade-opening Black Ships foray into Tokyo Bay in the early 1850s.

Iwasaki saw the American presence as a direct and consequential challenge. In a company declaration dated August 1875, he wrote: "Ever since diplomatic relations were entered into, we have found ourselves being belittled by the outside world . . . In particular the Pacific Mail Steamship Company's sailing through our waters is not only an affront to our empire but also an invasion of our rights . . . I believe we should defeat the Pacific Mail in order to regain our people's pride and redeem our rights. From this day on, I will demand [from the company] strenuous efforts day and night until the battle is won." With unabashed support from the central government in the form of contracts (not to mention the use of so many extra ships for free as a result of Mitsubishi's contribution to the expeditionary force), the company slashed prices on first-class passenger fares by 60 percent. The American company soon quit its routes, unable to compete.

The tone of Iwasaki's letters reveal the deep conservatism and nationalism of Mitsubishi and the Meiji Restoration in which it flourished. The strategy of close government relations coincided with an abiding suspicion of outsiders. The result was a corporatist state, in which government and business acted in unison, offering a single face to the world. To a lesser degree, Japan relies on a similar system of "political merchants" to this day, Mitsubishi chief among them.

This cozy relationship between government and business was key to the development of Japan's pre–World War II aircraft industry. Beginning in 1916, Mitsubishi Heavy Industries began building aircraft for the military in the city of Kobe. Between 1926 and 1945, it manufactured 17,250 warplanes. During its invasion of China, in 1937, its bombers set transoceanic distance records, averaging more than 1,200 miles on round trips to their targets.

The company had an extraordinary record in the skies, an accomplishment largely dismissed in the West. Mitsubishi produced the world's first operational modern carrier plane, the Type 96 fighter, an all-metal single-wing plane, whose flush-riveted construction was just a technological gleam in the eyes of American aircraft designers. The plane's chief engineer, thirty-four-year-old Jiro Horikoshi, led the team that created an even better fighter, which was without doubt the best carrier plane to emerge at the beginning of World War II: the infamous Zero.

As was customary, the designation for the new fighter was taken from the last digits of the Japanese calendar year, which was then 2600. The *rei-sen*, as Japanese pilots called it—the *rei* from zero and *sen* from *sentoki*, "fighter." The plane went into operation in 1940.

The Zero-sen was a slim, elegantly elongated plane with widely set landing gear that lifted its nose at a haughty angle. Its vertical stabilizer extended distinctively beyond its tail, making it appear stretched thin. In flight, the aerial attacker was known for its speed and ability to climb; in battle, it was known for its endurance and agility.

One month after it entered service in July 1940, the Zero set a combat flight record, traveling 1,000 miles to escort a Japanese bomber force on a raid in China. With coaxing, Zeros could stay aloft for half a day, twelve hours. By comparison, the best Western fighters, such as the Spitfire or the German Me-109, had half the range, about 600 miles.

Claire Chennault, who later went on to command the renowned Flying Tigers, sent photos of the never before seen plane and estimates of its performance to the U.S. War Department. Washington dismissed Chennault, calling his figures "bunk." They declared the plane an "aerodynamic impossibility." At no time during World War II was there a Western fighter that could match the first Zero for maneuverability.

In 1941, the Zero not only flew farther but flew faster than any plane in the U.S. arsenal. At 230 m.p.h., it could turn 180 degrees in just six seconds, while traveling only 1,200 feet forward. Astonishingly, it lost a mere 40 knots of forward airspeed in the process.

From the outset the United States underrated the Japanese, convinced that the plane was a knockoff from a Western design. Early Zeros did, in fact, have U.S.-made components, built under license from U.S. manufacturers. Instruments, for example, came from the Bendix Corp. and propellers from Hamilton Standard. Its 20-millimeter cannon was Swiss. Other parts were direct copies of American designs. In 1937, the Japanese purchased a Vought 143 fighter from the United States, and modified its landing gear for the Zero. The sum of those parts, however, added up to something very special: the Zero. Not even the vaunted British Spitfire, which won out in the Battle of Britain, could equal the plane.

Its designer rightfully boasted after the war that "there has never existed anywhere in the world a fighter powered by a 1,000 horsepower air-cooled engine that was faster than the Zero, even without comparable range and dogfight characteristics." When comparisons were made by the U.S. Army in 1942 between the best of this country's fighters and a captured Zero, their assessment left no doubt: "Never dogfight with a Zero" was the instruction that went out to U.S. fliers.

Not until the United States introduced the Grumman F6F Hellcat in 1943, with twice the horsepower of the Zero, did the airplane meet its match, but while outmuscled, it was not outmaneuvered.

What most impressed the first American experts to examine a Zero up close proved to be a harbinger of Japan's postwar economic resurgence. Rear Admiral William N. Leonard (ret.) recalled of the Zero: "The refined aerodynamic design *was not compromised by mass production.* Fit and finish of all plates, rivets, and accurate fit of fairings, engine cowl, access plates, canopy, and wheel doors were most faithfully executed" (emphasis added).

"Quality" itself was not a goal to Japan. Rather, such excellence was implicit in the precepts of Bushido, the warrior arts, and was embodied in the samurai sword, which, like the Zero fighter, was unsurpassed in the West. As that sword once dominated the battlefield, control of the skies now dominated the theater of war. Mitsubishi produced the blade known as the Zero, and it managed to mass-produce them without sacrificing quality.

In many ways, Tsutsui's FS-X paralleled the Zero program. In both cases, the aircraft engine design presented problems. In the 1980s, Japan lagged in engine production, as it did in the 1930s. Indeed, the nation did not make advanced jet fighter engines and planned to buy or license one from the West —probably from the United States—for the planned domestically built FS-X. The Zero faced a similar problem. Japanese industrial firms could not produce the high-powered aircraft engines the Zero required.

To understand the significance of this, it helps to know that fighters are designed around their engines, a fact which Tsutsui tended to overlook when he boasted that Japan was capable of producing an all-Japan fighter. Certainly, the engine was a limitation Mitsubishi's Horikoshi could not ignore when he designed the Zero. Nor could he rely on the West to provide the needed engines.

Because of engine problems, both planes had to depend on new materials for improved performance. Advanced plastic composites were at the heart of Japan's plans for its new FS-X fighter, and they were as well at the heart of the Zero.

In order to build a plane light enough to climb at almost 3,000 feet per minute and top-end at more than 310 miles per hour, the designers of the Zero had to trade weight for horsepower. Serendipitously, the Sumitomo Metal Industries approached Horikoshi with an aluminum alloy that offered the strength-to-weight ratios necessary to overcome his plane's bantam-sized engines. The alloy was called "Extra Super Duralumin" and was the composite material of its day.

Little more than thirty years later, the world's leading plastics firm, Toray Industries, told Laboratory Three that it had produced a tennis racket out of a new durable and stronger-than-steel material that might have an important role to play in aircraft structures. Toray was a member of the Mitsui group—like Mitsubishi, another of Japan's great "political merchants," *seisho*. From Toray's tennis racket, the all co-cured wing was born, a wing Mitsubishi hoped would revolutionize flight. Cast as a single unit, the wing promised a lighter, more efficient aircraft, not to mention ease of manufacturing. Thus, the close links between Japanese corporations, between tennis rackets and the tools of war, yielded the basis for a whole new aircraft. The Japanese called this process of developing military technology from commercial products "spin-ons."

Difficult requirements hemmed in designers of both the Zero and the FS-X. At the same time, it inspired them. In his memoir, *Eagles of Mitsubishi*,

Horikoshi recalls being stunned when confronted by the specs the military expected him to achieve: the new plane had to be able to intercept and destroy enemy planes as well as provide escort and defense for Japan's long-range bombers. To do this, it would have to fly at a maximum continuous power at an altitude of 10,000 feet for more than 1.5 hours. What is more, it had to be able to land at less than 67 miles per hour and take off in less than 230 feet into a 30-mile-per-hour headwind.

Similar rigorous requirements drove the FS-X. The Japan Defense Agency, led by Ryozo Tsutsui, called for a fighter that could carry four heavy antiship missiles and still have the agility to play the interceptor role. It had to have an extra-long combat radius—so great that it could take off from central Japan and fight battles beyond its northernmost borders. What is more, it had to land and take off from primitive or bomb-pitted airfields offering no more than 3,000 feet of clear runway. This it had to accomplish fully loaded with weapons, at air temperatures above 104 degrees Fahrenheit. (Heat cuts the lift a plane needs for flight.) And one more thing. The FS-X had to have a glass canopy capable of withstanding the impact of collisions with crane-sized birds as it traveled at nearly supersonic speeds, even though such a collision might well tear through the nose of the plane.

Finally, the very signature of the Zero fighter was its balletic dogfighting ability. Able to turn virtually on its tail to counterattack, the sleek interceptor was never outdone in this dance of death by any combustion-engine combat plane ever built.

The idea of fitting canards on the FS-X—small winglets that cut the air ahead of the main wing—and hot-wiring them to a computer was a bow to the philosophy of the Zero fighter. If the Zero was able to turn 180 degrees while traveling just 1,200 feet forward, the test-bed vehicle Mitsubishi built for the FS-X maneuvered so sharply it created a cloud about itself as its nose skidded into the contrails created by its exhaust.

There was one other element that the FS-X seemed to share with the Zero: Western doubts. When the designer of the Zero, Jiro Horikoshi, joined the Mitsubishi company, he was sent to tour the world's great aircraft manufacturing companies. Similarly, thirty years later, Ryozo Tsutsui would come to the University of Maryland to study aeronautics. The prevailing view Horikoshi found in the Western nations was that Japan was incapable of innovation. The Zero couldn't be built. Tsutsui met with similar stereotypes. Japan could not build the FS-X on its own.

The West could not entirely be blamed for such notions. The proposition that Japan was a copycat nation arose during the Meiji Restoration when industry geared up for the Industrial Revolution with all-Western hardware. Steam engines, ships, cannons, the internal-combustion engine were all imports.

Far less obvious in this nineteenth-century strategy was the outright determination to catch up and then surpass the West—and the manner in which this would be accomplished. In the case of the youthful aircraft industry, Horikoshi saw that "it would not take Japan very long to catch up with [Western] small-airplane technology *if we had proper government priorities and policy*" (emphasis added).

This was a suggestion with its roots in the Meiji era, in the *seisho*, the craft of the political merchant. Meiji bureaucrats and businessmen weren't simply on a Western buying spree. They were tough-minded traders who cut deals in which the Japanese could gain the engineering knowledge necessary to build their own steam engines to power ships and trains and cast the cannons to fight wars. The national goal was obvious: With time, all this matériel would be manufactured and ultimately designed in Japan. The men of the Meiji studied management, learned Western production methods, and then adapted all of it to the nation's commercial and security needs.

The elements so crucial to the success of the Zero—the lightweight engine, the reliance on new materials, the government's stiff requirements, Western-trained engineers—represented a design philosophy that was carried over into the FS-X. As Tsutsui himself would later explain to his Western counterparts, an aircraft that could meet Japan's requirements could meet any enemy, under any circumstances.

The Zero was built to achieve dominance in military conflicts. But here, finally, the Zero of old parted company with the new Heisei Zero. The FS-X was planned to achieve dominance in a much grander field of conflict—the great *economic* struggle that was emerging in the global marketplace. And as with the Zero program, few people in the United States would understand the significance of the FS-X until much too late—and some never would.

3

Congress Stirs

"We were told by Japanese aircraft industry representatives that military and civil aircraft are mixed throughout the production process. Japan's civil aircraft production reaps benefits from the advanced processes and technology used in military aircraft production programs."
—"U.S. Military Co-production Programs Assist Japan in Developing Its Civil Aircraft Industry," GAO, March 18, 1992

THE FIRST SIGNS of American worry about Japan's aviation ambitions surfaced in 1981. In a letter dated March 30, Sam M. Gibbons, the veteran Florida Democrat and chairman of the House Ways and Means Subcommittee on Trade, wrote to the investigative arm of the Congress, the General Accounting Office: "The Subcommittee on Trade has long been interested in U.S.-Japan Trade relations and in particular, the challenge in high technology trade presented by Japan."

Gibbons was one of those characters who appeared at each stage of the FS-X debate, serving briefly as a catalyst who energized, investigated, and defined the issues, but whose interests quickly became submerged in the murky and diffuse terms of the debate. Despite the potshot approach, the report he generated would have serious and reverberating consequences.

The craggy Gibbons, who some said resembled chicken king Frank Perdue, was a free trader to the bone. Though he would play no role in the rough-and-tumble of the FS-X deal, he was the man who set the terms of a debate that would later go off like a hand grenade in the Congress.

Gibbons came right to the point in the letter he wrote to the GAO that late March day. "I believe that in the coming decade, Japan will become a major competitor in aviation." That was a powerful statement for a man with Gibbons's free-trade credentials. It acknowledged that Japan's unfair trade practices *might* be creating a problem. However, that did not mean that he had plans to build a fence around U.S. industry. Rather, he wanted to take a sounding. As he put it, "to prepare for it creatively (rather than defensively and after the fact)."

Gibbons was an unlikely man to skip into the role of Cassandra on the issue of Japan's aviation ambitions. *The Almanac of American Politics 1992* likens Gibbons, with his penchant for free trade, to Cordell Hull, Franklin Roosevelt's Secretary of State, who believed that trade was the opposite of war, its antidote, the greatest of aims. Trade was the high tide upon which life's little boats all rose. Yet Gibbons was behaving more like a pragmatist than an ideologue in ordering up such a report from the congressional investigators. Not only was he looking past a free-trade utopia; he was looking past politics as well. His real fear, he wrote, wasn't trade with Japan as much as it was handouts, giveaways, bad deals.

"I am especially interested in the transfer of aviation technology to Japan," he wrote. The huge transfer of technology involved in the licensing of F-15 technology to Japan created a quiet storm within the Defense Department, with military experts fearing that the plane was simply too advanced to be produced outside the United States. Indeed, apart from its American manufacturer, McDonnell Douglas, only Japan built the radical new plane, which offered riches aplenty in manufacturing experience.

Japan's vision for aerospace was becoming increasingly plain to savvier elements of the U.S. government. In 1958 MITI wrote the Aircraft Industrial Promotion Law, which explicitly pinned the development of a commercial aviation industry on the successful development of a defense aircraft industry. Like any other nation, Japan recognized that it required a huge economy of scale to support a civilian aircraft industry, and the way to achieve that was through the military. The way an enterprise survived in the airplane business was through some sort of government dole, either in the form of a direct subsidy, as was the case with Europe's Airbus Industries, or through military projects, as was the case in the United States.

Gibbons wanted to know the quid pro quo for handing over the secrets of the F-15. "What did the U.S. receive in exchange for this licensing agreement . . . what future competition problems will it create . . . how does the licensing agreement coordinate as part of Japan's national policy to develop a world-class aviation program . . . ?"

At the time Gibbons wrote his letter, Congress was, if not on the lookout, then looking around warily for Japan's next offensive in the U.S. marketplace. The trade deficit between the two nations had grown steadily throughout the

1970s, and rose from $10 billion in 1978 to more than $16 billion in 1981. Already, steel, autos, semiconductors, and consumer electronics had been surrendered to or were under siege by competitors from Japan. Aviation was the next logical choice, which Japan made no effort to disguise.

Gibbons's letter asked the correct questions, and he was asking them of the proper agency. Located on the rough fringe of the capital's Chinatown section, the block-long neoclassical facade of the General Accounting Office looks more worn than old.

Starting out as an auditing agency in the early 1920s, the GAO began to change in the fat years after World War II. Less the bean counter and more the investigator, the agency, in its evaluations and analysis, targeted fraud, waste, and abuse. Its budget grew to $440 million a year.

The GAO represented government in the sunshine. There were no political employees in the day-to-day operations; only the titular head of the GAO, the Comptroller General, was a presidential appointee. With access to secret data, it ranged over Washington's bureaucracy. Without power to indict, it functioned more like an investigative reporter, exposing wrongdoing, acting as a watchdog over government agencies. The GAO produced 950 magazine-sized studies a year, nearly all bearing the same trademark true-blue covers, which many a bureaucrat came to loathe. Little escaped its scrutiny.

Critics, most notably Republicans, charged that the GAO tailored its findings to suit its requesters. Their point was that 80 percent of all GAO reports originated in congressional committees, and the chairmen who submit them are in most cases Democrats. At the very least, the Democrats had a powerful say in who and what got investigated. Republicans maintained that the GAO took a prosecutorial approach to its studies rather than an investigative approach, taking a case and setting out to prove it, instead of gathering evidence before it drew conclusions. More often than not, however, the GAO reliably unearthed the unwelcome truth. Seldom was it venal.

The Pentagon was a frequent target. Nearly one-quarter of the agency's 4,000 to 5,000 employees worked on Pentagon audits. Whether the GAO cast doubts on a new missile's test results or charged that there was an insufficient supply of regulation footwear in the strategic stockpile, it raised hell with the Defense Department. Invariably it made war planners look like crooks or dupes or double agents. Whenever the GAO probed, it seemed that the Defense Department's guns misfired and some bloated bastard got richer. Not yet over the embarrassment of the Vietnam debacle, the military suffered under GAO scrutiny, the brass's judgment called into question at every turn.

Now, with Gibbons's request, the Congress's sleuths delved into a heretofore little explored Pentagon practice: technology transfer. Whereas other nations guarded their industrial secrets as the keys to their national security, the Defense Department appeared to be putting them up for sale. The process in which this information was passed on was known as co-production.

The GAO's definition of co-production was turgid but enticing: It enables a foreign country "to acquire the know-how to manufacture or assemble, repair, maintain and operate . . . a specific weapon . . . it may extend to *a major manufacturing effort requiring the build-up of capital industries"* (emphasis added). In full-scale co-production programs, such as Japan's, the United States sold manufacturing data, machinery, tools, raw materials, finished materials, production components, subassemblies, quality-control procedures.

The United States had been engaged in such co-production programs for years with NATO allies France, Great Britain, Italy, and others. The GAO warned of the implications of such programs for American workers and, more importantly for military planners, the nation's industrial capacity. For their part, the Europeans did not engage in co-production of their own weapons systems on a scale even closely resembling that of the United States.

Arguably, the growing European challenge to the United States in aviation had its inception in co-production. Whether the benefits of co-production (common and interchangeable weapons for alliance partners, cheaper and more sophisticated weaponry) outweighed its dangers (eroding market share for U.S. manufacturers, the threat to second- and third-tier suppliers) was a constant source of debate. However, without a clear answer, the Pentagon plunged forward with similar and, in the case of the F-15, far more sophisticated ventures with this nation's number one industrial competitor: Japan.

Co-production was central to Japan's aviation plans. Knowing the "how" and, better yet, the "why" of design and manufacturing was the real value for the purchaser in such deals, particularly in the case of Japan. Prohibited by constitution and public law from reselling the tools of war, Japan's giant industrial companies could freely export the commercial products spun off from the co-production experience. The way Japanese factories were set up, it was only a walk across the design floor from military cockpit displays to civilian flight decks.

Unlike old-fashioned arms deals, in which the issue was strictly limited to the security community, co-production had a powerful and residual effect upon the civilian economy. For example, the air brakes used on Japan's revolutionary Bullet Train evolved from its co-production experience on the U.S.-designed F-86 Starfighter.

While this did not have a direct effect on U.S. air brake manufacturers, it contributed to Japanese excellence in railway technology. That had the direct effect of increasing Japan's competitiveness against the United States and other countries that did not have the benefit of the same co-production experience.

The GAO report that finally landed on Gibbons's desk a year later was a bombshell—but a bombshell that exploded with little notice. The chairman went through the motions of making a big deal of the report, but eventually let the matter lie. No doubt an angry controversy played an important role in submerging the report's findings. There had been heavy infighting at the GAO over the language of the report, which was eventually watered down. In its original form, the report found Japan had been targeting its aviation industry for development, though not necessarily in the predatory sense of targeting another nation's mature industry for market share. Still, this was too controversial a point to make at the time. In the published findings, the direct link drawn by the report between Japanese government contributions and the bead they had drawn on the aerospace industry was blurred by such terms as "government subsidy" and "government support."

Another reason the report did not have a serious impact at the time was that Japan was just too far away in the American mind. Adding to this official myopia was the long and seemingly insurmountable lead the United States held in aerospace. A conscientious reader of the report felt compelled to reject it on its face, because if it was correct, then the United States was in trouble, hurting itself through its own security policies. That meant Congress would have to act, and people in Washington are not wont to act.

Still, the GAO's key findings were instructive of the Pentagon's modus operandi. More important, they were signposts pointing to serious problems of continued co-production programs with Japan:

- The United States enters into military co-production agreements for defense reasons.
- Japan enters into military co-production agreements for economic reasons.
- The transfer of technology that is created flows one way, from the United States to Japan.
- These co-production agreements help Japan develop and expand its aircraft industry.
- The United States has not devoted enough attention to understanding the implications of the military co-production programs it instigates.

In fact, the United States did not worry about these military deals with Japan because the Pentagon saw no connection between a small rigidly structured fighter jet and a mammoth and flexible passenger aircraft. The GAO found quite a different view in Japan, however: "An official of Japan's MITI states that '. . . the development and manufacturing techniques of both [civilian and military aircraft] are closely related and technological spinoffs can be mutually anticipated.' " Some of the areas U.S. industry acknowledged as having commercial potential were composites, avionics, instrumentation, and propulsion. The report cites a Rand Corporation study in which an unidenti fied industry representative said, "We were paid to put them in business and we gave them everything we had."

This was especially significant because these were *components*, and as Japan's strategy in aerospace emerged over the decade, it would become clear that the future of Japanese aviation lay in these components. As was the case in Apple computers, the Japanese did not mind the American label on the box, so long as 70 percent of the *components* were manufactured in Japan. The implications of this strategy were plain for the thousands of U.S. subcontractors manufacturing components. As a result of co-production programs with Japan, they were now in competition with the Japanese government for their business, which was abetted in its aims by their own Department of Defense.

The GAO's findings concluded with a warning: The United States could no longer ignore the effects its defense policies were having upon the Japanese economy. As the GAO saw it, this was more than the advantage conferred on Japan by having the United States defend it, allowing Japan to spend a fraction of the fortune the United States spent on arms. This was more serious. The United States was helping Japan grow its aerospace industry by pushing co-production.

The GAO laid the responsibility for this dramatic development on the military. By ignoring the economic impact of its co-production programs, the report said, the Pentagon incubated foreign competition that might one day come home to bite it on its brass buttons. The Defense Department had "too narrow a perspective to adequately address the attendant domestic and international economic, industrial and labor interests," the report said.

The State Department also came in for criticism, largely for the same reasons the Defense Department did: its myopic view of co-production's economic impact. State played a key role because it authorized *all* co-production agreements. In the case of Japan, this was largely a rubber-stamping operation for the DoD's initiatives.

Despite the rigorous nature and explosive charges of the GAO report, the Pentagon and State Department officials at which it was aimed dismissed its devastating findings as the work of youthful amateurs.

Gregg Rubinstein, at the State Department, was an important focus of GAO attention. A foreign service officer on the Japan desk, he carried unique security credentials. He had been on loan to the Defense Department, where he aided in negotiating the government-to-government contracts (known as MOUs, or memorandums of understanding) with Japan that were at the heart of all co-production agreements. He thus had the unusual advantage of knowing the separate institutional viewpoints of each department on security issues.

Though he was of the State Department, Rubinstein had a penchant for the military. A measured man in his early thirties, Rubinstein was brainy and low-key. On occasion, he sported a beard and smoked a pipe. He spoke in perfect paragraphs and had a prodigious memory. A scholar in Japanese studies, he collected lithographs of Japanese naval battles. The F-15 was his case. As he recalled: "What attracted me to that job was a combination of both policy analysis and operational management, as well as actually getting involved in programs like the F-15. Given the substantive issues of defense technology in Japan and the combination of analytical and management work, it was all but irresistible to me."

While the official State Department reaction to the GAO report was forbearing, Rubinstein was rankled. He called the charge that the DoD was giving away U.S. technology "outrageous." He thought the study lacked objectivity. "They had a vested interest," he said, siding with critics of the GAO's methodology. "These reports from the GAO say what their committee chairman want them to say by and large." (Rubinstein's criticism overlooked the fact, however, that Gibbons was a devoted free trader.) In Rubinstein's eyes, the GAO saw all defense cooperation with Japan as dark and dangerous. "The GAO assumed that anyone who argued in favor of co-production had a terminal case of clientitis and had sold out to Japan." He believed the GAO had a "Buy American" bias.

Rubinstein ridiculed the GAO researchers for being naive. "These people are all political science types who may know a lot about Japan, but who know virtually nothing about defense technology—the industry, procurement, how systems develop. They have no firsthand exposure." To Rubinstein, they were amateurs playing at an expert's game.

Rubinstein believed with a deep and unflinching certainty that there was little risk in co-producing the F-15 with Japan. The technologies the United States was giving away were "mature," he said. No sensitive electronics were at stake. The Japanese would learn "metal bending," as opposed to methodology. The "know why" of aircraft design, he felt, Japan emphatically would not get.

This was not a view held by the Pentagon agency concerned with protecting military secrets, the Defense Technology Security Administration, which considered technology transfer risky business. Its director, Dr. Stephen Bryen, spoke out against the whole concept of co-production. He feared the damage it could someday do the aircraft industry.

Rubinstein disagreed. "The GAO report was one polemicist using a selective reading of the evidence. Technology release was very carefully reviewed. You have to consider whether U.S. industry was generally satisfied with these agreements. They were the ones who stood to lose. If the answer was yes, they were satisfied, then DoD had no reason to interpose. If there was some real problem, it would have been fixed in that way."

There was a gestalt aspect to co-production and a philosophy to which Rubinstein subscribed. As a process, it yielded common weapons among allies, a great logistical virtue. Henry Ford used to say, "You can have any arms you like, provided they're all the same." What is more, co-production strengthened weak economies susceptible to Communist influence—though it was a little difficult applying this rationale to Japan in the early 1980s, when it had become a capitalist miracle state.

Co-production grew out of the Pentagon's military assistance programs of the 1950s. At the time, Western Europe was rebuilding under the Marshall Plan and dollars were in short supply, though military budgets were expanding. Co-production cut those costs.

The important feature of co-production was standardization. In 1961, the Western alliance employed fourteen different types of small-arms ammunition, while the eight nations of the Warsaw Pact shared just one. As an ideal, co-production brought nations closer together, augmenting treaties and agreements through interdependence. In this, the gestalt of co-production was a close cousin to the utopia of free trade.

With the Warsaw Pact flexing its mushrooming nuclear muscles behind the Iron Curtain, the West was anxious to build up and modernize its militaries. Out of this combination of threat and penury, the Pentagon offered co-production as a compromise, allowing Europe to rebuild its industries and armed forces, while the U.S. Treasury reduced its foreign aid burden and U.S. arms manufacturers benefited their bottom lines through the sale of licenses. Government and industry in the United States made healthy profits from co-production through royalties, mark-ups, and equipment sales, business they might not otherwise have enjoyed.

Davi M. D'Agostino was the youngest member of the GAO team investigating the F-15. She twice interviewed Rubinstein. Then in her late twenties, she was born in Wichita, Kansas, and raised in Fort Lauderdale, Florida. A graduate of Tulane University, she took her master's in international security affairs at Georgetown, where she graduated in 1976. This was only her second case for the GAO. Before that, she had worked part-time at the Congressional Research Service, the information-gathering and analytical arm of the Congress.

When Rubinstein thought of the GAO's naiveté, he thought of D'Agostino. Part of her problem may have been that she looked a lot like actress Karen Allen, of *Raiders of the Lost Ark* fame. She had large brown eyes and a flashing smile—not the type to inspire fear in the heart of a seasoned bureaucratic warrior like Rubinstein. She was a woman confronting a male-dominated Pentagon bureaucracy revving up for the largest peacetime spending spree in history; co-production was an essential part of that program, providing economies of scale for U.S. planners. Gaining acceptance, let alone respect, would not prove easy.

D'Agostino was not without resources, however. She knew the arms trade, and had worked as an analyst for a large international weapons dealer in Washington. Her chief asset was her resourcefulness, her ability to ferret out alternative routes around problems, Rubinstein being one. He had attempted to block her trip to Tokyo to study the Japanese aviation industry, but D'Agostino outmaneuvered him. She was street-smart, a blue-collar tough with good instincts and a sharp mind. Her guiding principle was: "Where you stand is where you sit." The issues and opinions a person represents reflects on who they are. "I didn't go into this to make a case. My aim was to bring objectivity to DoD's co-production programs with Japan. Every word of the report was backed up by reams of evidence from Japanese and American sources."

The study arose, D'Agostino recalled, from the GAO's "burden-sharing" studies of the late 1970s. While trying to determine the degree to which allies shared in the common defense of the West, information was obtained by the GAO that indicated there were problems with co-production. Lots of U.S. technology was flowing overseas, with little drifting back in return. This was particularly true in the case of Japan. In 1978, huge transfers of defense industrial knowledge poured into Japan through co-production programs. The largest of these was the F-15.

She concluded from her study that Japan was committed to rebuilding its aviation industry and that co-production programs gave Japan the leverage to vault into direct competition with the United States. Moreover, the extent of Japan's financial backing—and thus the government's direct commitment to these projects—was not always clear. She found, for example, that funds for aviation appeared throughout the Japanese government budget, under such headings as agriculture, forestry, education. At the same time, Japan made no secret of its goals. For three decades running, Japan had been announcing its intentions in aviation.

D'Agostino personally wrote the damning third chapter of the report: "U.S. Military Co-production Programs Assist Japan in Developing Its Civil Aircraft Industry." She found that Japanese industry was making "large capital investments" in facilities and equipment. That Japan knocked down barriers between civilian and defense production, thus gaining economies of scale and synergy. She succinctly captured the strategy of the incipient FS-X program: "Technological innovations in the aircraft industry, electronics, communications, and alloy and composite materials production and processing are considered mutually complementary. *Aircraft production represents an integration of these new technologies*" (emphasis in original).

The Pentagon's Japan desk dismissed the report summarily, as had Rubinstein. "Trash," in the words of the man whose views would dominate U.S.-Japan security relations through the decade of the eighties, James E. Auer. The GAO researchers "were all in the their twenties." He didn't think they were dumb, but he dismissed their experience. "When those people were in Japan, who did they talk to, Ambassador Mansfield, or the man who mops his floor? It was a trash job."

Auer and Rubinstein would soon be in a position to closely view the very matters the GAO described in its report. Rubinstein would go to Tokyo to work on co-production programs at the embassy, and Auer would continue on at the Pentagon. As Dr. Tsutsui's work progressed on the FS-X in Japan's Laboratory Three, the two Americans would be on the front lines of the U.S. response, one that completely dismissed the findings of the investigative arm of the U.S. Congress.

4

The Little State Department in the Pentagon

"Did I convince Weinberger, or did he convince me? I don't know."
—JAMES E. AUER, special assistant for Japan, International Security Agency

T HIRTEEN THOUSAND LABORERS toiled mightily for sixteen months to complete the Pentagon, building it upon a piece of land known as Hell's Bottom in the Year of Our Lord 1942. As the Communists once noted about Wall Street, the Pentagon began at a cemetery and ended at a river. Taking its mystical Masonic shape from the five roads that bordered its original site, it was designed over one lone weekend in July 1941. One wonders if architect Hugh Pat Casey had been carrying the idea for the edifice around in his back pocket. Five nested concrete pentagons are interconnected by ten radiating corridors, so that no two points in the building's seventeen and a half miles of corridors are more than seven minutes apart. Old now, the Pentagon experiences an average twenty power outages a day lasting up to two hours each.

The bureaucracy at the Pentagon is no salute to its efficient design. The organizational chart of the Pentagon's staff is printed by the Department of Defense on a broadside of heavy gold-colored paper stock. The stacks of interconnected affiliations lined up in flow-chart fashion resemble lights burning late in the windows of a darkened office tower. The thin rows of print listing names and titles fit like narrow louvered blinds.

On one side of the graphic, which happens to be the left although it is descriptive of nothing political, sits the Office of Defense Policy. It is the tallest stack of names on the chart. Here, the "Little State Department in the Pentagon," as the sprawling and powerful International Security Agency is known, takes its place in the Defense hierarchy. The agency was responsible for selling arms, secret operations, and monitoring issues that ranged from the Soviet military buildup developing along the Pacific Rim to handling U.S. sailors caught pissing on the Brazilian flag in Rio de Janeiro. Here the air war against North Vietnam was conceived and what came to be called *The Pentagon Papers* were compiled and written.

The ISA was likened to the State Department because it was run on a "desk" system: Responsibility for key nations is divided into individual departments that are referred to as desks. There is a Japan desk at the State Department and a Japan desk at the ISA. In the early and middle 1980s, the agency's Japan department was a single desk run by one man, a gangling, professorial political appointee of the Reagan administration named James E. Auer. In the world of defense, Auer was the Pentagon's ambassador to Japan.

A retired navy commander, Auer was a graduate of the prestigious doctoral program at Tufts University's Fletcher School of Law and Diplomacy. The first American to have graduated from Japan's Maritime Self-Defense Forces Staff College, in 1977, Auer studied Japanese at a Jesuit university in the resort city of Kamakura, an hour's train ride south from Tokyo. To be awarded a degree, he was required to write six papers over the course of a year. Three of the papers were expected to be written in Japanese. Auer topped that, writing five papers in Japanese.

In fact, Auer set a strong example for the program. He was a trailblazer. In the early 1970s, an assistant to Melvin Laird, who was then Secretary of Defense, attended a briefing given by Auer. The talk was on expanding defense relations with Japan. It much pleased the Defense aide. "That's the best explanation I've heard yet of how the Nixon Doctrine is supposed to work," Auer remembered him saying. The remark represented a public pat on the back that became the lever Auer used to propel his career into high gear.

No one in the Pentagon boasted a wider, more detailed working knowledge of U.S.-Japan defense relations than Jim Auer. From 1971 to 1973, he served as political adviser to the commander of U.S. naval forces in Yokosuka, the giant U.S. base at the western entrance of Tokyo Bay. When the Nixon administration's National Security Council decided that for the first time ever a U.S. aircraft carrier, the *Midway*, would be homeported outside the States, and that it would be in Japan, Auer did much of the work that finally brought the deal off, winning a Legion of Merit for himself in the process. The medal is the highest noncombat citation given by the military.

Auer believed in Japan. He made no bones about it. "I am in favor of U.S.-Japan relations because I believe it is good for the United States and Japan. The United States ought to make up its mind: Is Japan our ally or not? If it is, we ought not to act deceptively toward it." In terms of U.S.-Japan relations that meant no bullying, no patronizing. He tried to be sensitive to the positions taken by his Japanese counterparts. Symbols were important to him. He took great pride, for instance, at how the carrier *Midway* had been maintained by its Japanese hosts. He liked to point to the fact that the great carrier lasted years past its scheduled retirement. That saved the United States big money and cemented an important working relationship.

Akahata, the newspaper of the Japanese Communist Party, once quoted Auer in its headlines: "American Defense Official Says U.S.-Japan Security Treaty More Important Than NATO." The article that followed surprised Auer with its accuracy. In fact, in a moment of archness, the lifelong anti-Communist considered writing a letter to the paper thanking them for reporting his speeches so faithfully.

Auer pointed out that Japan, with the good wishes of the Reagan administration, had evolved into the third-largest military in the world in dollar terms. By 1991, if all went according to plan, Tokyo would have three times the number of destroyers in the Pacific as the U.S. Seventh Fleet and as many fighter jets as the United States used to defend its own skies. In the Pacific that added up to more aircraft than the United States kept stationed in Japan, Korea, and the Philippines combined. Auer emphasized the great savings this allowed the U.S. military.

Though Auer always minimized his own clout, he had outstanding connections in the Pentagon and the State Department. He got his job at the Little State Department in the Pentagon through Michael H. Armacost, who would go on to become ambassador to Japan, replacing the legendary Mike Mansfield. Also interceding on Auer's behalf was Admiral William J. Crowe, Jr., who would become Chairman of the Joint Chiefs of Staff in the Reagan administration.

Auer was an articulate, affable man, with a pleasant face and thinning hair that formed narrow bands when combed across his scalp. His prominent nose was set off by glittering blue eyes and a ready smile. His voice was resonant with conviction, and his arguments were carefully drawn, entire of themselves, even where they were not persuasive. He would lecture, even preach on issues. Absent, however, from the Auer demeanor was the persona of the military man. There was no "Black Jack" Pershing here, although there was no lack of admiration for the man or the type.

In fact, Auer idolized his immediate superior, the Assistant Secretary of Defense for International Security Affairs, Richard L. Armitage, for his swashbuckling and derring-do. Armitage, the number three man in the Pentagon, was known for taking positions, going against the grain, and yet still managing to move controversial programs through the bureaucracy, getting his own way for the most part. A graduate of the Naval Academy in the same year as ex-Marine Oliver North, 1967, he had the ear of Secretary Weinberger, who held him in some awe.

Armitage had cachet throughout Washington, where he was something of a mythic figure. There were tales of Armitage slugging back Jack Daniel's straight from the bottle with Panamanian dictator Manuel Noriega. There was the rumor that he was the model for Colonel Kurtz in Francis Ford Coppola's film *Apocalypse Now*, a cinematic adaptation of Joseph Conrad's *Heart of Darkness*. Armitage denied this, although he did consult on the film. Fluent in Vietnamese, he served three combat tours advising the Vietnamese riverine forces, in the heart of Southeast Asia's darkness. There were those in the press and even those inside Washington's military establishment who considered him dangerous.

Armitage's weekly routine was legend. He left home before sunrise to lift weights in the Pentagon gym. On the job at 6 A.M., he would begin his day reading the overnight cable traffic from the embassies. Staffers expected calls from him at 7 A.M. to go over the issues confronting their desks. He regularly worked until 9:30 at night. He would be up again at 4:30. On Saturday mornings he was back in the office, usually dressed in gym shorts, a ball cap, a T-shirt, his feet up on the desk. Friday afternoons were Miller Time in his office and the whole staff came in to relax and talk about the week.

The Japanese especially admired Armitage, whom they saw as an American samurai. He was Japan's most influential advocate at the Pentagon. They described him as *naniwabushi*, a man who would lay down his life for another. This was a superlative compliment, the ultimate in comradeship and loyalty. To be *naniwabushi* was to be irreversibly humble and limitlessly courageous, generous and unutterably committed in the irreversible instant of death. Americans did not have a word for whatever it was Armitage had, but many in the Reagan administration, particularly Vice President George Bush, admired it.

The only thing bigger than Armitage's reputation was Armitage himself. Bald and pink, bright-eyed, he was a power weight lifter who toted up thousand-pound sets with presses, squats, and splits. With his bald dome and barrel chest, he cut a figure reminiscent of Mussolini. He had that thing the policy wonks on Capitol Hill most lacked: mystique.

Together, he and Auer enjoyed a direct channel to Secretary of Defense Caspar Weinberger. This was significant because information flowed from the staff upstream to the top. The linkages were powerful. Weinberger had an almost fraternal rapport with President Reagan. Thus the chain reached the top and formed an iron triangle with the State Department and the military side of the military-industrial complex.

Weinberger gave Auer much credit for the success of Japan's emergence as a military power. He called him a "brilliant, a leading expert on Japan" in his memoirs, *Fighting for Peace*. Many of Weinberger's positions on U.S.-Japan issues were scripted by Auer. Sometimes they were even co-opted by the Secretary.

Auer, for instance, often used a color photograph of the Northeast Asian region taken by satellite in polar orbit to illustrate Japan's strategic importance to the United States. In the photo, the four main islands are seen strung in a 1,000-mile scimitar-shaped arc around Vladivostok, home of the Soviet Navy. What was obvious from this view was that Japan was neatly positioned to slice off a Soviet thrust into the Pacific. The photo demonstrated the strategic importance of the inward-looking archipelago; a battle-ready Japan could seal tight the Soviet's sea gates to the Pacific. One of Japan's peculiarities and strategic advantages is that while it comprises little more land area than California, it is stretched into a narrow island chain ringing huge expanses of watery territory.

Secretary of Defense Weinberger thought that a powerful Japanese force in the East could also serve to keep the Soviets off balance in the West. Weinberger could not ignore the Soviet buildup in the Pacific. During the 1980s the Soviets raised 55 divisions of ground forces, more than 800 ships, and at least 3,000 fixed-wing aircraft for its Pacific war machine. A rearmed Japan meant that Soviet commanders could not ignore a second front. Although the phrase never really caught on, this was the Weinberger Doctrine, the stamp the Reagan administration put on U.S.-Japan defense affairs.

When Weinberger writes of these things in his memoirs, published in May 1990, he echoes Auer's satellite imagery, word for unattributed word in some cases. He begins his chapter on U.S.-Japan relations: "A line drawn west from the northernmost tip of Hokkaido Island intersects the east coast of the Soviet Union at a point three hundred miles north of the key Soviet Naval port of Vladivostok, the only ice-free port of the eastern USSR."

More than two years before, Auer had written in the April 1988 edition of *Current History*, a world affairs journal: "A line drawn due west from the northernmost tip of Hokkaido intersects the east coast of the Soviet Union, at a point 300 miles due north of the key Soviet naval port of Vladivostok."

Auer was modest and tactful about this. "Weinberger knew my name," he says. "Reagan never did. Weinberger had a lot of influence with Reagan. Did I convince Weinberger, or did he convince me? I don't know."

Sketchy evidence that Japan was going forward with plans to develop an indigenous fighter first began appearing on Auer's desk in 1983. Until that time, he had expected them to execute a twenty-four-plane purchase to make up for their shortfall of F-1 fighters, as they had announced the year before. The prospect was that this would result in a deal for a U.S.-designed aircraft. Now, it seemed, Japan had discovered that the F-1s on hand would last longer than expected. As a result, they would not have to purchase new aircraft for several years, when the entire fleet of F-1s would be phased out in favor of a replacement, the FS-X.

At approximately the same time, news of the F-1 decision reached the Little State Department in the Pentagon, purchasing orders and licensing requests for engines and avionics—mission computers, electronic warfare gear, electronic countermeasures equipment—began accumulating in the Defense Technology Security Administration. The role of the DTSA was to watchdog industrial secrets and technologies that affected national security. The pattern that emerged from the Japanese licensing requests suggested that Japan was exploring other possibilities than a direct purchase for its planned F-1 replacement.

Separately, Auer learned early in 1985 that the research arm of the Japan Defense Agency—the Technical Research and Development Institute's Laboratory Three—was at work on an internal study, initiated that January and published in time for the Prime Minister's cabinet meeting that September, that would claim that Japan had the expertise to build modern fighters on its own.

The CIA was also reporting on these developments and took a dim view of Laboratory Three's capabilities. In its own study, it concluded that Tsutsui's people did not have the technology or the experience to build an advanced fighter aircraft on its own. The agency raised questions about whether Japan recognized the magnitude of their problem. The report drew a picture of a Japanese military deluded by the success of its civilian sector, one that had not so much overestimated its abilities as it had underestimated the difficulty of its proposed undertaking. For one thing, Tsutsui had low-ball cost projections. Developing an advanced fighter costs between $3 billion and $5 billion, according to U.S. calculations and experience. The TRDI was budgeting $1.2 billion.

But more important, at least from a negotiator's point of view, was the CIA's determination that Japan could not build the plane *without U.S. technology.* Unless the United States was willing to back Japan's plans for domestic development, the project was doomed to failure. That would take billions of yen out of an already limited Japanese defense budget. That money could go to better uses, such as a U.S. fighter. Thus, the CIA determined that a domestic FS-X could not go forward. It was against U.S. interests.

That put the issue in the middle of Auer's desk.

The official U.S. position on this incipient program began to emerge in June 1985, when Japanese defense director Koichi Kato paid a visit to Secretary of Defense Weinberger in Washington. The scion of a samurai family, the forty-six-year-old politician enjoyed noting that he was a Harvard alumnus, as was Weinberger, although he only attended the university for one year. Kato was much Weinberger's junior, in terms of both age and government ranking. Kato had a lower rank because Japan's defense agency was not accorded the full status of a ministry by the postwar constitution. This, and the still fresh memories of the occupation, gave the Pentagon considerable leverage over Japan's defense forces.

Unlike defense secretaries in Washington, defense directors in Japan come and go, seldom lasting more than a year in the post. The position is largely titular. Although Kato served twice in the post, political observers were shocked by his appointment. So was Kato, who envisioned himself as a labor minister, or welfare minister, or even minister of agriculture. Never defense. He was seen by Prime Minister Nakasone, who had himself once been defense chief, as young and inexperienced.

No one doubted Kato's ability or talents, however. A stout and square man, Kato had a large mole on the edge of his nose that seemed to support his square eye frames. He had an extraordinary ear for English, which he spoke with great confidence and exuberance, his accent more British than American. This was perhaps the single most important qualification for a Nakasone defense chief. He could directly talk to the Americans, without the need for translation.

Leery of technical matters, Kato was acutely aware of his military's desires for domestic development. Most of all he was impressed with their enthusiasm and self-confidence. Though the industry represented the most narrow margins of the Japanese industrial complex, they exuded potential.

Despite his apparent Yankee orientation, Kato would have a hard time reconciling the home team's wishes with those of their patrons at the Pentagon. He knew that the FS-X was going to become a problem, and he recognized the growing perception in the United States that Japan was knocking at the door of America's last great, unchallenged manufacturing sector: aircraft.

When Kato arrived at the Pentagon that summer in 1985, he was greeted by a circumspect Caspar Weinberger, who figured that with the FS-X still in the incipient stages, he could afford to continue his policy of low-key caution. Weinberger had bigger fish to fry, for there was much the Secretary wanted from the director. High on the agenda was a hoped-for Japanese commitment to take part in Star Wars, the Reagan administration plan to create a missile defense umbrella for friend and foe alike. Also on the menu were sales proposals for the ultra-expensive AEGIS destroyer program and the equally costly AWACS early-warning plane. The Pentagon's business was selling defense.

Still, the intellectually bustling and intense Weinberger sought assurances on the FS-X. "Was it true," he asked Kato, "that Japan had already decided to go forward with domestic development?"

Kato told him no. No decision had been arrived at. Japan, he explained, was exploring three options for the FS-X—to buy a foreign aircraft, to refit additional aircraft that it was currently manufacturing, or to begin domestic development. He made plain that it was true that there was strong support for an all-Japan fighter. Industry, he said, was behind domestic development, as was MITI and the parliament. The project already had momentum.

Weinberger tried to be accommodating. He told Kato that he understood that the FS-X was Japan's project and that it would be paid for out of Japan's pocket. "This is a decision that is up to the government of Japan," he said. He told Kato that he would try to keep the issues of trade and defense from being muddied and mixed together. In other words, he would try to hold off the Congress. More important to the Japanese, he promised not to take the issue public, so that the matter would be settled quietly and without rancor.

In military terms, Weinberger argued that cooperation with the United States on the FS-X would assist in the interoperability of the nations' armed forces, returning to the notion that an ally's hardware should be shared. U.S. aircraft, for example, could augment Japanese forces in a time of war, if they shared the same weaponry and tactics. Interoperability was a potent and seemingly commonsense argument. It was also a not too subtle Buy American sales pitch; for this reason the Japanese, not unlike other U.S. allies, nodded in the direction of interoperability while trying to change the subject.

Weinberger, however, tried to keep his presentation fixed on the security angle. He wrote in his memoirs: ". . . FS-X was [Japan's] decision. I did not apply pressure as such, but gave them general performance information about American aircraft, public data concerning maintenance costs and the suitability of our various planes for their defense needs. I left them in no doubt that they should buy a United States plane. I shared with them our experience, and reminded them of the problems and very great expense that some of our allies had encountered in trying to build their own planes; specifically, I mentioned Israel's enormously expensive Lavi fighter planes, which the Israeli government later canceled at our urging."

In August 1985, two months after Kato called on Weinberger, Auer had lunch a few blocks from the Ministry of International Trade and Industry, in the Hibiya business district, with Takeshi Isayama, the ministry's director of the Aircraft and Ordnance Division. Isayama was held in high regard by Auer because he had a good feel for U.S. interests and was comfortable around Americans, having served as the Japanese consul in New York. Fluent in English, the smiling Isayama had a casual and appealingly easygoing manner. Problems between the two nations over issues such as the FS-X were not irreconcilable, as Isayama saw it. Cultural issues and differences in national character caused misunderstandings, but beneath it all the two peoples shared the common ground of human nature. He therefore understood the position

the United States found itself in—overstretched internationally, overbur-
dened financially, and overwhelmed by Japanese competition. Under the circumstances, he was surprised that the United States did not pursue the FS-X
more aggressively.

Meeting Auer for lunch was Isayama's idea, and he raised the subject of the
FS-X. He was curious about why there was no overt U.S. pressure being
applied. Why was the United States taking such a disinterested approach?

Auer responded that the United States did not intend to apply pressure.
"It's your money," Auer said. "Our two nations face the same Soviet threat."
Auer talked about the excellence of U.S. aircraft and reminded Isayama of the
political climate in both countries. He mentioned Japan's huge trade surplus.
"In the end," he said with genuine confidence, "the United States assumed
that this would be a decision made at the highest level of the Japanese government, which would have to take responsibility for that decision."

Isayama seemed crestfallen and replied with a half smile, "That's unfair;
that's the strongest possible pressure you could apply."

There was something Zen-like in Auer's approach—the force applied without effort. In a way, it was a Japanese response to a Japanese problem. While
Isayama claimed no recollection of the exchange, the message Auer thought
he delivered carried the full force of U.S.-Japan relations: Auer to Armitage
to Weinberger to Reagan. As Auer had put it, this was a decision that would
be made at the highest levels of government. If the United States was lying
low for now, it plainly intended to take the question of the FS-X all the way
to the highest levels in Washington and Tokyo.

As far as the Defense Department's ambassador to Japan, James Auer, was
concerned, his message to Isayama was as plain as the outcome of that message was predictable: Japan would mend its ways over the FS-X, and it would
get on board the U.S. program. Auer never dreamed that Isayama, MITI, or
the Japan Defense Agency had any other choice in the matter.

5

American Desires

"If Japan expects U.S. support for the FS-X program, there are certain requirements that would have to be met."

—GREGG A. RUBINSTEIN, Deputy Mutual Defense Assistance Officer, U.S. Embassy, Tokyo

JIM AUER trusted men like defense chief Koichi Kato. The Japanese leader seemed well attuned to the patron-protégé parallels of the U.S.-Japan relationship. Auer believed Kato would bring the Japan Defense Agency to its senses on the FS-X. Consequently, in the fall of 1985, the United States played a waiting game, giving the political forces within Japan's military establishment time to work. Beyond that, there was no plan. The United States was in a reactive mode.

The FS-X issue took more definite form in Japan that September, when the Prime Minister's cabinet officially began consultations on its next five-year defense plan, known as the Mid-Term Defense Estimate. What emerged from those deliberations held no surprises. The FS-X would go forward.

The official cabinet program called for the defense agency to explore three contingencies for the FS-X: buying a foreign aircraft; reconditioning an aircraft now in the Japanese arsenal; or domestic development. One of those three would be chosen, probably in the next six months—that is, by June 1986. With the annual security consultations between the two nations scheduled after the New Year, in January 1986, Auer and company had two months to arrive at a strategy to counter Japanese plans.

Gregg A. Rubinstein, the pudgy, bearded, pipe-smoking foreign service officer who was now at the U.S. Embassy in Tokyo, began framing a response to the FS-X immediately after the cabinet session. The cable he produced on the subject was not long in coming. Indeed, it was a matter he had been considering for months. As he saw it, two of the three options Japan proposed for the FS-X were throwaways—"straw men," as he called them.

In the first case, he argued, it was highly unlikely that Japan would buy 130 ready-made fighters—the number called for in the defense estimate—from the United States. At no time in the last twenty-five years had Japan made a large purchase of U.S. weaponry without something in it for itself, in the form of licenses or technology. Japan had a long-term strategy of building up its own defense industry. In every case but one, Japan produced its own aircraft from U.S. designs. Why would it now revert back to a 1950s strategy, especially when it envisioned a future for itself in the aerospace industry?

Just as unlikely, Rubinstein reasoned, was the call for an upgrade of an existing fighter, which happened to be an F-4J, a plane designed by McDonnell Douglas in the 1950s. If the FS-X was going to be an aircraft that would fly into the year 2030, a year 2000 aircraft as the Japanese called it, it made no sense to base it on technology that was already antique.

Both proposals were clearly designed for domestic consumption, he said, to make clear to Japan's defense-wary parliament and to its penny-pinching Finance Ministry that the air force had exhausted all the alternatives. The same rationale applied equally to the United States. The defense agency didn't want the Pentagon to think that it had been cut out of the deal without being given due consideration.

By the process of elimination, this left Japan with one remaining option: domestic development. Based on that assumption, Rubinstein's cable contained a simple and straightforward counterproposal. Whereas Japan traditionally manufactured U.S.-designed aircraft under license, through the process of co-production the United States should now offer the defense agency a sweetener and encourage Japan's military to take the next logical step. He called it co-development. All that it meant, in Rubinstein's mind, was the redesign of a U.S. fighter to Japanese specifications. Smaller co-development programs had had success in NATO. Although nothing on this scale had ever been attempted before, it was not seen as a complicated matter. An antitank missile had been co-developed; a new family of air-to-air missiles was being worked on. Co-developing the FS-X would be something on the order of updating an existing U.S. model aircraft based on Japanese technology.

Rubinstein never dreamed that so simple an approach could go out of control. Neither did anyone else in the U.S. chain of command. There were so many terms in use for defense cooperation—co-production, licensed production, joint production—co-development was just another variation on the same theme. In the minds of those on the U.S. side, co-development did not mean that U.S. designers would sit down with Japanese designers and create a whole new plane. They made it clear to the Japanese that was precisely what they wanted to avoid. In co-development, Rubinstein thought he was calling for a polite compromise, not a confrontation over national goals. "Co-production-plus" was how he saw it.

"Be precise. Avoid zeal." Those were Rubinstein's watchwords. He had adopted them from his college readings of Harold Nicolson, a British diplomat prominent in the creation of the Versailles Treaty ending World War I. Those accords failed, Nicolson wrote, because they lacked precision, an obvious diplomatic failure and one that constantly arose between the United States and Japan. The imprecision that killed the Versailles accords and bit at the ankles of U.S.-Japan relations derived from the same damaging tendency, and that was zeal. The greatest risk in pursuing an important negotiation was to turn it into a crusade. Be precise. Avoid zeal.

Rubinstein's office was on the seventh floor of the U.S. Embassy, two floors below the ambassador. This was the Mutual Defense Assistance Office, which acted as the liaison between American arms merchants and Japanese defense procurers. Rubinstein was the office deputy, its action arm.

On the bland wall across from his desk in Tokyo hung a print depicting the Meiji Emperor atop a white stallion. The Emperor was the symbol of Japan's nineteenth-century renaissance. In the lifetime of this one man (he was eighteen years old when he succeeded his father), Japan heaved itself out of the medieval knighthood of the Tokugawa era and went roaring into the Industrial Revolution. Under his chrysanthemum seal, the symbol of Imperial perfection, Japan adopted a parliamentary constitution and the military became a profession. The nation emerged as a world power, a testing ground for newly developed military technologies. It became the first Asian country in modern times to defeat a Western military power, the mighty Russian Empire.

Rubinstein found the lithograph in a Los Angeles shop that specialized in *objets de guerre*. He had wandered past the place by chance one day while traveling. After surveying the shop's racks of iron crosses and stacks of swords, he was on his way out when he glanced over the glass counter and recognized the Emperor Mutsuhito. Figuring the store owners didn't know about the print, he hid his surprise and inquired about it. The owners didn't seem particularly interested. It was some "Chinaman," he was told, and they quoted a price of twenty-five dollars. Down to his last twenty dollars, he offered a deal: Take the picture out of the frame and knock off five bucks. Rubinstein went home with an original lithograph, an official regimental portrait. It was a collector's item worth hundreds, maybe more.

Japan was not a foreign country to Rubinstein. His father owned a small electronics trading firm that introduced the first Hitachi products into the

American market in the 1950s, including the company's first transistorized radios. Educated at the University of Chicago, with a master's from Columbia University, Rubinstein was a product of the Reischauer-Mansfield era, a time after the war when Japan was viewed as America's understudy in Asia, our apprentice in Democracy and Capitalism.

Rubinstein's proposal for the FS-X grew out of a series low-level talks with his Japanese counterparts. "If Japan expects U.S. support for the FS-X program," he told them, "there are certain requirements that would have to be met." Chiefly that meant some kind of agreement between the two governments. The United States, he made clear, would not stand by as a passive participant. At the very least, he reasoned, Japan was going to have to buy the engines for the FS-X. Furthermore, it was already clear from the licensing requests the Japanese were submitting to the Defense Department that other, just as sensitive technologies would also be required. Japan, obviously, couldn't go forward with the program without U.S. help, and the United States was not going to give away technology without something in return. At least in Rubinstein's rational mind, this left little room for unalloyed domestic development, no matter what name was finally attached to the process.

Rubinstein's vision for the FS-X was elegant in the manner in which it negotiated the fine lines of U.S.-Japan security relations. It was a breakthrough. In a single package it presented the United States with the opportunity to bring Japan closer into the defense fold and make it more and more a European-style ally. At the same time, it would open up a two-way highway for technology between the two nations, instead of the present one-way street running from the United States to Japan, which characterized the postwar era. What's more, it could save the Pentagon and U.S. taxpayers millions, perhaps billions of dollars. Because if the project worked, Japan would fund a substantial portion of the cost of building the next version of a top-of-the-line U.S. fighter.

That was precisely what Rubinstein had in mind when he spoke about the co-development of the FS-X. The project would be a joint U.S.-Japan effort to build the F-16 Agile Falcon or the F/A-18 Super Hornet Plus, the drawing-board iterations of fighters currently in the U.S. arsenal.

Of course, as things now stood between the United States and Japan, Rubinstein would have been happy to take a lot less. Japanese law forbade the export of defense equipment. That meant any FS-X jointly built with Japan couldn't be exported to the U.S. military. That was an obstacle to be overcome, Rubinstein reasoned. Already the United States was the one exception to this law, although Japan could export only technology, not actual weaponry. And even that had yet to take place, despite serious negotiations and a host of technology agreements dating back to the 1950s. In fact, Rubinstein did not know what technologies he actually wanted to get from Japan, only that he wanted technology, any technology. So much for precision.

Gaining a two-way technology flow with Japan was potentially very significant, however, and worth the trouble. Industrial cooperation was the tool the Pentagon used in the hope of defining its relations with the Japanese, which, when they were not vague, were confusing. The word for ally, for example, in Japanese is *domei koku*. Nazi Germany was Japan's *domei koku* during World War II. In the postwar era, Japan has described its connection with the United States in treaty terms, a *joyaku*, a relationship. No reference by Japan to the United States as an ally, *domei koku*, has ever appeared in any document, not even in communiqués, the bulletins issued after talks between a nation's representatives.

Japan hovered in a defense netherworld, and the view of Japan as a close U.S. ally was not matched in Tokyo. Japan was clearly equivocal about its relations with America. For the public, the relationship was an economic benefit that threatened foreign entanglement, which they feared might lead their nation back down the road to militarism.

Although America was tremendously attractive to the Japanese imagination, the U.S. government was seen by the Japanese public as high-handed and coercive, constantly applying pressure to force Japan into agreements like the Mutual Security Treaty, or guarantees to guard its sea lanes out to a thousand miles. Whereas Japan was utterly captivated by American culture—indeed, Japan was as Americentric as America was Eurocentric—it was completely repulsed by America's international posture.

Japan's ambivalence was evident in the bureaucracy at the U.S. Embassy. The Mutual Defense Assistance Office, where Rubinstein worked, was unique to Japan, and it would become a focal point in the development of the FS-X. It was the only U.S. arms sales office whose number two officer was from the State Department, as opposed to Defense. Rubinstein was a foreign service officer seconded to DoD.

In Europe, the United States maintained an ODC at its embassies, an Office of Defense Cooperation, where alliance issues were coordinated. In less developed countries, the United States maintained MAGs, Military Assistance Groups, where the United States played defense analyst, arsenal, sponsor, and bodyguard.

Rubinstein's Mutual Defense Assistance Office was none of the above. As an institution, its functions were somewhere between a liaison for a First World industrial power, which Japan was, and an arms merchant to a Third World political backwater, which, arguably, Japan also was. Only in existence since the late 1970s, the Mutual Defense Assistance Office was temporary, jury-rigged, a mobile home to be abandoned for something bigger and better in the future. Indeed, no one quite knew how to refer to it. When it was used

as an acronym—pronounced EM-dow—it stood for the Mutual Defense Assistance Office. More often it got just three initials: the MDO, for Mutual
Defense Office.

Which is where the FS-X came in. It represented a point of demarcation, a
graduation out of the halfway house of the MDO and into the mainstream
Euro-alliance of the ODC. Rubinstein saw the FS-X as a crossroads in Japan's relations with the United States. The fighter project signified a time of
transition.

Washington reacted positively to Rubinstein's cable. At the Department of
State, Rubinstein's counterpart, John F. Scott, chief of the Political-Military
Section, had been thinking along similar lines. He agreed that a straightfor-
ward purchase of an American aircraft just wasn't a realistic expectation. The
same applied to upgrading a plane that was nearly thirty years old, the F-4J.
He, too, saw co-development as "the next logical step."

Scott took special notice of Rubinstein's budget arguments, which concentrated on Japanese defense expenditures. Since 1976, Japan had capped its
defense spending at 1 percent of gross national product (GNP), the total
value of the goods and services the nation produced each year. Though Japan's GNP grew at an astonishing 5 percent per year (the U.S. GNP grew at
about 3 percent) and defense spending was growing at about the same rate,
the amount of money available for the defense buildup the Reagan administration foresaw was short of the mark. There was no way, for example, for
Japan to fulfill its pledge to defend its sea lanes within the current budget
constraints. By comparison, the United States was sinking nearly 6 percent of
its GNP into defense.

But now, on top of its limited budget, Japan was proposing to invest billions in an FS-X program that essentially reinvented the wheel. Japan needed
to economize, not put money into expensive and risky defense programs like
this one. Fighter development was a tricky business, as evidenced by the failed
F-1, Japan's mostly homegrown supersonic fighter.

By entering into a deal with the United States for its next fighter jet, the
Japanese would get far more bang for the buck. A comparable U.S. aircraft
would cost less than half the price of developing the FS-X. There were more
important matters for Japan to spend its money on. The United States
wanted Japan involved in Star Wars, AWACS, and AEGIS.

There was a further consideration. As the State Department's Scott later
explained it: "The end result of domestic development would be an airplane
that was not necessarily either compatible with or interoperable with the U.S.
[military]. In the context of a bilateral security relationship, the two militaries
had to be able to operate together, to communicate together, and have a
sense of one another's strategy and tactics. Those are both areas that we had

set a lot of stock in." It came down to this, in the view of the State Department: If Japan really wanted a strong defense, the answer was to Buy American.

In Japan, the response appeared positive, at least from Japan's frugal, budget-guarding Ministry of Finance. They made no secret of what the future would hold. An official of the ministry was quoted in November 1985 in the *Tokyo Shimbun*, a second-string Japanese daily: "The Department of State and Defense's opposition to *kokusanka* [domestic development] is explicit, and the Ministry of Finance wants no deepening of the trade friction because of this issue."

Still, the United States did not press the matter of the FS-X, and the Japan Defense Agency misconstrued whatever hints Rubinstein and Auer tossed across the bargaining table—or, more precisely, the sushi bar. This was confusing to the Japanese, and was widely perceived as being tacit encouragement from Auer, who was considered a close friend of Japan.

Just five months after Auer met over lunch with the MITI representative and unveiled what later came to be called his "no-pressure pressure" strategy on the FS-X, arrangements began for a Weinberger visit to Tokyo the following spring. In these talks, Japanese representatives in Washington came away surprised that the FS-X was not listed for discussion. The impression of U.S. disinterest was augmented once again when there was no request that the FS-X be on the official agenda for the annual security meeting to be held three months hence, in Hawaii.

Auer's strategy was taken as a sign that the United States was not going to press Japan on domestic development, which was good news to Japanese defense officials. The indications were that the FS-X would follow in the same domestic development footsteps as its predecessor, the bumbling F-1. There would be little interference from the United States. Washington seemed willing to allow Japan to build its second-tier support fighters at home.

What Japanese representatives arranging the Weinberger visit did not realize was that the Rubinstein cable detailing the U.S. response to the FS-X—the co-development plan—had only just arrived in Washington that October, less than four weeks earlier. It was still circulating through the bureaucracy and still under discussion. A U.S. response was certain to be forthcoming in January, when Japanese and American defense officials would be meeting in Hawaii.

The 800-room Japanese-owned Ilikai Hotel in Hawaii was the site and common ground for U.S.-Japan defense gatherings, a halfway meeting point on Japanese real estate situated on U.S. territory. Held on a regular yearly basis, the Security Subcommittee of the Security Consultative Group, known more practically as the SSC, gathered to discuss the working issues of the security relationship.

Originally aimed at informal talks about common defense concerns, the SSC had grown increasingly elaborate and ritualized over the years. Meetings were attended by the commander of the Pacific Fleet, the U.S. ambassador to Japan, the Japanese deputy defense chief, staffers for both sides (Auer and Rubinstein among them), and hordes of Japanese press covering every word and nuance of the proceedings. Typically, most of the discussion across the tables is polite and formal. The real business was transacted after hours.

The January 1986 convocation was the sixteenth such parley of the SSC, which was a creation of the U.S.-Japan Mutual Security Treaty of 1960. Held over three days, the meeting's big news was that there was no news at all. Security relations couldn't have been better, participants judged. Things were going in the right direction. U.S. ambassador Mike Mansfield gave his blessing to the new five-year defense estimate enacted in September and praised Prime Minister Nakasone for reappointing Koichi Kato as director of the Japan Defense Agency. Richard Armitage, the number two man at the meetings on the U.S. side, pronounced his pleasure with the new $147.2 billion five-year defense budget and reassured his Japanese counterpart that the pressures building in Congress to link the growing U.S. trade deficit with Japan to defense issues could be handled. This was taken as an assurance on the FS-X by the Japanese.

Indeed, the FS-X did not come up in the formal sessions, but after hours was a different matter. Richard Armitage broached the subject with his Japanese counterpart, the don of the Japan Defense Agency, Seiki Nishihiro. They spoke over dinner.

Nishihiro, aged fifty-six, was the most important Japanese defense official to emerge in the postwar era. He was a central figure at the defense agency because he was a seminal figure. A man of immense intelligence and unswerving integrity, he represented the first official of the defense agency to rise through the ranks to the principal position of policymaker. Whereas nearly every other post at his level was staffed by an official from one of the ministries, owing to the defense agency's second-class citizenship under the peace constitution, he alone was JDA-born and -bred. If the Japanese military was ever to ascend to the honored ranks of a ministry, its reinstatement would be based on the example of Nishihiro. People called him Mr. Japan Defense Agency.

A self-contained man, quiet, Nishihiro was a scholar of the Meiji Restoration, the period when Japan surged into the ranks of modern nations. Some on the U.S. side puzzled over him and dubbed him a sphinx. Popular and well regarded, especially by younger agency officials who saw their futures embodied in his career, he was known to enjoy drinking and gambling, male pursuits endorsed among the general populace.

Graying and deliberate, Nishihiro was a heavy smoker who would often squeeze three or four emptied packs of Japanese Mild 7 cigarettes into cellophane accordions in the course of a day's meetings. This was in stark contrast to the weight-lifting, fitness-conscious Armitage, who definitely did not smoke.

Attention to health was not something the middle-aged bureaucrat Nishihiro and the tough combat veteran Armitage had in common. Defense was. Armitage spoke of Nishihiro as the top planner in the defense agency. As he put it: "He's about the best strategic thinker that I've run across. I'm not limiting myself to Japanese strategic thinkers either. I know my own limitations, and I know what I do well. I recognize it in others when they have a talent. Seiki Nishihiro has a very great ability to see the big picture, a broad picture. He may be the finest strategic thinker I've seen."

Armitage flattered the modest Nishihiro, who demurred at the compliment. "I simply told Armitage about the history of the power balance in East Asia. Probably the United States did not pay as much attention to East Asia as they paid to Europe. We were looking at this Cold War from the Asian side."

Nishihiro proceeded under the assumption that, within limits, Armitage was being entirely candid with him. "Mr. Armitage was always clear about U.S. interests, and he understood Japanese interests. He sought compromise." The two men trusted one another.

The position Armitage took on the FS-X seemed to reflect that understanding, the pursuit of compromise. Armitage did not try to force the issue. He did point out that U.S. support for the program would come with a price —namely, U.S. participation. The new concept of co-development was brought up at the meeting, but it was not spelled out, other than to suggest a program that went beyond the standard licensed co-production programs between the two countries.

Nishihiro emphasized that Japan's three choices for the FS-X—foreign purchase, aircraft upgrade, domestic development—were really much more narrowly defined. "I made it clear to Armitage," he said, "that Japan wasn't looking to buy a plane right away. We wanted a plane in the year 2000. We didn't want something we could get in 1986. We wanted something better than that.

"I also told Armitage that if he couldn't get the United States to understand this, it would be a problem, because if it came down to buying the FS-X, then we would look to Europe as well."

The conversation had reached an impasse. The net effect, however, was the continued low-pressure approach Armitage's assistant James Auer had begun in Tokyo: The United States would take the position that this was Japan's decision, that this was Japan's money, that the FS-X was Japan's responsibility. Armitage held up the stick of co-development and called it a carrot.

Nishihiro took the long flight back to Tokyo contemplating a way to make Armitage's carrot palatable for domestic consumption. There was still a chance, he thought, that the United States would keep its word and not mix up trade with defense requirements, as Armitage promised during the formal SSC sessions.

What is more, agreements often changed in their implementation. One nation's co-development program could be seen by another as domestic development. At least that was how Nishihiro responded at a budget hearing in the upper house of Japan's parliament three months later.

Questioned about whether the defense agency was considering a collaboration with the United States on the FS-X, Nishihiro replied somewhat Talmudically, "Yes, [there is the choice of joint development] but is that not also a form of domestic development?"

In fact, Nishihiro was personally skeptical of the domestic development faction led by Ryozo Tsutsui. He referred to them in Japanese as *wagama*, "selfish." As he saw it, "they could not really build the plane if they could not build the engine, any more than they could build a house without knowing how to lay the foundation."

This represented a deep split on the Japanese side over how to proceed on the FS-X. At virtually the same moment as Nishihiro was speaking before the Diet, Japan's Air Staff Office was making it clear to visiting American defense officials that they discouraged any thought of a joint program. Indeed, the U.S. side returned from Tokyo convinced that Japan was about to go its own way on the FS-X.

The situation was less confused than it seemed, however, for Nishihiro was the man in charge and his actions spoke louder than his equivocating pronouncements. While speaking ambiguously of compromise, he opened the door to joint development by extending the deadline on the FS-X selection process for one year, just days after his discussions with the parliament.

For Auer, this was the first break. "Had the decision been made in 1986" to go forward with the FS-X, "there was a stronger chance that the Japanese would have been for domestic production. By delaying it a year, all the deadlines required to do that were becoming more difficult."

That May, Auer's co-architect on FS-X policy, Gregg Rubinstein, wound up his three-year tour in Tokyo. Rubinstein returned to Washington satisfied that the United States was on the correct course with Japan over the FS-X: low-key, but firm in its efforts to steer Japan off domestic development.

What Rubinstein did not foresee was that his replacement as the deputy at the Mutual Defense Assistance Office would take a very different view of the FS-X program. Nor could he imagine that the tentative truce he had worked out at the embassy between officials from State and Defense was about to break down into guerrilla warfare and change the course of U.S.-Japan relations.

6

An Airport Theory
of Nations

"The airport is Japan's most heavily guarded institution, surrounded by several rings of tall electrified fences that continue deep into the ground to discourage tunneling. All passengers and well-wishers are scrutinized and sometimes searched by the police when entering the airport grounds."
—KAREL VAN WOLFEREN, *The Enigma of Japanese Power*

SITTING MID-DECK on the wide-bodied jet, Gregg Rubinstein's replacement at the Mutual Defense Assistance Office adjusted his heavy body in his narrow seat and thought about the blood pooling in his legs. Kevin Kearns's face was impassive, drawn; his small mouth was pinched shut over the cleft of his chin. The time was August 1986.

Almost fourteen hours out of Detroit, the cabin of the aircraft had become an island of tedium. It was worse for the Northwest Airlines passengers like Kearns, who had boarded at National Airport in Washington, D.C. They had already endured the hour-long leg from the capital and an endless two-and-a-half-hour layover in the Motor City. Japanese businessmen who were regulars on such excursions referred to them as kamikaze flights. Somewhere midway over the Pacific, about ten hours into the flight, passengers developed the claustrophobic feeling that they were suffocating on recycled air; that the plane's portholes had shrunk to the size of bottlenecks. Even the weary flight attendants appeared to be at their wits' ends as they made their last pass through the cabin before final approach.

Over the past eleven years Kevin Kearns had visited seventy-five countries, many of them as a foreign service officer. Just weeks before coming to Tokyo, he had been to the Philippines to monitor the presidential election. He was coming off a much longer tour in South Korea. He'd had stints in Honduras and El Salvador. On the heels of the U.S. invasion of Grenada, he was a member of a five-man team that got Congress to appropriate $15 million for the Caribbean peacekeeping force. These were trouble spots, and Kearns was in the security business.

The evening was overcast when the plane touched down, the sky the color of metal machine parts. The last light before nightfall revealed the letters NARITA formed by a green hedge on the taxiway. Next to it was the same word in Japanese. This was the New Tokyo International Airport at last.

The plane stopped on the tarmac and parked, and the flight attendant announced that a bus would transport passengers from the plane to the terminal. No jetways were available. For the passengers, this meant walking down a long stairway in a humid August drizzle and crowding into a bus, a nearly insufferable humiliation after so tedious a flight, particularly when downtown Tokyo was two hours away by turnpike, and the irksome process of baggage retrieval and customs still lay ahead.

There were those in the U.S. government who argued that such inconveniences as Narita offered were not an act of incompetence on the part of the Japanese, but their intention. Kevin Kearns faintly considered this as he rode the crowded bus. The mix of wet clothes, tired bodies, and stale cigarette smoke—the Japanese were compulsive smokers, and by the end of the flight the ashtrays at the rear of the plane by the lavatories spilled over—mingled with the smell of exhaust fumes. It was true that Japanese aircraft always seemed to get a place at a jetway, while more often than not U.S. carriers idled on the tarmac or had to bus their passengers to the terminal.

Kearns had a pet theory, a kind of "airport theory of nations," as he called it. He believed that airports revealed important information about a people, their government and bureaucracy, their economy. Thirty minutes in the airport and you had a good sense of how a country was run, he would say. It was an idea he took only half seriously, more of a there-is-truth-in-jest analysis, something on the order of first impressions. Such analytical shorthand came with the itinerant life of a foreign service officer. "An airport was often a visitor's first introduction to a nation and its institutions," Kearns said. It's the first glimpse an outsider gets of its bureaucracy, its city services and transportation.

Narita presented Kearns with a startling series of contradictions. It serviced the capital of one of the world's great trading nations, yet it had one single runway for takeoffs and landings. It worked only half the day, closing down at 11 P.M., not to reopen again until seven the next morning.

Narita had its good points, though. The baggage area, for instance. Luggage carts stood waiting and available, a courtesy and not a rental. Service in Japan is free and offered willingly, indeed dutifully. And while the baggage carousels resembled those at any large international airport—Kennedy or Charles de Gaulle—there was never any fear that luggage would be stolen or lost, at least not on the Japanese end of the transaction.

Trustworthiness and efficiency are emblems of the Japanese character. In Tokyo restaurants, for instance, it is considered an insult to calculate the receipt or to count change. Cheating, even innocent miscalculation, is unthinkable.

Of course, Kearns did not deduce all this at once. In his immediate surmise, Narita and, by extension, Japanese society appeared rigidly ordered. You make it through the airport, he thought, and you realize that everything is set and controlled centrally—a precision operation. The taxis, for instance, were immaculate, air-conditioned. The drivers wore ties and white gloves. The back door swung open by remote control to admit passengers. This was a far cry from his experiences in Thailand, where the hacks hustled for the whorehouses. There was nothing Third World about Tokyo.

Maneuvering into the antimacassared interior of the compact taxi was not an easy operation for Kearns. He was a large man—six feet two inches, 240 pounds—a nearly sumo-sized passenger. He resembled a young Sydney Greenstreet. The wire-rimmed glasses he wore appeared small, the size of bottle caps, in proportion to his pudgy face. They lent him an innocent, bookish air.

The world Kearns saw through those bottle caps was not the world of an innocent, however. It was a regional battleground. A deeply conservative man, Kearns expected to confront intrigues. He looked for subtexts, nuances. He had his causes: staunchly anti-Communist, antiabortion, profamily. He loathed the put-down-America crowd. Though he approached Japan positively, he was innately suspicious.

Kearns brought a different set of experiences to the job than his predecessor. Whereas Gregg Rubinstein was a Japanophile, Kearns was more of a Latin Americanist. Kearns could be confrontational; Rubinstein was politic. Kearns was a lawyer, trained in argument, unlike the diplomatic Rubinstein, who had been schooled in foreign affairs and had made a study of Asia. Kearns embraced zeal; Rubinstein preferred to avoid it.

For the most part, Kearns had been working the world's trouble spots; he was a field man. Rubinstein had a flair for security matters, but he was more abstract and less hands-on. He was a desk man. When he left Tokyo, Rubinstein was just thirty-three, a time when a person's career takes shape. Kearns was nearly forty when he arrived in Tokyo, a time of now-or-never in a career, a restless time, a time of reassessment, reordering.

The FS-X pointed up those keen differences. Kearns was 180 degrees opposed to the U.S. program as conceived by Rubinstein and Auer. It seemed to him that the Pentagon had already overreached itself with its co-production policies with Japan, which he saw as giveaways of U.S. technologies. Why push the idea even further into the unknown territory of co-development?

Unlike Rubinstein, Kearns did not see the value in cooperation, at least not with Japan. Step by step, the United States had marched down a one-way street in deals like this one, always giving technology and never getting technology. Though he understood that the United States had far more to give, he was convinced that Japan's interests weren't in their defense, but in building up their commercial opportunities in aerospace, particularly in aviation.

To Kearns aviation was the ultimate high ground. Not only was it a symbol of technological excellence; it was America's leading export. A healthy aviation industry was central to national security. What was the point of encouraging Japan to move into yet another industrial field, particularly this one? The goal of defense cooperation was not to set your allies up to compete with your private sector. Yet that's what he witnessed taking place in programs like the FS-X.

Rubinstein was wrong about defense cooperation with Japan. For if it was true, Kearns reasoned, that Tokyo genuinely was concerned about the Soviet threat, why would they squander huge junks of their small defense budget on a long-shot deal like the FS-X? For half the price, they could buy all the security they needed from Uncle Sam.

Such differences as there were between Kearns and Rubinstein were not a minor matter. They introduced the element of antagonism into a U.S.-Japan relationship that was already straining to be redefined—at a crossroads, as Rubinstein believed. Now it was the conservative Kearns who was in control of the position that handled the business of arms sales to Japan. As deputy of the Mutual Defense Assistance Office at the embassy, Kearns was in a position to challenge not only the FS-X deal but the people who were engineering it: the State Department, the Defense Department, and the whole Japanese military establishment.

Kearns first came to the FS-X in May 1986, three months before his arrival at Narita, when a meeting was held at the Pentagon with a Japanese team assigned to study FS-X options. Attendance at the gathering was part of the preparation for his new position at the MDO, replacing Rubinstein. Both men attended the meeting.

Before arriving in the United States, the Japanese team assigned to study the FS-X had traveled to Europe to visit Panavia, the consortium that built the Tornado, which was now a mainstay of the Royal Air Force. The aircraft was under consideration along with two U.S. planes, the F-16 and the F/A-18. The Japanese team had made a grand tour of the United States on their way to Washington, from north to south and sea to shining sea. Along the way, they visited Westinghouse Electric, in Baltimore, as well as Hughes

Aircraft, on the opposite littoral, in Los Angeles, to study U.S. developments in advanced radar. They traveled to McDonnell Douglas in St. Louis to study the F/A-18, then down the Mississippi to General Dynamics in Fort Worth to study the F-16. They visited the United Technologies Pratt & Whitney plant in West Palm Beach, Florida, and then on to General Electric's Aircraft Engine Group in Lynn, Massachusetts, to study engines, tracing a route up U.S. Highway 1 along the East Coast.

This was a busy time for U.S.-Japan relations. Just a month earlier, in April, the long-awaited visit to Tokyo by Secretary of Defense Weinberger took place. That meeting, the first major U.S.-Japan security discussion since the SSC in Hawaii that January, produced a grab bag of discussions. There were talks about Japan's guarantees to guard its sea lanes out to 1,000 miles, progress in Japan's participation in Star Wars, and arm twisting on the 1 percent ceiling on defense spending.

Once again, as Japan had come to expect, the United States brushed off the FS-X. Weinberger was quoted during his visit in the *Japan Times*, an English-language newspaper published in Tokyo: "The U.S. government has no intention at all of interfering with the Japanese government's decision making process on FS-X introduction." That was big news in Japanese defense circles. Weinberger had once again publicly opposed linking trade and defense. As he saw it, the rationale for a defense budget was not Japan's trade balance with the United States; it was the 2,000 Soviet aircraft within striking distance of Tokyo. The key, Weinberger emphasized, was that Japan got the best fighters available.

A few weeks later, at another high-level U.S.-Japan conference, Prime Minister Yasuhiro Nakasone came to Washington to meet with President Reagan. This time the subject was trade. Nakasone gave the President a gift of a Sony Walkman TV, one of the consumer electronics products that had driven the U.S. television industry to its knees. It was an interesting memento, considering that the United States was still trying to sue Japan over low-balling TV prices to drive U.S. manufacturers out of the market. The trade deficit with Japan had soared 40 percent in 1985 over the year before, reaching nearly $47 billion. Massive dumping of Japanese computer chips (selling below cost in order to gain market share) was starving U.S. high-tech companies. U.S. construction firms found themselves unable to get work on the $5 billion island being built in Osaka Bay for the city's new international airport. And U.S. cellular phones were kept off the hook by trade barriers, as were supercomputers and satellites.

In neither visit—Nakasone's or Weinberger's—was the FS-X linked to trade. The clear message was that the FS-X was strictly a defense matter. Trade would not be used as a lever to get Japan to buy American fighters in order to balance the deficit. That was real encouragement to Japan's FS-X faction. Treated as such, the FS-X could be handled by the defense agency as any other defense matter would. It could be forestalled, giving the FS-X enough time to become a domestic project, a fait accompli. Only if the fighter plane emerged as a political issue, if it were to commingle in the red ink of the U.S. trade deficit, would it become a problem.

Surely, reasoned Ryozo Tsutsui and the all-Japan faction, if there was going to be an opportunity for the FS-X to turn into a political issue, it would have come during either Nakasone's trip or Weinberger's visit.

Thus the FS-X study team arrived in Washington confident that this was the last hurdle before domestic development would be authorized in the next budget, which was scheduled for completion in less than three months.

The big meeting at the Defense Department was held in a small, drab auditorium in the B Ring, one of the outer loops of Pentagon power. The setting was nondescript in a military way: drop ceilings and folding chairs. The room was painted the same color as the rest of the Pentagon, a dry yellow. There was a speaker's podium where presentations were made, an overhead projector, and an easel for visual aids. Meetings were conducted like workshops, informally, with individual presentations followed by a question-and-answer period.

The meeting struck Kearns as being strange from the very start. He had the sense that he was witnessing grand Kabuki, the formalized all-male folk theater of Japan. Seven months had passed since the Nakasone cabinet had announced the three options for the FS-X, and the United States had yet to get its first glimpse of the operational requirements for the fighter. The U.S. side still had no idea of what Japan expected the FS-X to be. What range would the plane have? Would it be an interceptor or strictly an attack air-craft? What kind of weapons would it carry?

Interestingly, one of the principal architects of the U.S. response to Japan's plans for the FS-X, Gregg Rubinstein, shared Kearns's assessment of the meeting. He had always thought the option to either buy or upgrade a plane for the FS-X was a "straw man." The Japanese side seemed engaged in a great charade.

When the requirements for the FS-X were finally unveiled by the Japanese study team, Kearns and Rubinstein were astonished. The defense agency called for an airplane that was unique in all the world. Certainly nothing like it existed in the U.S. inventory. Or the Soviets'. Or the Europeans'. "This was strictly a paper airplane," Kearns later recalled. It resembled the stuff of argument more than the stuff of military requirements.

The most obvious physical difference from anything currently in any nation's inventory was the plane's canards, little duck wings placed ahead of the main wing. Canards had been dismissed years ago by the U.S. planners because whatever they added to a plane's maneuverability was useful in only about 5 percent of combat situations. In return, the plane paid a high price in added weight and drag which affected 100 percent of overall performance.

Another unusual requirement put forward by the Japanese was that the plane had to be able to take off fully loaded with weapons and fuel on a 3,000-foot runway in 104-degree temperatures. Most military airfields in Japan were 6,000 to 10,000 feet long, and there was no record of 104-degree heat in Japan in thirty years.

Two Japanese words summed up what appeared to be emerging on the easels and overhead projectors used by the Japanese presenters that May: *tatemae* and *honne*, the difference between an explanation and the unspoken reason behind it.

To the Japanese, the proper explanation is crucial. Some would say that, indeed, reality could at times appear to be negotiable. *Tatemae* is the facade, the pretense, the official and acceptable rationale of why things are so. It is the balm that makes for harmony. *Honne* was its opposite. It represented what was really going on: one's true feelings.

Tatemae and *honne* did not equate with ulterior motives, however. They figured much more in maintaining smooth relations, in avoiding conflict, in reaching a consensus. Much that takes place in the way of communications between Westerners and Japanese is *tatemae*. Whereas the Americans prefer candor—we say we "bare our chests" or we "wear our hearts on our sleeves" —the Japanese respond by sipping tea, nodding in agreement, and then going their own way. The effect can be disconcerting.

Japanese defense officials had made this special conciliatory trip to Washington to show their attention to U.S. concerns over the FS-X. It was meant to be polite. They feared giving the appearance of being ungrateful to the United States, which was their single biggest trading customer. As well, the Pentagon was their greatest defender. Indeed, the United States had rebuilt Japan. To simply reject our aircraft without sincere effort (*tatemae*) would have been unthinkable, even if those efforts were designed to make it impossible to buy U.S. planes (*honne*). Hence their many-sided qualifications for this plane, which Kearns labeled derisively and for all time as "the 64 parameters," a phrase Rubinstein came to accept.

"We went from being ready to help Japan in a cooperative project if the terms were correct to believing that they're just playing us along," Rubinstein said. "It was then we began to think that they just wanted our technology."

Both sides were now talking past each other. The United States told the Japanese that they should not go forward with the fighter until the program had been given a thoroughgoing threat assessment. That meant a clear picture of the strategies and forces it would be fighting.

Japan replied that it could not do a threat assessment without full U.S. intelligence, which the United States supplied strictly on a need-to-know basis. The Japanese contended that they did not need a "world-class fighter," but wanted a second-tier support aircraft, a successor to the domestic F-1 project.

The United States pointed out that its fighters could easily be modified and could serve a variety of missions. They argued for some kind of mutual, joint program, a co-development scenario.

The Japanese worried that joint development would bog down over how much work each nation would get. Besides, there was a basic problem with U.S. aircraft. American F/A-18s and F-16s were too small, the Japanese side said, and the F-15 was too big and expensive.

The official record of the FS-X deal written by Captain Andrew J. Button, the officer in day-to-day charge of the program through 1988, notes parenthetically: "I believe they still thought they could wrap up their study by the end of July with a domestic fighter solution." In other words, the U.S. side failed to win their point for co-development.

The Japanese side did not quite slam the door in DoD's face, however. Without making any promises, they said they would be willing to consider proposals from U.S. industry for U.S. aircraft, but that the deadline if the United States wanted to put their planes in the contest was June 30. The Defense Department would also have to provide a letter by the same date, supporting joint development with U.S. industry. A late filing would result in elimination.

The Japanese concluded the meeting by asking U.S. defense officials not to discuss "the 64 parameters" with U.S. aerospace contractors. The defense team explained that Japan's secrecy laws prohibited the defense agency from dealing with contractors before an official proposal was released. They asked that DoD treat U.S. contractors in the same way.

The explanation is perplexing because Mitsubishi Heavy Industries, Mitsubishi Electric, Kawasaki Heavy Industries, and others had long been involved in developing the systems that were to be plugged together into the Japanese domestic version of the FS-X. Indeed, such close cooperation between the defense agency and private industry was emblematic of Japanese defense policy. In a case study of Mitsubishi's role in the procurement of the Patriot air defense missile, the MIT-Japan Program observed, "Mitsubishi Corp. was involved in the decision before the [Patriot] system itself was developed in that it was *actively involved in J.D.A. drafting of systems requirements*" for more than twenty years (emphasis added).

Such relationships were typical. If this was the case with the FS-X—and there is no reason to assume that it was not—then the instructions of the Japanese team deliberately and directly undermined the ability of the U.S. contractors to make successful presentations on the FS-X.

The request clearly left Kearns puzzled, because it did not make sense.

How could U.S. contractors be expected to submit their proposals, particularly on such short notice, if they could not be apprised of the elaborate requirements of their Japanese customers?

The fact was, such notions of good business practices ran counter to common Japanese business practices. The contractors in Japan probably had a very good idea of the needs of the Japan Defense Agency, as the Patriot case made clear. Kearns got on the shuttle bus back to the State Department that evening knowing that it was only a matter of time before the other shoe dropped—which it would, soon after he arrived in Tokyo.

7

The Sound of One Shoe Dropping

"Foreigners . . . have had to tighten belts in this city, where a cup of coffee routinely costs the equivalent of $4 and taxicab meters start at $3.10."
—CLYDE C. HABERMAN, "Embassies Face Hard Times in Costly Tokyo," New York *Times,* August 16, 1987

B Y THE FALL of that year, 1986, Kearns was well settled in Tokyo; in all, he found that life at the embassy was not bad. The high cost of living was another matter, however. Prices were out of hand, and that was particularly evident in real estate. It was so bad that even nations struggled to pay the rent. Some, like the Ugandans, had to close down their embassies or make special arrangements for their diplomats. The Peruvian Embassy cut corners on heat in the winter and air conditioning in the summer. The Venezuelan ambassador moved from his house to an apartment to keep within budget, and Haiti struggled on with just one diplomat at work in an apartment building shared by thirteen other foreign missions.

Not all the embassies were hurt by Tokyo's hyperinflation in real estate. The Australian Embassy carved off part of its grounds, hoping to cash in on the so-called price bubble. It got its asking price too, something in the neighborhood of $700 million for less than an acre. The land encompassing the Imperial Palace, a parcel about half the size of New York's Central Park, was estimated to be worth the total value of all the land in Canada, plus the state of California.

The U.S. Embassy was like an island of calm in this tedious and overworked boomtown. A modern, copper-colored, nine-story filing cabinet of a building, it was located in an area convenient to the Nagatacho, Tokyo's

Capitol Hill. Here, the streets, both narrow and wide, were lined with restaurants and crowded with cars. For the most part, the city's thoroughfares were clear of litter, except for the flattened white cigarette butts scattered everywhere underfoot, blown into drifts at the curb. They formed a trail leading from the embassy toward Hibiya Park, in the direction of the all-powerful ministries of the bustling Kasumigaseki district.

The U.S. Embassy was a hardworking embassy. To keep up with the Japanese meant long hours, often until 8 P.M., at which time the unofficial business of business dinners began. This routine was repeated two or three times a week, maybe more. An old Japanese naval ditty had a refrain: "Getsu, Getsu, Ka, Sui, Moku, Kin, Kin." Monday, Monday, Tuesday, Wednesday, Thursday, Friday, Friday.

The zeitgeist of the embassy emanated from its renowned ambassador, Mike Mansfield, there since 1977 and nearly eighty-three years old in October 1986. Mansfield was a legend. He had played an important role in convincing President Truman to allow the Japanese to retain their beloved Emperor, and he viewed postwar Japan as a great experiment. The Japanese came to love that in him, that faith. To say "Mansfield" and "Japan" together in one breath worked like an incantation, evoking his now famous phrase about Japan's significance to America: "The most important bilateral relationship in the world . . . *bar none*."

Although nagging trade friction had grown into the single largest issue facing the embassy, Mansfield would not descend into haggling. He was constantly forbearing and took a positive approach toward Japan. He could point out that on his long watch the Japanese had continued their dazzling economic miracle, having risen phoenixlike from a bombed-out wretched ember of a nation into the second-largest economy in the world. What he saw at the end of his glorious career was that his loftiest goals of a peaceful and prosperous Japan had been fully realized.

Mansfield, however, preferred to cultivate the vision he had for Japan, rather than adjust it to the realities of new era. Thus, in its relations with the United States, Japan continued to be seen and treated as a fragile developing nation, long past the time it had become a fierce and flexible global competitor.

By that October, Japan had surpassed the United States as the leading nation in international banking. Japanese purchases of U.S. Treasury bills financed the national debt. The yen surged 40 percent in value against the dollar. And Japan was on a high-tech rampage. The big news story in October 1986 was that the Japanese computer giant, Fujitsu Ltd., was making a tender offer for Fairchild Semiconductor (which happened to be owned by the French), one of the founding firms of Silcon Valley. As Mansfield saw it, U.S. companies were not competitive and trade barriers were few.

The argument defied reality. Japan's telephone company, for instance, could not buy U.S. communications satellites because it had to purchase them through the Japanese government. A separate law said that the government could only purchase satellite equipment from a Japanese firm. Catch-22. Thus there were no trade barriers blocking American companies from potential clients like the phone company, Nippon Telegraph and Telephone (which, incidentally, also happened to be the largest communications company on earth), just a monumental quirk in the law.

In 1985, when the U.S. Congress threatened legislation to open up Japan's telecommunications markets, Mansfield actually came to Tokyo's defense. He told the Washington *Post* that he was "disturbed at the way Japan is being made the scapegoat" for the United States' $123.3 billion trade deficit, $36.8 billion of which resulted from trade with Japan. The usually laconic Westerner waxed loquacious. "The relationship [between the United States] and Japan is too valuable, too strong, *too precious* to let differences of the moment create a situation which we will be sorry for in the future" (emphasis added).

The deficit *that* year turned out to be a prodigious $46.6 billion, up an astounding 27 percent over the unprecedented levels Mansfield quoted, and it was headed higher. As changes in the value of the dollar, wrought by the 1985 Plaza Accords, brought U.S. trade into balance with the rest of the world, America's trade deficit with Japan continued to balloon.

But as issues of the deficit loomed larger, Mansfield seemed to grow more distant. Perhaps he was lowering his profile. A cruel rumor circulated that he had grown senile. For certain, much of his work was delegated. The Deputy Chief of Mission, the embassy's number two man, substituted for the number one man. Mansfield was for display, like running up the flag, or the Lenin tomb. He symbolized America's unrelenting "bar none" relationship with Japan. He was an oracle. And as he saw the trade problem: "The Japanese market is not as closed as many Americans think, and ours is not as open as many people say."

The embassy reflected this pallid and protective view of affairs. It was a place where no one made waves. A foreign service officer was expected to keep in his place. People said it was a "good news" embassy, where Japanese promises took precedence over Japanese deeds.

The Chrysanthemum Club, as the Japanophiles and Mansfield loyalists who ran the embassy were derisively known, were an exclusive and insistently insular group. They made it axiomatic that unless a foreign service officer spoke Japanese, it was not possible for him to grasp the subtleties of this ancient society in which they worked, let alone the lacquered manners of its mandarins. The club shared the Mansfield vision, which, as Kevin Kearns came to see it, meant that they subordinated U.S. interests in favor of their larger concern for U.S.-Japan relations. In this the embassy's staff functioned more as American missionaries than international emissaries. The Mansfield vision was blurred by sentimentality.

The Chrysanthemum Club had a peculiar effect on the embassy's bureaucracy, particularly at the Mutual Defense Assistance Office, where Kearns worked. Conceived as a temporary patchwork between the departments of Defense and State, Kearns's office had never been fully accepted into the diplomatic community. It functioned under the cold gaze of the more powerful and well-established Political-Military Section, which shared the ninth floor with the ambassador. The MDO was on the seventh floor.

There was a lot of chafing between them. Though it was the Department of Defense that coordinated military policy, it was the Department of State that elaborated U.S. policy. They spoke for Washington. The Mutual Defense Assistance Office fit between those two responsibilities. Principally, the job of the MDO was facilitating arms sales. That was its bailiwick. Problems of technology and business were also generally beneath Pol-Mil and thus fell to the MDO.

The higher-ranking section, however, lived in constant fear of being blindsided by the smaller seventh-floor office's billion-dollar arms dealings. To protect its interests Pol-Mil would often pull rank on the MDO. The moment, for example, one of the MDO's high-priced defense matters became sexy and politically charged, Pol-Mil took over. The run-up in high-tech arms transfers during the Reagan years raised the flag on these otherwise recondite weapons agreements, attracting Pol-Mil and irritating the MDO.

A tentative truce had been struck between the two sections in the early eighties by the diplomatic Gregg Rubinstein. He recognized the unfortunate netherworldly position his office occupied in the embassy pantheon. Rubinstein wanted to change that, and to use the FS-X as his vehicle. But where Rubinstein kept a finger in the wind, Kearns was more likely to stick his finger in someone's eye.

"A person with drive and ambition doesn't get ahead by pushing paper at the State Department," Kearns would say. "Why go into foreign service if all you do in your career is to go back and forth to Tokyo. The idea is to get out there in the world and to see what people are made of. These guys who sit around spewing the latest foreign policy theories ought to get out into the real world."

The Pol-Mil Section was run by the Chrysanthemum Club, the embassy insiders, the stewards of what the Japanese called *nichibei*, the U.S.-Japan relationship. For an outsider like Kearns, who was not a "language officer"—that is, he did not speak Japanese—who also had ambitions in the policy arena, it made for some lopsided discussions. Kearns was not one of the boys. Bureaucratic rivalries exacerbated personal differences. As the FS-X grew into a larger and more complex issue, Pol-Mil tried to move in. Kearns found himself and his office screened out, reduced to the role of messengers, the Rosencrantz and Guildenstern of the arms trade.

It had been a busy summer in Tokyo for the FS-X, and by the time Kearns arrived in August 1986 events had moved forward quickly. The June deadline for the U.S. contractors to submit their proposals for the FS-X had been met.

Indeed, the package of information had been hand-delivered by the MDO. There was symbolism in that. The packet contained proposals from General Dynamics and McDonnell Douglas and a letter from the Pentagon supporting co-development. Its delivery was a demonstration that the United States was now augmenting its concerns about the FS-X with action supporting the interests of U.S. industry. The links up the chain of command were being formed on the proposed high-tech fighter. The Defense Security Assistance Agency, which had charge of the FS-X at the Pentagon, clearly now had the backing of Richard Armitage, the powerful assistant secretary in charge of policy, the man who had pledged that January that he would see to it that trade issues would not be linked to security issues. Washington was getting more aggressive.

Separately, days after the June deadline, a rare double election for the upper and lower houses of the Japanese parliament was held. This had the potential to move the FS-X issue in the United States' favor. The forces of Yasuhiro Nakasone scored a resounding victory, and the ruling Liberal Democratic Party—which, as observers often noted, was neither "liberal" nor particularly "democratic"—won substantial majorities in both houses. This not only meant another term for Nakasone; it gave him a broader base of support from which to work, or so the United States surmised. A strong Nakasone government augured well for larger Japanese contributions to defense cooperation.

But this was not the direction Nakasone seemed to be heading in when he installed a new director at the Japan Defense Agency, Yuko Kurihara, the man who held the post before Koichi Kato, from December 1983 to October 1984. Kurihara had long experience in Japanese politics, beginning with the agricultural organizations that dominate the government. In the late 1970s, he was in line to head the Foreign Ministry, but lost out to a change in administrations.

The key to the Kurihara appointment (as with his predecessor, Koichi Kato) was his membership in the Miyazawa faction, one of five large factions that make up the ruling LDP. Factions matter less for policy than for fund raising; pork-barrel politics is a high art in Japan, more so than in the United States. But factions are not entirely without political significance.

The Miyazawa faction represented the more international, more pacifistic side of the conservative ruling party to which it belonged. Therefore, an appointment by the hawkish Nakasone of a dovish Miyazawa man mitigated against any public fear that might arise of a tilt back toward the terrible militarism that undermined the nation in 1930s and 1940s.

The faction—named after the would-be Prime Minister Kiichi Miyazawa, who headed it—was a midsized group that rallied under the banner of "Small Defense; Great Economy." The Kurihara appointment meant that no matter how far Nakasone hustled down the road toward alliance with the United States, Japan's business interests would be placed ahead of its defense establishment.

Still, Kurihara and Weinberger endeavored to become friends as well as successful counterparts. Kurihara was closer in age to Weinberger than Koichi Kato. Both men were personages of strong and grave convictions. Weinberger found Kurihara refreshingly candid, a characteristic that was familiar and comfortable to him, similar in style to Washington's power brokers. For his part, Kurihara was impressed with the solidness of Weinberger's character, his deep strength.

A one-day September meeting between the two men was arranged in Washington, though it was largely ceremonial, a photo opportunity. Kurihara performed the usual wreath layings at Arlington and held the de rigueur press conference on the thirteenth floor of the National Press Club. There, true to Miyazawa faction form, Kurihara attempted to dispel any hope for a major breakthrough by the Nakasone administration on defense policy, saying, "The fact that the LDP won 304 seats does not mean that we in Japan can do anything we like."

Privately, where the talks between Weinberger and Kurihara were substantive, they focused on Japanese military spending. Weinberger relentlessly hammered away at the same series of issues that came up time and again in his talks with Japanese leaders. At issue, as always, was Japan's 1 percent limit on military spending. Star Wars was also on the agenda. As Weinberger saw it, the big election victory had indeed given the hawkish Nakasone administration the mandate it needed to spend more on defense, disclaimers before the press club audience notwithstanding.

Weinberger played his Congress card, warning that American lawmakers expected Japan to pay more of its own way on defense. In fact, days before the Kurihara visit, Senate Minority Leader Robert Byrd wrote President Reagan about the unhappiness on Capitol Hill over Japan's puny efforts in its own defense.

On the FS-X, Weinberger was pragmatic. He believed, in fact, that Japan had long-range economic goals embedded in its defense plans. "A military aircraft industry is something they could have done very easily over a long period of time and at enormous cost, not to mention enormous political difficulties," he said. But he told Kurihara that there was too little money available for the defense agency to pursue such goals.

Weinberger spoke of the FS-X as a way around Japan's spending limits. He restated what would become the U.S. position in the coming months, explaining that it would cost less to buy a U.S. fighter than it would to develop one domestically. It only made sense, he argued, for Japanese aircraft to be "interoperable" with U.S. aircraft, that the bullets and missiles they fired be interchangeable.

This represented the third occasion on which the Defense Secretary had raised the murky issue of co-development in meetings with Japanese defense directors. Although it was the first time he had spoken about it with Kurihara, the Japanese defense chief seemed to feel the pressure.

Kurihara was in no position to take sides, however. Instead, he boosted the arguments of the all-Japan team, but did not rule out U.S. aircraft from consideration. He pledged to expedite the McDonnell Douglas and General Dynamics proposals for the FS-X that had been languishing in Tokyo for two months, since they had been dutifully submitted under the June 30, 1986, deadline. Still, he pressed for domestic development. Building its own fighter was a way for Japan to become more independent militarily, Kurihara maintained, and thus more secure, as the United States wished. Surely Weinberger could not argue against such an aim.

Concessions on the Japanese side emerged from these talks. Within weeks after Kurihara's return to Tokyo, the Nakasone cabinet gave the Reagan administration's Star Wars program its first foreign endorsement, although they did not actually sign on to the quixotic program. And over the coming months, Japan's defense budget actually breached the unbreachable 1 percent limit for the first time, by a scant thousandths of a percent (.004). Although less than 1 percent would actually be spent, the United States, of course, chose to ignore these facts in favor of their symbolism.

Kurihara also made good on his promise to consider U.S. interests in the FS-X by finally freeing up the proposals made by U.S. defense contractors in June. The not surprising explanation DoD received for the delay was that the evaluation was more time-consuming than expected. Whatever the reality, after the Kurihara visit, U.S. contractors finally received an invitation to present briefings on their proposals to the Japan Defense Agency in Tokyo the next month, in October 1986.

Kearns's conflicts with his superiors at the embassy had their origins that October, when General Dynamics and McDonnell Douglas journeyed to Tokyo on a sales mission. The purpose of the autumn meetings, held at the invitation of the defense agency, was to outline the new versions of the F-16 and the F/A-18 that would be available for co-development. This was the realization of Rubinstein's strategy, which envisioned a Japanese-funded Agile Falcon or Super Hornet Plus.

However, neither McDonnell Douglas nor General Dynamics was afforded detailed mission requirements on which to base their FS-X briefings. This was because the Defense Department had agreed to honor Japan's request for confidentiality that May, when Kearns first was introduced to the FS-X at the Pentagon. At the time, the Japanese negotiating team had expressed concern that DoD might give U.S. contractors an unfair bidding advantage over their Japanese counterparts.

The glaring problems which that pledge of confidentiality created for the U.S. side became immediately clear when General Dynamics arrived in Tokyo to make its presentation. Until now, the company did know that a twin-engine design was a basic requirement for the FS-X. Japan, defense agency officials explained, was a densely populated island nation, and the safety of an extra engine was paramount.

The last single-engine fighter Japan bought, the Lockheed F-104, was a rocket-fast spear of a fighter; the gleaming edges of its stubby seven-foot wings were so sharp that they had to be carefully sheathed to protect ground crews from beheadings. It flew like a prodigious dart at Mach 2.5, and was difficult to control. For certain, no fighter was less forgiving of its pilots or more prone to crashes. Japan wanted no more of that, and single-engine planes were out.

Representatives from General Dynamics had three proposals under their arms when they arrived in Tokyo that fall. They had plans for an F-16 XL, a unique prototype aircraft with a delta-shaped wing, known as a cranked arrow. There was also an F-16 SX-2 made from one-third composite material by weight, and an SX-3 that was nearly half composites.

All of these had but one engine. Indeed, that was all General Dynamics built—single-engine fighters.

Here was the other shoe dropping. For more than a year, General Dynamics had been putting out feelers about Japan's plans, taking briefings at the Pentagon, and getting encouragement from defense officials to push forward with its proposal for the FS-X. Now, four full months after they had submitted their plan to the Air Staff Office, six months after the Japanese study team had visited their factory in Fort Worth, the company was at last learning that the Air Self-Defense Forces were not interested in a single-engine plane! Why, then, was General Dynamics here? Why did Japan even bother to invite them?

General Dynamics was stunned.

Kearns called a halt to the proceedings. David Wheaton, the head of the General Dynamics marketing team in Tokyo, told Kearns that the company simply wasn't interested in developing a twin-engine version of the F-16.

They had considered it, once; but decided against it. Besides, the real benefit to General Dynamics of an FS-X deal was in modifying the single-engine version of the F-16, the lightweight Fighting Falcon that was now an air force standard in fifteen countries.

We're not prepared to brief on a twin-engine plane, Wheaton told Kearns. We were never told about the requirement, and if we had been, we wouldn't have left Fort Worth.

For more than six months, Kearns had known about the requirement for the twin-engine aircraft, and that U.S. contractors could not be told about this and the other specifications. Now he was face to face with the consequences of that knowledge. He had the unfortunate experience of falling victim to an ambush he had been obliged to help set. The petard wasn't his, but he got hoisted on it. Until now, he had been an outsider learning the Japan game. Now he had been set up by that game.

Kearns struggled to keep General Dynamics from flying off at the edges. Adjourning the meeting into the private offices of the leader of the Japanese team, General Hossho, Kearns eked out a flimsy compromise. Since the *actual purchase of a foreign aircraft* for the FS-X had yet to be officially ruled out as one of Japan's three alternatives, General Dynamics's F-16 should not be eliminated. After all, it had been one of the planes the JDA had announced was under consideration.

The ploy worked. The next day, General Dynamics tried to cement its fragile position when Charles Anderson, its top marketing engineer, arrived in Tokyo and joined the talks. Purely by serendipity, it turned out, Anderson had been head of engineering on General Dynamics's program to explore a two-engine version of the F-16. He had written articles on his findings and had even built a mock-up of the plane, known as the SX-4. It would do for now.

Caught out by the Japanese, Kearns found himself caught up in the drama. He was deeply troubled by what he saw as more Japanese Kabuki, more theater. "It seemed that the Japanese were using these briefings to grab all this technical information for their own use." As Kearns saw it, the Japanese had rigged the entire event for failure. "The U.S. contractors thought they had come to Tokyo for a general sales briefing, and then they were forced to respond to very specific performance parameters. They couldn't do that. They didn't have the staff. They felt set up."

To Kearns, the Japanese seemed far more organized than they actually were, however. In fact, they were deeply divided, between the policy side led by Seiki Nishihiro, and the Technical Research and Development Institute led by its *éminence gris*, Ryozo Tsutsui. Precisely what was taking place in Tokyo was not clear, but time was critical, and Nishihiro was stalling.

In November, one month after the U.S. contractors made their presentations in Tokyo, Nishihiro allowed yet another decision deadline to pass. At the same time, however, he kept open the possibility that Tsutsui's team could still win the battle for domestic development. They would have one more chance. A meeting was scheduled at the Pentagon in December. It represented a last-ditch effort to try to win the U.S. side over to an all-Japan FS-X program. The leader of the Japanese team would be none other than Ryozo Tsutsui himself, the father of the FS-X.

8

A D-Day in December

"In plain kitchen English, Tsutsui was saying, 'Fuck you very much.'"
—A background comment from a U.S. participant at the December 1986 meeting at the Pentagon

THE DECEMBER 1986 meeting at the Pentagon shaped up to be a dogfight for Ryozo Tsutsui, the father of Japan's FS-X program. But he thought he could win it, and he had reason to be optimistic. He had been encouraged by the low-key U.S. response to Japan's domestic development plans. Time after time, the likes of Auer and Armitage and Weinberger had promised that they would not tamper with Tokyo's affairs. Though the don of the defense agency, Seiki Nishihiro, had dealt Tsutsui a setback by delaying the decision on the FS-X, it stood to reason that Nishihiro had little choice. Brusqueness would only anger the Americans and would serve little purpose.

Tsutsui had succeeded in forging a neat and convincing case for the FS-X. Step by step he had exhibited Japan's ability to build this new Zero. As he predicted, the development program at Laboratory Three surged forward on schedule. His budget predictions looked good. He'd built up a track record. Just a year earlier, Laboratory Three and Kawasaki Heavy Industries delivered, on time and on budget, the T-4, a state-of-the-art intermediate trainer. "It replicated in miniature all aspects of the FS-X program, but with less demanding technology," noted an MIT-Japan Program study.

By way of contrast, an American effort to build a similar craft, the Fairchild Republic T-46A, had cost five times as much as Japan's model. What was particularly embarrassing about the episode for the United States was that the

T-46A made its appearance in *the very same* month as the Japanese plane, which was making its debut a month early. But there was more. A long, hot summer passed before the U.S. plane actually made its maiden flight in the late autumn, limping along six months behind the T-4. And lateness was the least of the U.S. aircraft's problems. The T-46A was such a disaster the program was finally and humiliatingly canceled at a cost of tens of millions of wasted dollars. In the final analysis, the American trainer had all the appearances of a flying pork barrel, powered by Senator Alfonse D'Amato. Fairchild was located in Long Island, New York.

For the first time, the two nations' defense sectors had gone head to head on an aircraft development project, and Japan looked like the big winner.

Everything was ready for the FS-X program to begin according to Tsutsui's plans—except for the political will to go forward. And even there Tsutsui had reason for optimism: Prime Minister Nakasone had himself served in 1970 as the director of the defense agency. Indeed, the very concept of domestic development on which the FS-X was based was institutionalized during his tenure. As the future Prime Minister then put it: "From the standpoint of autonomous defense, it is desirable for Japan to be defended with equipment developed and produced by Japan alone. From this point on [July 18, 1970], the development and production of military equipment will be limited to Japanese industries as a matter of principle."

What is more, after his term at the defense agency, Nakasone went on to become minister of international trade and industry, the head of MITI, which had written the Aircraft Industrial Promotion Law in 1958. This made him well acquainted with the importance Japan placed on its ambitious aviation priorities.

Tsutsui even thought that the hawkish Nakasone had carved out a bargaining position for the FS-X with the big concessions he had made to the Reagan administration on defense. Nakasone's new defense budget, for example, was groundbreaking, because it shattered the 1 percent cap on military spending, one of Japan's most sacred symbolic barriers. Nakasone had also agreed to endorse Reagan's pet Star Wars project, even at some risk to his own political standing at home.

Still, Nakasone offered no guarantees. His nickname in the Nagatacho was the Weathercock. Nakasone had strong convictions, which he sometimes acted on, but he was no iconoclast. An intensely political man, there was no telling which way he would be driven on an issue. Especially when the risks were as large as those in the U.S.-Japan security relationship.

The numbers spoke for themselves. Each year the government of Japan bought a billion dollars' worth of U.S. military equipment, more than Great Britain, France, and Italy combined. At the same time, the United States ran a $56 billion trade deficit with Japan. While this 56 to 1 ratio did not exactly represent a direct quid pro quo, the link was often stated and well acknowledged. In return for strategic security the United States allowed Japan to get away with a host of economic sins, misdemeanors, and outright felonies.

This put Tsutsui on a narrow ledge. Until now, he had managed to keep his own carefully developed domestic constituency intact—the defense agency, the Air Staff Office, the pilots, industry, certain of the ministries. That could be threatened by U.S. meddling. In order to hold on to his constituency, he would have to find a way to keep the Pentagon from turning the FS-X into a political issue. Thus far, the tough requirements put out by the Technical Research and Development Institute had sufficed to fend off the Americans. Now he had to take his case before the court of final appeals: the portentous Pentagon.

The December 1986 showdown meeting, which would decide the future of Tsutsui's program, was held in a small Pentagon auditorium a softball's throw from the Defense Security Assistance Agency offices, the Pentagon organization that supervises and negotiates all foreign military sales. The room, which was arranged as a theater, sat about forty people on folding chairs. There was a low stage, a podium, and a screen with an overhead projector for visual aids. It had all the elements of a corporate meeting, with presentations followed by challenges. Day one was the plenary session, after which the sides broke up into specialties—operational requirements, technical feasibility, cost estimation—for individual sessions. They would meet for a week.

From the outset, Tsutsui felt put upon and badly outnumbered. The forty seats in the room were filled with uniformed military from the U.S. Air Force and the U.S. Navy, as well as their cadres of civilian consultants. Only six other Japanese officials backed Tsutsui.

The purpose of this large American force was to make plain the seriousness which the United States attached to the matter. There were technical experts from the Defense Security Assistance Agency, the green-eyeshade boys from acquisitions, experts from Program Analysis and Evaluation, who decide on threats and countermeasures. Jim Auer was there, the Pentagon's leading expert on Japan. Kevin Kearns came from Tokyo. Also there was Captain Andrew Button, USN, who had day-to-day hands-on charge of the bolts, brochures, forms, paper, and files of the program. His boss, Tim Tyler, was also there, brimming, intense, his ruddy complexion a bit more florid than usual.

This forty-man U.S. team was seen by Tsutsui not as an affirmation of U.S. interest, but rather as a form of U.S. pressure, bullying. When the United States wanted its way with Japan, it simply leaned its great weight against the narrow island chain. The Japanese word for this was *gaiatsu*, external pressure.

During the meetings, Tsutsui sat stiffly in his chair. He looked fifteen years younger than his fifty-eight years. Trim, handsome, his body was a series of acute angles—thighs to shins, upper arm and forearm. He spoke in English, although without full confidence. As he later recalled his approach to the meeting: "It was important for the DoD to understand that our plan was not so bad, that our technology planning . . . not so bad. I think that after that they changed their tactics." In fact, the DoD would harden its position.

The outnumbered Tsutsui was accompanied to the meeting by a team of only six advisers, but Tsutsui felt confident he had brought with him the cream of Japan's aerospace crop: members of the FS-X study group, advisers from TRDI's Laboratory Three. They would confront the Americans head-on and attempt to win on details during the individual sessions, when numerical superiority would matter less.

As the meetings opened, Tsutsui's English turned out to be not as good as advertised. He used the wrong adverbs, and replaced adjectives with nouns. At times he seemed to speak phonetically, butting consonants against vowels instead of uttering words whole. This perhaps accounts for the *Rashomon*-like nature of the week that so many who attended experienced, where the sum of seven days' efforts seemed to get lost in the translation—some thought intentionally.

At first, Tsutsui argued determinedly that the FS-X was a "low-side fighter." That meant that it was not designed to compete with the best the United States had to offer, the exotic ATF, the Advanced Tactical Fighter, then under development by the U.S. Air Force. FS-X stood for Fighter Support Experimental. The key word was "support." It was not supposed to be the elite among military aircraft—an air-superiority fighter—it was to be flown in "support" of ground troops and naval formations. It was to attack enemy shipping, and then rise to dogfight if necessary.

Tsutsui often said that support fighters should be of Japanese design; more advanced fighters would be purchased from the United States. The F-1, he noted, was a support fighter built in Japan; and the F-15, the air-superiority fighter, had been license-produced from McDonnell Douglas. Tsutsui pointed out that in the 1970s, the DoD had allowed Japan to build the F-1 on its own. The FS-X was merely the follow-on, he said.

The U.S. side rejected such logic on its face, because of its failure to take into account the threats such a plane might encounter. A fighter, in the DoD's eyes, wasn't developed merely for the sake of updating or experimenting with new technology; it was developed to meet an ever changing threat. Such was U.S. doctrine, the rationale behind the Pentagon's armament decisions. For a nation like Japan, which was attempting to develop an aviation industry, economic and technological considerations naturally took precedence over specific mission criteria—at least on the ministerial level.

Indeed, it seemed at times that defense wasn't the issue at all in the FS-X talks. Without the FS-X, Japan feared for the very future of its planned aviation industry.

James Auer knew Tsutsui and respected him, but he also had his doubts about him. Tsutsui was a nationalist who once joked that the only thing Japan should import from the United States was scotch. Auer saw Tsutsui as "competent" but "arrogant," the rare Japanese who was willing to tell the United States it was wrong. "He thought we were wrong even more frequently than we were," Auer recalled. "But he had much more influence than the typical person in that job, because he spoke English and because he was so outspoken and . . . and just *good."*

Auer also knew Tsutsui's presence had symbolic value. Like his counterpart on the policy side, Seiki Nishihiro, Tsutsui had come up through the ranks of the JDA. He was not an import, seconded from one of the ministries, as so many high-ranking officials were in the JDA, rotating in for a year or two before rotating out again. He was JDA through and through, there from beginning to end, and, like Nishihiro, he represented the hope that the defense agency might one day rise to autonomy and be granted the full ranking of a ministry.

Still, Auer was convinced that Tsutsui would not have the final say on the FS-X. There would be a political solution. He'd seen it all before. An issue would rise up the political flagpole until all concerned saluted to U.S. demands. And Tsutsui needed U.S. technology, principally the engines, if he wished to build the plane at all. Though it would be argued that the Japanese could turn to Europe—indeed, Auer argued as much at times, when it proved convenient—no one actually thought they would dare. The obvious reason was trade: Japan's obeisance to a U.S.-made defense helped guarantee free and open access for the stunning $81.9 billion worth of imports it sold in the American marketplace. Whereas Tsutsui strove to keep the FS-X from becoming a political matter, Auer counted on it as an inevitability.

The December meeting was to be one of those confrontations that in retrospect emerged as a turning point. Captain Button, the coordinator for the Pentagon's FS-X program, later wrote in a paper for the War College that "the tone of the meetings was cordial and the exchange of information was candid; however, *the results of the discussions did not gain DoD consensus* on Japan's domestic development proposals" (emphasis added).

Button's comments grew more critical. Japan's proposed cost estimates "for development were understated by a factor of *two or three.* There appeared to be no consideration for the additional cost and technical risks of incorporating complex, highly integrated systems nor the appreciation of large amounts of composite materials" (emphasis added).

In fact, the characterization of the meetings as "cordial" was largely diplomatic, a courtesy, because it ignored the strain many participants on the U.S. side felt. Tsutsui recalled the questioning by the United States on the first day as "harsh."

No one felt those muffled tensions more than Button's boss. Tim Tyler had been involved in many of the big U.S. arms deals of the eighties, chief among them the Israeli Lavi and the sale of the AWACS aircraft to Great Britain. To him, this was as strange a meeting as any he had attended. "I don't know how many times in the history of man that I've seen the Japanese coming over here to tell us to 'stay out of our sandbox.' That does spark interest," he said.

A natty dresser, Tyler was closer in appearance to a Wall Street investor than a mid-level DoD bureaucrat. He wore bright foulard ties and crisply starched blue oxford shirts with white French cuffs and collars. Of medium height and medium age, he showed a wave of pink jowl beneath his immaculately shaven chin.

Tyler was a man of great color and a salesman who had his lines down pat. "The plane Tsutsui wanted to build," he said, "was going to come in three times the cost and twice the weight he predicated. That was absolutely rule-of-thumb numero uno."

For his part, Tsutsui was as bold as he was blunt. The only work the United States could expect to get on this fighter is the engine, he firmly told the U.S. side, and then Japan would expect to eventually license-produce that. Which is to say, Japan would ultimately manufacture the engines, providing only royalties in return.

"Tsutsui sort of took the gloves off because people started pressing him during that briefing," said one DoD official at the meeting.

If there was one thing felt with deep and unanimous conviction on the U.S. side, it was the low-ball cost estimate Tsutsui put forward for the project: A sporty $1.2 billion price tag was all he projected for the FS-X. That number became a nagging source of conflict. Tsutsui and his team wouldn't budge from it. Nor would the Pentagon budge from its estimate. They pointed out from long experience that developing a fighter produced a voracious cash sink. Every program encountered embarrassing overruns, costs soaring into the $3 to $6 billion range. This was many times Tsutsui's projections. The French had spent $5 billion on their plane. The Israelis were up to $4 billion on theirs before it was scrapped in the fall of 1987. The Swedes, the people who build Saabs, could not avoid similar problems.

Tsutsui made clear that Japan was not Sweden.

The United States countered by trying to finesse Tsutsui. The DoD suggested a study group be formed to evaluate the American program against the Japanese program.

Tsutsui dodged. He said he was in favor of setting up a group to study the relative technologies of both countries, but he did not want his project included in the evaluation.

No one raised their voice, but statements grew clipped and arguments grew more pointed. Kearns sat sternly, his face reddened, his voice low and commanding. He was uncategorical. "Your numbers are so far out of any other nation's experience in building aircraft that it's clear you don't have adequate information," he jabbed. "How can you make a decision without the facts?" What he did not say was that he thought that the Japanese team's presentations had been amateurish and the overall level of work sophomoric.

Tsutsui buttressed his arguments by pointing to Japan's manufacturing prowess, unsurpassed, indeed unchallenged in the world. "The T-4 trainer," he told the DoD, "was within 1 or 2 percent of its development estimate, and it was delivered one month ahead of schedule." He made it clear that in a separate development, when Japan created the software for its fly-by-wire study prototype—a computer-flown aircraft—it worked the first time.

So firm was Tsutsui's presentation that even would-be supporters on the U.S. side became angered. Jim Auer was annoyed at Tsutsui's insistence on proving that Japan could build its own fighter. Why was the FS-X issue coming down to a matter of international macho? Auer later recalled that Tsutsui and company could not have it both ways. They couldn't argue on the one hand that they wanted to design and build advanced fighter jets, the most lethal weapons evolved by humankind, while still standing atop the soapbox of the peace constitution, preaching that Japan did not want to become a major military power.

Then again, Auer remained unswervingly confident that the Japanese would finally act in their own self-interest and come to terms with the Pentagon. They would not, he was convinced, endorse the ambitions of a few Mitsubishi engineers or Ryozo Tsutsui over their single most important trading customer. "I couldn't imagine the Japanese being dumb enough to go ahead and build their own fighter while they've got a $50 billion trade surplus with the United States," Auer recalled. "That would be sticking their finger in the eye of their most important customer for their video-cassette recorders.

"Policymakers in Japan had to be thinking that they will unnecessarily piss off the United States. This was not critical to their industry. HDTV may be. But building 120 fighter airplanes, is that critical? Should you fuck up the whole rest of your relationship with the United States? How many billions a year do they sell here for that—to make twenty engineers at MHI happy? The Japanese were smart. They did their homework, and they knew that these kinds of security issues meant a lot to the United States." Auer had little doubt that Nishihiro would understand that influential people in the United

States would read a dust-off in favor of domestic development "as a sign that the Japanese really are SOBs."

In this way, the trade-defense link remained tacit, implicit and ever present, prodding. Armitage would not link the two in his talks with Japanese officials in Hawaii and after, nor would Weinberger; yet Auer never had a doubt that when the chain of command was pulled, the political process would prevail. So even while the Pentagon insisted that it would not intervene in Japan's affairs by linking trade and defense, Nishihiro and those above him understood all too well that this silence had a pernicious eloquence.

One evening, after the two sides had broken up into committees to review Japan's position on the FS-X, Tsutsui sat down for drinks with General Phil Gast, the Air Force three-star who ran the Defense Security Assistance Agency, which had charge of the FS-X on the American side. The conversation began by skittering around issues of substance before finally settling for a time on the pitfalls of language and translation. The tension already apparent in that day's meeting was worsened by serious communications problems. In a conversation that was lubricated by cocktails but still quite sober, they acknowledged their difficulties.

Tsutsui confessed to Gast that earlier in the day, during the briefings, he had grown upset with him over some of his comments about Japan's calculations. Later, in discussions with his staff about the day's talks, Tsutsui said he learned he had completely misapprehended Gast's message. He misunderstood the point. That, in fact, it was just the opposite of what the general had actually intended.

The anecdote made a strong impression on Gast, but as the talks wore on, it became clear that their differences went beyond language. Knowing that they were talking past each other did not prove to be a remedy, and the Americans grew increasingly angered by Tsutsui's intransigence. Words like "disingenuous" surfaced to describe Japan's tactics and "arrogant" to describe Tsutsui's manner.

Tsutsui apparently did not realize the depth of this American anger, or he naively chose to downplay it to his superiors. For Tsutsui had stepped over the line by seeming to preach technical prowess to a U.S. team that harbored no doubts about its own unquestioned superiority, not just over Japan but over any and all comers.

"Tsutsui had never really done an airplane, never done a first-rate frontline fighter. He had no comprehension of what it took, and this is where there was a tremendous communication gap. He had no comprehension of the nature of the problem of integrating a modern weapon system," said a DoD official.

Back home, Tsutsui reported to the don of the defense agency, Seiki Nishihiro, that his mission had been accomplished. The briefings had been detailed and the United States understood Japan's position, he said. Each of the team leaders on the subcommittees were confident that the DoD understood the position of the Technical Research and Development Institute and the staff at Laboratory Three. Some of Tsutsui's advisers told him that they had the clear sense that there were those on the U.S. technical staff who endorsed Japan's presentation.

But if Tsutsui dimly believed he had made his point to the U.S. side, he was wrong. Just the opposite had taken place. Tsutsui had no idea of the impact he had had on the Pentagon, having provoked and alienated even the mild-mannered Auer, possibly Japan's single biggest rooter in the Defense Department. Now there was no one for the Japanese side to turn to in the Pentagon on the matter of domestic development, at the same time that the FS-X was about to explode in the proper laps of the State Department's Chrysanthemum Club.

9

Sounding the Alarm

"What if Weinberger should read [Kearns's cable]? We have to manage the U.S. response."
—CLYDE V. PRESTOWITZ, JR., *Trading Places*, 1989 edition, quoting an official of the U.S. Embassy in Tokyo

KEARNS BEGAN setting off alarms over the December meeting with Tsutsui at the Pentagon as soon as he got back to Tokyo. By all evidence, Kearns learned, the way in which Tsutsui had portrayed the results of his trip had been interpreted as a victory for domestic development. When Tsutsui told his superiors that his mission had been accomplished, and that the United States now understood Japan's position, the JDA seemed to think that meant that the Pentagon was on their side.

Less than a month later, in January 1987, during the seventeenth annual meeting of the Security Subcommittee, Auer and Armitage attempted to rectify the misunderstanding over breakfast with Nishihiro. Later that afternoon, Kearns, who had not joined the morning meeting, stood with Auer on the balcony of his room at the Ilikai Hotel, to get a fix on the vice minister's position. "I remember Auer's words, the exact phrase he used," said Kearns. "He told me, 'Nishihiro will pull our chestnuts out of the fire.'"

Back in Tokyo after the Hawaii talks, Kearns learned that this was not the case at all, and he took matters into his own hands for the first time. Though he was merely a deputy in the Mutual Defense Assistance Office, he confronted Nishihiro himself over the matter. Kearns was outranked. Nishihiro was the equivalent to an American Assistant Secretary of Defense. His counterpart was Richard Armitage, not a foreign service officer seconded to the Defense Department on a two-year rotation.

Still, Nishihiro met with Kearns, as he met with other American defense representatives at Auer's rank (which was below him), Kearns's rank, and lower. As ever, Nishihiro struck Kearns "as a sphinx," silent, unreadable. The defense agency's policy director told Kearns that he thought there was *no* problem with Washington, that the two sides understood each other, and that the FS-X would go into Japan's next defense budget. Kearns understood this to mean that Japan was about to go its own way on the new fighter.

But what Nishihiro told Kearns could have meant several things: A budget was necessary whether the FS-X was built in Japan, or licensed from the United States, or purchased from Panavia, the European fighter consortium. The FS-X had to be paid for somehow. But to Kearns, budgeting for the FS-X meant budgeting for domestic development. He was convinced that Nishihiro still did not understand the depth of the United States determination to put off Japanese plans for domestic development.

As Kearns recalled, he wanted to leave no doubt in Nishihiro's mind about where the United States stood. "I told him that the Americans had not accepted the Japanese position at that meeting. I told him that the Pentagon thought the cost estimates were inaccurate."

Nishihiro was shocked. "He just exploded," Kearns says. "The sphinx exploded. This wasn't what he wanted to hear. He told me, 'If what you say is true, then the whole trip to Washington was worthless.' "

To what extent these matters were clearly communicated between Kearns and Nishihiro is not certain. Nishihiro spoke no English, and Kearns, no Japanese. Roy Aka, an American of Japanese descent who worked at the embassy in Tokyo, served as a reliable translator, according to Kearns.

As Kearns saw it, the problem between the two sides arose because Tsutsui misreported the meeting, and now Japanese plans were accelerating even faster in the direction of domestic development.

To some extent, the external evidence seemed to support Kearns's view. In February, on the heels of the Hawaii meetings, Japanese defense officials announced that a consortium of five companies, led by Mitsubishi Heavy Industries, had organized into an FS-X working group. They planned to produce an issue-settling report in March proving Japan's progress in aviation technology, and thus its ability to successfully build the FS-X without U.S. help. The timing of the report positioned it to coincide with—and to potentially short-circuit—a return meeting between the Air Self-Defense Forces and the American contractors, General Dynamics and McDonnell Douglas. A creature of the defense agency, the industry consortium could be seen as a signal that the JDA was now backing Japanese industry as heavily as the DoD was backing U.S. industry.

But Kearns also overlooked important evidence of Japanese intentions that mitigated against an all-Japan fighter. Back in December, around the time of Tsutsui's visit to the Pentagon, Prime Minister Nakasone made a subtle but important shift in the three choices Japan had long advertised for the FS-X— domestic development, foreign purchase, updating an existing aircraft. The key term "domestic development" was modified. Now Japan called only for the "development" of the FS-X. That meant that while the FS-X would be an all-new plane, it would not necessarily be an all-Japan plane. This was a high-level echo of Nishihiro's remarks before the upper house of the parliament a year earlier, when he said, "Yes, [there is the choice of joint development] but is that not also a form of domestic development?"

Nakasone's decision represented the first official acknowledgment, at the highest levels of government, that Japan had acceded to the Pentagon's quiet demand that joint development be added to the three choices. And while the precise term wasn't invoked, significantly the phrase "domestic development" lost its original meaning.

Thus despite Kearns's anxious reports, the United States continued taking a gingerly approach to the issue, the low-pressure strategy advocated by Jim Auer. In January 1987, when confusion over the Tsutsui meeting at the Pentagon was its peak, Secretary of Defense Caspar Weinberger received a visit from Japanese lawmakers. What was the U.S. position on the FS-X? the delegation wanted to know. Weinberger's reply was full of low-pressure inscrutability: The FS-X, he said, "was a Japanese aircraft to be paid for out of Japanese funds about which Japan must decide."

Such comments discouraged Kearns. As he saw it, even the Europeans, who were trying to market their Tornado fighter, were taking a more aggressive position on the FS-X than Washington. They made clear to Tokyo that they would take up the issue directly with Prime Minister Nakasone at the Venice economic summit coming up that June. The United States did, however, tighten its cinch on the FS-X deal two months later, in March, when Japan's air chief, Hitoshi Omura, met with Richard Armitage in Washington. Armitage told Omura that he feared domestic development might produce another inferior aircraft like the F-1. Ironically, in just a few days, the last F-1 was about to roll off Japanese assembly lines. Only 77 planes were built out of a projected 100, an acknowledgment on the part of Japan that the plane never measured up as a fighter. That couldn't be allowed to happen again, not with the FS-X, Armitage insisted.

Separately, deteriorating relations between the United States and Japan conspired against the FS-X. The U.S. International Trade Commission found Japan's computer chip industry guilty of dumping their product in U.S. markets, and President Reagan was forced by congressional maneuvering to slap a

100 percent tariff against Japanese chip imports, something that had never before happened in the postwar era. Japan was stung.

Shintaro Abe, one of Japan's most powerful politicians, hurried to Washington to try to mend tattered relations and to prepare the way for a state visit by Prime Minister Nakasone in February. At the time, Nakasone hoped to address a joint session of Congress, offering a plan to curb the burgeoning trade gap. The centerpiece of his plan was a promise to pass a domestic spending package through the parliament in order to get Japanese consumers to buy more U.S. imports.

Making amends with the United States was not going to be easy for Japan, however. Sensitivities, which were already running high, quickly began to take a personal turn. Nakasone himself drew a bead on the U.S. Trade Representative, Clayton K. Yeutter, singling him out for meddling in Japan's internal affairs. Yeutter, testifying before the Senate Finance Committee, had declared that Washington's trade balance with Tokyo would worsen because of Nakasone's policy. He pointed out that an unpopular tax pushed by the Prime Minister's office would reduce domestic consumption and with it demand for U.S. products. Nakasone shot back condescendingly that Yeutter "should increase his study of Japan's tax system reform."

Even Japanese business began squirming under increasing U.S. pressure. Fearing negative publicity, Fujitsu Ltd. dropped plans to purchase Fairchild Semiconductor. Reagan's Central Intelligence Agency director, William J. Casey, sniped that Japanese investment in U.S. computer firms was a "Trojan Horse." Though Japanese real estate purchases in California, New York, and Texas continued apace, the welcome mat was wearing thin, particularly on Capitol Hill.

Congress grew increasingly intolerant of Tokyo's recycling of trade dollars into new U.S. investments, which had the potential to skim off the cream of the U.S. technology crop. Talk of retaliation rose from a murmur into open debate. An amendment to the Omnibus Trade Bill nearing completion that year in Congress empowered the President to single out whole nations as unfair traders. In the past, the dubious honor was reserved for individual industries, as illustrated by the dumping case against Japan's computer chip manufacturers. Called Super 301, the powerful new measure was aimed directly at Japan, whose trade deficit with the United States now topped $51 billion.

Worse matters were yet to unfold, as the United States pressed its back channels for information about a $16 million machine-tool sale to the Soviet Union that appeared to be a violation of Tokyo's security arrangements with the United States.

For its part, the Chrysanthemum Club at the embassy was working overtime to keep "the relationship" from boiling over, which created an unexpected obstacle for Kearns. Cables Kearns wrote warning about the urgency of FS-X developments were increasingly worked over or even gutted. While typically such "memos" were vetted for accuracy or tone, Kearns believed that his memos were being vetted for ideological reasons.

To Kearns it seemed that the Pol-Mil Section was pulling rank on an already oppressed Mutual Defense Assistance Office. In charge of the section was a thirty-eight-year-old foreign service officer named Chris LaFleur. Two years Kearns's junior, LaFleur had moved smartly up the career ladder to his current post, although he had no experience in military affairs. He seemed to show even less interest in the FS-X. Indeed, he rarely attended meetings on the plane, not even the key meeting that October, when representatives of General Dynamics and McDonnell Douglas came to Tokyo. However, when Kearns attempted to take charge of the matter, cabling policy suggestions back to Washington, LaFleur raised objections.

Kearns attributed LaFleur's balkiness to his membership in the Chrysanthemum Club. "LaFleur is their fair-haired boy," Kearns would say. It was no secret at the embassy that LaFleur had married well in Japanese society, very well indeed. LaFleur was the son-in-law of one of Japan's most powerful officials, sixty-seven-year-old Kiichi Miyazawa, a man in line to succeed Nakasone as Prime Minister. (He assumed the post in 1991.) At the time, the gnomelike Miyazawa, who was Japan's well-regarded minister of finance, served an unprecedented simultaneous term as Deputy Prime Minister. Miyazawa's ministry had a crucial stake in the FS-X, since it controlled the nation's defense budget. Miyazawa also clearly understood the importance of aviation for Japan's future, having served as minister of international trade and industry in 1970, the year MITI first targeted aviation as a *kiban gijitsu*, a key technology.

Miyazawa was an intellectual, a veteran politician known for his command of English. Legend had it that as a college student Miyazawa ate all the pages of his English dictionary in his fervor over the language. Unusually well regarded as a bureaucrat—most politicians were mere figureheads—Miyazawa had actual power. He was also a force in ruling party politics, which was important to the FS-X because each of the men who had directed the defense agency during the program had come from his faction of the ruling party. That included the current defense chief, Yuko Kurihara.

Like most Japanese public officials, Miyazawa was beholden to a constituency. Japanese politicians generally represent entire industries, such as telecommunications, construction, or transportation. In return, they are rewarded richly in the form of campaign contributions, a massive and little regulated source of free-floating yen.

Significantly, Miyazawa's constituency was the Mitsubishi company. His connection was similar to ones in the United States, where, for example, Senator John Danforth is regarded as the senator from McDonnell Douglas and Sam Nunn is known as the senator from Lockheed. Miyazawa was the minister from Mitsubishi, and Mitsubishi stood to become the prime contractor on the FS-X and gain handsomely.

LaFleur's marriage to Miyazawa's daughter raised some eyebrows, because of the importance of family connections within Japan's ruling class. Even today marriages are often arranged and possess an almost contractual quality. They are as much mergers as romances, even when they are romances.

Among politicians, marriages are a kind of glue. The process is like grafting. Influence is the product. "Among top bureaucrats, politicians and businessman, marriage facilitates the building up of informal contacts with the elite. [Ruling party] politicians reinforce their positions by marrying the daughters of older, influential politicians, then match their own sons and daughters with the children of prosperous and influential businessmen. The resulting networks are known as *keibatsun*," writes Karel van Wolferen, in his influential book *The Enigma of Japanese Power*.

LaFleur made no secret of his connection with Miyazawa, and this created a problem of image for LaFleur, who was generally well regarded by his peers. If he took a position on a crucial issue, his motives could be left open to interpretation by opponents like Kearns, particularly when those were issues of great moment between his father-in-law's ministry and his employers at the embassy. The FS-X was one of those issues.

In 1986, when the Deputy U.S. Trade Representative, Michael B. Smith, arrived in Tokyo and requested a briefing from the Pol-Mil Section on the FS-X, LaFleur refused. The attempt at bureaucratic strong-arming was largely a turf matter, however, involving concerns that the USTR would invoke the link between trade and defense. Neither the Pentagon nor the State Department much relished the idea of having the government's commercial agencies like the USTR and the Commerce Department meddling in their sandbox.

So bad was this intradepartmental brawling that representatives of the USTR and Commerce complained that throughout the FS-X debate they had the clear sense that the Japanese were better informed about the DoD's or the State Department's intentions than they were. "The Japanese were always in the know about our government's positions ahead of us," said a former officer in the Trade Representative's office. "If we had a closed-door meeting, they would learn the details within hours."

LaFleur's refusal did not sit well with a man who thought trade matters were his bailiwick. Ambassador Smith, as he liked to be known, was a vinegary personality and a thirty-year veteran of the trade wars. Considered by many to be America's "toughest and most respected trade negotiator," he had negotiated more than 400 international agreements. By his own estimate, this surpassed the record of any other U.S. official, past or present.

One of the trade areas Smith specialized in was aviation. His office was hung with dozens of shining plastic aircraft models, of the sort presented as mementos by the manufacturers. He had negotiated many of this nation's major aircraft agreements, and was a bitter opponent of Europe's government-subsidized Airbus Industries. Japan, he thought, represented a new and perplexing challenge all its own, and the United States had to take care in handing over hard-won, taxpayer-financed technology.

Cantankerous and combative, Smith responded to LaFleur by picking up the phone to Washington and calling his boss, Clayton Yeutter, a member of the Reagan cabinet. The angry Yeutter told Smith that if there was no briefing by the end of the day, he would personally go directly to the President. Informed of the USTR's position on the FS-X, LaFleur quickly relented and a briefing was scheduled.

Witnesses interviewed about these events said that Smith was worried about LaFleur's Miyazawa connection and intentionally arrived early to do some reconnoitering. Although there is some dispute on the matter of whom Smith actually talked to before meeting LaFleur, it was Kevin Kearns who recalls briefing the Trade Representative. The message Smith got from Kearns was that elements in the Defense Department were deeply concerned about the deal. On this point, however, Kearns was largely on his own, bluffing: He was the "elements" in the DoD that were concerned about the deal.

The disparity between Kearns's informal briefing sharply contrasted with the "happy face" LaFleur painted on the deal. As LaFleur described it, the FS-X was a program that would build interdependence between the United States and Japan. He said that the two nations shared a special responsibility toward each other and that the deal would benefit both countries. The United States would get new Japanese technologies, and the Japanese would participate in a new era of cooperation.

Smith, who was known for his directness, barked that LaFleur's briefing was full of "horseshit." In a later interview, Smith spoke about the FS-X agreement as conceived by the Pol/Mil Section: "It had more damn holes in it than a fishing net." Smith refused to confirm or deny the meeting or the account of it for the record. He was candid, however, about the embassy's role in the FS-X project. "Sometimes it seemed that Japan had two embassies working for them—ours and theirs."

Smith says he had been prompted to bring up the matter of the FS-X on his visit to Tokyo by representatives of General Dynamics and McDonnell Douglas. In visits with him at his office, they made clear that they had lost faith in the DoD's low-profile approach to Japan's new aircraft. Indeed, the contact with Smith marked the beginning of a broad offensive mounted by the two U.S. aircraft firms to get Japan involved in a co-development program. They were taking the issue before the USTR, the Commerce Department, the Defense Department, but, most important, to the U.S. Congress.

Notice of the defense industry's newfound concern for the FS-X deal arrived on a letterhead from the Senate's Committee on Commerce, Science, and Transportation, dated March 5, 1987. Addressed to Secretary of Defense Caspar Weinberger, it was written by John C. Danforth, the senior senator from Missouri. Danforth represented the two St. Louis constituencies vying for billions of dollars in work on the deal, General Dynamics and McDonnell Douglas, both of which had their home offices in his state. Danforth was the man Japanese defense chief Kurihara most worried about.

As the ranking minority member on the influential Commerce Committee, Danforth led the Republican side on trade matters. He was known as a "trade activist" who believed that Japan's import barriers could not be allowed to stand. Much of the tough trade legislation that emerged in the Congress over the decade bore Danforth's sponsorship. He called for quotas on Japanese auto imports in 1981 that resulted in an agreement on voluntary restraints on Japanese auto exports. He favored a reciprocity trade bill that linked the openness of U.S. markets to the openness of our trading partners' markets. The 1984 Trade and Tariff Act carried a Danforth-designed Trade Estimate Report, which required the Commerce Department to list the trade barriers faced by U.S. exporters. He was the central figure in the 1988 Omnibus Trade Bill then embarking on its route into law.

Danforth's formal three-page letter to Weinberger began: "The United States Government will shortly be conducting discussions with the Japanese on the procurement of a jet fighter, the FS-X . . ." The tone sharpened from there, stabbing directly at the trade-defense jugular. If the Japanese are allowed to develop their own plane, he continued, "it will not only exacerbate existing trade difficulties, but will belie all Japanese claims that they wish to rectify the current imbalance."

With his coarse gray locks carving across his brow and his chalk-stripe suits, John Claggett Danforth, aged fifty-two, could muster a fine righteousness. One of the giants of the Senate, he was an establishment man with the look of Episcopalian lucre. (His grandfather founded Ralston Purina.) An ordained and practicing Episcopalian priest, known on occasion as "St. Jack," he resonated reason and goodwill in his thinking. Danforth was a man who knew the deep roots of his own convictions and indignations. He relied more on his "moral inventory" than any "political calculus" for his judgments, wrote *The Almanac of American Politics 1992.* New York senator Daniel Patrick Moynihan would say to him, "Good morning, Your Grace." Danforth would respond, "Good morning, my son."

The FS-X was surely a pressing constituent issue for Danforth, but it was also a matter he took personally, as his letter made clear. "Another favorite Japanese excuse is being applied to this situation. They claim that American planes cannot meet their specified needs. However, U.S. manufacturers have stated clearly their willingness and ability to modify their planes to meet the Japanese criteria—even though some appear to be little more than glorified non-tariff barriers." The United States should make clear, he wrote, "that the only way Japan can claim sincerity in its concern over the U.S. trade deficit is to stop stonewalling on this procurement."

The strongly worded letter continued: "American producers want to sell a high-tech product the Japanese government freely admits it wants. It is a quality product offered at a competitive price. The Japanese produce nothing that comes close. Our technology, cost, and ability to deliver promptly are superior."

For years, Japan had claimed it did not buy American goods because they lacked quality, or because the Japanese made a better product at home. This simply was not true in every case. They may have had a point about shabby American workmanship when they cited the problems with Detroit's auto sales. But they were wrong when they bypassed U.S. telecommunications satellites in favor of their own, or U.S. cellular phones, or fighter jets.

Danforth concluded his letter with a full-throttle threat: "Once the outra-geous nature of Japanese intentions becomes clear, Congress will accurately see this move as 'business as usual' in Japan. Unless the administration inter-venes with vigor, the inevitable political backlash will be well deserved."

A significant amount of time passed before Weinberger replied, indicating he did not see the same urgency in the FS-X as did Danforth. Thus, one month and three days later, the Secretary offered a broad, casual two-page reply that began informally "Dear Jack" and was signed in the style of an old school chum: "Cap." In between Weinberger confidently made the point that he had been looking out for the senator's constituents. "We have been work-ing closely with our major aerospace industries to ensure that they have proper access to the Japan Defense Agency with their proposals." Danforth must have been wondering why, then, those same contractors were worried enough to humble themselves before him.

Weinberger spelled out the U.S. approach. America's primary concern, he wrote, is that "Japan's defense forces be interoperable with our forces" (by now the requirement for "interoperability" had become a code word for co-development) "and that the replacement fighter be cost-effective and within the means of Japan's limited defense budget. . . . We have worked for a long time to ensure that Japan receives all relevant technical data so that it will be able to consider and weigh each of the U.S. alternatives available to it in order to make an informed decision." Significantly, Weinberger did not write of the Japanese alternative of domestic development. The omission signaled that such an alternative was not being entertained by him, let alone acknowledged.

In the end, Kearns was reprimanded for his visit to Nishihiro by the Deputy Chief of Mission, the embassy's number two man in Tokyo, Desaix Anderson. A foreign affairs veteran, the fifty-year-old Anderson was a thorny defender of the Mansfield vision. He was of a different generation from Kearns; World War II and its aftermath were the stuff of his youth. Kearns, the baby boomer, grew up on Eisenhower and Elvis.

Anderson's old-school loyalty clashed with Kearns's entrepreneurship. Kearns defended his actions as a forthright and necessary appraisal. Someone had to let Washington know what was going on in Tokyo. Kearns told Anderson, "Nishihiro was the one to see on this matter, and it was my job to do it. I'm not the problem. The problem is that the Japanese don't want to get the message. They don't want to hear this."

Anderson was furious. He told Kearns that he was not to see Nishihiro again. The vice minister was too far above his rank.

There was a second confrontation between the two men when Kearns cabled back to Washington that he was having problems making Nishihiro understand the U.S. position. Kearns learned that Anderson edited the text, moderating its tone. Kearns thought it had changed the very meaning of the cable, and he protested to Anderson.

Anderson dismissed Kearns. You're just a technical expert, he scolded, and technicians do not make U.S.-Japan policy.

Kearns did not raise his voice, but grew dark and caustic. His voice dripped contempt. "First of all," he replied, "I'm forty years old. I'm a lawyer. I've run a successful political campaign in the United States. I've been legislative council to a state senator and spent the last ten years in the foreign service. So maybe I know something about politics and policy. What's more, there's no way that the United States can make policy on an issue like the FS-X unless it *understands* the technical problems involved."

Kearns's cable warned of Tsutsui's misrepresentations and Nishihiro's failure to grasp the Pentagon's position that December. He said Nishihiro was out of touch and the FS-X was about to go forward as a domestic program. "When you write cables about the attitude and approach of the Japanese to these negotiations with the United States, you find that it's very difficult to get them cleared by the embassy."

Anderson thought the language of Kearns's cable could be damaging. He worried what would happen if it was read by Weinberger. He told Kearns, in essence, you don't understand U.S.-Japan relations; you're not a language officer, and you're not here to make policy.

Kearns told Anderson that he had it wrong, and he shot back: "You can't make policy here if you don't understand the technology." As he later recalled: "State Department political officers have a real disdain for business or economics or anything technical. Policy wasn't based on fact for Anderson; it was based on maintaining the good feelings in the U.S.-Japan relationship, and trying to preserve that at all costs. And it didn't matter what the cost was to the American side."

Kearns's tour at the Tokyo embassy was just six months old and already he was on notice that he could not meet with Japanese officials above a certain rank and that he could expect to have no input on policy. But Kearns was an ambitious man who believed in personal initiative. What he couldn't accomplish within the system, he could accomplish by other means. At least Kearns now knew what he was up against and who his real enemies were.

10

Dondi at the Boei-cho

"The Sullivan mission said there's no good Japanese technology. The United States is more advanced. That meant that we would get nothing out of joint development, but stood to give away a great deal."
—KEVIN KEARNS

DONDI was a popular comic strip character in the 1950s and 1960s. He was an urchin, a spunky orphan, part of the human sweepings left in the aftermath of World War II. Aged eight or nine, he was "adopted" by the good-hearted and indulgent GIs of the occupation. He became their mascot. Chewing gum and chocolate bars were his Stars and Stripes. Panel after cartoon panel, installment after installment, Dondi evoked the gallantry and homespun wisdom of the unshaven Yankee conqueror. Not to mention the worldly and clever antics of little Dondi.

By comparison, Alvin Cullum York was the laconic hero portrayed by Gary Cooper in the 1940s movie *Sergeant York*. Single-handedly, the brave Tennessean annihilated 25 German soldiers and captured 132 others on October 8, 1918, in the desolated Argonne Forest of France. Awarded the highest medals for bravery by his own government and by the French, York became a symbol of the daring and inventiveness of the U.S. Army. He epitomized the redoubtable courage and Yankee grit of the valiant doughboy.

Couple poor little Dondi and towering Sergeant York in a mutual security pact and an image of the U.S.-Japan defense relationship emerges. The stalwart sergeant extends his beneficent and protective Garand bolt-action rifle protectively over the tattered, shivering, and vulnerable Dondi, his requisitioned oversized overseas cap adorably askew.

Dondi, of course, could never be expected to defend the good sergeant, nor would he have to, such was the invincibility of the legendary York. Dondi would merely have to emulate him, donning his surplus clothes and military gear and embracing the great democratic spirit that he fought for.

The Sergeant York–Dondi bond well suited both the Pentagon and the Boei-cho, Japan's military nerve center in the heart of Tokyo's youth-oriented entertainment district, Roppongi. Particularly on the U.S. side, Japan was viewed as a combat urchin, the stumbling but too-clever-by-half protégé. The Japanese Air Force, for example, though well equipped, was seen as cautious, more skilled at formation flying for parades than air-to-air combat. The U.S. Air Force referred to them condescendingly as "taxi drivers." The same with the army, who were at their best cleaning up after typhoons and earthquakes, the occasional volcanic eruption. They were not expected to keep pace with their night-fighting crack American counterparts.

Only the Maritime Self-Defense Forces got credit as a fighting unit from the U.S. Navy. "Our guys don't have to slow down to allow them to keep up with us on maneuvers," said Jim Auer. Still, the navy was a bathtub-sized force in comparison with the huge flotillas the United States put to sea, a two-ocean navy with enough airpower to cover the entire globe.

Whereas the State Department was devoted and accommodating to Japan, the Pentagon was patronizing, and thus each was in its way protective of its quasi ally. In the FS-X, Foggy Bottom functioned most of all as a buffer to the Pentagon's increasingly pressured prodding. Sergeant York wanted Dondi to come to his senses. The domestic development charade had gone far enough.

Four months had passed since Tsutsui's December foray into the Pentagon, and now the hardening of the U.S. position was well underway. Kearns's cables were having their desired effect, despite the concerns of conservative embassy officials, such as Desaix Anderson. When Assistant Secretary Armitage, Jim Auer's boss, learned that Nishihiro had not in fact grasped the degree to which the Pentagon opposed Tsutsui's December performance, he fired off a letter to Nishihiro. Said a source close to Armitage, "Rich didn't just tell Nishihiro, 'No,' he told him, 'Hell, no, we don't accept Tsutsui's analysis.'" In addition to his epistolary efforts, Armitage pushed for a U.S. evaluation team to assess how far Tokyo had progressed in its aviation technology.

The mission slated for that spring in 1987 was headed by Assistant Deputy Under Secretary of Defense for International Programs and Technology Gerald Sullivan. Sullivan's mission to Tokyo that April was to find out just how good the Japanese really were, to test Tsutsui's bravado.

————

Sullivan was a thirty-year veteran of the Pentagon and the technical director for U.S. Air Force projects. In his unique and influential position, he was at the absolute edge of aerospace defense technology. With his long experience in international programs—research and co-production projects with Europe —he understood the obstacles and opportunities latent in what he referred to as "industrial cooperation," a DoD euphemism for weapons development. He had engineering degrees from Georgetown University and the Massachusetts Institute of Technology. A native of Kansas, he was out of the same heartland mold as the good Sergeant York.

Everything about Sullivan said engineer. He would wear paisley shirts with a tweed jacket, disdaining fashion. His lean build seemed pared down. A man of essentials, his thin blond hair was cut manageably short. He looked to be in his gung-ho prime, not a worn-out thirty-year veteran. There is a tough-mindedness about engineers like Sullivan, perhaps the result of having a career grounded on numbers, facts, and natural laws. Sullivan was prickly with that faith, like a man crouched down over his own set of facts. Sullivan could be cold and smart, but with no bias other than his personal integrity. He was widely respected at the Pentagon, and even though Kearns and Sullivan were at odds on co-development, Kearns saw him as "the clean career bureaucrat." He completely trusted Sullivan's judgment on the state of Japanese technology. Indeed, that judgment became an article of faith for Kearns.

Sullivan was one of four Pentagon decision makers with direct authority over the FS-X. The others were Auer, whose job was to keep the FS-X focused between the narrow lines of policy, General Phil Gast, who watched over the contractual agreements and negotiations, and Richard Armitage, their boss, the final authority before the Secretary of Defense.

"Phil Gast and I are very close friends," said Sullivan. "We worked together on a lot of these sorts of things before. We have no problem in this, and the same thing with Rich Armitage. So there was an easy amount of trust on our side."

Sullivan's job was to study and evaluate the technology and engineering of the FS-X program. He knew fighters. In the end, his mission would mark a turning point in the FS-X debate. His findings would become the foundation upon which the United States built its arguments against an all-Japan FS-X. Forevermore, after his visit, when the question of Japanese competence in aerospace arose, both opponents and proponents of the deal would turn to Sullivan's findings for support.

By and large, Sullivan took a jaundiced view of the Japanese defense industry. He believed that their weapons firms made their investments in order to subsidize technology developments they wanted for their commercial markets. They called this "dual-use" technology, which could be "spun off" from the military sector to the commercial side, as the brakes used on the U.S.-licensed F-86 fighter were spun off into the brake system for the *shinkansen*, known as the Bullet Train. In the other direction, such dual-use technologies could also be "spun on" from the commercial side to the military sector, which was more and more the case in Japan. A chip used to regulate the fuel intake of an automobile, for example, might have applications in the fuel-injection system on the engine of a battle tank.

The Sullivan mission to Tokyo took place over an eight-day period beginning April 18. The initial meetings were held at the Japan Defense Agency, in the Boei-cho, Japan's Pentagon equivalent. They were largely a rehash of previous parleys; the two sides clawed over the airplane's mission, its tactics, its technical requirements. Once again, they fought to a draw.

Day two found Sullivan and company still in the white tower blocks of the Boei-cho. Much as in Laboratory Three, the decor here made the wilting Pentagon appear by comparison to be a great and venerable plantation. From across the street, at the Mrs. Fields cookie shop, the defense agency's offices were barely noticeable. There was just a long, low wall with plane trees growing along the sidewalk. The interior of the agency was even less impressive. The corridors of the dimly lit air staff's headquarters were stacked with unused furniture and cardboard boxes. Tan metal lockers lining the walls gave it the appearance of a basement gymnasium changing room. Dusty pipes ran across the ceiling.

Sullivan found the air staff officers he spoke with rigid in their support for domestic development. This was a new generation of airmen, who, unlike their predecessors, did not feel beholden to their American benefactors. Though the relationship remained York-meets-Dondi, this was a newer, older Dondi. Now a teenager, the urchin had his own car and was after his own hot rod.

Sullivan argued that they were approaching the FS-X more like a technology test bed than a combat fighter. It looked like something they wrenched together in the garage from parts purchased at various speed shops. He hammered at them about the real purposes of their work: the mission. The mission should define the aircraft's technology, not the other way around, he told them. He also played a policy card, making clear to the air staff that the FS-X would have to be viewed as an integral part of the U.S.-Japan relationship, not just as a weapons system.

The U.S. team had requested visits to the member companies in the Japanese FS-X consortium—Mitsubishi Heavy, Kawasaki Heavy, Fuji Heavy, Ishikawajima Harima Heavy, and Mitsubishi Electric. Only visits to Mitsubishi Heavy's Nagoya plant and Mitsubishi Electric's plant in Kamakura were allowed. (Tsutsui, however, said this was not the case, and that the U.S. side was able to visit any plant they wished.)

It was no secret that Tsutsui was infuriated by the U.S. visit and its findings. Indeed, back in December at the Pentagon, he had expressly ruled out the very sort of mission on which Sullivan was now embarked. This was precisely what he had hoped to avoid.

The focus of the U.S. visit was on Japan's aircraft and avionics firms. At Mitsubishi Heavy Industries, Sullivan got a look at where the FS-X was heading. The cockpit of the plane—which existed as a computer simulation of dials and displays performing an ersatz mission—proved a disappointment, despite a flourish or two. In mock-ups Sullivan saw, the Japanese employed the latest flat-panel display technology, using laptop-style screens as opposed to conventional TV screens, thus saving precious weight and space.

While displays in the F-16 were not as advanced as the flat-panel displays at Mitsubishi, it wasn't for lack of technology. There simply wasn't enough money around to switch the F-16 from video to flat panels. What was more, the F/A-18 was already flying with flat-panel displays. In other words, what the Japanese were showing was hardly leading-edge technology.

In Sullivan's view, the only striking difference between the FS-X and other generic aircraft was the use of canards, the little winglets canted upward beneath the cockpit. The Japanese were enamored of them. Sullivan was not. He told the Japanese plainly: "Everything that you've got here has been done. You're not making any advances, not in computers, not in the plane's dynamics. You're going to take ten years to build a plane that's no better than the most advanced planes that we're flying today. Right now." As for the canards and the computer technology that went along with them, he was equally unenthusiastic. "You just don't get your money's worth from it," he told them.

(A drawing obtained by Michael Green, a Ph.D. candidate from the Johns Hopkins School of Advanced International Studies, who worked for the defense caucus of Japan's ruling Liberal Democratic Party in the middle 1980s, shows the FS-X as it appeared in 1985 under the designation JF-210. It bears a striking similarity to the projected F/A-18 Super Hornet Plus, proposed by McDonnell Douglas. Both planes had canards and, more distinctively, a "cranked arrow" main wing.)

Two Japanese technologies did prove interesting to Sullivan, however. The first was a new wing the Japanese were developing. The actual composite material from which it was to be made was nothing new, but the process of molding the wing as one solid piece was.

Until now, the United States built wings in sections and riveted them together, using some composite parts. The Japanese were experimenting with molding the whole wing from composites and curing it all at once like a clay model, complete with chambers for holding fuel, running electronics, seating activators, incorporating hydraulic systems. Only the top skin of the wing was riveted on for access and maintenance.

The problem with the Japanese wing was that it was a "rigid box" structure and not "air-elastic"—that is, it did not shape and move with the forces applied to it. The Japanese wing was stiff, forming a rigid box. All fighter wings are stiff, but are still air-elastic. A co-cured air-elastic wing was possible, Sullivan thought; the question was whether it would hold together. The work Mitsubishi Heavy was doing "was good for an R&D program," he concluded, but it was hardly earthshaking.

The other technology that attracted Sullivan was an active phased array radar, which was really many smaller radars working independently and in concert, like the compound eye of an insect. Indeed, the Japanese referred to the radar as "the eye of the dragonfly." The engineers from Mitsubishi Electric had a test unit flying using a cargo plane as a test bed, but it proved difficult to make the modules work together and the radar was back in the laboratory for repairs and reevaluation.

Sullivan did not question the ability of the Mitsubishi Electric engineers to produce the radar; he simply doubted its usefulness to the FS-X. "You don't need a sophisticated, high-powered phased array radar for the kind of missions you've proposed for this plane," he told Tsutsui. "You can tweak out the radars we've got on our current aircraft and perform the mission." By "tweaking" Sullivan meant minor modifications or even adjustments. In other words, the radars available on U.S. aircraft could already do everything Japan hoped its phased array would do in terms of mission.

Sullivan was not entirely critical, however. He was impressed with the modules the Japanese were producing for the phased array. Each module was an actual radar that employed gallium arsenide circuitry in place of silicon circuitry. This ensured that its components would remain functional even during the paralyzing electromagnetic pulses broadcast by nuclear blasts. The problem was cost. According to Sullivan, "to do this right would take a thousand modules [to create an array], and the best price you can get for a module is a thousand dollars each. That's too expensive for a tactical radar."

Sullivan told Tsutsui: "We can believe that Melco [Mitsubishi Electric] will do a better job of miniaturizing these modules than the United States. We can believe that Melco will make them more reliable and produce them more cheaply. That's their forte, and they'll probably do it. On the other hand, we in the United States have been building and flying tactical radars for a long time. We know what they have to do in combat. A radar is not just a device that transmits and receives. What matters is how this information is processed, how it links to the other systems in the fighter, and we have the combat experience to know how to do it."

The radars, the wings, and the canards were the signature of Tsutsui's FS-X. Taken separately, as Sullivan was doing, these technologies may have been "merely" state of the art. The key in Tsutsui's mind was that the FS-X brought them all together, integrating them into a fighting system. To his way of thinking, the whole was far greater than the sum of its parts. It was that synergy which would make the FS-X the equal of anything flying in the year 2000, Tsutsui believed.

After nearly a year of meetings with the Japanese over the FS-X, Sullivan had sized Tsutsui up as a game player. As he saw it, Tsutsui's gambit to win the FS-X for domestic development was to envision a unique airplane for a unique Japanese mission. Sullivan countered the Tsutsui strategy by attempting to dismember those elements of Tsutsui's FS-X that made it unique. Sullivan's endgame concentrated on software. "Software is a bitch," Sullivan later recalled telling Tsutsui. "And this one, this radar which had a thousand modules to coordinate, is an even bigger bitch. Each one of those units is sending signals and receiving them, processing information and evaluating it. It's one of the most awesome tasks you could think of for a computer programmer. And no nation comes close to the United States in software development. Hands down, across the board, that's where we are the best."

Japan's ability to reliably manufacture the tiny modules combined with America's preeminence and experience in software—and here was a core belief of Sullivan, his main argument to Tsutsui—would make a formidable product to compete on world markets.

Sullivan reportedly even went so far as to urge Tsutsui to join with the United States in developing the next-generation Advanced Tactical Fighter, and then to modify the ATF for Japanese use.

Sullivan's appeals were heard beyond the Boei-cho, in the influential ministries which acted like the fingers in the glove that was the Japan Defense Agency. Until now, the Ministry of Finance, under Kiichi Miyazawa, had kept a low profile on the FS-X. The expectation was that they would have been more active opponents of domestic development because of the obvious cost problems involved in the project.

Sullivan's logic pried at those institutional interests overseen by Miyazawa. Using Japan's own estimate of a $7 billion budget to build a mere 120 planes, Sullivan was able to show that the FS-X was more than twice as costly as the F-16, with the FS-X arriving on the runway at $70 million per copy and the F-16, with all the bells and whistles, arriving years earlier at less than half the price, about $30 million per copy. That was the kind of argument that tended to sway the Ministry of Finance.

Other institutional interests, such as the Ministry of Foreign Affairs, had always been more forthcoming to the idea of a co-development with the United States. Like the State Department, its counterpart, the Gaimusho, as the ministry was known in Japanese, lived in the thrall of its own policy, referred to in Japanese shorthand as *nichibei*, the "relationship," the U.S.-Japan relationship, our single most important bilateral relationship *bar none*, according to Ambassador Mansfield. For the Gaimusho, there were larger matters at stake in the FS-X than the ambitions of a group of enthusiastic engineers at one of the heavy-industry companies. The ministry worried about the effects of the FS-X on *nichibei*, especially with Prime Minister Nakasone's visit to Washington just days away on April 29.

In the final analysis, what mattered most in the Sullivan mission was the determination that Japan lagged behind the United States in advanced fighter technology. As Sullivan himself put it: "The Japanese were not providing us with anything new or unique." Here the Pentagon had proved correct in its prospective estimate of Japan's defense industry. The Defense Department's concerns that an all-Japan FS-X would turn out to be a costly and inferior weapon facing a major Soviet buildup and modernization in the Pacific proved justified.

At the same time, however, Sullivan's findings revealed the small or nonexistent gains co-development held for the United States. It answered the question "What would we get out of this?" with the impolitic reality: "Nothing." Without Japanese technology flowing back across the Pacific, the deal represented small potatoes—just 100–170 planes—for the United States' contracting partner. And while defense in the Pacific would be bolstered, the Soviets were supposedly adding hundreds and hundreds of new planes to their arsenal. The fact of the matter was plain: Like it or not, the FS-X was shaping up to be a far better deal for the Japanese than for the United States. That meant industrial benefits and new technology that would bring Japan closer to the threshold of becoming a competitor with the United States in yet another field, this one producing our single largest export.

11

The Silence of the Subs

*"We Japanese who put our companies' fortunes in front of our country's are begin-
ning to realize that the security of our nation is the security of our company."*
—An unnamed source in *The Wall Street Journal*, August 4, 1987

S ULLIVAN THOUGHT the Japanese really weren't up to the task of
building the FS-X on their own," recalled Jim Auer. "At least they
were not up to building the aircraft they needed to counter the Soviet
threat. Sullivan came back and said that they have less technology than he
expected. He was really surprised."

So was Auer. "I wouldn't have been in government if my job had been in
arms sales. I have no interest. I got involved in the FS-X because it became a
political issue. I was never involved in it for the damn technology; I don't
know whether something's high-tech, low-tech, mid-tech."

Which is precisely what Kearns feared, that key people in the FS-X deliberations didn't actually grasp the problem, which was the degree of technology the Japanese would be getting in a co-development deal.

To some extent, Auer understood that he was in over his head. For him, the
FS-X was a large and complex responsibility on top of a behemoth burden:
U.S.-Japan security relations. Whereas dozens of Pentagon staffers covered
Italy, France, and Great Britain—nations whose *combined* military purchases
from Uncle Sam totaled *less* than Japan's—Auer was on his own. As Japan
completed one of the largest military buildups in the world during the 1980s,
Jim Auer commented on the overload: "Putting one guy in that job, given the
sophistication of our defense relationship, was cruel and unusual punishment."

One of Auer's chief assets in dealing with Japan was his silent partner in Tokyo, a man named Hideo Kimura, political operator par excellence. Those in Auer's circle considered Kimura to be a man of some genius and deep loyalty. Kimura would have a powerful impact on the FS-X in his role as a go-between for Auer and the Japan Defense Agency. His role in assuaging doubts on the Japanese side over co-development, and in placating the United States over what came to be known as the Toshiba affair, was substantial because it bore fruit. In the case of Toshiba, Kimura managed to get the Pentagon to back off Japan's case; and with the FS-X, Kimura succeeded in getting the Japanese air staff to listen seriously to Auer.

Hideo Kimura was a real-life Dondi. In fact, if Dondi had been Asian and grown up in modern Japan, he would have been very much like Hideo Kimura—a proud nationalist who knew how to deal with Americans, who considered them friends but was not averse to telling them what he thought they were doing wrong.

Kimura received his first direct impression of the fearsome American conquerors on a rainy day in 1946. He was a little boy, hungry, aged six, with a long walk to school. The roads from his home to class were rutted and worn by the ravages of the war. Worst of all, in the awful heat of the June rainy season, he had to wear a heavy black rubber raincoat. The slicker was so outsized it touched the ground. He nearly disappeared inside it, swallowed, soaked with perspiration, and struggling uncomfortably under its great bulk.

One humid day, when the rain pelted the road to school into a slithering red channel of mud, he felt himself snatched up from behind and deposited atop what he immediately recognized as a jeep. The Americans. Other Japanese children were already on board. The *gaijin*—these foreigners—were so big! They gave him chocolate and chewing gum and took him to school. Thereafter, they always saved him from his heavy black raincoat and the long trek to class with a speedy bouncing ride in the jeep.

Like the charming comic strip urchin Dondi, Hideo Kimura discovered that GIs were gentle conquerors. They were gruff men, but they were there to help. In Yokosuka, where he lived, these men were mostly sailors. The city was on a beak of land that guarded the entrance to Tokyo Bay. Just thirty miles distant from the capital by sea, it was then many hours away overland. Yokosuka had been hard hit during wartime bombing raids because it was an industrial center, home to Japan's largest shipyards.

Kimura never forgot those early days after the war. The kindness of the Americans affected him deeply, and he was grateful. As he grew older and the American occupiers evolved into Japan's defenders, he went into politics.

A graduate of Sophia University, a Jesuit school in Tokyo, Kimura worked in the 1970s as a political secretary for a well-regarded Diet member, Eki

Sone, of the Democratic Socialist Party, a small right-of-center, pro-American political party. The DSP often lined up with the ruling Liberal Democratic Party on matters of national security.

Sone was important to the U.S. military because he was one of the key representatives from Kanagawa prefecture, where the U.S. Navy and the U.S. Air Force had bases. In his case, it was perhaps more significant that he had been in the Foreign Ministry prior to entering elected office. The ministries held the power, and that is where Sone had his contacts, his pipeline, in Japanese his *paipu*.

Sone's preferred liaison among the Americans was Jim Auer, who, even in the early 1970s, was among the most prominent security hands guiding the levers of U.S.-Japan relations. During a flap over a U.S. Army ammunition depot in Sone's district, Sone and Kimura drove to Yokosuka for talks with Auer. They met Auer outside the base and retired to a restaurant. Sone wanted Kimura to act as an intermediary because Kimura spoke English. Sone introduced the two men: "Mr. Auer, I would like you to meet Mr. Hideo Kimura, the notorious Mr. Kimura."

"Why notorious?" inquired Auer.

Replied Sone, "Notorious playboy!" Here was truth in jest. Kimura was partial to good food, to Rémy Martin, and to the good life in general. Though Auer was a conservative man, he was not unaffable. Though his uniforms sometimes seemed too loose and large for him, he was sophisticated and worldly. He was an officer. Kimura immediately gathered that Auer could be a very important man to get to know.

Though a "notorious playboy," Hideo Kimura was not a flashy man. He did not boast diamond cuff links. Nor did he wear the silk-suit signs of success seen in the Orient. Most often he sported a prêt-à-porter navy-blue blazer with brass buttons. He smoked heavily, but his lighters were disposable, plastic. He jiggled his legs nervously as he talked, and would slouch back in his chair, a lounge lizard's pose.

He was a boyishly handsome man with a dark complexion. His hair was too long for a typical Japanese salaryman and slid into his eyes, fanning open like a bird's wing to reveal shafts of gray. His ever ready smile was lit by a row of silver-capped molars. Like other things about him, they were not gold.

Born in Yokosuka, Kimura was the son of a successful innkeeper, and while the family was not well-to-do, Kimura never seemed to need money. Even after his political mentor, Eki Sone, died in 1979, Kimura would sip cocktails in the pricey Highlander Bar of the exclusive Hotel Okura. He never seemed to work, at least not any regular hours. That, and his many connections within the U.S. military, made one wonder if he had clandestine interests. And if he did, whose? In some ways, he was a perfect double agent, not in an official spooky manner, but more casually, as people who have broad connections serve at times as agents in the national interest.

When Kimura's patron died in 1979, it was Auer who kept Kimura in politics. He did this by asking favors of Kimura, as though the political secretary still had influence. Thus, Auer became the first big link in Kimura's network as he tried to keep his political career alive.

In 1981, for example, Auer's boss, Richard Armitage, made the first high-level visit to Japan on behalf of the Reagan administration. A major move was underway by the new President to build up Japan's defensive capabilities, an effort that eventually gave impetus to the FS-X. However, Ambassador Mansfield's embassy didn't accept the Reagan plan, at least as it was being implemented. It wasn't that Auer and Armitage and company were being aggressive; they were just asking for too much too quickly, in the embassy's view, risking the "relationship."

As Secretary Weinberger described the problem in his memoir, *Fighting for Peace:* "Our State Department offered some opposition to meetings of the type I proposed. It was never really comfortable with the idea of the Defense Department's meeting with officials of other countries. State also felt that defense was a sensitive area in which Japan had to set its own pace without help from us."

Auer found a way around the embassy blockade through Kimura, who provided a back channel into Japan's military establishment. Kimura knew people, and while he had no "official" position, Auer treated him as an equal. "Hideo," he would say, "a political secretary can do anything." Presumably, Auer took this to mean even when Kimura was not a political secretary.

"A political secretary . . ." became a running joke between the two men, their bond. Auer would use it in a variety of circumstances, from opening channels for Armitage to finding funds for official but unauthorized dinner expenses. Kimura came to believe that "a political secretary can do anything."

April 1987 was a cruel month for the FS-X, and Hideo Kimura found himself standing on ground zero. A news leak from the Foreign Relations Committee of the U.S. Senate became a headline in the Detroit *News* that sent shock waves through Tokyo. The story, which appeared in April 1987, said that militarily sensitive high-technology machinery had been sold to the U.S.S.R. by a well-known Japanese electronics firm: Toshiba.

The machinery had allowed the Soviets to mill new propellers for their submarines, making them far quieter, and Soviet subs suddenly began showing up without warning off the coast of Maryland. By improving their propellers, the Soviets achieved the watery equivalent of stealth aircraft for their submarines.

By some estimates, the damage caused by the $17 million Toshiba sale to the Soviets would cost the United States some $30 billion to overcome with new technology and increased surveillance. Because of its timing, as well as its entanglements, the Toshiba affair had a profound effect on the outcome of the FS-X deal; in part because of Hideo Kimura.

The illegal sale was revealed to the Western alliance in December 1986 by a disgruntled employee of a trading company involved in the deal. The powerful Ministry of International Trade and Industry was immediately notified of the disastrous transaction. MITI responded by making phone inquiries but essentially sat on its hands. After six months, in June 1986, the Pentagon placed a direct call to MITI and got a similar response: a promise of action but no verdict of wrongdoing.

That winter, a high-level Pentagon delegation traveled to Tokyo to get some answers but were dismissed by indignant Japanese officials. As an American participant at the meeting recalls: "It was a very nasty meeting. I was very depressed by it. If you went to look in some transcript for the angry words in the exchanges, you won't find them. It was just the atmosphere and the arrogance of the Japanese, and the sense of 'Who are you Americans to come and tell us? We don't need to listen to this.' "

Three times the Japanese turned down U.S. requests for an investigation of Toshiba Machine, a subsidiary of the Toshiba Corporation. Though Defense Secretary Weinberger interceded in the affair through his friend, the director general of the defense agency, Yuko Kurihara, Tokyo merely called Toshiba executives in for questioning. No real response was forthcoming.

Indeed, nothing happened in Japan until the U.S. press got hold of stories leaked about the affair by the Senate's Foreign Relations Committee. In turn, the news set off a feeding frenzy in the Japanese media. Within a month after the first stories began to appear, on April 30, 1987, raids at the headquarters of Toshiba Machine, as well as at C. Itoh & Co. and Wako Koeki Co. (the trading companies working for Toshiba Machine and their Soviet partners), resulted in the arrest of 52 managers and 50 of their deputies.

In Tokyo, punishment was swift, if light. Toshiba Machine was banned from exporting anything to the Soviet Union and thirteen other Communist countries for one year, which was expected to mean a loss of sales of about $36 million. Toshiba Machine's president, Kazuo Iimura, resigned. C. Itoh was barred from exporting to the same countries for three months, losing a mere $2 million in sales. Wako Koeki, whose representative in Tokyo had blown the whistle on the deal, was given a "serious warning," according to a Foreign Ministry official. There were also official denunciations. Prime Minister Nakasone labeled Toshiba's actions an "act of betrayal," and Hajime Tamura, a MITI minister, called it "an unforgettable criminal act."

For the most part, however, Japan saw the Toshiba affair as an American plot. The chairman of the giant Mitsui trading firm told the Japanese press that Toshiba "was made a scapegoat for economic friction or for the failure of the Pentagon" to make better detection devices. Elsewhere, it was said that the Toshiba affair was designed to gin up funding for a new class of more silent Sea Wolf attack submarines to be built by General Dynamics. Even the repentant Nakasone saw ulterior motives in Washington's condemnations. He made a direct link between the FS-X and the Toshiba deal, arguing that the DoD used it to give its plan for co-development new leverage.

Washington was indignant. In July 1987, eight congressmen, led by Republicans Helen Bentley of Maryland and Duncan Hunter of California, sledgehammered a Toshiba tape recorder on the Capitol grounds. Hearings in the House and Senate churned out legislation calling for a ban on all Toshiba imports to the United States—television sets, personal computers, semiconductors, microwave ovens—at a potential cost to the company of $2.5 billion a year.

Toshiba countered with a lobbying blitz. More than $16 million and maybe as much as $30 million was spent by Japan and its U.S. surrogates to convince Congress not to take vengeance and ban Toshiba. That was the one thing that loomed large about the whole affair: the first-class Japanese lobbying effort. Republican Jake Garn, the senior senator from Utah, who led the campaign against the electronics giant, told Stuart Auerbach of the Washington *Post*, "In all the 21 years I have been in public office I've never seen a lobbying campaign so orchestrated at so many levels." In fact, there were some levels Garn never saw, like the level Hideo Kimura worked at.

Hideo Kimura took a different route amidst the sprawling lobbying effort mounted by the Toshiba Corporation: through Jim Auer. Kimura became involved in the Toshiba controversy one evening on the train on the way home from Tokyo to Yokosuka. His seat companion, by chance, was a vice president of the Toshiba factory near where Kimura lived. It was late in the evening and both had been to dinner with associates. Both probably had their fair share of drinks, as is customary in Japan when doing business over dinner. Feelings were heightened, and as they spoke about the Toshiba affair, the executive became emotional.

With tears in his eyes, he told Kimura, "I sincerely hope that the recorder the Congress smashed was not made by Toshiba America." He feared that the wrong company was being blamed for the sale to the Soviets. "It is so sad for those U.S. employees" to be blamed, he said.

The Toshiba executive's sincerity moved Kimura deeply, and he told the executive that he wanted to help. He had friends in Washington, Kimura said, in the Congress and in the Pentagon. Early in July, when the crisis between the United States and Japan deepened and the chairman of the Toshiba Corporation was forced to resign, Kimura went to work for the firm. Like many

Japanese who saw the resignations at Toshiba as *tsumebara*, a suicide that is forced on someone, Kimura was angry at U.S. pressure tactics.

Kimura flew to Washington to plead his case. His chief contact was Jim Auer. Kimura told Auer that if Toshiba was cut off from its American market, more than 3,000 Japanese workers stood to lose jobs. That would have serious repercussions because many of those people lived in and around Yokosuka, where Toshiba had several factories and the U.S. Navy had its great base. Auer was sensitive to such concerns because of his work getting the Japanese to accept the carrier *Midway* there. He knew how uncomfortable Japan's locals sometimes were with the U.S. military presence. The protests could be terrible, Kimura warned.

America did not realize the extent of Japanese anger over Toshiba, Kimura said. The bashing on Capitol Hill, the forced resignations of the company executive, all looked like American strong-arm tactics, meddling in Japan's sovereign affairs. He reminded Auer that the U.S. air base at Atsugi already had problems with local people over noisy night landings. It could get worse. How much angrier would those people be if they lost their jobs as well to a Pentagon plot.

Until now, Auer had given his Japanese friends little comfort over the Toshiba affair. In April, he told Japan's largest daily, the *Yomiuri Shimbun*, which often lines up in its views with the conservative ruling party, that Soviet subs were much quieter since the Toshiba incident. In effect, Auer was on board with the Defense Department's assertion that the Toshiba affair had done Western security a serious harm.

The Pentagon had taken a very tough stance toward Toshiba, killing a huge and important deal with the Japanese firm for $104 million worth of laptop computers. These light and portable electronic marvels were the hottest segment of the personal computer market, and the Pentagon's buy could have made Toshiba *the* leader in the laptop pack. As it happened, the contract went, instead, to the Zenith Electronics Corporation, a firm which badly needed the order and surely considered it poetic justice. For nearly a decade, Zenith had led the fight in Washington to demonstrate that America's consumer electronics market was being bullied out of business by Japanese trade tactics.

To get the Pentagon out from behind the barricades, Kimura invited Auer to meet informally with Toshiba officials in Japan. Auer did so. As he recalled, "To my knowledge Hideo has never worked officially for Toshiba Machine." (Kimura, as noted, said he worked for the Toshiba Corporation.) "All I did with Hideo was to meet informally with a person from Toshiba. They said that they wanted to improve their image. I said that I recommended that Toshiba become a model supporter of COCOM," the Paris-based body created to keep sensitive technology out of Soviet hands. "Toshiba chose to do that, but I doubt that it was because of me."

Auer says, "The big issue in 1987 was whether there was linkage between what Toshiba did and quieter subs. I've always said the same thing on that score. The simple thing that I said to *Yomiuri* was that in fact the numbers of quieter Soviet subs increased after the period that Toshiba Machine did what they did. Therefore that was one indication that there was direct linkage between what they had done."

After that spring, Auer's comments on Toshiba began to change, however. On the cost and damage of the affair, Auer's stance seemed to soften. The damage was in the millions, he said, not the billions, which was what was being advertised all over Washington: "The U.S. Navy and DoD never supported any of those claims," he says. Here, however, he was directly contradicted by Fred C. Ikle, the Under Secretary of Defense for Policy, who, while discounting the $20 to $30 billion figure, told the Washington *Post* that "the breach is 'very serious' and probably will cost 'billions' to correct."

By the next winter, February 1988, as the House moved on a Senate bill to ban Toshiba's products in the United States, Auer's boss, Richard Armitage, wrote a letter on behalf of Toshiba, representing his view as that of the Defense Department. Parts of the Armitage letter were quoted in the Los Angeles *Times:* "The Japanese government has taken legal and administrative actions of unprecedented dimensions . . . The companies involved have been punished; the GOJ [government of Japan] has strengthened its export control law, making it closer to ours, and the Toshiba Corp. has instituted a tough new export control policy that has become a model for Japanese industry.

"The real question is the effect of U.S. legislation on future Japanese behavior," Armitage continued. "Actions by the U.S. government against Toshiba would be interpreted in Japan as motivated by trade imbalances, rather than by national security concerns, and would weaken our efforts to strengthen [export regulations]."

After the Armitage letter, the Pentagon essentially dropped out of the Toshiba fray. Though the President signed tough legislation in August 1988 that dealt harshly with Toshiba—banning the Toshiba Corporation's products for sale to the U.S. government, and all U.S. imports from its guilty subsidiary, Toshiba Machine—the company had escaped from multibillion-dollar multiyear penalties. Had the DoD remained adamant, the outcome might have been different.

Deborah Sparr, an assistant professor at Harvard Business School, wrote: "Armitage, encouraged by James Auer, one of the Pentagon's top Japanese specialists, worried that any public sanctions against Toshiba would lead to increased congressional involvement in export control policy. Armitage wanted to see the technology diverters punished, but not at the risk of diminishing the Pentagon's maneuverability in the area of technology export."

In the end, Armitage was compelled to write an embarrassing retraction to the letter he wrote on behalf of Toshiba Machine. "I think Armitage was misled by Auer," said Dr. Stephen Bryen, Ikle's deputy in charge of technology security.

Still, Kimura's connection to Auer had proven valuable. He succeeded in throttling back Pentagon pressure. After all, the DoD was the injured party. Without the Pentagon leading the charge, reaction was defused.

Ultimately the Toshiba affair had a profound effect on the negotiations over co-development because it galvanized and organized those elements on the Hill who saw Japan as welshing on its defense commitment. No longer would Weinberger be able to keep the elected from barging around the issue. Congress would have its day.

The Toshiba affair had another effect, this one more direct though more subtle. Jim Auer had gone a long way for his friend Hideo Kimura simply by agreeing to meet informally with Toshiba officials. Those same officials certainly must have drawn some connection between their meeting with Auer and Armitage's correspondence with Congress, which took much of the heat off the corporation. As a result, the esteem for Kimura and his influence over the United States grew. This helped him and his career as a "political secretary who could do anything." Now he owed Auer something in return, and obligations such as these are not taken lightly in Japan. The payoff would come later with the FS-X, when Kimura would intercede with the air staff on behalf of his friend.

12

June 1987: The Power Play

"When viewed in a purely political context against the background of the Toshiba Machine Tool case . . . autonomous development of FS-X was clearly not in [MITI's] or in Japan's interest."
—MICHAEL J. GREEN, *Kokusanka: FS-X and Japan's Search for Autonomous Defense Production*

THE UNAVOIDABLE PRODUCT of any major defense project—no matter how crucial to a nation's well-being—is a conspicuous heap of cold hard cash. By Japanese estimates, in the case of the FS-X that was about $7 billion, a number that the more sophisticated Pentagon bidders scoffed at, believing the FS-X would be more honestly priced at a bloated $10 billion. Even at the low end, however, the FS-X had to be among the richest weapons deals of the decade, and one that would keep paying well into the next.

From the beginning, both the United States and Japan discussed this bounty in terms of strategic policy—the Soviet menace, the defense of the home islands, mutual security pacts. The cause, of course, was noble and true, and the ends were just plain obvious: yen for dollars. This fact is usefully kept in the forefront of any explanation about what was actually taking place at any given moment between the two sides. For the profit angle tended to get overshadowed by ponderous talk of "rationalization, standardization, and interoperability," or it disappeared into labyrinthian dialogues about "roles and missions." Those issues were relevant and important and, finally, secondary to the inescapable business at hand, which was business.

So much was at stake that in the spring of 1987 Caspar Weinberger unexpectedly announced that he was making a special trip to Tokyo.

Stunned already by the Toshiba affair, Japan was jolted by news of the Secretary's sojourn. No such trip had been scheduled and no indication of a Weinberger visit had been given at the annual security meetings held in Hawaii that January. News of the trip came in a missive from Weinberger to his counterpart, Yuko Kurihara, just days before a scheduled visit to the United States by Japan's Prime Minister, Nakasone. The traffic across the Pacific was getting heavy.

Weinberger had invited himself, leaving Japan little time to prepare for its guest. The flustered Japanese parried by dispatching high-level emissaries to Washington, one after another. First to arrive was General Shigehiro Mori, a man whose post at the Boei-cho was the weak equivalent of the powerful Chairman of the Joint Chiefs of Staff, America's highest-ranking military adviser. His job was to lay the ground for the Weinberger visit and to probe for any mines that lay in wait for his boss, Seiki Nishihiro, who was due in Washington in a matter of hours.

Though the official purpose of the Nishihiro trip aimed at developing an agenda for the Weinberger visit, the United States was anxious to puzzle him out on the FS-X. Back in January of that year, 1987, at the annual meetings held in Hawaii, it appeared that Nishihiro would be the salvation for Armitage and Auer, "pulling their chestnuts out of the fire." Now he had become something of an unknown quantity, as a result of the apprehensions expressed by Kevin Kearns in his cables from Tokyo. If Nishihiro had indeed embraced Ryozo Tsutsui's position, a confrontation could well be in the offing. Kearns had insisted that Nishihiro was pushing for domestic development, and that he had gotten the wrong message about the December meeting at the Pentagon from a dissembling Tsutsui. Thus even though Armitage had personally written Nishihiro, making plain his own account of the Tsutsui visit, the situation was fluid and there was only one way to be certain of Nishihiro's thinking: pin him down.

In fact, Nishihiro arrived in Washington personally opposed to the U.S. concept of co-development. Yet he was politically prepared to bend whatever terms were arrived at in Japan's favor, which is to say, toward making a joint project as much as possible a domestic development project.

The reality was that for him both plans under consideration—the air staff's and Washington's—were flawed and failed. There was no way, for instance, that he would be interested in buying U.S. aircraft off the shelf, as Senator Danforth was demanding. Japan would not need a replacement airplane for ten years, which was when the FS-X would be available. Buying planes off the shelf meant Japan would have to take possession in three years, increasing the size of its air force by a third more planes, which was one hundred more fighters than the U.S. Air Force kept in defense of the continental United States. Nothing in Japanese defense plans allowed for that.

Furthermore, Nishihiro didn't want to cast Japan's fate with the United States on a co-development deal, because the FS-X was to be a year 2000 aircraft, and the United States was offering modifications of designs that first emerged on U.S. drawing boards in the 1960s and 1970s. They would be old before they were new.

Complicating this unpleasant menu of choices, Nishihiro could not ignore the will of Washington, what Tokyo referred to as *gaiatsu*, outside pressure. To hear those at the defense agency describe it, the Japanese government was virtually an indentured servant to U.S. security interests. That was Japan's dilemma. The United States had to be made to understand these issues, Nishihiro thought, or serious problems would arise.

Richard Armitage's large Pentagon office quickly smelled from the smoke of Nishihiro's Mild Seven cigarettes, though the first cellophane pack had yet to be crushed empty on the coffee table. Nishihiro puffed and talked, listened and puffed, his hair as gray as ash, his suit dark.

Jim Auer, who sat by Armitage, thought he heard Nishihiro taking a position in favor of domestic development, although he could not be sure. Indeed, he was never sure where Nishihiro stood on the matter. Though Nishihiro's opinion counted for a great deal at the defense agency, he spoke here for the consensus, not for himself. This was not just Japanese political practice; this was what a man of his rank did.

Armitage, who could be boyishly charming—basketball with the guys, Miller Time on Fridays, free weights and power lifting, baseball caps and shorts in the office—could also be coldly professional. His voice was high, a tenor, yet it was coarse, the sound of wet gravel underfoot. His mission today was fairly simple: to put an end to Japan's hopes for domestic development. He told Nishihiro that an independent FS-X program would have grave consequences for U.S.-Japan relations. In other words, proceed with domestic development at your own risk. The FS-X was a litmus test, Armitage declared.

With that single phrase, the constant American promises that the United States would not meddle in Japan's internal affairs were broken.

Unflappable, Nishihiro merely puffed on his cigarette. He surely had to have expected something like this. After some stony consideration, he told Armitage that there was still room for agreement. Japan would be willing to cooperate with the United States on the FS-X, provided that co-development would be *genuine* co-development. That meant an all-new aircraft, a plane that the United States and Japan developed together from concept through design, testing, and production.

This was the best of the compromises Japan could hope to get from the

United States. This was what Nishihiro's boss, Yuko Kurihara, wanted. In fact, this was not a new position for Japan, but one that had been percolating up in calls and cables at the staff level for some time.

But such a concept had never had appeal for the U.S. side. For good reason, Armitage knew what he did not want. He referred to the findings of the Sullivan mission that spring and told Nishihiro that the tactical situation Japan faced didn't warrant a whole new aircraft. It was not timely, and it was not cost-effective. He countered with a sweetener. He said that Japan could modify and co-develop the next generation of the McDonnell Douglas F-15 Eagle, the F-15E Strike Eagle, a plane so advanced that it had yet to enter service in the U.S. military. Learning how to build a plane like that from the ground up would constitute a major leap forward for Japan in all levels of aerospace development.

That seemed to interest Nishihiro, and the meeting ended on a positive note. If the United States could offer Japan the opportunity to work on the F-15E, then an agreement might be possible. Nishihiro also hinted that time pressures might be easing. Though June remained the official deadline for a budget decision on the FS-X, it was not necessarily the drop-dead date.

In essence, Armitage and Nishihiro had reached terms. The director of the policy bureau accepted in principle a joint U.S.-Japan program. The details were left wide open, and the devil is in the details, but as the Pentagon's day-to-day officer on the FS-X program later wrote: "After a lengthy discussion, the two officials agreed on the benefits of building the FS-X based on an existing U.S. fighter . . ." Now it was up to Weinberger to strike the deal.

Weinberger came to Tokyo that summer to confront Prime Minister Nakasone over the Toshiba debacle and to settle the FS-X matter once and for all. Unemotional, methodical, Weinberger characterized U.S. losses in the Toshiba affair as "severe." The Soviets were more dangerous than ever, he told Nakasone. He used Congress as a cudgel, warning that the Democratic-controlled legislature was a big stick that was rapidly slipping from his grasp. The implications for the FS-X were plain to Nakasone.

Weinberger stacked his demands on the table. He told Nakasone he wanted punishment for Toshiba's behavior, rehabilitation of Japan's export policy on dual-use items that had military applications, and money. That meant that he expected people at Toshiba Machine to be fired (they later were), but, he added, it should be done as part of a positive housecleaning effort. He didn't want to see sophisticated machine tools sold to our mutual enemy. The goal now had to be to help the United States regain its lead in submarine technology, which he thought Japan should pay for. He suggested an "intensive" research program to improve undersea detection undertaken in cooperation with the United States and funded by Japan.

Surprisingly, Nakasone seemed to Weinberger to be relieved by these demands, as if he had been prepared for worse. Weinberger had anticipated that the Prime Minister would react by deferring the matter, explaining that it would have to be taken up with his cabinet. Instead Nakasone leapt at the proposal. "We will do this," he promised. Nakasone even threw in clearance long sought by the United States to make use of a Japanese navigational system that the navy needed for its minesweeping operations in the Persian Gulf. Now at last routes around the combatants' minefields could be more accurately drawn and followed.

The United States was deep into a perilous escort operation in the Middle East, protecting shipping that was frequently attacked by both hair-trigger combatants in the Iran-Iraq war. Japan was one of the chief beneficiaries of that U.S. protection, since it imported more than half of its oil from the region. To Washington's consternation, Tokyo had refused to participate in these defensive operations. What was even harder to understand, it declined to sign a multinational security agreement to keep Japanese technology out of the war zone. Thus, it was willing to pay tribute to the warring parties while withholding assistance from its defenders, notably the United States. Still, Weinberger seemed pleased by this Japanese token.

Later that evening, Weinberger held the climactic FS-X talks with the head of the defense agency, his friend Yuko Kurihara. A posh setting was prepared, in the penthouse suite of the august Hotel Okura, where the dutiful and energetic bellboys rehearsed their smiles and perfected their bows before mirrors. The two defense leaders and their staffs gathered in the Imperial Suite, where the likes of Henry Kissinger and Rolling Stone Mick Jagger stayed when they were in Tokyo, at a chic $3,846 per night.

When Weinberger entered the elegant reception room he was surprised to find Kurihara already sitting at a long table surrounded by defense and Foreign Ministry officials. Kurihara was his usual composed self, more poker-faced than inscrutable. He sat stiff and handsome in his chair. Tanned from hours on the golf links, his skin glowed.

By contrast, Weinberger's tallowy complexion had turned to paste, and he hunched over in his dark suit, exhausted perhaps by the thirteen-time-zone trip to Tokyo. Kurihara's large staff surprised Weinberger, who felt outgunned. This was a bad omen, he thought. It appeared to him that an offensive was underway, and he feared that Kurihara would use the budget deadline—due in a matter of days—to announce the final decision to go forward with a domestic FS-X.

The Secretary considered himself a formidable adversary in debate. Indeed, prominently displayed on Weinberger's office wall at the Pentagon was a group photo depicting an evening in 1984 at Oxford University, when he stood against the famed British Marxist E. P. Thompson and debated whether the foreign policy of the Soviet Union and that of the United States are equally immoral. His opponent wore a sackcloth suit to represent the masses. Weinberger wore a tux, because his father had once told him everybody looked the same in one, making all men equal. In the end, Weinberger vanquished the Brits *and* the Reds that night.

Now, facing Kurihara and his minions, Weinberger decided on a preemptive strike. The FS-X, he told Kurihara and company, "went right to the heart of the U.S.-Japan relationship." This was serious talk. Coming from a man such as Weinberger, it carried the full weight of U.S.-Japan relations. Armitage and Auer had made the FS-X a litmus test, and here Weinberger made it a "very stiff litmus test." Though he recited the standard arguments about "reinventing the wheel" and "the economies of working with the United States," Weinberger made it clear that domestic development would create serious political problems in the United States. In other words, the FS-X represented *an absolute test* of Japanese allegiance and reliability.

Kurihara never had much choice in the matter. There was no percentage in alienating the United States, even over a reborn Zero fighter, with all the prestige and honor that entailed. Pride was one thing; national prosperity quite another. Though his large staff far outnumbered Weinberger's men, Kurihara now looked like the one who was surrounded. In whatever direction he turned, the FS-X left him in a box. On the U.S. side, Kurihara worried about Congress, particularly Republican senator John Danforth, who led the charge for an off-the-shelf purchase. Danforth was one of the toughest trade advocates in the Senate, and an offense on the FS-X—which was a direct attack on two of his constituencies—could have much wider ramifications for other irritating and potentially explosive issues: supercomputers, satellites, semiconductors. The problems over Toshiba in the Congress were bad enough already and threatened to get worse.

At home, Kurihara faced strong pressure from Japan's powerful industries, particularly the mighty Mitsubishi company, an old and loyal government friend. The chairman of Mitsubishi Heavy Industries, Masao Kanamori, had announced just weeks earlier, at the end of May, that "Japanese government leaders need to discuss the FS-X from the higher viewpoint that Japan foster its own aerospace industry and build its own defense capability."

More powerful forces pressed in. Like the American State Department, the Ministry of Foreign Affairs put the U.S.-Japan relationship upon a precious pedestal. They wanted no confrontation. They very well understood what was taking place in the United States—the seething over Japan's behavior in the Iran-Iraq war, the chronic problem of Japan's limited commitment to mutual security.

Backing the Ministry of Foreign Affairs was the Ministry of Finance, which controlled the defense agency's budget. While it continued to maintain a low profile, it wanted more bang for the buck and had little interest in spending capital on the ambitions of a bunch of technocrats.

Finally, there was MITI. Until the Toshiba affair surfaced in the spring of that year, 1987, MITI's small but chic Aircraft and Ordnance Division had dominated the issue and supported domestic development. Along with Mitsubishi, they were Tsutsui's strongest allies. The division had great influence because it administered the Japan Defense Agency's purchasing arm, the Equipment Bureau. In effect, they were the ones who were actually buying into the FS-X deal and promoting Japan's aviation development. They provided the economic springboard from which to finance and implement the long-term goal of commercial aviation.

But the Toshiba affair had cornered MITI, leaving it in an untenable position. Its International Trade Administration Bureau, which had jurisdiction over the glamorous Aircraft and Ordnance Division, was responsible for maintaining happy trade relations between the United States and Japan. For them, there was no question about what was more important, a domestic FS-X or $112.3 billion in bilateral trade. The International Trade Administration Bureau was now dead center on the FS-X issue, supporting the Finance and Foreign ministries in the push for co-development.

Not to be overlooked in this was the philosophical change that had overtaken the powerful ministry. In the struggle between priorities and foreseeable realities, MITI changed its aviation agenda in 1986. The new aircraft law it announced revealed a new strategy for competing in the global aviation market. The emphasis now would be on sustaining commercial ambitions through providing components and subsystems. Instead of building a commercial fleet from the runway up, Japan would become the world's supplier of high-quality parts, from wings to tail assemblies, from radar to navigation aids. This approach mirrored what evolved in the FS-X the year after the aircraft law was changed.

In the final co-development agreement, a U.S. plane would be the model, but its key parts and components would be made in Japan. MIT's Richard Samuels referred to this process in a paper on Japanese aviation entitled "How to Succeed Without Really Flying." It should be noted that the area in which civilian and commercial aviation technologies most easily mingle is that of subsystems, components, and materials, which are considered the "backbone" of the industry.

Kurihara reached for a compromise. He told Weinberger that Japan had no interest in buying a U.S. aircraft, and that domestic development was not a necessity. If the United States and Japan combined technologies, he said, they could build a better fighter.

This was an implicit acceptance of the U.S. call for joint development, vague as it was. Depending on the manner in which joint development was implemented, it could still be a domestic project, built entirely in Japan. That gave the politician Kurihara something to sell to the ministries, the defense agency, industry, and even Tsutsui.

Back in January of that year, during the annual meetings in Hawaii, Armitage had talked to Nishihiro about a Japanese company acting as the prime contractor on the program, making Japan the leader in the project, a first for the two sides. Kurihara's formulation was another way of saying the same thing, and Weinberger had no problem with that. The FS-X could be an all-Japan project, the Secretary said, as long as U.S. companies participated in the program and got a sizable chunk of the work.

Here the two men seemed to reach terms. Kurihara said that co-development might be acceptable to Japan if it incorporated leading-edge technology from both countries. As Weinberger put it, by way of agreement, "the FS-X program should employ the best technologies of both nations." Though neither man grasped the implications of their similar phrases, those words represented common ground, granting U.S. participation in the FS-X, while allowing Kurihara to argue that this was still a domestic development program.

But what was it that those two leaders were agreeing to? "The best technologies of both nations"? Perhaps in the case of Kurihara this made sense. The United States invested upward of $30 billion a year in defense research. Surely the Pentagon had treasures aplenty to offer.

To Kurihara, co-development was *tatemae*, the means of pretense and expediency that concealed the ends and inner aim, *honne*. Thus, when Kurihara said co-development, he meant domestic development. He believed that "a rose by any other name . . ." He would push for Japan to get access to all the data and experience that went into developing the top aircraft the United States had to offer and then modify it according to their own needs. Hardly a surrender, the plan was to outflank the United States. Like a judo combatant, Kurihara hoped to use his opponent's advantage to bring him down.

But what of Weinberger? Did he not see himself peering down the barrel of a one-way deal? After all, the Sullivan mission had returned from Tokyo just two months before, having proven that Japan needed U.S. assistance on the FS-X precisely because *it had no technology to offer*. What did Weinberger think he was getting?

"They never defined the meaning of 'best technologies,' " recalled Kearns. "Weinberger didn't know what the fuck it meant. No one had thought this through. If you say what are the best technologies, and if they're all on the U.S. side, as the Sullivan mission showed, it means that the Japanese are going to build a U.S. aircraft. It's a slippery decision."

Clearly, Weinberger was less interested in the technology than he was in gaining U.S. participation in the deal. This is the core of it. What Weinberger wanted more than anything was a guarantee that Japan would remain tied to the United States for the next five to ten years. Co-development would keep Japan in lockstep with U.S. defense planning until virtually the end of this century. Here was the Cold Warrior at work.

Weinberger would later argue that letting Japan build the FS-X on its own would quicken its arrival as a competitor in aviation. That was debatable, but Weinberger reasoned that the Japanese were going to become our competitor in any case—which was not debatable. So the larger goal was to keep them tied to the United States, dependent on us, for as long as possible.

Global competition was really not the issue for Weinberger, who was hard-driven by his implacable concerns about the menace of global Communism. For what Weinberger feared more than giving away technology, or the advent of a new international competitor for our largest export industry, was the Soviet Union. Whereas the Secretary might allow Japan to skitter out from commitments to its allies in the Persian Gulf, he would tolerate no compromise on the Communist threat. Here Weinberger's zeal for the cause of anti-Communism overcame all logic.

Important as it was to keep the extraordinary value of the $10 billion FS-X deal at the center of any and all developments, the weight and force of ideology could never be entirely discounted. At this crucial moment, for Caspar Weinberger, those strategic concerns, those nightmare fears of Red Armies encamped all over Asia, were paramount. He would have been better off staying focused on the dollar signs.

In the final analysis, the vague formulation of "co-development" and "best technologies" ignored a fundamental rule of economics: Never create competitors. But such logic and fact would have to be ignored if Weinberger was to get what he really wanted: a U.S. role in the FS-X, which guaranteed that for the next ten years Japan would maintain its island fence around the Soviet exit points into the vast blue Pacific.

"Be precise. Avoid zeal." That was the injunction of the man who brainstormed the notion of co-development, Gregg Rubinstein. That was how to deal with Japan, he was convinced. But now the zealous anti-Communist Caspar Weinberger had embraced the cloudiest of definitions for co-development. Thus, though Weinberger had won the day, he had also fumbled the deal. For the murky terms he and Kurihara tangled out that evening would obscure any virtue either side hoped to gain through cooperation. Co-development was a political grab bag, a Pollyanna's term fit for a political settlement. Such vague notions had in the past been the bane of U.S.-Japan relations, and now they would haunt the future of the FS-X, and set the stage for disaster.

13

A Beauty Contest

"I never saw myself doing an end run on the State Department. My loyalties were with the Pentagon. FS-X was our football."
—Kevin Kearns

NISHIHIRO, the brilliant strategist and revered don of the defense agency, accompanied his director, Yuko Kurihara, to Washington in September 1987. This was Kurihara's third and final visit to the United States as defense chief before leaving office that November. Defense directors seldom stayed on more than a year. U.S. Secretary of Defense Weinberger, who also retired that November, spent nearly seven years on the job and had to acquaint or reacquaint himself seven times with Japanese military leaders.

"The power of the defense chief depends on the individual and his relationship with the Prime Minister," said Jim Auer, the Defense Department's ambassador to Japan. "Kurihara happened to be a strong politician who had a very strong relationship with Nakasone. That made him more powerful than your average defense minister." That did not mean defense chief and the Prime Minister were friends; it meant that they accepted each other.

Nishihiro and his boss were a study in contrasts. Twice director of the defense agency, Kurihara was not a military man as was the don. Though he aspired to become foreign minister, Kurihara had been appointed to his post because he came from a faction within the ruling party that played dove to the Prime Minister's hawk, thus calming Japanese voters' skittishness about the ever dangerous military mind.

The aristocratic Kurihara came from the farm, although he appeared more the silvery plantation owner than the muddied sharecropper. In his elegant manner, he recalled the chairman of the Senate Finance Committee, Lloyd Bentsen. He was an ambitious politician who rose through the ranks of farm organizations known as the *Nokyo*, the grass-roots party machine that kept the ruling party in power. Proportional seating in the parliament provided sparsely populated farming villages with the same number of representatives as an overpopulated district in teeming Tokyo. The *Nokyo* delivered those few crucial and powerful voters.

The real military man was Nishihiro, who looked like a bureaucrat and smoked like a politician, but was at heart a samurai. The details of Japan's defenses had been calculated on his watch for decades. Like a great admiral or a great general, he was a noble. "Mr. JDA." Someday he would retire from office and take work with one of Japan's great corporations, an event known as *amakudari*, "descent from heaven." His boss, Yuko Kurihara, had no such luxury. He would soon have to get back on the hustings and scramble for campaign funds for reelection.

As a farewell gift to Weinberger on this, his last trip, Kurihara crossed the blue Pacific bearing a valuable *omiyagi*, a souvenir for the Secretary. Jim Auer remembered how Kurihara presented what was for Japan a great concession, saying stiffly and officially, in translation, "We are giving up domestic production and are accepting your suggestion that we modify a U.S. aircraft."

Recalled Auer: "There was no point up until August or September in 1987 that we knew for sure which way this would go. But we thought we were going to win, and we were right. We were very excited." No bottles of champagne were uncorked, however. There was just the traditional formal dinner for visiting dignitaries in the Secretary's private dining room at the Pentagon, a favor returned the next evening at the Japanese Embassy. Auer celebrated by telephoning Senator Danforth's office to break the big news. "I told them they would hear the announcement the next day." Here Auer was being politic, hoping to secure Danforth's support for the deal, which he got, at least initially.

Separately, Nishihiro called on Armitage at his Pentagon office to break the news. "There was no elation," recalled Armitage. "This was business." Nishihiro requested that General Dynamics and McDonnell Douglas come to Tokyo in October to clear up last-minute technical details before the final selection of a U.S. aircraft was made.

Though Kurihara's concession on co-development was great, it was really just a big dance around a little fire. American officials celebrated what should have been obvious. The fact is, the broad swatches of the agreement had been decided months before, when Weinberger met Kurihara in Tokyo. This final agreement really only fixed two, albeit crucial, decisions: There would be no independent Japanese fighter, and the FS-X would be based on a model of a

U.S. aircraft. The rest remained to be done or undone. As it turned out, the widespread satisfaction over the deal proved premature. It was as if the shoemaker had tied the laces on a new pair of brogues before the leather had been cut, put on a last, and sewn.

Content with the accomplishment of having crafted a $10 billion weapons deal for the two lame-duck defense chiefs, Auer and the DoD flattered themselves. They were gambling on a thimblerigged game of semantics typed out in two complex languages, which they proudly called an agreement. The sizable bet was that the United States would again control the action on the FS-X through political pressure. But as events unfolded, chaos quickly reigned. The same uncertainties and vague formulations that allowed the deal to be consummated now threatened to consume it.

By that October in 1987, Kearns had become virtually persona non grata at the embassy. His back-stabbing fight with the Chrysanthemum Club over the FS-X and other issues had carved its way through embassy ranks. The number two man in Tokyo, Deputy Chief of Mission Desaix Anderson, banished Kearns from the ninth floor, where the ambassador had his offices. He forbade Kearns from meeting with Seiki Nishihiro, on the pretext that the Japanese policy chief was too far above his rank.

The embattled Kearns defied the order. He had come to see the FS-X co-development program as an economic threat, and thus a policy threat to the United States. He would say, "This was an economic battle between the United States and Japan and technology was the weapon." Losing such a fight, Kearns feared, meant more than jobs. "There's a saying the Japanese have about flying geese. It is a Confucian proverb about hierarchies and the relationship between superior and inferior. To really understand it, you have to recognize how the Japanese treat their subordinates; which is to say, badly, as inferiors. Look at Korea, China." Third-generation Japanese whose families were from Korea had to be fingerprinted and carry identification cards.

One encounter with the chief of the embassy's Political-Military Section, Chris LaFleur, whom Kearns disliked, and not just because he was married to the daughter of Japan's influential Minister of Finance, made plain the wide discrepancy in vision between Kearns and his peers. LaFleur, trying to understand why Kearns was so unhappy with developments, said, "The defense agency has selected a U.S. airframe. This is what we wanted from the deal. Why are you so upset?"

"Because," snapped Kearns, "the issue isn't just the airframe. It's American jobs." With so vague a definition as co-development lacing up the incipient accord, Kearns worried that all work on the FS-X could still wind up in Japan.

Kearns saw a nefarious pattern emerging. Mitsubishi Heavy Industries was slated to be the prime contractor in the chevron flight of co-development. A U.S. aerospace firm would be the subcontractor, handing over to Japan its design plans. The symbolism was as bad as the fact. Here, indeed, the United States was already cast in the role of subordinate. For the first time, a Japanese company would assume the role of prime contractor for a frontline fighter aircraft. Did this augur a deal in which Japan would act as prime contractor for a commercial aircraft? Was this a precedent, the beginning of the end?

Kearns did have some allies at the embassy. In the crucial days of the FS-X negotiation, he managed to have his protégé in Washington detailed to Tokyo to work with him at the Mutual Defense Assistance Office. Craig Richardson, who considered Kearns his mentor, knew well the problems of the FS-X, having followed the issue for nearly the whole year Kearns was in Tokyo from his own unique perspective in Washington.

Once Richardson had been Kearns's intern at the State Department. Now he was back in government as a Presidential Management Intern, part of an exclusive fast-track training program for federal officials sponsored by the Office of the President. The two-year apprenticeship allowed federal agencies to pick up warm bodies without having to worry about staffing restrictions. It gave the intern the opportunity to rotate through government before "landing" in the agency of his choice to begin his career.

By the time Richardson arrived in Tokyo, he had spent seven months auditing the Japan account at the Defense Security Assistance Agency, which had charge of the FS-X program. Unlike most other management interns, however, Richardson was no passive player content to impress his superiors. Rather, he saw the jobs he took as opportunities to seize the reins of policy. With a presidential boarding pass, he traveled through the defense landscape, sizing up issues such as the FS-X. Richardson had been able to use his position as a PMI to move through government like a mole. Now he would become Kevin Kearns's agent.

Just twenty-five years old, Richardson was a blond bear of a man with large white teeth and peaches of fuzzy baby fat for cheeks. Well scrubbed, conservative in a conservative administration, he appeared to be a perfect fit for the PMI profile. A graduate from the intellectual paradise of Pomona College in California, he had a master's degree in international affairs from Princeton's prestigious Woodrow Wilson School of Public and International Affairs. Articulate, kinetic, sure of his thoughts, he considered himself a true patriot, a man of zeal.

Already, he held the State Department, where he was presently ensconced, in disdain. "Foggy Bottom played by the three C's," he said in a voice that sometimes rose an octave in exasperation: "clientism, careerism, and conceit." The first, clientism, he ascribed to human nature. "That's when you get immersed in another nation and lose touch with 'they' and 'we.' Soon America becomes 'they.' " The hostage syndrome. He sensed that acutely soon after he arrived in Tokyo. "You begin to feel like you want to deliver for these people, your Japanese friends." He and Kearns were determined to remain unbound by the elaborate sash of Japanese influence that girdled the American Embassy.

In preparation for the October selection of a U.S. airframe on which the FS-X would be modeled, Captain Andrew J. Button arrived in Tokyo. He was new at the Defense Security Assistance Agency. He had come to the Pentagon expecting to get a job as an assistant, not running the day-to-day business of a program like the FS-X. Of the three courses the U.S. government offered in foreign military assistance, Button only had time to take the shortest and most general. Having no experience as a negotiator or systems supervisor, Button knew nothing about Japan beyond the buddy-buddy world of the military. He had been a pilot stationed in Tokyo for a time, not a negotiator.

Button had never delved into the all-important policy side of the U.S.-Japan relationship, much less an issue as sensitive as this one, which had risen to the Secretary level. Nor had he credentials to manage a complex $7 to $10 billion program—one that would earn the Pentagon $30 million over the first five years—let alone the first program of its kind in U.S.-Japan history.

An affable man with thinning hair and a soft middle, Button was self-effacing and nonconfrontational. He had no pretenses about himself: "I was a fairly new captain assigned to the [Defense Security Assistance] agency, and probably for that reason, if for no other, I was picked to pick up the new job and move out with it."

Button saw the Tokyo trip as part of a simple decision-making process, a choice between two fighters. "These meetings had the potential to play one U.S. contractor against the other, putting the U.S. firms at a disadvantage," he later wrote.

This did not shape up to be a complex groundbreaking trip to Tokyo. As he saw his job: "The meeting was only to allow industry to provide the information that the Japanese need to complete their study." Essentially this was a beauty contest, and the Japanese were to choose between the two most glamorous finalists, the wasp-waisted and elegant F-16 or the grande dame of the skies, the soaring F-15.

Worth noting was that the State Department was largely out of the loop on the meeting. Had the embassy in Tokyo taken the trouble to send someone from the Pol-Mil Section to the negotiations, they might have had some control over events. Though this was a deal valued at more than $7 billion by conservative Japanese estimates, and U.S. companies stood to gain more than a billion dollars in work, the Pol-Mil Section sent no one. In Tokyo, Button was joined by Kearns, Kearns's boss, Walter Dziedzic, and the newly arrived Richardson. Meetings were held in the windowless crisis management center of the Japan Defense Agency.

Craig Richardson remembered the extraordinary security they went through entering the building to begin the talks. It made him think of the line from the Stanley Kubrick movie *Dr. Strangelove:* "You can't fight in here; this is the war room!" The building's walls were insulated with metal to prevent eavesdropping.

This was a setting for something larger and more elaborate than a mere beauty contest. There was a plenary meeting, followed by expert sessions, one targeted at technology and one focused on finance. Whereas the Japanese side had teams of specialists in technical and financial issues, the United States had Button, a grudging Kevin Kearns, the intern Richardson, and Walter Dziedzic, the senior member of the group, who saw his job as providing a messenger service for the Pentagon. Richardson and Kearns decided to follow the money, to pay closest attention to those meetings where jobs and dollars were at stake.

What had been advertised as a beauty contest ended in a nitty-gritty negotiation, for which the U.S. side was obviously not prepared. The Japanese essentially called for major concessions from the U.S. contractors. They wanted all funds and all patents that emerged from the development process to revert to Japan. What is more, they demanded that all work on the aircraft be done in Japan, as was the case in early co-production agreements with the United States. They expected that all present and future technology for the American aircraft would be available to the Japanese FS-X team. And for this, Japan would pay $500,000 per plane, $60 million for 120 planes valued at up to $30 million a copy.

(Japanese sources say these terms have been misrepresented by Kearns. The lead Japanese negotiator had prepared a two-page eight-paragraph framework on what Japan wanted in the MOU. This was not meant to be the opening of negotiations, as Kearns surmised. "There was nothing eye-catching or surprising about the framework," said a Foreign Ministry source. "Its terms were general, not as specific as they have been portrayed.")

If the terms were absurd, so was the U.S. reaction. As Kearns recalls, during a break in the talks, General Dynamics vice president Charles Anderson said he had spoken with his home office in St. Louis and that his company was prepared to accept the terms. That is, General Dynamics would send a dozen engineers and all the blueprints for the latest version of the F-16 SX-3 —a plane so advanced that its first version had not yet been introduced into the U.S. arsenal. Richardson estimated that the actual cost to U.S. taxpayers to develop this plane in all its iterations and elaborations had been close to $7 billion.

"General Dynamics didn't pay for this technology," he later said, "and now they were prepared to hand it off for a dime on the dollar. U.S. taxpayers footed the bill. What did GD care if they gave it away for $60 million? It was money in their pockets."

The baleful Kearns told Anderson, "This may be General Dynamics' position, but this is not the U.S. government's position. We won't allow it."

As Kearns recalled: "At that point, what I saw was total disorganization on the U.S. side. I saw General Dynamics ready to collapse. It was a very dicey time. Essentially we had gone through this whole long two- or three-year process to wind up with a full transfer of technology and no value-added work for the United States. This in a year where we had a $56 billion trade deficit with Japan."

In fact, Richardson said, "Kevin was bluffing when he told Anderson that the U.S. government would not permit such an agreement, because there was no U.S. government position. We were winging it."

Logically, in the absence of official instructions, Kearns or his boss might have called for a recess in the talks, a pause to request instructions. After all, this was to be a beauty contest. That's what Button had come out to referee. Now, obviously, it had turned into quite another matter.

But that didn't happen. On the night the Japanese presented their framework for negotiations, Kearns and Richardson stayed at the office late to compose a cable to Washington. "We saw this as an opportunity to keep the issue from rising up the ranks of the embassy, where we would lose control. We were afraid that we might get railroaded by our own side. Tactically, for Kevin and me, it was great. We could step into the breach and make policy that would never have been made if it had been thoroughly deliberated in Washington," Richardson said.

Kearns said he hoped to "lay down a marker on workshare," in order to get the best terms from the Japanese. As he saw it, he was now negotiating the contract, though that was not his job as Deputy Mutual Defense Assistance Officer. Nor did he have experience in such negotiations, although he recalls playing a secondary role in the sale of F-16s to Korea.

In an effort to keep the initiative, Kearns and Richardson prepared a cable, which was later sent by Button to his boss in Washington, John Tim Tyler. Ruddy-faced and brimming with self-confidence, some said self-importance, Tyler had been one of Tsutsui's harshest critics after the December 1986 meeting at the Pentagon. At the time, the natty Tyler had warned that "the plane Tsutsui wanted to build was going to come in three times the cost and twice the weight."

The fax that was sent to Tyler was transmitted over an unsecured line. This was a risk Richardson said they took in order to keep the initiative away from the State Department. To properly make the fax secure meant encryption and that meant review, which would have brought the very people who were already censoring Kearns's cables into the chain of command. Kearns was not worried about interception. "We were only telling Tim what the Japanese told us. Obviously there were no secrets here."

Whereas the Japanese were trying to steal the initiative on Washington by turning the beauty contest into a negotiation, Kearns and Richardson were trying to stampede the Pentagon into what they considered to be the appropriate response.

In Washington, Tyler felt "blindsided" by the news that the Japanese had presented General Dynamics with a framework for the contract negotiations. He said, "This was almost like a Pearl Harbor tactic."

Tyler felt that he could not postpone the Japanese initiative. "It was coming from too high up in the government," he said. So, knowing that Button had gone out to Tokyo barely trained to be a referee, he now empowered him to become a point man in a $7 billion deal for a high-technology fighter plane, a deal for which there was no precedent.

"I pretty quickly perceived that we had some stuff to gain by coming right back at them," Tyler said, describing his sense of urgency. "Remember, we'd been thinking about how to negotiate this deal for some time. We wanted to out-MITI MITI all the way on this one," he said, referring to the reputation of the Ministry of International Trade and Industry for efficiency and quality work. As he saw it, he was firing a shot back across their bow by refusing to give in to their demands.

Tyler's reply took one working day, laboring at what he characterized as "the bureaucratic speed of heat." He said, "Suddenly they realized we weren't going to be a patsy on this, especially since they got a response so quickly. I mean, that's unheard of. Think about the history of the U.S. government, how many times a friendly foreign power has sort of laid a major demarche—which is in effect what this was—on the table and had a reply within thirty-six hours?"

The stampede spread. Glenn Rudd, Button's boss and the man who would become the lead negotiator in this matter for the U.S. side, signed off on Tyler's return cable. As it turned out, having recently taken charge of the FS-X program, he never seriously questioned the switch the Japanese had pulled. "It wasn't really high on my scope until about that point in time," he said. Rudd's first major action on the FS-X was when he signed off on Tyler's dotted line. The lack of continuity proved disturbing. Rudd wound up entrusting Pentagon interests—not to mention corporate interests—to an inexperienced four-man U.S. government team.

"One of the things that I knew," Tyler continued, "was that Americans suffer in any negotiation with foreigners. We generally tend to go in and table our third fallback position. Americans are then terribly surprised that the foreign negotiator doesn't fall over themselves accepting our position. Americans have a hard time comprehending that if we say A, the foreigner says B. And maybe you have to go to A prime or, you know, B minus or something like that. You have to negotiate. We generally don't leave ourselves negotiating room.

"So when I crafted the cable back—you know, essentially to Andy Button —with a formula of 40 to 70 percent of the development phase, I admit that it was with a certain amount of malice aforethought. I just knew that handing the Japanese a demand that we wanted 70 percent of the work would absolutely blow their tiny minds."

Tyler's boss, Glenn Rudd, who approved the memo, was skeptical of the workshare concept. "Workshare, in the percentage sense, was something that we had never done before, for a couple of reasons. Up to this point, Japanese co-production had been of existing items, and we decided what items we wanted them to co-produce and what items we didn't." There was no need for percentages.

"Tim had the idea for percentage workshare," Rudd says. "What I wanted out of this thing, even at the time we were talking percentages, was to develop an annex to the MOU [the contract between governments] which would actually lay out agreed tasks for the Japanese to do and the American contractors to do, which wouldn't necessarily target a certain percentage. I'm uncomfortable at targeting percentages."

In effect, Rudd did not want to find himself in a position where the U.S. government was guaranteeing work and profits on behalf of an independent U.S. corporation. In this, Rudd echoed the Reagan administration, which looked on international trade agreements that assigned percentages of work —as opposed to allowing the "invisible hand of the marketplace" decide who gets the jobs—as "managed trade."

The idea behind the negotiating range was clearly to start at the high end and then to give ground gradually, trying to get as much as possible, but not less than 40 percent of the development phase. Button, however, forgot to negotiate, and Tyler's all-day effort ended in an astonishing blunder.

The Pentagon cable went to Button. He then literally handed it over to the Japanese negotiator. As Button himself recalls, this was the actual paragraph as written by Tyler. "I just sort of cut the paragraph off and gave it to them."

This incredible act, as it turns out, was not atypical. Having the actual U.S. document helped the translation and cleared up the ambiguity of spoken language and simultaneous translation. However, Button, as Kearns recalls, immediately undermined his own position and Tyler's intentions by telling the Japanese that these numbers represented a starting point. In other words, the United States envisioned a range of work for its demands. Now the Japanese both saw that range and knew that the low end could be hammered down in talks.

But just as important, Japan learned for the first time that "workshare" was to be a U.S. negotiating point. This was particularly significant because the United States did not know with surety that "workshare" would be incorporated into U.S. demands. It had been talked about, but Rudd had qualms. So Japan learned at approximately the same time as Washington what the U.S. negotiating strategy was to be.

The attempt by Kearns and Richardson to seize the initiative on policy had backfired horribly. "It was a gamble," Richardson said. "I think we were mistaken. We actually believed that we could get a majority workshare for the United States."

14

Kurihara's Choice

"Corruption in Japan had always been specially associated with deals with arms companies: before the First World War, Vickers had bribed a Japanese admiral to get an order for a battle-ship—a scandal which had toppled the prime minister . . . Aerospace was specially tempting to the Japanese, as for Britain and France, as a means to deploy their skills to pay for raw materials; they resented having to import all their commercial airliners from America (the extortion of bribes may have been partly an index of that resentment—a kind of extra tax on foreigners): but no thriving aerospace industry could be built without a defense base."
—ANTHONY SAMPSON, *The Arms Bazaar*

O N OCTOBER 23, 1987, less than a month after the co-development agreement was reached by Weinberger and Kurihara, the Japanese officially announced that the General Dynamics F-16 would be the model on which the FS-X would be based. The response within military circles in both nations was astonishment. The plane had been given virtually no chance of being selected. Certainly no American official guessed the F-16 would win. As Jim Auer put it: "I have no idea why they chose the F-16. I don't think anyone does."

In Japan, the news of the selection was endlessly rationalized and circularly explained, but there was agreement on only one point: The F-16 was cheaper. All that can accurately be said about the final choice of the F-16 was that it had been made by Yuko Kurihara. "This was my choice," he declared without equivocation.

The surprise decision by Kurihara to select the General Dynamics F-16 as the model for the FS-X program raised many eyebrows but no serious questions. The bitter fight over co-development had demoted the issue of which aircraft got chosen to the scrap heap of extraneous details, even though that choice was largely what the shouting had been all about, and, more important, where the money was, some $1 to $3 billion or more in revenues over the decade to the U.S. winner. This was, after all, the largest single weapons purchase the Japanese would make in their prodigious decade-long buildup of the 1980s.

Despite the lack of scrutiny that followed the final aircraft selection, no one seemed entirely satisfied with the explanations that were proffered for the choice of the F-16. Neither the Japanese nor the Americans said they fully understood the decision-making process, not even those at the highest levels of government, including the don of the defense agency, Seiki Nishihiro. General Dynamics said it was as shocked at the choice of its plane as was McDonnell Douglas, which never quite got over it.

Many rationalizations for the selection of the F-16 were offered. The most logical among them figured that the F-16 was relatively cheap, easy to reinvent as a domestic development project, and that the crucial issue of single-engine versus twin-engine design was easily settled. Over its illustrious lifetime, the F-16 had proved to be as safe and reliable as its twin-engine counterparts, perhaps even more so. What's more, the Japanese had never dealt with General Dynamics, and this would give them yet another opportunity to study the methods of one of the world's leading aircraft designers and manufacturers.

There was never a suggestion that untoward influence may have affected the decision. Indeed, the vast sums of money that might have enticed an eager manufacturer into sweetening the deal in favor of certain influential individuals were discounted. The logic was that the fighter plane manufacturers were already rolling in cash and overwhelmed with work. They didn't need this deal. Though downsizing was inevitable after the Reagan buildup and already on the horizon, manufacturers' back orders were sizable. Why risk an international bribery scandal to build just 130 airplanes?

The same logic applied to the Japanese, who were said to have learned their painful lessons about bribes during the infamous Lockheed scandal of the 1970s. Kakuei Tanaka, the most prominent political leader of the postwar era, a man known as the Shadow Shogun, was brought down as Prime Minister for allegedly accepting $1.8 million in bribes. The payments were made by the Lockheed Corporation to influence Japan's All Nippon Airways to purchase its L-1011 Tristar wide-body jet. The hideous affair stretched over two decades. No Japanese leader would dare tread over such ruinous territory again.

The seeming lack of a financial motive in the FS-X deal and the supposedly prohibitive fear of exposure were compelling arguments against hanky-panky taking place in the F-16 selection; but they were weak explanations for a decision that ultimately defied the most powerful forces in the Japanese defense establishment. The F-16 was opposed by the redoubtable Ministry of International Trade and Industry. The most prominent figure in the Japan Defense Agency, Seiki Nishihiro, opposed the choice of a single-engine aircraft. And Japan's leading industrialists, led by Mitsubishi Heavy Industries, studied the issue and strongly recommended the McDonnell Douglas plane. What's more, as Andrew Button recalled, McDonnell Douglas had made clear to the Japanese that they were willing to accept as little as a 30 percent share of work, whereas General Dynamics and the United States held out for 40 percent.

By logic alone, the choice of the F-16 was not just irrational, it was downright fishy. To this day, officials at McDonnell Douglas say they do not understand why on the day of the crucial announcement of the aircraft decision their commercial partner in Japan was a no-show. According to a Tokyo-based McDonnell Douglas manager involved in the deal, his company completely lost contact with the representatives of Nissho Iwai, the trading company that had been representing them in Japan for a decade.

The McDonnell Douglas manager, who has now retired from the firm, says his company never got a satisfactory explanation about Nissho Iwai's behavior, though it was almost unthinkable that a Japanese company would behave so badly in so critical a situation to so large and important a customer. As the McDonnell Douglas manager saw it, this was more than a matter of bad form. Nissho Iwai's disappearance represented some sort of manipulation, a sign that all was not in order regarding the F-16 decision.

McDonnell Douglas was a big and bitter loser in this and surely had an ax to grind, which may explain the finger pointing at its trading company. However, this self-interest does not alter the fact that the decision to drop the F/A-18 from the competition appears to be without solid basis.

In August 1987 (two months before the beauty contest in Tokyo), defense chief Yuko Kurihara essentially eliminated the McDonnell Douglas F/A-18 from consideration for the FS-X and substituted for it the McDonnell Douglas F-15. The F-15 was highly touted by the U.S. side in the FS-X debate, and it was the plane favored by Seiki Nishihiro, Mr. JDA. However, the substitution hides the significance of demoting the F/A-18 from consideration.

Despite the fact that the F-15 was a McDonnell Douglas aircraft favored by high-ranking defense agency officials, it was an unlikely choice for the FS-X. Japan's own pronouncements, predilections, and preconditions for its new support fighter make this plain. Above all, the F-15 represented by far the most costly of Japan's choices. With the Ministry of Finance already glowering over the deal, the defense agency was in no position to purchase the most expensive machine on the sales lot.

The F-15 was a red herring, because it offered Japan so little of what it said it so much wanted. There was practically no new technology for Japan to learn in the F-15, which everyone on the Japanese side agrees was the whole point of the FS-X process. Indeed, it was the defense agency's antagonism over its already ongoing F-15 *co-production* program that had led to the decision to build a domestic FS-X.

Japan had been privy to the innermost secrets of the F-15 for most of the decade—with the exception of the controversial black boxes—during which time they co-produced the plane in Nagoya. What would they learn by redeveloping the plane that they hadn't already figured out? According to the GAO, the Japanese eventually wrung from the U.S. Air Force every secret about the airframe of the F-15 that they needed to know. For a nation intent on pushing its aerospace industry in the international arena through domestic development, seeing the plans for the F-15 was as useful as déjà vu.

What is more, had the F-15 been adopted, it would have had the effect of reducing Japan's strategic options, by reducing the "mix" of the aircraft in the nation's inventory. The F-15 would have left the Japanese Air Force with only two plane types after 1995, F-15s and F-4s. And the F-4 would soon be retired.

Finally, the F-15 was an air-superiority interceptor, and the FS-X was to be a specialized plane for air-to-sea attack. Though versions of the F-15 could do the job, Japan consistently argued against having a top-of-the-line FS-X. Japan made the point that the most advanced aircraft, planes of the F-15 type, would be left to America to develop. The whole idea of domestic development was to provide a niche for Japan in second-tier aircraft. Indeed, they had invented the designation "support fighter" for just that purpose.

By dropping the F/A-18 from consideration, Japanese defense experts were left with a choice between two of the very things they said they wanted least: a single-engine aircraft and the most expensive air-superiority fighter flying.

The fact was, the F/A-18 was the perfect choice for the FS-X and the aircraft Japan's influential industries said it wanted. So, then, why did defense chief Kurihara decide to drop the F/A-18 from the competition, when it was the one airplane that came closest to fulfilling Japan's dream of a domestically developed aircraft? Kurihara says he did it because "the pilots didn't like the plane." As one U.S. aviation consultant commented: "If that was his reason for dropping the F/A-18, it would mark the first time in history that a government listened to its pilots when selecting equipment."

Indeed, early Japanese drawings of the FS-X, known then as the JF-210, bore a stunning resemblance in form to an advanced version of the F/A-18 known as the Super Hornet Plus, the very plane McDonnell Douglas was angling to sell as its model for the FS-X.

Though it was argued that the F/A-18 was a navy aircraft and the FS-X was to be an air force model, this argument ignores the fact that influential and landlocked buyers like the Swiss, who also worried about single-engine fighters tilting over their tiny homeland, chose the F/A-18 for their air forces. Israel, a nation which may well have the best air force in the world, is considering buying $2 billion worth of the "navy" planes.

Unlike any available versions of the F-16 offered by General Dynamics, the F/A-18 Super Hornet Plus had canards, the little winglets set ahead of the main wing. The Japanese coveted canards, believing that they held the secrets to greater maneuverability, the signature of Japanese designers since the days of the Zero.

The F-16 had no canards, and U.S. defense officials and General Dynamics officials made no secret of the fact that they didn't see a place for canards on the aircraft. Given the shape of the crucial air intake on the F-16, there was no strong point available to affix them to.

Not only did the F/A-18 offer a basic design that fit Japan's plans for domestic development of the FS-X; it offered two engines. Since the chase for the FS-X began, Japan had been calling for a two-engine fighter. Reliability was not assured simply by statistical measures; it was based on the hard fact of having an extra motor in case one broke. Indeed, the reliability argument of single-engine aircraft had long been raised to counter the twin-engine requirement. And it had been ignored by Japan for these selfsame safety reasons. What is more, of all the irrational requirements Japan had called for in the FS-X—Kearns's infamous "64 parameters"—the one demand that the United States acknowledged had validity was the call for twin engines.

The importance of a twin-engine aircraft in the FS-X debate cannot be overstated. So strong was the Japanese demand for a two-engine design that General Dynamics had tried to withdraw from the FS-X competition just five months before their plane was selected, because they could not put such a design forward.

In March 1987, General Dynamics had asked for and *received* from Secretary of Defense Caspar Weinberger permission *to take the F-16 out of competition* for this reason. Thus, for all intents and purposes, GD had dropped out of the deal. The company was unwilling, it said, to get involved in the development of a twin-engine version of their plane. What is more, they acted on those intentions that August, when Japan's FS-X Joint Study Team visited General Dynamics' Fort Worth plant.

In fact, according to Joseph Jopeline, a General Dynamics vice president who had worked on the project since 1985, the company's offices in Tokyo were being scaled back because of their belief that the FS-X would be a twin-engine aircraft. GD gave up the apartment it kept in Tokyo and brought home its American representative, leaving the office to its Japanese manager. The company was in retreat. "There was not enough business," lamented Jopeline.

Incredibly, some argued that General Dynamics' reluctance to go forward with a twin-engine version of the F-16 was an example of sterling character, which much impressed the Japanese. According to this version of events, so pleased were the Japanese with General Dynamics' austerity and determined courage that Tokyo decided that this was the company they wanted to work with. If such reasoning is to be accepted, then it must be believed that Tokyo committed their national security and treasure to the tune of $10 billion just to be on the side of the more noble-seeming defense firm.

The fact was, General Dynamics didn't really need the FS-X deal, or want it. Money had been rolling into the company for fighter development throughout the Reagan years. Besides the F-16, which filled their mile-long factory floor, General Dynamics was building the AX advanced stealth fighter with McDonnell Douglas, which potentially was worth $50 billion. They were shoo-ins for the Advanced Tactical Fighter program, which they would share with Boeing and Lockheed, and which had the potential for another $50 billion. The numbers were limitless. They could hardly keep up with the work, much less manage a project with Japan, a nation with which they had little experience.

To the bitter end, the informed wisdom in the aviation industry was that the F/A-18 would win. It was increasingly price-competitive because of the yen's dive against the dollar. Indeed, the press wrote off the F-16 as early as March 1986, when Japan carved in stone its requirement that the FS-X be a twin-engine plane.

As the authoritative *Aviation Week & Space Technology* put it in March 1986: "The Japanese [military] has narrowed its foreign selection *to a twin-engine vehicle, and the F-18 appears to be a front runner*" (emphasis added).

In his dissertation on the FS-X, Captain Andrew J. Button, who served as the Pentagon's day-to-day operator on the FS-X program, wrote: "As an observer [of those meetings on the FS-X], it seemed clear to me that the Japan team favored the baseline fighter that offered Japan the most work. Initially, this looked to be the F/A-18. However, the twin-engine F-16 (called the SX-4) might have been more attractive to the Japanese industry team had not GD decided to withdraw that option the week prior to the [Japanese FS-X study group's] visit." He concludes: ". . . no one believed that the single-engine F-16 had a real chance to be selected." When the Fort Worth fighter won the competition, Button remarked to a General Dynamics representative, "This was the greatest case of negative marketing I've ever seen."

Finally, the decision to go with the F-16 represented a direct blow to the influential and much courted Ministry of International Trade and Industry. The man in charge of aircraft at MITI at that time, Takeshi Isayama, puzzled over the choice of the F-16. "The Japan Defense Agency always said it wanted a twin-engine aircraft. The pilots were clearly in favor of two engines [here he contradicts Kurihara's explanation]. We don't really know what happened."

The most interesting result of eliminating the F/A-18 was the effect it had on the Mitsubishi group of corporations, the single most important and influential defense concern in Japan. Mitsubishi Heavy Industries had hoped to continue its relationship with McDonnell Douglas, and saw the F/A-18 Super Hornet Plus as a more advanced plane to work with electronically than the F-16. The F/A-18 also employed more advanced composite materials. In fact, the Private Industry Joint Study Group on the FS-X, created by Kurihara's JDA, *recommended that September that the defense agency adopt the F-18.* Mitsubishi Heavy led this group of five Japanese firms that would build the FS-X (Mitsubishi Heavy, Mitsubishi Electric, Fuji, Kawasaki, and Ishikawajima Harima).

In Kurihara's three principles for the selection of the FS-X (that the FS-X must be superior militarily to anything in the air; that the DoD's understanding on the matter must be gained; that industry pressure—from the United States and Japan—would be ignored) he promised that no industrial interests would be considered in his final selection. Surely he was sticking to his word when he dropped the plane Mitsubishi Heavy wanted.

And yet one key business interest was ultimately and unexpectedly very much favored by Kurihara's elimination of the F/A-18, apart from General Dynamics. That was Mitsubishi Corp., the giant trading company. Had the F/A-18 stayed in the competition and been selected by the defense industry, the opportunity to produce the FS-X, the new Zero fighter, *would not have been* an all-Mitsubishi project, as the original Zero had been. Though this mattered less to Mitsubishi Heavy Industries, which was primarily concerned with its own profits and technology development, it mattered a great deal to Mitsubishi trading.

The august Mitsubishi trading company, one of the original three diamonds of Mitsubishi (the name means "three diamonds" in Japanese; the three included Mitsubishi Heavy, Mitsubishi Bank, and Mitsubishi Corp., the trading company), stood to lose out if a McDonnell Douglas plane was selected. McDonnell Douglas was already represented by one of its archrivals, the Nissho Iwai trading company. What is more, Mitsubishi trading was the only member of the corporate inner circle that stood to gain new revenues if

General Dynamics won the competition. Mitsubishi Heavy and Mitsubishi Bank stood to gain in any case.

Typically, a trading company earned 2 percent of any deal it brokered. In return for this money, it provided services to General Dynamics to help it in its relations with the defense agency: permits, contracts, logistics, translations, technology transfer—all the esoterica that comes in dealing with a foreign nation's legal and financial system. Mitsubishi Corp. was one of the few trading companies in Japan with a high-level security clearance. In a $10 billion deal for the FS-X, if General Dynamics earned $3 billion, the trading company might reasonably expect to realize substantial profits of up to $60 million and potentially more. With the elimination of the F/A-18 from the competition, the door was now opened for the last of the three Mitsubishi diamonds to join the FS-X constellation.

What must be understood about the relationships among the Mitsubishi companies is that they are part of a *keiretsu*, an industrial grouping peculiar to Japan that centered on a bank and included a heavy industry company and a trading company. Each member of the *keiretsu* functioned autonomously, in its own best interests. At the same time, the individual companies deeply identified with a common cause: the *keiretsu*—in this case Mitsubishi, whose traditions went back more than 130 years. Such *keiretsu* are bound by cross-shareholdings among each of the member companies. The three diamonds of the Mitsubishi group hold a total of about 20 to 30 percent of the *keiretsu* stock. For example, about 20 percent of Mitsubishi Heavy's stock is held by members of the *keiretsu* (among them, Nikon cameras, Kirin beer, Mitsubishi cars). In addition to cross-ownership, they have board members in common. Their leaders meet regularly each month at their so-called Friday Club. As a group, the Mitsubishi *keiretsu* accounts for an astounding 10 percent of Japan's GNP.

Though the fact was largely unrecorded, Mitsubishi Corp., the trading company, had fought a very hard behind-the-scenes battle to be a part of the Mitsubishi FS-X group that would build the new Zero. It did this by trying to keep General Dynamics from dropping out of the deal. A win by the Fort Worth company was their only hope of getting participation in the FS-X program and joining with their *keiretsu* brothers in the new pride of the Japanese Air Force and aviation industry, the FS-X.

David Wheaton, General Dynamics' leading marketing man on the program, recalls being awakened in the middle of the night by an urgent telephone call from a Mitsubishi representative pleading with him to get his company to adopt a twin-engine version of the F-16. "If you could do that," he recalls being told, "Mitsubishi Corp. felt certain the deal would go in favor of General Dynamics."

Hironori Aihara, the handsome and urbane director of Mitsubishi Corp.'s

Aerospace Division, recalls how he had tried pushing Wheaton toward the design, telephoning him and encouraging him. At about this same time, Mitsubishi Corp. opened offices in the Dallas–Fort Worth area, home to the F-16 and General Dynamics. This was a clear indication of their eagerness to take part in General Dynamics' business, if the company was selected to build the FS-X.

The most tempting aspect of this argument is that it all potentially devolved on one man, defense director Kurihara, who made the decision in favor of the F-16. By his decision to eliminate the F/A-18, he opened the door for General Dynamics to take the prize no one expected it to win.

With the exception of the Prime Minister, Kurihara was the only major politician involved in the deal. This is significant, because Japanese politicians have a desperate need for cash flow. What is more, Kurihara was leaving the defense agency in November and would soon face the costly process of re-election. He would not get *amakudari*, the revolving door enjoyed by Japan's leading bureaucrats. (After the FS-X, for example, the defense agency don, Seiki Nishihiro, went to work for Tokyo Marine and Fire Insurance, a member of the Mitsubishi *keiretsu*. Tsutsui went to work for Kawasaki Heavy, the number two subcontractor in Japan on FS-X.) Kurihara had to consider his own future.

The costs of political office in Japan are astronomical, as they are in the United States. But worse, the Japanese government provides only a small stipend to politicians to maintain their Diet offices, barely enough money to hire a secretary and one assistant. To be an effective legislator, an elected official needed dozens of people to run the office. Still more cash was necessary to disburse among constituents, to ease the pain of funerals or to heighten the joy of marriages. As finance minister Miyazawa put it: "The hugeness of the money required is beyond anyone's honest toiling work."

This made the political process ripe for corruption. And unlike in the United States, where the Federal Election Commission tracks campaign contributions and makes them accessible for public examination, no such records exist in Japan. Millions and millions in invisible and illegal campaign funds are thus easily available to grease the wheels for politicians, who typically pass their seats on to their sons, like endowed chairs.

In fact, as the FS-X deal was coming to its conclusion, a major stock-for-influence scandal was coming to light in Tokyo, involving not only Prime Minister Nakasone but also his finance minister, Kiichi Miyazawa. This was not the first time Nakasone had been alleged to have been involved in influence peddling. Indeed, during the infamous Lockheed scandal, when Nakasone served as minister of trade, he was purported to have made a crucial phone call to Prime Minister Tanaka that swung the deal in favor of Lockheed.

The finance minister, Kiichi Miyazawa, was also hip-deep in what came to be known as the Recruit Cosmos scandal. He was tainted and on the take, and had to resign his office. This reflects on the FS-X, because his ministry controlled the purse strings of the defense agency. In fact, his influential ministry opposed the F/A-18 because of its high cost.

But more, the last two defense chiefs—Kato and Kurihara—both came from Miyazawa's faction. Ostensibly their appointments had been to counteract Nakasone's hawkishness. But both defense chiefs served terms in the crucial years when the FS-X was being debated: 1986 and 1987. These were the very same years of Miyazawa's greatest influence over the budget process as head of the Finance Ministry. What good would such connections be if they did not provide members of the faction the opportunity for success? In other words, Miyazawa faction members not only mitigated Nakasone's hawkishness, they opened the door for the defense agency (which Nakasone had once led and was unusually close to) at the tightfisted Finance Ministry. They were in a position, thanks to Miyazawa, to help Nakasone get what he wanted.

Explaining his decision to drop the F/A-18, defense director Kurihara said, "Industry is only concerned with its profits. Mitsubishi Heavy Industries pushed the F/A-18 because it required a great deal of remodeling to develop it into an FS-X. Their profits would have been huge. And I vowed in my three principles that I would not be influenced by corporate interests."

None of this long logic adds up to evidence for a bribe, however, or even a large campaign contribution. The smell of sulphur does not always imply the presence of the devil. At the same time, the argument asks a necessary question in any transaction, and that is: Who benefits? In this case, the chief beneficiaries of Kurihara's choice were General Dynamics and Mitsubishi trading. What did Kurihara get for vastly enriching the bottom lines of these two giant firms? By whatever evidence might possibly exist, *nothing*. He did his duty as he saw fit. But what he did ignored or defied virtually every rational interest in Japan's defense bureaucracy, from the powerful Ministry of International Trade and Industry through Japan's largest and most influential *keiretsu*. As the much respected Seiki Nishihiro lamented years later: "It was a pity we selected a single-engine aircraft."

BOOK TWO

The Fight

15

Mutiny in a Hot Tub

"The FS-X debate was important because it suggested a potential revolutionary change in U.S. attitudes and policies in the direction of responding directly to the Japanese challenge."
—CLYDE V. PRESTOWITZ, JR., *Trading Places*, 1989 edition

A MAJOR THREAT to the FS-X deal began to take shape one evening in Potomac, Maryland, the quiet Washington suburb that had once been hunt and horse country. Indeed, Auer's hopes for a simple solution to the complex deal would be undermined here even before the final contracts for the FS-X were signed in late 1988, even before Auer had time to retire in peace.

Potomac was one of the capital area's prestige addresses. The powerful and the famous made their homes here. R. Sargent Shriver, Jr., for one, a man of the Kennedy clan, famed for leading the Peace Corps and lately as muscleman Arnold Schwarzenegger's father-in-law. His white clapboard manse stood back of a high grass-covered berm, a great green wave looming over the choked two-lane blacktop bounding one side of the property.

In the real estate surge of the late 1980s, Potomac chewed up most of the horse meadows, with their vanishing-point white rail fences, and cemented a gridiron of roads servicing dozens of tony subdivisions. New-home prices soared to six and seven figures. Developments with names like Falconhurst were hammered up like stage sets, their price tags in the vicinity of $3 million a parcel. Middleweight boxing champion Sugar Ray Leonard made his home here. Elsewhere in Potomac, Wonder Woman Lynda Carter and her wealthy financier husband, Clark M. Clifford protégé Robert A. Altman, built a Euro-castle. And a private deer park.

This was Washington's answer to Beverly Hills.

Just north of the feisty waters of the Potomac and the enchanting locks of the old C&O canal that runs in peaceful parallel with it, the upper-middle-class development of River Falls was built in the early 1970s. Set amidst the tame hills that ripple outward in the river's wake, it is a pricey collection of $500,000 Federal and Colonial homes. These were elegant domiciles without heritage, where the assistant secretaries, the policy-level people in business and government, made their Beltway nests.

Here, late on a clear midnight in deep December 1987, beneath River Falls' native American beech and tulip poplar, Clyde V. Prestowitz, Jr., for-mer Assistant Secretary of Commerce, settled chest-deep into the bubbling waters of the family hot tub. His guest at this ungodly hour was Craig Rich-ardson, recently returned from his tour of Tokyo as Kevin Kearns's agent in the FS-X affair.

Richardson had been anxious to reach the schedule-bound Prestowitz and so was obliged to settle for the midnight shift. The hot tub was Prestowitz's idea, a practice he brought home from his years in Tokyo as a graduate student and later as a businessman. Steeping in deep tubs is a bedtime ritual in Japan, the equivalent of a sauna for the Finns. For Prestowitz, the tub was a way to unwind. He did not think twice about inviting a stranger to join him for a midnight dip.

A bully-faced man with a no-nonsense manner, Prestowitz was of an age, forty-six, that appeared neither old nor young, an age that didn't call atten-tion to itself. It was an age of influence but usually not power. He might have climbed the Commerce Department's ranks to the influential office of deputy had it not been for the ideological range war that was Reagan trade policy. Prestowitz chafed against the administration's notion that the invisible hand of the marketplace was the ultimate and unbiased broker and that govern-ment meddling inevitably warped economies for the worse. His experiences in Japan had convinced him of that ideological error.

Kearns had gotten wind in Tokyo that Prestowitz was writing a book describing his battle in the trade wars, and that Japan was his focus. Kearns wanted to create a swell of opposition against the budding FS-X deal, and he told Richardson to contact Prestowitz when he got back to the capital. The hope was that their experiences in the FS-X deal might find their way into Prestowitz's text. That would be one way to raise the profile on a transaction that they saw turning against U.S. interests.

For Richardson the visit was a desperate move. "I was convinced that the Japan club had a stranglehold on policy," he said. "I was convinced that the system was broken, from the inside, and that there was no way it was going to correct itself of its own volition. What was happening in Tokyo was not good for the republic."

Prestowitz told Richardson that he knew about the FS-X. He had read in the Washington *Post* about the unanimous vote in the Senate calling for Japan to buy a U.S. jet off the shelf, and had followed the October 1987 Kurihara announcement. Until now, listening to Richardson, he had not been aware of the shenanigans involved in the deal.

Prestowitz was impressed with Richardson's information; the fact, for example, that the costs for developing the FS-X were going to be far above projections. Richardson seemed to have good insights into the tensions between the embassy and the DoD as well. The problem for Prestowitz was that his book was nearly complete. Publication was just months away, set for the spring of 1988. There was a chance, however, he told Richardson, that he could add a page or two.

Richardson had hoped for more, but he said that he understood. At least Prestowitz was willing to listen. Richardson relaxed in the steaming water and looked across the hills rising back of Prestowitz's home.

Slowly, in a methodical, articulate narrative, Richardson unraveled his story about events in Tokyo, focusing on the crucial October meeting at which Japanese negotiators had overwhelmed the U.S. side. Richardson did not elaborate on his and Kearns's efforts to seize the initiative on policy. Rather, he focused on U.S. ineptitude and lack of preparation. How, for instance, the DoD had sent a team of amateurs to confront more than fifty Japanese experts, technicians, and trained negotiators. How a General Dynamics vice president had nearly agreed to outrageous Japanese demands, and how, finally, Button had handed over the U.S. negotiating position without bargaining.

When Richardson mentioned the name of the Japanese negotiator, Prestowitz wanted to groan. He knew the man well. Masaji Yamamoto was one of the shrewdest, most senior negotiators in the Japan Defense Agency, Prestowitz said. He was a MITI man seconded to the military to make certain that a balance was struck between his ministry's industrial aims and the nation's defense needs. He was the toughest of men and among the highest-ranking of Japan's trade elite.

Yamamoto had been Prestowitz's chief antagonist in the long, bruising battle to get Japan to stop its slash-and-burn forays through the U.S. semiconductor market. In meetings with Prestowitz, Yamamoto was always quiet and courteous but as tough-minded and calculating as he was thorough and bent on the details. Prestowitz recalled that Yamamoto was an expert Go player, an ancient board game similar to chess in its emphasis on planning and strategy. The Japanese had been playing Go for twelve centuries.

Prestowitz was gloomy. To have a man like Yamamoto face off against a navy captain whose only experience in Japan was antisubmarine warfare was a genuine mismatch. The last thing that the Pentagon should have done was to allow such a lightweight to go up against a heavy like Yamamoto. To think that no one in the DoD had objected made Prestowitz shudder.

There was genuine concern on the part of Prestowitz that the nation was in grave economic danger. He told Richardson that the stock crash that October signaled the end to what had been an American century. He ticked off the signs: In 1986 America's trade balance in high-tech goods—computers, scientific equipment, communications gear—tipped into the red for the first time ever. By some estimates, 40 percent of the advanced electronics in U.S. defense systems were made in Japan, and would go to 55 percent in the next five years. In just the last year, the United States had become the world's largest debtor nation, and lost its lead to Japan as the leader in international banking. Japan was now the world's largest creditor nation, and the Japanese surpassed America in per capita gross national product. The French were saying that the United States now had *two* central banks, the Federal Reserve and the Japanese insurance companies.

Prestowitz suggested that Richardson read a new book that came out while he was in Japan, entitled *The Rise and Fall of the Great Powers*, by Yale professor Paul Kennedy. The book was being widely circulated and much debated in Washington power circles. It commented directly on their discussion. Kennedy had written: "Precisely because a top-heavy military establishment may slow down the rate of economic growth and lead to a decline in the nation's share of world manufacturing output, and therefore wealth, and therefore *power*, the whole issue becomes one of balancing the short-term security afforded by large defense forces against the longer-term security of rising production and income."

Richardson finished his description of the farcical October meeting in Tokyo with an equally disturbing account of its follow-up in Washington a month later. Immediately after returning from Japan in late November, he scheduled a briefing with the director of the Defense Security Assistance Agency, General Charles Brown, and his deputy, Glenn Rudd, the man now in charge of the FS-X. Richardson's purpose in the get-together was to attempt another end run on the U.S. embassy by going directly to the top of the DSAA, which had charge of the FS-X program. He told the director and his deputy about the events that took place that October—the near-sellout by General Dynamics, the overwhelming presence of the Japanese negotiators, Button's handout. Worst of all, he concluded from Japan's most recent moves that a new strategy was emerging, in which Japan agreed to co-development but structured the deal to allow domestic development. Something had to be done. As Richardson turned to General Brown to get his response, he discovered the general dozing.

Prestowitz knew a good story when he heard one. As a young man, still in graduate school, he worked nights reporting for the Honolulu *Star-Bulletin*. At first he slogged through police blotters and obituaries, but as the Vietnam War began rumbling more loudly over the Pacific horizon, he grew ambitious, camping out for arriving military brass stopping off on the island.

On one occasion, he parked himself at Hickam Field to track down World War II hero General Maxwell Taylor, who was on his way to Saigon via Honolulu on behalf of President Kennedy. Told that he could not see the general, who was relaxing on the tennis courts, Prestowitz proved himself to be enterprising. Instead of putting his car in reverse and heading back to the office empty-handed, he set out in search of Hickam's tennis courts. Spying the elegant, silver-haired general at play, he staked him out, trailing him as he made his way back to the locker room. When Taylor emerged in swimming gear and started toward a stretch of Waikiki Beach, Prestowitz plowed through the sand, notebook at the ready, and got his interview.

Though more than twenty-five years had passed, Prestowitz brought that same reporter's sensibility to the book he was working on. "I had been standing at ringside for four years watching the Roman Empire crumble," he said. The story begged to be told.

When *Trading Places* finally appeared that spring, it turned out to be a seminal, iconoclastic work, casting the troubling disparity in U.S.-Japan commercial relations in new and revolutionary terms. Instead of lavishing praise on the Japanese for their innovative management style and then heaping blame on American corporate managers for their lackluster showing, *Trading Places* drew on Prestowitz's own experiences to reveal a Japanese economic system rigged by government subsidies and private sector cronyism. Case by case, he demonstrated how the protection of domestic industries and the systematic assault on foreign market share had skewed the principles of free trade in Japan's favor.

Bad American management was not a sufficient explanation for a $57 billion trade gap, particularly when a devalued dollar was equalizing trade with European partners. Japan presented a special case. "Not only was I in Europe in the early 1970s when American business expanded vigorously there," wrote Prestowitz, "but I have also managed companies in Japan and have seen Japanese executives up close. While some are excellent, the percentage of outstanding Japanese managers is no greater than what I observed in France, Belgium, or Italy, and certainly not [greater] than in the United States."

There was a more fundamental difference, crucial to understanding what was actually taking place between the United States and Japan. "Few, if any, American companies can compete with the Japanese in the areas the latter deem important," Prestowitz declared. This was a heretofore unheard-of remark about Japan, at least from a former government official. Those areas included semiconductors, the seed corn of virtually all modern manufactured goods and machine tools, implements fundamental to industrial society. Then there was steel and textiles, autos and consumer electronics, the finished goods of international trade. Largest of all was aerospace, which was at the heart of the FS-X debate. Manufacturing, Prestowitz reminded his readers, not just "service industries," created the jobs people needed to reach for the American Dream.

Prestowitz managed to deliver on his promise to Richardson that night in his hot tub. His discussion of the FS-X, though brief, read like an indictment. Prestowitz reached for the core issue: technology flow. "The agreement of 1983 for transfer of dual-use technology from Japan had not yet resulted in any flow of technology to the United States," he wrote in preface to his argument. "One reason was that the agreement could be activated only when the United States specifically identified a technology it wanted from Japan. But since there was no mechanism to make it aware of what technologies Japan had, there was no mechanism to identify those that might be desired."

Unlike most academics writing about Japan, Prestowitz brought wide-ranging expertise to the problem. His mix of talents was rare. Fluent in Japanese, he could discourse also in French, Dutch, and German. He had a strong academic background as well as a long record as an international businessman. With these qualifications, combined with his five and a half years in government in the top echelons of the Commerce Department, he brought a formidable perspective to an issue that most people only parsed.

Though Prestowitz was only vaguely aware that Richardson and Kearns were embarked on a mutiny aimed at defeating the FS-X, he succeeded on his own in defining the problems that would soon return to haunt the program: fears about Japan's targeting of the aerospace industry; the use of co-production programs with the United States to build up Japan's industrial base; the exploitation of defense relations with the Pentagon for economic advantage; the DoD's failure to monitor its agreements or implement its initiatives; the dangerous crossover taking place between military might and economic security.

"While the U.S. has sought security by giving away technology," Prestowitz wrote, "Japan has sought it by hoarding technology, even from the United States, its primary source. This has been the strange denouement of the concept of economic security. In a sense, the United States, the defender of Japan, has become its target, not in any sinister sense or even by plan: it was a result inherent in the logical dynamic of [co-production]." Co-development, Prestowitz feared, which went beyond mere co-production, took defense cooperation entirely too far in Japan's direction.

———

Prestowitz was a lifelong Republican who believed himself to be part of the party's conservative wing. He was a liberal, however, in the sense that he believed that there is a role for government in economic policy. His conservatism revealed itself on social issues. He believed in patriotism, and thought that people had an obligation to serve their country, ideals not limited to conservatives but loudly claimed by them. He opposed abortion, but kept his mind open. He would say that what he really wanted to do in his work now that he had left government was to revitalize the American Dream.

At the Commerce Department, Prestowitz was considered a maverick, a contrarian. He lacked the strong political connections to make a real go of his post. He could also be difficult to work for, and would alternately burden and then ignore subordinates, while taking the credit himself. He had practically no concept of time and would allow appointments to drag on and overlap, creating havoc for others. Rude would have described him, except that his poor manners were unconscious. Prestowitz often seemed preoccupied.

Because he rarely missed an opportunity to take a jab at the sanctity of U.S.-Japan relations, he was characterized after the publication of *Trading Places* as a "Japan basher," a term of accusation designed to echo British racists who engaged in "Paki bashing." The phrase had been coined in the early 1980s by Robert Angel, the former president of the Japan Economic Institute, a well-regarded Washington-based think tank funded by Japan's Ministry of Foreign Affairs. The aim of the phrase was to discredit critics of Japan by insinuation and innuendo.

The phrase quickly became identified with Washington *Post* economic columnist Hobart Rowen. According to Rowen, he had been accused of originating the phrase by Democratic congressman Richard Gephardt. To Rowen, who was an apostle of Reagan-style laissez-faire economics, a Japan basher is "someone who is so critical of Japan that he proposes remedies that are extreme."

Ad hominem by design, the phrase "Japan basher," with its resonances of racism and homophobia (gay bashing), had the effect of branding its victims and reducing serious and important debate to name calling. Though attempts to label Prestowitz a Japan basher were many, the former assistant secretary managed to dodge them all. For his book was as much a best-seller in Japan as it was at home. Prestowitz's critique of Japanese trade practices, though sometimes harsh and usually draped in the American flag, was not aimed at the Japanese people but at their bureaucrats and their industrialists, a combination that was often indistinguishable. Indeed, his toughest attacks were aimed at Washington.

In Japan, Prestowitz came to be identified as a member of the "Gang of Four," a group of foreign commentators intent on debunking Japan, Inc. The others with whom Prestowitz was associated were: James Fallows, the Washington editor of *The Atlantic*, author of *More Like Us*, published in 1990; Dutch journalist Karel van Wolferen, author of *The Enigma of Japanese Power*, published in 1989; and Professor Chalmers Johnson of the University of California at San Diego, author of *MITI and the Japanese Miracle*. *Business Week*, which plied the cutting edge of U.S.-Japan business affairs, regarded the four affectionately and dubbed them "revisionists." Senator Danforth of Missouri preferred to call them "trade activists." Of course, it was the more negative and memorable "Japan basher" that stuck.

The idea central to the four writers was that Japan was not like the United States; it was not a nation that aspired to American-style social and political organization. It was its own nation. The revisionists rejected the State Department view that Japan was evolving in the image of an American-style political and economic system. Japan's economic structures had served it well, they argued, why should it change? Where Japan, for instance, could afford to have ten-year visions for their companies because of low-cost loans and administrative guidance from the government, U.S. companies were more nearsighted, trapped by their institutional investors into accounting for their performance from annual report to annual report, blindered by what may be called their 10-K vision.

While advocates of Reagan-style free-trade ideology argued that the consumer is the ultimate beneficiary of Japan's market-gouging tactics, the revisionists countered that they were missing an obvious point. By winning U.S. market share, Japanese products were eating up American jobs. Without work Americans became less formidable consumers. Whereas consumers benefited from underpriced Japanese products in the short term, they paid dearly in the end. These critics pointed out that under the right circumstances government could have a very positive and sustaining effect on business. America's much lauded space program was one such example, as was Washington's agricultural program. The popular mortgage deduction is industrial policy in the service of America's chief archetype: the American Dream, a home for every family and a chicken in every pot.

This is why the FS-X became such an important issue to the revisionists. As Prestowitz later put it: "The FS-X debate subsumed more completely, and demonstrated better than any other single incident, the fundamental inconsistencies, misperceptions, mixed motives, bureaucratic struggles, conflicting objectives and ambitions, fallacies and evolving dynamics that bedevil the U.S.-Japan relationship . . ."

16

A Coup for Congress

"What would ensue would be one of the most vitriolic debates in the history of U.S.-Japan relations . . ."
—MICHAEL CHINWORTH, *Inside Japan's Defense*

THE MOMENTUM for the mutiny that began in the hot tub of Clyde Prestowitz bubbled over with the return of Kevin Kearns to the United States from his assignment in Tokyo in July 1988. Whereas his predecessor, the popular Gregg Rubinstein, had stayed three years in the embassy's Mutual Defense Assistance Office, Kearns stayed but two, so bad were his relations there. Also back in Washington was Kearns's cohort, Craig Richardson, who monitored the FS-X from his office in the State Department's Intelligence and Research Division. The pair's plan was to take the FS-X fight to Congress, which would review the FS-X under the Arms Export Control Act.

Kearns had applied for a State Department fellowship that would allow him to work on Capitol Hill as he saw his days in Tokyo drawing down. Such fellowships were widely available at State, where the apprenticeship approach toward career and workplace prevailed. The object of going up to the Hill from Foggy Bottom was practical: to soak up the workings of the Capitol, the who and how of selling international policy.

Kearns approached the Congress as a way to right what he saw as the wrongs of the FS-X, and, he had to admit, politics was his first love. After Kearns graduated from law school in the 1970s, he managed a state senate campaign in New York. The candidate was an Orthodox Jew running on the

Conservative ticket (the state has a Conservative Party) who shared Kearns's deep opposition to abortion.

Typically, voter turnout is so small for a state legislative election that capturing a single apartment building's voters could swing the results either way. The problem for Kearns was that registered Democrats outnumbered Conservatives four to one. It would take more than one apartment building to carry the seat. It would take block after city block of votes.

Kearns delivered. He succeeded by mustering a full third of registered Conservatives to the polls, while the complacent opposition managed to turn out their usual 5 percent of registered Democrats.

Although it was a small race, it was a significant achievement, and one Kearns touted. His candidate's victory was substantial and unexpected. The campaign represented the sort of all-out, headlong exploit that signaled Kearns's organizational skills and powers of persuasion. After eleven years of having to pocket those talents, as he made his way laterally through the ranks in the State Department, he now had a mission: the FS-X.

In March 1988, while he was still based in Tokyo, Kearns began scouting Congress. He wanted a job on the Senate Armed Services Committee, which had been tracking the flight of the FS-X deal. In a congressional bureaucracy dominated by lawyers, the Defense Industry and Technology Subcommittee had Ed McGaffigan, a physicist and a science whiz who had spent years in the Soviet Union studying its technology, in the fearful years after Sputnik, when for the first time in the postwar era America's technology lead seemed in jeopardy. The FS-X was full of technical issues—computer source codes, composite technology and materials, radical new flight dynamics—which would be well understood by the techy subcommittee staffer.

McGaffigan worked as Senator Jeff Bingaman's legislative assistant on national security. He had been following the FS-X deal for the senator for more than a year. Whereas the FS-X had been a constituent issue for Senator Danforth of Missouri, the advanced fighter targeted the sensitive realm of technology transfer for the junior senator from New Mexico. McGaffigan recognized that Kearns would be a key ally of the subcommittee as the FS-X taxied onto the congressional runway.

Yet McGaffigan, however sympathetic, could not accommodate Kearns. The subcommittee staff already had its share of interns, all of whom would still be in place when Kearns returned from Tokyo.

The disappointed Kearns turned his attention to his number two choice, the Senate Foreign Relations Committee, which had jurisdiction over foreign military sales. He made contact with the committee in April when William Triplett, Senator Jesse Helms's rod and staff in Congress, was introduced to him through a mutual friend at the embassy in Tokyo. A man of medium height, Triplett wore suits in defiance of style. Some appeared to be as old as he, aged forty-five. His black hair was trimmed short and combed to one side. His stodginess proclaimed his conservative credentials.

Triplett had been following Japan for years and had recently been after a high-tech issue to address. He was a gifted staffer, "a rabble rouser," as Senator Danforth's aide Susan Schwab described him, not without affection. For his part, Triplett called Schwab "La Susan," because she could be brash and formidable. It was Schwab, who had once served the State Department at the Tokyo embassy, who first introduced the FS-X into Triplett's lexicon, long before he ever thought to take it up in committee. The two senior staffers often worked together and consulted on U.S.-Japan issues.

Triplett had a curious reputation on Capitol Hill. Jesse Helms was the provocateur, Triplett his press agent. Reporters loved him, because he was always concocting news, although it was sometimes difficult for reporters to distinguish between Triplett's brainstorms and his leaks. Having served the committee for five years and Helms for three, he had become a political force in his own right. He knew how to bring attention to otherwise obscure issues, which the FS-X was at that time.

Triplett's former boss and friend, the Deputy U.S. Trade Representative, Michael Smith, had been hammering at him informally for months to turn his attention to high-tech trade matters. Triplett had been focused largely on the low-tech side, on the corrupt and exclusionary Japanese construction market in particular. The city of Osaka—a huge and ancient port town on Japan's Pacific coast—had a $5 *billion* project to construct an international airport right in the middle of the city's large and busy bay. U.S. companies, while allowed to bid on these projects, lost out because of the *dango*, a bid-rigging process that was, apart from being illegal, obviously also trade-exclusionary. At the same time, Japanese construction firms were in the incipient stages of plowing under their American competition on big U.S. construction jobs.

Smith told Triplett that the Japanese construction industry was not the big problem; Japan's inroads into high technology were. High tech was the high ground on which both the United States and Japan had staked their economic futures, and the United States was losing the competition, and losing for the wrong reasons.

Not only did Smith have a point, Triplett thought, he had the ability to make Triplett cringe, which was no small feat, considering that Triplett was a former military man assigned to the CIA. "Smith just kept beating up on me, saying, 'Triplett you're missing the boat. The country is going to wrack and ruin and it's all your fault.' " Smith had similarly bulldozed Chris LaFleur when the Japanese finance minister's son-in-law refused to brief him on the FS-X.

For Triplett, the FS-X proved just the high-tech solution he had been looking for. It made the Deputy U.S. Trade Representative happy, for one thing. Aircraft and aerospace were considered by Smith to be the jewels in America's trade crown. More important, Triplett now had a personal *cause*. A man of zeal, Triplett believed that there was no better fight than a righteous fight. That was the FS-X pure and simple; and Kevin Kearns was just the rebel to go along with it. The mutiny had reached Congress; Kearns joined Triplett on Helms's staff.

Triplett was something of an ironic figure in the FS-X battle, in that he got his start in Washington toiling as a lobbyist for Japan. His boss was Bill Tanaka, the powerful Washington attorney who helped Japanese business carve out the legalisms and legislation that paved Japan's way into the American market.

H. William Tanaka, sixty-six, was senior partner in Tanaka, Ritger & Middleton. For thirty years he and his firm consulted for the embassy of Japan. A Nisei—second-generation Japanese-American—he was born in Los Angeles. He was declared an enemy alien as a teenager when World War II broke out. The family was evicted from their home and placed in concentration camps, along with 120,000 other Americans of Japanese descent. By the end of the war, however, Tanaka's fortunes had changed. He joined the Office of Strategic Services, granddaddy to the CIA, where his job was to interrogate Japanese POWs.

When the new Bush administration entered office in November 1988, Bill Tanaka was offered a position as the President's supervisor of Asia-Pacific affairs. He turned the job down. That was his style. His opponents supposedly called him "the man in soft shoes," although he testified before Congress more than a hundred times on U.S.-Japan trade issues. His clients were the powerful Electronics Industries Association of Japan, the Japan Automobile Manufacturers Association, Brother International Corp., and Minebea Co.

Triplett founded the Tanaka office that represented American Honda Motor. During those crucial years when the car company's future in the United States teetered in the balance, Triplett's job was to clear the legislative highways for the arrival of the "Honda, the Car That Sells Itself." The auto company had been well served by Triplett, as Honda's burgeoning market share in the eighties made plain.

Before Honda, Triplett had been Tanaka's attorney for the Japanese television manufacturers, handling "dumping" cases. "Dumping" was the accusation that a nation's products were fetching prices below fair market value. The tactic was aimed at sponging up market share by flushing the competition out of business. The initial financial costs for dumping products into a market were high, but in the long run it led to profits, sometimes to market dominance, for which Japanese companies seemed to aim.

"I got to a point where I was not pleased with what I was doing," Triplett says. "I was having trouble justifying it to myself. By the late 1970s there was no American TV industry left. Now I was going after the auto industry. I was part of the problem, not part of the solution."

The turning point came in Paris. On a trip for his Japanese clients, Triplett got into a conversation about buying influence in Washington. Finding himself on the defensive, he attempted to switch the attack. "What would happen," he asked, "if a certain anti-American trade minister left office in France and got hired by Ford or Milliken to help them gobble down the markets of mature French industries?"

By way of reply, he got a cold and calculating stare. His French counterparts dismissed the notion. "Such a thing would never happen in France," they said. "Never."

"Never?" Triplett asked.

"No one would ever again answer the minister's telephone calls."

Kearns came to work for Triplett in July 1988. "This was Kevin's chance to right wrongs," Triplett says, "to get out his sword and go after things. The State Department, where he worked, is a stifling bureaucracy. It's a place where they hire people to check the width of margins on outgoing mail." Triplett believed Kearns's purposiveness partly arose from his past. "Being Catholic didn't help. He needed a way to express himself. Kevin gets offended, as I do, by serious wrongs."

The plan was to turn Kearns's mutiny against the U.S. Embassy in Tokyo into a Capitol Hill-style Rolodex rebellion. "I showed him *Hudson's,*" Triplett says, holding up a copy of the press guide to Washington. "That's the bible. I taught him how to talk to the media."

Timing was a problem, however. By arriving in July, Kearns came as Congress was winding down; many key people were just too busy to meet with him. A monthlong recess followed, wiping out any momentum Kearns might have generated in that first rough month. On top of that, September signaled the final stretch run for the presidential campaign, which meant Congress broke camp even earlier than usual. "There wasn't a lot of time to work the issue," Triplett says, "but what Kevin did was to write the memos to Helms, and get Helms's education up to speed on this stuff."

The goals Triplett and Kearns set were modest initially. Triplett says that he would have been satisfied if they got Congress to think more seriously about the aviation industry, to consider the implications of helping Japan become an aggressive competitor. "We didn't think that we could stop the train," Triplett says. "We thought maybe we could make the train somewhat better."

Their aim was to keep the Pentagon on its toes as it negotiated the government-to-government contract for the FS-X. They wanted the defense people to think that Congress was looking over their shoulders every minute. Triplett, however, was less than confident. "As a practical matter, Kevin and I were *bluffing*," he says. "That's what it amounted to. We didn't have the horses at the time. Most of the bad guys downtown [at the State Department] who were involved in this knew that we were bluffing too."

But Kearns and Triplett were far from alone in their opposition to the FS-X. They had allies in Congress, chief among them Ed McGaffigan, Senator Bingaman's lead staffer on the Armed Services Subcommittee on Defense Industry and Technology. McGaffigan was a whiz on technology policy who had long been concerned about the FS-X.

Back in the spring, in May 1988, McGaffigan told Kearns, Congress had sent "guidance" to the Pentagon—an early warning on upcoming legislation —saying that they would be required to consider the effects of deals like the FS-X on the broader U.S. economy. The plan was to use the Defense Authorization Act of 1989, which blesses the Pentagon's yearly budget, as the battering ram.

As the report that May scoldingly put it: "The committee is disappointed that the Department of Commerce has not been involved in the review of bilateral MOUs . . . This lack of interagency consultation within the U.S. government can lead to the perception, if not the reality, that U.S. economic interests, and in particular the effects on the U.S. industrial base, are not given great enough weight in these negotiations.

"The committee therefore has included a requirement in section 805 that the Secretary of Defense consult with the Secretary of Commerce on the negotiation or renegotiation of such MOUs and fully utilize the resources of the Department of Commerce . . ."

The FS-X was prominent among the report's concerns. It specifically stated: "The U.S. government should not enter into a memorandum of understanding with the Japanese Government on the FS-X/F-16 that simply transfers American technology and jobs to Japan with nothing more than a license fee in return."

With the publication of the report that May, the Pentagon was on official notice that Congress was monitoring their negotiations with Japan for the FS-X. McGaffigan and company were a step ahead of Kearns and Triplett. Indeed, they had actually set a deadline on the deal. If the negotiations for the FS-X continued past October 1, 1988, when the bill became law, the Commerce Department would be required for the first time to be included as an adviser in the MOU. This was a trap set for the Pentagon.

As the clock ticked down toward the October deadline, the talks between the Pentagon and Japan over the FS-X ground to a halt. What had appeared in June to be a done deal was now stuck over what was standard language in other agreements similar to this one. As ever, the United States expected access to any new technology that grew from licenses the United States sold. And free of charge. Such technologies that were due back to the United States were referred to as "derived technologies."

The Japanese had a real problem with this, arguing over the distinction between what technology was derived and what was not. This was a crucial point for Japan, because nearly all technology is at some level *derived*. Considering Japan's long and successful record deriving new products from old technologies, a wealth of innovation was at stake for them. In particular, Japan feared that the terms set by the United States would designate the radar planned for the FS-X as derived technology. The plane's inertial navigation system, electronic countermeasures, and mission computer software were also considered *nonderived* by the Japanese. The issue was thus still very much up in the air.

For its part, the DoD did not press the matter of terminology with Japan. The Pentagon reasoned that it was better to let the Japanese settle this on their own. Glenn Rudd, who was now in charge of the FS-X negotiations at the Defense Security Assistance Agency, argued for patience. "Internally we told ourselves time is on our side, not theirs," he said.

In fact, the limits set by the Defense Authorization Act did not enter Rudd's mind. Time was on his side, he believed, because Japan would have to begin the serious work of building the aircraft sooner rather than later if it hoped to have a prototype ready to fly in 1993. Rudd's view assumed the primary concern of the Japanese was military applications, not aerospace development. "We sat there and we did not push them," Rudd said. "We didn't want to give them an excuse to make things more difficult."

Kearns brought several key ingredients to the budding congressional insurrection. The most obvious was his knowledge of the deal. As the deputy chief of the Mutual Defense Assistance Office in Tokyo, he had witnessed the development of the FS-X program from both sides of the Pacific. He attended all the key meetings. In May 1986, for example, he was at the Pentagon when Japan proposed its impossible requirements for the FS-X, which Kearns succeeded in characterizing and spoofing as the "64 parameters." He was there at the infamous December 1986 meeting, in which Ryozo Tsutsui of Japan's Technical Research and Development Institute claimed Japan could build a better support fighter on schedule and more cheaply than anything the United States had to offer.

With Kearns acting as interpreter, there was no way that the Pentagon could ply the Congress with half-truths and extravagant predictions. They might argue with Kearns and take issue with his explanations, but few could say they had seen more of the FS-X program since its inception. Only Jim Auer, at the "Little State Department in the Pentagon," had followed the program as long. But Auer was preoccupied with his personal life. By the time Kearns came back to Washington, Auer had taken retirement to teach at Vanderbilt University.

Politically, Kearns brought the Republicans into the FS-X coalition. He was a charm for McGaffigan. For while Democrat Jeff Bingaman worked well with his senior Republican counterpart, John Danforth, Kearns brought in Jesse Helms and the minority staff of the Foreign Relations Committee. With the Republicans on board, center and right, there was a chance at confronting the President.

"Kevin was able to concentrate on the FS-X," says McGaffigan. "When committee schedules forced the FS-X onto the back burner for some of us, Kevin was there to follow it." Kearns kept close contact with Senators Bingaman, Byrd, Dixon, Danforth, D'Amato, Helms, and all their staffs. When the Pentagon gave a briefing on the FS-X, he would correct the record and often refute the DoD spokesman on issues. The staffs relied on him.

Finally, Kearns had a virtual front-row seat at the ongoing government-to-government negotiations for the FS-X through his young protégé at the State Department, Craig Richardson. Both men knew all the current players in Tokyo and Washington personally. So as the deal progressed closer and closer to the fateful October showdown with Congress, Kearns's mutiny seemed to be turning into a revolution.

17

The Sound of One Hand Washing the Other

"As Glenn Rudd once said to me about our success in Congress, 'You caught us with our pants down.'"
—KEVIN KEARNS

IF THERE WAS ANYTHING about the FS-X negotiations that gave Kearns comfort, it was the presence of Glenn Rudd, the deputy director of the Defense Security Assistance Agency, which handled the government-to-government negotiations on the FS-X. Gritty and well seasoned, Rudd was no apologist for Japan. He was not a member of the Chrysanthemum Club and bore none of the romantic attachment Jim Auer brought to his relations with Tokyo. But Rudd had other liabilities that worried Kearns. The problem was that Rudd put business ahead of economics. The perspective he brought to defense cooperation was based—obviously and as it should have been—on the Soviet threat in Asia. Unfortunately, this ignored the trade balance with Tokyo.

Rudd had the jowly face of a weary hound dog. The bags under his bulging eyes sagged onto his cheeks. Only Seiki Nishihiro on the Japanese side smoked more cigarettes, but only Rudd smoked the lethal red soft packs of Pall Malls. Balding, in his fifties, he had a neighborly manner. Nothing about him betrayed his high office, or the billions of dollars in contracts that ended with his jagged signature. He simply saw himself as the chief bureaucrat in the labyrinth of procedure he administered at the Defense Security Assistance Agency.

Rudd did not seem to have pretensions. He was his own man who wore short-sleeve shirts in the dead of winter. He slouched in his chair when he talked, and his body had a limp look. This was misleading, perhaps, because he was an alert and guarded man. In his line of work, the object was to get as much as possible and to give as little. He was America's lead negotiator for Foreign Military Sales, both in Europe and in Asia. Even as Rudd draped one thin leg over another, he was at complete attention. The languid posture concealed a sharp and appraising mind. Asking him a question was like tossing a stone into still water and not seeing a ripple. His gap-toothed smile, so disarming, was used more for effect than expression. It underlined points; it demurred; it politely said "no comment" and "no way" and "fuck you."

As deputy director of the DSAA, Rudd had the final nod on the FS-X before it went up the chain of command from his boss to the Secretary of Defense. Though he rarely took personal control of deals now that he was deputy, he decided to take charge of the FS-X after Craig Richardson confronted him with the experiences he had with Kevin Kearns in Tokyo. "I have sign-off authority on messages," Rudd says, describing the sort of powers he held over his FS-X working group, led by the blustery Tim Tyler. When, for instance, Tyler responded at "the bureaucratic speed of heat" to the fax sent off by Kearns and Richardson while the Japanese deliberated over their choice of U.S. aircraft, Rudd took responsibility for what had the appearances of a stampede. "I signed off on that message," he said. For better or worse.

This put Rudd at the controls on the FS-X, though he tended to understate his role. "The basic framework of the arrangement was done by Rich Armitage and Mr. Nishihiro," he said, "not me." Those two decided, for example, that the FS-X would use American engine technology and Japanese radar and stealth technology. But the all-crucial line-by-line terms of that agreement were handled by Rudd. This was significant because for all intents and purposes the FS-X had no precedent. As Jim Auer, the man who got the concept of co-development going, stated it: "An arrangement of this magnitude had never been negotiated before." Rudd's responsibilities were huge. The terms of the deal literally had to be teased out step by step.

Those who knew Rudd considered him solid stuff. He was respected both inside and outside of the Pentagon. Highly professional, shrewd, hardheaded, he had a disarming aw-shucks style. Even the angry Craig Richardson, Kevin Kearns's cohort, who generally had a low opinion of bureaucrats, liked Rudd. "I think he is a patriotic fellow, a well-intentioned fellow, and an able bureaucrat," pronounced Richardson. Tim Tyler, who worked for Rudd and assisted him during the FS-X negotiations, called him "the best closer I've ever seen." This was a salesman's term, "closer." It referred to a dealer who not only got his terms but landed the all-crucial agreement as well.

But Rudd's approach to the FS-X was self-limiting. He worked for economies of scale, common weapons systems, strengthening allies. The industrial advantages conferred by the agreements he so well negotiated were not a concern. Gaining Japanese technology was a *low* priority for Rudd. "Technology was not at all a driver of the FS-X deal," he said. "If we would have been sure we wouldn't have gotten anything in the way of technology from Japan, we would have still done the same deal." Surely Rudd had read the report of the Sullivan mission and entertained no illusions about Japan.

What Rudd wanted from the co-development of the FS-X was business, pure and simple. Business did not mean that he viewed the agreement between the United States and Japan in a global context of international competitiveness—that is, examining the technologies and their impact on Japan's learning curve and America's industrial base. He didn't think about potential competitors. He thought about work for U.S. contractors and their employees, including their subcontractors. He wanted to keep Japan from taking its business to Europe.

Rudd took assurance in U.S. technical superiority. The United States invested billions upon billions more defense dollars in research and development than Japan. How could Japan compete? he reasoned. It was ridiculous to even imagine it. What's more, the United States had fought two major wars and several minor wars over the last forty years. American weaponry had withstood the test of combat all over the world. The success rate of U.S. aircraft in the Middle East alone was staggering: more than a hundred enemy shoot-downs without a single loss. Japan had no such experience. What could they teach the United States?

Rudd embodied the genuine disdain in which the Pentagon held Japan's defense technology. The phased array radar, for example, that Japan touted for the FS-X was described in private as a costly "piece of shit" by the Pentagon. An analyst for Rudd's DSAA described Japan's relative position: "They were five years behind Texas Instruments," and Texas Instruments lagged behind Westinghouse and Hughes, both leading manufacturers of radars. While there was some interest in how Japan manufactured the fast (gallium arsenide) circuits used in the radar, the system it fit into was far behind that of U.S. electronics firms.

Masaji Yamamoto, Rudd's high-ranking counterpart in the upcoming FS-X negotiations and the Go expert Clyde Prestowitz so much feared, brought a very different approach to the table. As he told the Japanese press in the days before the final agreement was reached: "It is desirable to always see progress of defense technologies as an extension of consumer technologies . . . In the future we have to invest in [defense] with well-defined targets based on consumer technologies." While the Pentagon was drumming up a little business for a few defense contractors and worrying about the machinations of the Soviet Union, Japan was bargaining for the keys to the kingdom of aerospace.

———

Negotiations for the FS-X contract opened in the United States on a chilly Tuesday, November 24, 1987, while Kearns was still stationed in Tokyo. Talks were held in the E Ring of the Pentagon, which looked into the central courtyard, now a chilly tableau of bare branches and empty park benches. The meeting room was dominated by a long mahogany conference table. On the U.S. side were Jim Auer (not yet retired), Glenn Rudd, and Captain Andrew Button, among others. The Japanese were led by the Go master Masaji Yamamoto, who was joined by a representative from the Ministry of Foreign Affairs, as well as legal and technical experts from the defense agency.

At issue were the terms of the government-to-government agreement known as a Memorandum of Understanding. Such an agreement, which is the core document in nearly all co-production agreements the United States maintains with dozens of nations, covers the treatment of classified components and data owned by the U.S. government. In addition, the MOU sets the conditions for commercial licenses, as well as financial terms. Most important in the case of the FS-X, the MOU establishes the rules for technology transfer—which technologies will be available and how.

A simple strategy emerged for the United States. First, Rudd wanted a steering committee to be established, made up of members from both sides, to handle technology transfer issues. The rules under which they worked would be based on technology transfer agreements signed with the United States and Japan in 1983. In Rudd's mind, using these agreements would make plain to the Japanese that we expected their technology to flow back to the United States.

Another principal aim of Rudd's team was to counter Japan's opening thrust that October, when the United States was either "blindsided," caught flat-footed, off balance, or stampeded at the Tokyo "beauty contest." In a tête-à-tête between Rudd and Yamamoto just before the group convened in the Pentagon's central ring, the two men agreed that a joint steering committee made up of U.S. and Japanese representatives would control the project.

Masaji Yamamoto brought a far different view of Japanese defense to the FS-X talks than Rudd did. Whereas Rudd approached defense cooperation through security interests, Yamamoto held the door wide open to Japan's broad commercial development strategy, which was the principal focus and purpose of the ministry he served. Unlike Rudd, he was not a career official in the defense agency. He had been seconded to the JDA from the Ministry of International Trade and Industry.

Yamamoto's team opened the talks by reiterating their October demands— all manufacturing to be done in Japan, only development agreements are open for talks, the United States will supply all data and technology for the

F-16 at a royalty fee of $500,000 per plane. The meeting quickly bogged down.

The determined Japanese attempted to steal a march on Rudd. The broad terms outlined by Yamamoto's people were based directly on the DoD's own Security Assistance Manual, which stated that royalty fees in cases like this were $500,000 per aircraft.

This put Rudd off. He replied sharply to the Japanese. We at the DSAA basically wrote the manual that you're referring to, he said. We'll tell *you* what the manual says, and we can proceed from there.

Yamamoto, who had been quiet until this point, letting his lieutenants press the issue, spoke up calmly. We need to step back for a moment, he said. He reminded the negotiators of their mission. We can no longer deal in terms of nostalgia, he said, recalling that the FS-X was supposed to represent a new level of cooperation between the two countries.

Rudd declared that before the United States could even begin to reach agreement on a framework for the agreement, four requirements had to be met. One he had already succeeded in winning, which was the concept of a technical steering committee. But he also wanted U.S. contractors to get a share of the work on this program, anywhere in the neighborhood of 35 to 45 percent. That principle was nonnegotiable. So was the flow-back of Japanese technology under previous U.S.-Japan agreements. And he wanted to be certain that the United States would also get workshare in the *production* phase of the agreement. He said there was the clear danger that having negotiated a development agreement, the Japanese could go off and produce the plane on their own. "We weren't going anywhere until these four principles were taken care of," Rudd recalled.

On the very day that co-development was agreed upon, Ryozo Tsutsui, the father of the FS-X, was promoted to director of the Technical Research and Development Institute. This was no reward. The promotion fettered him in obligation, effectively taking him out of the still contentious debate in Japan over co-development. For while the two governments had reached agreement, there was still a strong hope among its supporters that the MOU negotiations would fail and the FS-X would be resurrected as a domestic development project.

But now the father of the FS-X had been neutralized. He was no longer in a position to play advocate for his beloved program. As director of the TRDI, his responsibilities encompassed larger concerns. He had to think of the welfare of the other laboratories and services when he slugged it out with the defense chief over budgets and appropriations. He took a pledge: "We will see the FS-X through to a successful development." When he later recalled his pledge and pronounced the phrase in English, he sat a little straighter in his chair and paused for effect. The samurai fell on his sword. The voice of duty hushed the man of zeal.

The grumbling over Kurihara's choice did not end with the purge of Tsutsui, however. Indeed, tensions continued to mount in Japan as Rudd and Yamamoto worked on the MOU. One obstacle on the Japanese side was the Air Staff Office, which had strongly argued for domestic development. The top officers there wanted to shoot down the deal as much as Kearns and Richardson wanted to shoot it down on the U.S. side.

The Japanese Air Force played a game of dodges, at every opportunity avoiding grounds that would allow Yamamoto to reach a settlement. They shunned Jim Auer, for example, because they felt he had betrayed them. Auer had been the center of Japanese defense relations. Without him, contacts remained at the margins. No settlement was easily possible.

One key official who ducked Auer was the influential General Hideaki Tamura, the man who spoke for the Japanese pilots as well as for the young officer corps that had emerged in Japan over the last decade. These were the people who dreamed of a new Zero. Tamura was a close friend of Ryozo Tsutsui, and he had direct lines to Yamamoto's office. He was a natural conciliator. Had Auer been able to reconcile with the Air Staff Office, the problems of Yamamoto's negotiating team would have been vastly simplified. But Tamura treated Auer like the plague.

Having Tamura in favor of Kurihara's co-development would be a salve, and the man who led the effort to win the influential general over was none other than Hideo Kimura, Jim Auer's closest friend in Japan. ("A political secretary can do anything.") His absence to this point in the contentious FS-X issue had almost become conspicuous.

Kimura maintained that he had been avoiding the issue of the FS-X out of loyalty to Mitsubishi, a company he respected for its selfless nationalism. This loyalty was strengthened by a personal bond he had with a former naval admiral, a man named Yaita, who joined Mitsubishi Heavy Industries after retiring from the military service.

Yaita, who was also friendly with Auer, asked Kimura why he was not more involved with the FS-X. "Is it because of your loyalty to me?" Mitsubishi Heavy, of course, had the most to gain if Japan rejected the idea of co-development. Kimura did not want to oppose the company's fortunes or those of his friend. He told the admiral, yes, he was staying away from the FS-X out of loyalty to him. Yaita replied, "You should do what you believe." In an indirect and very Japanese way, the admiral was telling him to help Mitsubishi by not becoming involved. Thus, Kimura divided his loyalties in favor of the admiral, Mitsubishi, and Japan.

Later, it was at the admiral's direction that Kimura began steering a different course. Kimura's new orders came when an angry split within Mitsubishi

Heavy Industries surfaced in Nagoya, where the company built its planes. According to Kimura, a top engineer at the aircraft plant became drunk after a company meeting on the deal and, knowing that Yaita was a friend of Auer's, called the admiral in the middle of the night. Auer was seen by some Mitsubishi men as the demon in Kurihara's design for co-development. "Admiral," the inebriated engineer snarled, "you are paid by Mitsubishi. How can you be friends with a traitor like Auer?" Yaita was stunned. Drunk or not, the engineer, a man high up in aircraft management, was way out of line. Instead of getting angry, the admiral decided he would make certain that the company went forward in the service of the government. He called Kimura the next day. "Hideo," Kimura recalls the admiral's commanding him, "go your own way on the FS-X."

Kimura insinuated himself into the FS-X debate almost by accident, during an argument he had with a lieutenant on the air staff. Disdain was Kimura's tool. He declared: "The Maritime Self-Defense Forces," Japan's navy, "know how to deal with the U.S. Navy. But the air staff does no *nemawashi* with the U.S. Air Force. No wonder they look on you like taxi drivers." (*Nemawashi* literally means "root binding"; in political usage it means getting all your ducks in a row and achieving consensus before making important contacts or undertakings.)

This approach by Kimura was insightful, both in the sense of arousing the young lieutenant with the verbal equivalent of a smack on the face, but also in its deft perspicacity. The reason the Maritime Self-Defense Forces got along so well with the U.S. Navy was the *nemawashi* it did through Jim Auer. Auer was a navy man. He helped homeport the aircraft carrier *Midway* at Yokosuka. He had been a classmate of many of Japan's naval officers during his days at the Japanese naval academy. As the political officer in charge of Japan for the Pentagon, Auer had given the Japanese Navy someone who understood their needs and whom they could approach.

When, for example, the United States wanted to sell AEGIS-class destroyers to Japan—a ship designed to protect the carrier formations Japan did not (yet) possess—Auer's influence was crucial. The Japanese claimed that the hulls on the ships were too large for the smaller Japanese seamen (even though young Japanese were growing far taller than their parents, who were raised during the shortages brought on by World War II). Gangways were too wide, they said. Controls were ergonomically incorrect.

Whereas the DSAA was incredulous at such complaints, which bordered on the absurd, Auer sought compromise. What if Japan redesigned and built the ships' hulls at home? The electronics system—which was AEGIS—could be bought from the United States and mounted on the Japanese hulls. In a broad sense, the solution paralleled the one Auer had carried forward for the FS-X co-development. That deal, too, went through.

That is the power of *nemawashi* that Kimura pointed out. The Japanese Air Force did not have that same relationship, he said, suggesting that the situation had to be changed in order to settle the FS-X to everyone's benefit. He told the young lieutenant that had the air staff played its cards right, the U.S. Air Force might have taken up their cause over the FS-X and everything might be different today. Maybe they would have gotten a twin-engine plane; maybe they would not have had to stand for co-development. The air force was stupid, Kimura concluded.

As it happened, a second air staff officer overheard Kimura's tirade. He was an aide to General Tamura. The staff officer challenged Kimura. Haranguing a junior officer was one matter, daring to say those same things to those in charge was another. "Why don't you try saying that to my boss," Kimura recalls him saying. Kimura said he would be glad to oblige. After all, "a political secretary can do anything."

(Auer scoffed at the account of the Tamura story. "Do you mean to tell me that General Tamura would ignore the Office of the Secretary of Defense?")

The game of bluff ended in a two-hour meeting between Kimura and the general. Kimura talked about his background, and made his argument for breaking bread with the U.S. Air Force. Though Tamura disagreed with Kimura's analysis, he seemed to accept the inevitable and in time agreed to meet with Auer. Kimura gives himself the credit for this breakthrough, and considered, in his mind at least, that he had delivered the quid pro quo for Auer's help in the Toshiba affair. As he put it: "I was the ham in the sandwich."

On June 3, 1988, the Japanese press reported that the FS-X MOU was a done deal. The financial wire of the Kyodo News Service, Japan's version of the Associated Press, wrote: "Japan and the United States have reached agreement on the framework for the joint development of Japan's next-generation support fighter, dubbed the FS-X, defense agency director general Tsutomu Kawara said Friday."

Consensus came during a meeting in Tokyo between Japan's new defense minister, Kawara, and Frank Carlucci, who had taken over from Caspar Weinberger as Secretary of Defense. According to the Japanese press story, the two sides were expected to sign the MOU at the earliest possible date.

In the agreement, the Japan Defense Agency would run the project and a Japanese company would be the prime contractor. The defense agency would pay all costs. Japan would not have to negotiate a production contract until the development phase was complete. The United States appeared to get its way on the basic issues involved in the technology transfer.

The only sticking point seemed to be workshare, with Japan calling for 65 to 70 percent of the work and the United States demanding 40 percent. The way Carlucci and Kawara got around it was to avoid specifying the exact percentage in the MOU. It represented a major concession on the Secretary's part. The final compromise would have to come from Japan, and that would be the recommendation that Japan go forward with the agreement.

By September 1988, when the Japanese still did not respond, the United States was concerned. Word was that the Japanese were haggling over the terms of technology transfer, the problem of derived and nonderived technologies. Rudd feared they were dragging their feet. Ahead loomed the October 1 deadline set by the Defense Authorization Act of 1989, although that was the last thing on Rudd's mind. His chief worry was pressuring the Japanese. They could easily balk and accuse the DoD of being high-handed and trying to pressure them into an agreement. He decided to say nothing to Japan, gambling that his discretion would be rewarded with an agreement. As the negotiations developed and September stretched toward October, the last thing on Rudd's mind seemed destined to become the first.

18

The Grandfather Clause

"In my perspective, what turned me against these folks at the Pentagon—and I'm a reasonably moderate character; I'm not viciously partisan—but what pissed me off was that they just disregarded [the Senate's] advice."
—Congressional staffer speaking on background about the FS-X

GLENN RUDD said that he saw the October 1, 1988, deadline as just another date on his calendar. Indeed, he didn't even bother to pencil it in. "We considered at the time the legislation [Defense Authorization Act of 1989] was passed that this thing [the FS-X] was a done deal. I'm not even sure it [the agreement] wasn't initialed by then. It obviously wasn't signed, but it was completely negotiated. We just didn't consider that this would be a problem."

That was a bad mistake, and the Japanese would later shout betrayal. Rudd pleaded innocence. "This just wasn't on my scope," he said, drawling out the word "scope" for emphasis. He recalled that he didn't push the Japanese to reach a decision over the five-month period in which they deliberated because he feared they might interpret queries from him as more American pressure, the much resented *gaiatsu.*

At his rank as the number two man in the Defense Security Assistance Agency, Rudd was beyond getting down in the trenches and taking on the day-to-day responsibilities of a negotiator. Rudd's job description did not call for him to gauge wind direction and velocity on Capitol Hill. That responsibility was delegated. In this case, the task fell to Rudd's deputy for planning, Tim Tyler. That Rudd was involved at all in the negotiations says something about the growing concern on the U.S. side for the way the program was developing.

Rudd became involved because of orders he received from Assistant Secretary of Defense Richard Armitage. "Rich called me and told me he wanted this thing to stay in political channels. I more or less matriculated into the role [of negotiator]."

Craig Richardson pointed out that Rudd got involved in the FS-X after Richardson told him about the "beauty contest" in Tokyo. Richardson had told Prestowitz of Rudd's reaction to this wake-up call, and he used it in his book *Trading Places:* "Although [General] Brown fell asleep in the briefing, Rudd was visibly upset and screamed at the chagrined Button [who had shared his notes on the U.S. negotiating position with his Japanese counterpart], 'We have to get smarter.'"

Clearly, the message Rudd was now getting from his lieutenant, Tim Tyler, was that the FS-X deal was on track. As Rudd put it: "We didn't think at the time that Congress was going to create a serious problem about the MOU. We thought we had basically satisfied them," adding with candor, "We were pretty apparently mistaken."

Tim Tyler was completely confident that he had Congress under control. After all, the FS-X was too big a project and the DoD was already too far along in the negotiations to turn back now. At the very least, they had a powerful argument to grandfather in an agreement that had been "initialed" before the advent of the new law.

Tyler could not have been more wrong. If anything, Congress had been banging the drum, declaiming and making great stage gestures at the FS-X for almost two years. Even worse for FS-X proponents was the call for Department of Commerce participation in the Defense Authorization Act of 1989, which augured that most vicious of battles, a bureaucratic turf war. Tyler misread the political semaphore. Starting in the summer of 1987, the Senate voted 96–0 to demonstrate their desire that Japan should buy the FS-X from a U.S. aviation contractor. Unanimous votes in the Senate are always meant to be red signal flags.

Dismissing the ballot, Tyler said, "I saw it as a free vote." It carried no political baggage. "You can engage in some free Japanese bashing but still have no practical effect. Who isn't for jobs, motherhood, and apple pie? When Congress is really concerned you'll know it because they hold hearings and debates. Not bed-check votes."

In March, Senator Jeff Bingaman signaled the Pentagon again, blasting the FS-X in hearings in which Robert B. Costello, the man in charge of buying and developing America's weapons at the Pentagon, voiced support for involving the Commerce Department in MOU negotiations.

Costello said in his written statement to the subcommittee that he was worried that America's technical superiority was on the wane: "We, as a government, need to do more to pursue the economic benefits that the MOUs offer our industries. We are actively working with the Department of Commerce to remedy this shortcoming. We must all work toward insuring that our industrial base can compete in a global economic market."

In fairness to Tyler, it should be pointed out that the acquisitions side of the Pentagon represented by Costello also wrote MOUs, but only those involving cooperative agreements in which costs were shared. Such agreements were exclusively, or almost exclusively, with Europe. The DSAA, the side of the Pentagon where Tyler worked, wrote those that did not involve the use of DoD funds. The FS-X, for instance, was to be paid for entirely by the government of Japan.

Thus, while Costello's side of the Pentagon may have supported a role for Commerce, such as the one described in the 1989 Defense Authorization Act, Tyler's side did not. The Pentagon's policy side despised the Commerce Department for its Bureau of Export Administration, which the DoD saw as a pipeline for exporting U.S. high-tech commercial goods to Soviet bloc nations.

In a paper Tyler circulated privately, he blamed the cry in favor of Commerce on news stories. The media, he wrote, portrayed Commerce "as the protector of defense technology. That is curious when you think about it, because it is the Defense Department that has the procedures in place and the technical expertise to evaluate and protect sensitive technology. In fact, for virtually the entire eight years of the Reagan administration, the press relished reporting about a running battle between Defense and Commerce over the issue of protecting technology—back then Commerce was for selling; Defense was for protecting."

Commerce was two-faced. "How long have they licensed this relationship between Boeing and the government of Japan?" Boeing had extensive coproduction agreement programs with Japan for a number of aircraft, among them the giant 747. "I mean, if Commerce is so concerned about the Japanese eating our lunch in the commercial airline industry, why the hell do they continue to license Boeing to do business with the Japanese?"

Tyler's institutional concerns focused strictly on a need to protect national secrets; he expressed little understanding of the impact such secrets had on the economic side. He continued in the next paragraph: "To the watchful eye, this apparent role reversal might be worth wondering about. Could it be that the Defense Department has suddenly forgotten about the need to protect its family jewels—and had passed this baton to the Commerce Department? It does not seem likely. The Defense Department, in the early 1980s, moved to establish the Defense Technology Security Administration (DTSA). The DTSA was, of course, involved in the FS-X from the very beginning and did have a representative on the team that negotiated the Memorandum of Understanding. The DTSA is also the agency that reportedly spearheaded the efforts within the executive branch to induce Commerce to control dual-use technology in the interests of national security."

In fact, Tyler's agency deliberately kept the Defense Technology Security Administration away from the FS-X deal. Dr. Stephen Bryen, director of the administration, stated flatly, "We had to struggle internally to be put on the FS-X team. Our agency was screened out of almost all technology deals like this. That was controversial then and controversial now. Since the FS-X, it's all been downhill. There's virtually no role for the DTSA on technology transfers."

In January 1988, in an effort to have a voice in the FS-X negotiations, Bryen wrote a memo to Fred Ikle, the Under Secretary of Defense for Policy at the Pentagon and Richard Armitage's boss. Bryen cited a list of serious concerns, culminating in his worst fears: "While the current [FS-X] program is called joint development, it provides Japan with complete authority for design and configuration decisions. Since the Japanese have already decided that most major components [of the FS-X] will be Japanese (apparently forgetting years of U.S. industry assistance) there may not be much left for our defense industries."

Tyler was intent on ramming the FS-X through Congress, even ignoring face-to-face warnings on the fighter by Senator Bingaman's lead staffer on technology issues, Ed McGaffigan. According to McGaffigan, Tyler had briefed him and other staffers throughout 1988 on the developments in the FS-X negotiation. Time and again, McGaffigan said, Tyler was advised of their concern and warned of the impending October deadline. "Tyler just wasn't a good listener," McGaffigan decided.

Tyler interpreted events differently. "We were aware that Commerce was fiddling with the FS-X behind our backs, but I don't recall that McGaffigan made a special point of going to the mat over this."

McGaffigan may have been less clear on the matter than he realized, for Rudd backed Tyler's assessment. "I briefed McGaffigan a time or two myself," Rudd said. "I don't really recall that he brought up the legislation in a way that I would have taken as threatening the FS-X arrangement."

Tyler's view was widely shared in the DoD. Jim Auer, the man who engineered the FS-X deal, could not imagine that this was an issue that would arouse Congress. As Auer later wrote, the FS-X negotiations had begun "a year before Congressionally mandated consultations with the Department of Commerce *became an issue*" (emphasis added).

Auer continued: "Bureaucratic disputes over turf aside, the most basic issue of disagreement between Defense and Commerce on foreign military sales in the past had been over technology security, *i.e.*, Commerce arguing for greater freedom to sell and the Pentagon arguing for the need to protect sensitive technology."

In other words, both Commerce and Defense saw one another as sieves for technologies flowing out of the United States, to the industrial advantage of other nations: what amounted to an American industrial policy for its trading partners. Probably both were right. Commerce provided and encouraged a flow of finished high-technology goods to Iron Curtain countries, and Defense provided the underlying technologies, the know-how and sometimes the know-why, of leading-edge weaponry to allies like Japan, who saw themselves as industrial competitors.

By his own admission, Auer had little experience in arms sales, and perhaps was unqualified to assess the FS-X's chances in Congress against the Defense Authorization Act.

If these men on the Pentagon's policy side were getting incorrect readings on the direction Congress would take on the FS-X, the Senate staffers felt that they were being led astray by the Defense Department, and blamed Tyler. Said one, "Tyler would brag to us in his briefings that he had snookered the Japanese in negotiations—that was the word he used, 'snookered'—and when we later looked into the program he described, we found that he had sold off the farm."

Misjudging the mood of Congress was excusable; alienating those in influence in Congress was not. Congress felt patronized by the DoD. The ever-present silk handkerchief ballooning from Tim Tyler's breast pocket became a much-commented-upon symbol by the legislative staffs, a magician's prop. The confidence and salesmanship that had served Tyler so well within the Pentagon's world of weapons contracts turned on him before Congress.

On November 29, 1988, Ambassador Mike Mansfield signed an Exchange of Notes in Tokyo on behalf of the United States, making the final agreement on the FS-X official. Five months had passed since the usually accurate Japanese media advertised the program as a done deal. Two full months had passed since the Defense Authorization Act had gone into effect. And still Rudd did not worry. As he saw it, the FS-X was packaged and ready to go. "We figured the Commerce Department would have a role in future programs," he said, "but not in this one."

The final agreement called for 130 to 170 planes to be built (more than is commonly acknowledged), the first four prototypes to begin flying in 1993; production was scheduled to commence in 1997. The $1.2 billion development budget—considered staggeringly and unrealistically low by virtually everyone on the U.S. side—promised $440 million for U.S. contractors. General Dynamics actually expected to rake in at least $1 billion on the program. At the time of production, a second MOU would be negotiated, with the

United States getting roughly the same amount of work as in the development phase. Japanese technological developments derived from General Dynamics would flow back to the United States free of charge. Homegrown Japanese technologies developed through the program could be licensed, assuming Japanese contractors were willing, a likelihood that denied precedent.

There were actually five parts to the package that represented the full U.S.-Japan agreement. There was an Exchange of Notes, signed by foreign minister Sosuke Uno and Ambassador Mansfield. This was the only public document. The MOU itself, which was the second part of the agreement, was kept secret at the request of Japan. Typically, MOUs signed between the United States and other cooperating countries were public documents. Only Japan cloaked such accords.

The third document, a "side letter," was more controversial. Side letters were stratagems Clyde Prestowitz described in his book *Trading Places* as "a favorite device of the Japanese bureaucracy." According to Prestowitz, side letters allowed the Japanese to be conciliatory *(tatemae)* while publicly proclaiming steadfastness on the issue (more *tatemae)*.

When Prestowitz's book made public the existence of a side letter to the Semiconductor Trade Agreement, the Japanese denied its existence. Finally, a Japanese magazine obtained a copy of the letter and published it. Forced to acknowledge the note, the Ministry of International Trade and Industry said it did not represent a commitment on the part of the government of Japan! "The episode greatly undermined the credibility of agreements negotiated with Japan," wrote Prestowitz.

The text of the MOU said that the United States was to get between 35 and 45 percent of the work on the plane, but this was intentionally left vague. It was settled through the side letter to the FS-X agreement, as reported by Peter Ennis of *Tokyo Business Today*. The letter spelled out that the U.S. contractors were to get a flat 40 percent, including royalties.

The two remaining documents in the FS-X agreement were a set of minutes of the negotiations, and the terms both governments set for the contracts between private companies, known as the Licensed Technology Assistance Agreement (LTAA).

The Japanese, who were very good at—and took great pride in—understanding the drift of U.S. politics, thought that work on the program could now go forward. There was no indication of trouble. Nothing premonitory. They were obviously not getting any signals from the Pentagon about congressional interest. Everything seemed in order. The U.S. government had simply entered into an agreement with the government of Japan. The few stories that appeared in the press about the FS-X seemed to fade deeper and deeper into the business section, much like depth charges, as it happened.

———

The decision whether to polish off the FS-X during the last stages of the Reagan years depended not on the Defense Authorization Act, as it turns out, but on another law, the Arms Export Control Act. For both the Pentagon and the Department of State, which also regulated the issue of overseas arms deals, notifying Congress had potential pitfalls.

The crucial choice of when to spring the FS-X on Congress fell that December to the *acting* Under Secretary of State for Political Affairs, Michael H. Armacost, at age fifty-one a veteran diplomat, number three man in the Reagan State Department, and longtime Japan hand.

Armacost, who managed the day-to-day business of the department and its regional bureaus, faced a simple choice: inform Congress of the FS-X deal under the Arms Export Control Act or try a tactic to block out Congress. He could argue that since the FS-X was not an arms transfer but a licensing agreement, the authority to vote it up or down fell outside their purview. However, cutting out Congress on a technicality like that could make for irritations. There would be cries of foul. Alternatively, notifying Congress quickly might play into the hands of those who opposed the FS-X.

There was, however, also a sizable advantage in moving forward speedily, in the last weeks of December, and notifying Congress. Timing was everything. If Armacost moved to inform Congress at the right moment, while the Reagan administration was still intact, the players who created the FS-X deal would still be at their posts.

There was an even more practical reason for hitting Congress in December: recess. With the inauguration little more than six weeks away, Congress would surely take time off. Since the act provided a thirty-day period for review, and the legislators were about to take two weeks off, the small amount of time left for them to take up the FS-X after they returned was not worth fighting for. Congress would be forced to shrug and pass on the fighter.

Thus could Armacost railroad the FS-X through. There was nothing to stop it. Acting quickly also had the virtue of making moot the provision in the Defense Authorization Act that compelled the Pentagon to consult with Commerce. The lack of time would take its toll on both Bingaman's initiatives and the Arms Export Control Act, and Congress could not complain that the administration had failed to properly notify them. It would be a fait accompli.

Armacost did none of the above.

Instead of cutting the FS-X off before trouble could start, he opted to play the percentages, gambling that the DoD would be able to keep the FS-X from causing trouble in Congress, and he elected to wait.

The reason for taking the political high road appeared to some in Washington to be self-interest. Armacost topped the short list of likely successors to the legendary ambassador to Japan, Mike Mansfield, who would retire in

January 1989. By making peace with Congress, Armacost ensured that he would not be held to account for the FS-X by a vindictive Jesse Helms on the Foreign Relations Committee—now staffed by Kevin Kearns—should he face confirmation. If Helms took vengeance and put a courtesy "hold" on him over the FS-X, he could wind up behind a desk looking out over D Street in Foggy Bottom, as opposed to a desk with a view of the Hotel Okura in Tokyo.

Although two high-ranking Bush-Reagan officials believe Armacost chose to delay notifying Congress in order to assure his confirmation as ambassador, Armacost denies this. "There is no truth to the rumors," he wrote, but he did not explain *why* he did not notify Congress of the FS-X when the Reagan administration was still in power.

Whatever the truth, delayed notification had the profound effect of taking the FS-X out of the familiar hands that had guided it through the Reagan years and plopping it down in the lap of a new and uninstructed Bush administration. This would have not been an outsized problem for a simple arms deal. But nothing between the United States and Japan was simple, and crouching unforeseen in the distance was an angry Congress waiting to spring its trap.

Another force not easily reckoned with arose over the pending FS-X deal. During the Reagan years, there had evolved in Washington a loose association of ranking administration officials who looked on Japan as an unfair trader. Much like the revisionists—who were largely media types and academics—these administration insiders saw U.S. policy toward Japan undermining American industry. In their view, Japan's markets were unconscionably closed to U.S. products. They referred to themselves lightheartedly as the Black Ships Society, in recognition of Commodore Matthew Perry, who tried to open up a closed Japanese market 130 years earlier. The name neatly paralleled the Chrysanthemum Club. But fearful of being tagged Japan bashers, the group never formally adopted the name or used it much outside their inner circle.

Certainly one recognizable member of this Black Ships Society was Clyde Prestowitz, author of *Trading Places.* His boss, Lionel Olmer, the military man who retired to sell Motorola products in Japan, was also considered a member, if member is even the correct word. The group met casually and infrequently. The telephone and fax constituted their real tie. Among the people associated with the group was Joseph Massey of the U.S. Trade Representative's Office, who early on expressed concern over the FS-X deal. Another was John Richards, Deputy Assistant Secretary in the Commerce Department's Office of Industrial Resource Administration, who stood to take charge of the FS-X under the Defense Authorization Act. Deputy U.S. Trade Representative Michael Smith was included.

One of the members of this loose association who played a principal role in the FS-X deal was Maureen Smith, the Deputy Assistant Secretary for Japan at the Commerce Department's International Trade Administration. Smith first began following the FS-X in the Japanese press during the middle part of 1987. In fact, she first informed Clyde Prestowitz of the program. In the early 1980s, she had been one of Prestowitz's closest subordinates.

Smith said she had heard jokes about a Black Ships Society in the Reagan administration, but "to my knowledge, no such group existed." However, Smith was very open about the close working relationship among Reagan administration officials in attempting to reshape U.S.-Japan policy. "The group," she called them. "In the first year of the Reagan administration, five cabinet officers in succession went to Tokyo and told them that this trade balance"—edging toward a disreputable $57,766,631,255 in 1987—"was not going to stand." She gives credit to President Reagan. "He didn't go out and say get tough on Japan," she said. Reagan was, after all, a paragon of free and open trade. "But it could not have happened if he had not wanted it. Reagan worked by putting people in place who knew what to do. Lionel Olmer, for example, knew exactly what U.S. industry needed in telecommunications."

As the United States and Japan slogged out the contract negotiations for the FS-X into the fall of 1988, Smith began searching around for a copy of the agreement, the terms the Japanese press said had been reached between Secretary Carlucci and foreign minister Uno, and initialed as early as June, according to Glenn Rudd. She worked independently, she said, unaware that the Defense Authorization Act would soon empower Commerce. "I framed my inquiries in terms of the FS-X program's implications for U.S. competitiveness."

She continued: "Someone gave me the name of Karl Jackson," who was the Deputy Assistant Secretary for East Asian and Pacific Affairs in the Defense Department, her counterpart. "I telephoned him and told him I was in Commerce; I told him who I was; and I told him I wanted to see a copy of the MOU. I was plain as day, I said, 'Karl, I need a copy of the MOU.' "

Jackson seemed to be obliging. He would be happy to send it over, he told her. The problem was that it was locked up in a safe at that moment.

Smith continued: "I said, 'Well, OK, I don't need it this instant but get me a copy and courier it over to me."

Jackson had more problems, he said. The two people who knew the combination to the safe were not in. One was on a two-week vacation and the other was in the hospital.

A twenty-year veteran in government, Smith had a suggestion for Jackson. "Karl," she said, "suppose the Secretary of Defense called and told you he needed the MOU on his desk in five minutes. What would you do?"

Jackson replied that he was sorry, the information was classified.

The Pentagon's strategy was plain: they would stonewall. There was little Commerce could do, at least officially. On the other hand, Smith said, "there are a thousand ways to get a document. There are a thousand ways to get at somebody. If someone in Washington thinks they can stonewall a legitimate request, they're dead wrong."

The bureaucratic potshots fired by Jackson and Smith proved to be the opening volleys in a dirty little war fought across the Potomac between the civilian business suits at the Defense Department and the security wonks at the Commerce Department. The tensions between the two sides had been cranking up since the middle 1970s, when the military began giving away jobs and technologies—commercial considerations in which Commerce thought it should have a say—in order to win overseas military sales.

Maureen Smith was introduced to both Craig Richardson and Kevin Kearns through Clyde Prestowitz. She was one of the first people Richardson met after returning from Tokyo in December 1987. In turn, Smith arranged a larger briefing with Richardson for other members of "the group," to update them on what was actually taking place inside State and Defense on this $10 billion deal.

For the first time, those in the Reagan administration who worried about the implications of Japan's economic power for U.S. security began to see the FS-X as something more than just another program that licensed away U.S. technologies to Japan. This aroused suspicions. Co-development looked and sounded like a whole new level of cooperation, with serious economic ramifications. Just what was the Pentagon allowing General Dynamics to sell to Japan? Were they *teaching* them *how* to build a world-class fighter? The Commerce Department decided it had to know what was on the table in this revolutionary new program.

Neither Maureen Smith nor John Richards, who would later become the Commerce Department's liaison with the Pentagon, much considered the Defense Authorization Act. As Richards recalled: "I had never heard of the law, and I wasn't concerned about it." They were pushing this on their own, angry over what they were learning from Kearns and Richardson.

In October 1988, before the United States and Japan had finished negotiating the government-to-government contract, Richards telephoned the Pentagon to request a briefing. The flamboyant Tim Tyler, who had become the Pentagon's top internal spokesman on the FS-X program, was assigned to talk with Commerce. Just as he had with Congress, Tyler was not worried that Commerce would have any significant impact on the deal. He recalled thinking at the time, "Aw shucks, here's something else that's going to cause a delay with this thing [the FS-X]."

The DoD saw Richards's call as an upshot of the Defense Authorization

Act, and they responded for that reason. At the same time, however, the act was vague about what the role would be for Commerce. Defense would not take it on itself to set broad limits by embracing the new law. Rather, the goal was to contain Commerce, especially on the FS-X.

Still, Tyler arrived at Richards's office planning to be accommodating. He wanted to let Commerce know what a good deal this was. He even brought along six unsigned copies of the MOU to give out.

But Tyler suddenly had second thoughts. Standing in the outer offices, as he was about to go in and brief John Richards, it occurred to him that he didn't owe Commerce anything. Commerce was always trying to meddle in the DoD's affairs. "This was a done deal last May," he told himself. "We shouldn't have to go with a begging bowl to these guys." Handing over an unsigned MOU could only cause trouble. Commerce could begin raising questions about difficult and hard-won compromises that had already been settled. They could pick on anything.

Using a telephone in one of the carrels outside Richards's office, Tyler rang the Pentagon's lawyers, the General Counsel for International Affairs. Should he give Richards the MOU?

"Do not pass on those MOUs," Tyler recalled being told. His instructions were to brief Commerce; leave the briefing material if asked, and no more.

Once again, the Pentagon made a conscious decision to keep Commerce away from the FS-X deal. But this was only a delaying action. As Commerce grew more insistent, and the issue threatened to become openly contentious, Tyler finally provided Richards with an unsigned copy of the MOU. This was in mid-December, however, weeks after the actual documents had been signed in Tokyo.

When Richards finally realized that he had been given a mere draft MOU and that he had been "snookered" by Tyler, the skirmish escalated into general warfare. The Secretary of Commerce-designate himself would be called up, and the FS-X would be added to the portfolio of issues Robert A. Mosbacher would champion before the President, who also happened to be his best friend, George Herbert Walker Bush.

19

The Baker Gambit

"Many have spoken of the Pacific Century and the Pacific Rim as the world of the future. One thing I think is certain: The world's economic promise to the end of this century depends on how well the United States and its Pacific partners manage their affairs."
—Statement of Secretary of State-designate JAMES A. BAKER III

THOUGH SOME SORT of congressional showdown over the FS-X was possible, Kevin Kearns was not optimistic. Events were not conspiring in his favor. The Pentagon was calling his bluff. He didn't have the horses, and the men in uniform knew it. If anything, circumstances tilted toward quick Bush administration approval of the FS-X. On January 10, 1989, Reuters News Service reported that Noboru Takeshita, Japan's Prime Minister, would be the first head of state to visit with the new President after the inauguration on January 20. The likelihood was that Takeshita would get Bush's handshake on the fighter program and the battle would be over, the end of everything, for, surely, Oval Office support would weigh heavily against serious opposition on the Hill.

In early January 1989, Kearns stood outside the rooms of the Armed Services Committee talking with Ed McGaffigan in the marmoreal half-light of the gray-on-gray Russell Office Building. The sound of heels clicking on the polished floors and the low rumble of conversation filled the hall.

Kearns was looking for something to grab on to, some hope. "I said to Ed, 'I don't know the Senate that well. You've been up here for years. What can we get out of the FS-X?"

"He said, 'Well, maybe the best we can get out of it is that they won't do it again. Maybe we can get a letter, either an individual or joint letter from my boss [Democrat, Bingaman] and your boss [Republican, Helms] and one or two others that says we're laying down a marker now. Don't do this to us again. Don't negotiate it in this way. Don't cut out the Commerce Department, etc., etc.' " Kearns laughed sardonically. "He offered me several lists of don'ts." There was no humor in this, however. "This came as a rather severe disappointment."

Back in the offices of the Foreign Relations Committee in the gleaming Hart Office Building, Kearns asked for Bill Triplett's prognosis. Kearns said, "I can't take the FS-X any farther. I can't set the world on fire with it. It's a mistake. It's a bad deal for the United States, but I've been working on this thing up here on the Hill for five or six months now. I think we're going to lose this one. I can't figure out anything else to do."

Triplett agreed.

Kearns said, "What advice do you have? Is there something that we should have done that we didn't? Some avenue of attack that we didn't see?"

"No, I think you're right. I think we'll have to live to fight the next battle," Triplett replied.

The end was in sight, Kearns realized. "I had invested almost three years of my life at that point trying to make sense out of this FS-X thing," Kearns said. "I thought about it and thought about it, and I said I have to give this one more try. It's just too important to let go by without any real public debate."

At one time, Kearns appeared to have three options for prying the deal apart—the new defense act, the export control laws, and congressional rumbling. None now seemed to amount to much.

There was, however, one possible way to straight-arm the new administration. Kearns called it "the Baker vehicle." That had possibilities, Kearns decided. He had to get Triplett to go along. The problem was that Triplett had gone to Paris for meetings on another issue and he would not return until January 18, 1989.

Said Kearns, "This all came to me after Triplett left, when the administration notified the Foreign Relations Committee that it needed an early confirmation of the new Secretary of State. I remember thinking during that time that maybe here's an avenue, the Baker hearing."

On January 17, 1989, there would be a confirmation hearing for the Secretary of State-designate, James A. Baker III. The nominee would be questioned by the Foreign Relations Committee, where Triplett's boss, Jesse Helms, led the Republican minority and where he derived much of his power over U.S. overseas policy.

The Reagan administration got a strong flavor of that authority frequently over its eight years in power. Secretary of State George Shultz, in particular, knew Senator Helms's special kind of wrath. The senior senator from North Carolina pelted incessantly at Shultz with the use of a senatorial courtesy known as a "hold." The device gives individual senators the right to "hold" a presidential appointee from nomination, keep him in a bureaucratic limbo until the senator satisfied his personal objections. "Helms used it constantly," as Hedrick Smith noted in his book *The Power Game*. In June 1985, twenty-nine Shultz appointees were held hostage by Helms while he tried to impose his own people on the department.

This was something any secretary up for nomination would have to consider as he sat before the Foreign Relations Committee. The difficulty would be getting Helms to think enough of the FS-X in order to raise it as a question. There was also the sensitive matter of what response Baker might give. If he knew about the FS-X, he might oppose it, and Helms wasn't going to hang the Secretary of State on one little issue. On the other hand, there did not seem to be much else Kearns could do to stop the program. Time was running out. Just a week earlier, on January 10, the agreement between General Dynamics and Mitsubishi Heavy Industries was signed. The contractual process was now complete. There would be no more chances after this.

It was the final hour for James A. Baker III. Two full days of confirmation hearings before the Senate Foreign Relations Committee were coming to an end for the Secretary of State-designate. His was the first hearing for a Bush administration cabinet appointee, called ahead of schedule, even before the new President was inaugurated. Indeed, the formal nomination papers had yet to reach the committee. As Baker said the day before, arching for some leavening humor to launch his opening statement: "I think every administration aspires to hit the ground running instead of just hitting the ground."

It could be said at this late hour that the hearings had gone well for Baker —no fireworks, no faux pas, no headlines. He had managed to neatly lay out the administration's international game plan in a way which few could argue with, a fair test of statesmanship by itself. In fact, there was nary a clash, nary a question that shook the calm, almost convivial atmosphere. Baker told Congress that neither he nor the administration was seeking confrontation. His tenure, he promised, although not in so many words, would not be a reenactment of the Reagan years, a time of stonewalling and deception. His predecessor, George Shultz, had placed the blame for U.S. foreign policy failures on a "chaotic Congress."

Baker came before Congress as the peacemaker.

Mary McGrory, the Washington *Post*'s liberal conscience, described Baker in performance at the proceedings as the "handsome, hard-nosed, affable . . . [former] star of the Reagan team." Secretary of Treasury from February 1985 to August 1988, Baker served Reagan as chief of staff before that. These hearings were going so smoothly, McGrory compared them to a "Republican campaign event that [Baker] had planned himself."

Democrat Claiborne Pell, chairman of the committee, was hard put to find differences with the Republican appointee. "It is interesting to note," he said through the slosh of his Rhode Island accent, "there are now fewer partisan differences in the area of foreign policy than I can recall in quite a while." This was truly a moment of congressional ecumenism.

For his part, Baker showed that he had grasped the assessment others held of him. He had been able to weave that into a deft self-analysis. "Some have described my philosophy as pragmatic," he told the committee. "I would like to say that labels can be misleading. I am actually a Texas Republican, all of whom are conservative. I will admit to pragmatism, however, if by that you mean being realistic about the world and appreciating the importance of getting things done."

Even the large hearing room-cum-auditorium where Baker sat before the Senate panel partook of the salutary atmosphere. Room SH-216 of the spectacularly modern Hart Office Building was an architectural extravaganza of political management, the physical embodiment of modern public policymaking. The inconspicuous marquee in the hall outside said simply "Central Hearing Facility," but SH-216 was as much a stage set, a made-for-TV location, as it was a court of opinion.

You entered in three stages. A large U-shaped foyer opened onto a wide skylit hall—a gangway, really—and then another foyer with closet-sized workspace and finally the auditorium-sized hearing room, with its rows of dark blue modern metal stacking chairs for the spectators. It was theater as well as stage. At the front of the hearing room, a magisterial white marble wall, the size of a Diamond Vision scoreboard, loomed above all in audience. This slab made for a dramatic backdrop, shot through with dark green veins and emblazoned with an overdrawn seal of the Senate: a bald eagle streaming a golden banner between beak and talon that read *E Pluribus Unum.*

Much of the apparent bonhomie taking place between the committee and the appointee was aimed at the ranking minority member of the panel, the conservative senior senator from the state of North Carolina, Jesse A. Helms. Part demagogue, always an opportunist, the senator could be a political nettle, but Baker had to assuage him. He needed Helms. At the very least, he needed him to mind his own parochial business and not impose his pet fetishes upon international affairs. That was no small thing to hope for. Baker had made a courtesy phone call to Helms, an act above and beyond the call of duty, to say that while the two would not agree all the time, he looked forward to a good working relationship. Luckily for him, Helms bore an olive branch, going out of his way in the most chivalrous manner of a southern gentleman to exude: "Mr. Chairman, I thank you [for the introduction] and I join you of course in welcoming Mrs. Baker, a lady whom I admire very much, and also their son Jamie is seated right behind Mrs. Baker. We welcome him too. I know that you are proud of your husband and your dad." Honor a man's family and you honor the man.

He offered Baker a forecast, his own prognostication: "Mr. Chairman, Herman Talmadge [a footnote-sized senator from the 1950s, whose career sank on his financial improprieties] used to say that the State Department had a South American desk and an African desk and a European desk and what it needed was an American desk. I have a hunch, Mr. Secretary, that your desk is going to be an American desk."

Helms and the State Department were old enemies. In his righteous far right fervor during the Reagan administration, Helms had declared Baker's predecessor as Secretary of State, George Shultz, a dupe. Helms could be even more obdurate if the individual in question had a connection with former National Security Adviser Henry Kissinger. Kissinger was despised by the senator for his aspirations for détente with the Soviets. With a raft of ambassadorial appointments ahead of him, Baker wanted Helms in his camp.

As the hours of the confirmation hearing rolled to the end of day two, it was clear that each man had been seeking the other's wavelength, a very favorable sign for Baker. He and Helms could use each other. But while Baker had managed to keep Helms affable, that did not mean he would be able to keep Helms under control. The senator was a rogue. Helms could not resist the role of provocateur, which was his special genius: he liked to toss Molotov cocktails.

For Baker, things had gone well so far, and Kevin Kearns desperately needed to change that.

Jesse Helms stood in the hallway just inside the tall redwood doors that led to the hearing room and the Secretary of State-designate. Helms lit a cigarette, and Kevin Kearns watched him puff contemplatively, large, loose-limbed. The senator appeared worn from the two-day grind of testimony.

There was a theory on Helms's staff that it was better to let some questions wait until the nominee had been ground down by hours and days of grueling testimony. For that reason, they would often save their toughest questions for last, when a nominee's guard would most likely be down. On the other hand, if you asked a question early, you were more likely to get better press. Kearns had missed that opportunity. Now it was a matter of whether his question about the FS-X would be seen as something important enough to spend time on in the waning minutes of the nomination hearing. Triplett counseled asking questions late. It seemed to him that nominees would agree to almost anything just to get the process over with.

Kearns was plainly worried. Helms's whole staff had submitted their own agendas for the senator's attention, he knew; he figured Helms had a broad-ranging agenda. Worse, the FS-X wasn't actually an issue, so there was a question of which one of Helms's manifold constituencies he could play to. What sort of mileage could Helms get out of it?

Kearns wanted Helms to ask the question in such a way that it would force Baker to look into the FS-X plans before the new administration simply signed off on the deal, as was about to happen. For days he had been crafting the questions which he now held before him on two sheets of paper.

Bound by committee protocol, Kearns was almost completely dependent on one person, Helms's deputy staff director, Darryl D. Nirenberg, the man who managed the hearings for Helms's staff. Nirenberg made the legislative paper move on Helms's committee, though he was not a foreign relations player, as might be expected. Nirenberg's committee background was in agri-culture, and he had followed Helms into foreign relations after the Republi-cans lost the Senate in 1986.

What Nirenberg brought to the staff, in place of international expertise, were his skills in administration. He thought of himself as a packager, a technician who knew what to do when his boss's work got stalled in the gearboxes of Washington's power train.

Nirenberg was an attorney, a man of medium height, in his middle thirties. His hair was black, almost matte black, and his skin was very white. A pleasant man, his office was decorated with GOP coffee mugs shaped like elephants, Bubba baseball caps, and a framed Doug Marlette political cartoon of his boss, tooting along in the kiddie seat of a giant automobile representing the Foreign Relations Committee. "Vroom! Vroom! Beep! Beep!" says the sena-tor from North Carolina in the caption.

Nirenberg kept the proceedings on track by setting priorities. He paid special attention to the questions the staff generated for him and the commit-tee. That made Nirenberg one of the prime keepers of the gate. He was the man you had to go through, the one you had to sell, if you wanted to get an issue before the Secretary of State-designate on this day.

And Nirenberg was a stickler about questions. A question was a tool, he would say, the jimmy on another man's opinions, something to pry open the canned remarks. With Baker out front, this was big-game season, a chance to draw out a future Secretary of State on policy. The answers to the secrets of the universe all depended on the right question.

Kearns turned from Helms to Nirenberg. Ahead of Kearns stood a dozen staffers, people with more seniority and more clout on the committee. As Triplett recalled: "Baker only testifies once a year, and all these staff guys, including me, are all jumping up and down like terriers trying to get Helms's attention—my question, my question . . ." Most had issues that would be-come an important part of their congressional agenda for the next year, or longer—the Contras, El Salvador. Kearns was low man on the committee totem pole, an intern, with only months to go before his fellowship ran out.

Kearns had held out hope until now, but in a matter of minutes the final gavel would nail down the end of the hearings. Helms was taking his last puff before beginning his final round of questions. If Kearns missed this opportunity, everything he had worked for these last two and a half years would be lost. Congress would embark on its traditional honeymoon with the incoming President, and auld lang syne would reign for a hundred days. That would be enough time for the Defense Department to close the FS-X deal.

Already, Senator Terry Sanford, the mild-mannered liberal Democrat who lived in the shadow of his North Carolina Republican counterpart, had made plain he was supporting Baker as the nominee. Committee chairman Pell nearly let slip his own endorsement, telling Sanford, "I am almost in the same position." The end of the hearings was now clearly in sight.

Kearns tried one last time to call on Bill Triplett, who had returned from Paris for the hearings. In the hubbub of the confirmation, he was not to be found. Kearns finally caught up to him by telephone in his cluttered fifth-floor office, where he had retired for a little peace and quiet. "We've got to get Helms to ask the question," Kearns told him. "We're going to miss the train."

Triplett glanced at his watch, it was after three in the afternoon. The hearing would surely not last more than an hour. "Nirenberg's about to go out into the hearing room," Kearns said, "you've got to talk to him."

Nirenberg took the call. "Darryl," Triplett began, "Kevin will burst a blood vessel if the senator doesn't ask Baker about the FS-X."

Nirenberg paused. He thought they had already asked the FS-X question. No, Triplett said. Nirenberg could see that Kearns was about to begin jumping up and down. "Darryl," Triplett said, "do the deed."

Nirenberg turned to Kearns, who showed him his question. Nirenberg was shocked. He looked over the two typed sheets of paper and shook his head. "Kevin, we only have time for one question," Nirenberg said. "The senator gets fifteen minutes after Biden, and that's it." Now, in a race against the clock and the long-winded junior senator from Delaware, Nirenberg and Kearns whittled away at Kearns's FS-X question. They did their work with a felt-tip marker, ripping the text to shreds, paring the question to what Nirenberg thought was its essence. Kearns kept one eye on the strokes of Nirenberg's pen and the other on the strokes of the clock.

Each senator had fifteen minutes to ask their questions. In the hearing room, Senator Joseph Biden was on his last question, attempting to corner Baker on the issue of Star Wars, the Reagan missile defense plan. By this point, Biden's questioning had grown so chummy and lackadaisical that he didn't seem to care if he got his answer. He made a point about his objections to the Star Wars plan and beat a hasty retreat, ending with a joke and not with the jugular. "That," Biden declared mildly, "is the appropriate role [for the United States on Star Wars], in my view. But I can see the chairman is about to hit my knuckles with his hammer, so I am going to stop."

Nirenberg and Kearns entered into the quiet of the hearing room just as Biden was wrapping up. Suddenly the both of them were in the glare of the dazzling white TV lights. Baker sat swimming and composed like a man afloat in the midst of it all. Nirenberg leaned right over Helms's shoulder as soon as he walked in and dropped Kearns's question on the bench before him. Kearns sat back of the senator, among the staffers privileged to have their questions under examination.

"Mr. Secretary," Helms began, reading and ad-libbing the words Kearns and Nirenberg had prepared, "last week, General Dynamics and a Japanese company, Mitsubishi Heavy Industries, signed a little old agreement to produce in Japan a modified F-16 fighter aircraft, which the Japanese call FS-X. The program is a new type of cooperative venture between allies and it is supposed to be a model for the future and all that.

"Nevertheless, I wonder if I might encourage you to delay sending the notification up here to the Congress for, say, a couple of months, until your team—your team—is in place and you have had a full opportunity to review this proposed program and in order that you would be able to enthusiastically or otherwise recommend it . . .

"Would you consider that?"

Baker had paid close attention to Helms as he spoke. His response was guarded, politic. "I'd be glad to consider that, Senator," he replied amiably, adding a canned caveat applicable to most instances where unexpected issues arose: "Of course, it would be subject to the President's determination."

That was it, all Baker said. Baker had not even heard of the FS-X. He hadn't been briefed. It probably never appeared in the briefing books stacked nearby.

Kearns recalls, "The thing that I remember most was that Baker had this uncanny knack of being able to read and speak at the same time. He's answering a question but he's also flipping pages in his briefing book and then reading. And I remember thinking I could never do that. It was clear he'd read the briefing books thoroughly, because throughout the hearings he would flip to sections and, while he was talking, scan. When Helms asked the FS-X question, Baker's hands didn't go to the book. He had been paying intense attention because he knew the answer wasn't in the book. And he understood he was getting this request from Helms." Kearns was seeing two and a half years of effort suddenly gel before his eyes.

Helms spoke again. "Of course," he allowed, he didn't mind if Baker talked it over with Bush, that was the whole idea of asking. Then he reminded Baker that he took the issue seriously. Helms said, "I think you would be well advised to go a little bit slow and make sure you know what you were doing."

Kearns was stunned. The entire pithy exchange was a mere 185 words. So minor a moment was it that no one in the public media managed to record it. It did not make the evening sound bite announcing Baker's bravura performance before the committee. The New York *Times* did not bother to include the comment to Helms among selections of transcript it published the next day. The Washington *Post* overlooked it too, as did every other major newspaper in the United States.

Oddly, the FS-X did not pop up in the hearings for Secretary of Commerce-designate Robert A. Mosbacher, who had been gearing up for questions about the program for weeks. Indeed, he and his staff would soon lead the way in the inquiry into the deal. But during his confirmation hearings, the opportunity to comment on the deal did not arise.

Some days later, however, in post-hearing questions submitted by Senator Danforth, Mosbacher signaled that he was focused on the FS-X and would pursue the matter under the Defense Authorization Act. "I fully support the intent" of the law. "I plan to take this up with Secretary-designate Tower as soon as possible . . . No single agency alone has the breadth of expertise or authority to determine the importance of these technologies to our industrial base."

The next day, when Tower faced the Armed Services Committee, Senator Bingaman raised the FS-X issue. The handsome young senator minced no words. "Senator Tower," he began, "last week the General Dynamics Corporation signed a licensing agreement where it essentially became a subcontractor to Mitsubishi, to engage in the co-development of the new aircraft fighter, the FS-X, and in doing so to transfer to the Japanese the technology that we have in the F-16." The fighter he referred to was so advanced that the first production model of the F-16 C/D Block 40 rolled off the assembly lines less than a month before, in December 1988.

"Are you familiar with the case?" Bingaman asked.

Tower's hair, slicked straight back from his round face, glistened like streams of West Texas crude in the video lights. Just the day before, Tower had made a courtesy call on Bingaman at his office in the Hart Office Building. The young senator had first served on the Armed Services Committee when Tower was its chairman. This was a chance for the Secretary-designate to address Bingaman's concerns out of the glare of TV cameras and senatorial scrutiny.

Tower reminded Bingaman of the talk. "Senator, you and I discussed this yesterday, and I must admit that my first enlightenment on this subject was my discussion with you yesterday." Bingaman, obviously, did not plan to let up on this one.

Tower acknowledged Bingaman's gambit. "It is a matter of more than passing importance, in my view," he said, "and one that I promise you I will give my attention to, from the standpoint of what the national security implications are."

Now Tower took the opportunity to campaign for himself with the committee. "As a resident of a state [Texas], and indeed a city [Wichita Falls, near Austin], that is in the high-tech business, I am concerned about technology transfer . . ." But he was noncommittal. "I do thank you for bringing it to my attention. I am sorry that I cannot give you an enlightening answer on it right now. But it is a matter that, based on my conversation with you, I would tend to have some apprehensions about."

Two days after that, on January 27, 1988, when U.S. Trade Representative–designate Carla Hills came before the Senate's Commerce Committee, Senator Danforth said he was worried about the trade implications of Pentagon policy. "What do you think specifically of the FS-X agreement . . . ?"

Hills did not fully grasp the problem. She replied that she thought that "the decision did not go through the ordinary interagency process." She then pledged, if confirmed, "to ensure that we do have a well-coordinated trade policy where we do get the input from those agencies that have expertise in a variety of areas across government."

Finally, the January 30, 1989, issue of *Newsweek*, in a side bar crouched in the lower right-hand corner of page 34, there was a brief article entitled "A 'Little Old Agreement' on the F-16," and it began: "Get ready for the Bush administration's first foreign policy controversy."

20

A Shot Across the Bow

"We were looking aggressively for articles that challenged the sanctity of U.S.-Japan trade relations."
—David Ignatius, editor, Outlook, Washington *Post*

SUNDAY, JANUARY 29, 1989, was a gray but warm winter day in Washington. This was "Death in Venice" weather, a tubercular season that bred new and spectacular genetic permutations of the flu. Everyone was sick, hacking at their colds on the Metro, sniffling their way through the Redskins games.

Readers opening their Sunday morning papers who turned to the Washington *Post*'s Outlook section saw a disheartening headline in the corner of page 1: "Giving Japan a Handout: Why Fork Over $7 Billion in Aircraft Technology?"

The article's author, Clyde V. Prestowitz, began: "First it was TV sets, then VCRs, then semiconductors. Now, unless Congress and the administration act quickly, the United States will shortly give Japan a big boost toward its long-sought goal: leadership in aircraft manufacture, one of the last areas of American high-technology dominance."

With the Toshiba controversy still reverberating in the public mind, word of the dangerous new deal arrived like news of the Soviet Sputnik in 1957, unexpected and startling evidence that America's technological supremacy was under attack. How could this happen? The deal, Prestowitz wrote, "will transfer technology developed at great expense to U.S. taxpayers at very low cost to a country whose primary interest is not defense but catching up with America in aircraft and other high technology."

Deputy Outlook editor Jodie Allen had not heard of the FS-X until she edited Prestowitz's article, but she regarded the news as explosive. "Clyde really moved the dial for a lot of people on trade issues," she recalled. Prestowitz was saying things few people in Washington dared to say about trade with Japan. According to the *Post*'s Allen, the article generated strong attention and a powerful sense of urgency around the capital.

Timing was crucial. In just four days, Prime Minister Takeshita (who had replaced Nakasone in November 1987) would be visiting Washington, and that would surely have an impact on the FS-X deal, which the two leaders were certain to discuss.

According to a *Wall Street Journal* article that appeared two days after the Prestowitz piece in the *Post*, the Japanese government was under intense pressure at home to conclude the FS-X agreement during the Prime Minister's stay. "The Japanese faced a deadline of their own, on March 31, 1989," the *Journal* concluded. If they missed their deadline the defense agency "would have a difficult time retrieving the $80 million of FS-X earmarked money . . ." That could doom the project and provide the JDA with a way out of an accord it never wanted.

The article continued: "Japanese opposition parties, no fans of the FS-X program, will insist on more details of the unprecedented collaboration with the U.S., a demand that could put considerable political pressure on the ruling Liberal Democratic Party.

"As a result, Japanese Prime Minister Noboru Takeshita, during his scheduled visit to Washington later this week, may try to nudge President Bush to act quickly to formally notify Congress of the deal."

As Kevin Kearns discovered in the first days after the Baker hearings ended on January 18, the printed word is a powerful tool of influence. "The way this town works," Kearns said, "if a national news magazine said there's a controversy on the FS-X, you would clip it and send it around with a dear-colleague letter. An article like that validates what you're doing."

Videotape did not allow for niche-marketing a policy. "Even though Peter Jennings covered the FS-X during his broadcast one night [January 27, 1988], it was no use to us. TV is an evanescent medium. If a story is sustained day after day, TV has an impact. When it's thirty seconds of talking heads, it just doesn't have the same impact as something in print. You can't use it. You can't show it. You can't fax it around the Hill, and that's what counts."

There was also a lesson in geometry for Kearns, the way opinion builds in Washington. He recalls, "The ratios were one-two-four-twelve. I had one guy, Helms, ask a question to Baker." January 18, 1989. "That makes two. Then I had four senators on a letter I drafted to the GAO asking them to investigate the FS-X from the tech transfer point of view." That was January

30, 1989. The letter to which Kearns refers, to the Comptroller General at the GAO, Charles Bowsher, pointed out that the FS-X had cost taxpayers over "$5 billion"—money spent to produce the technical package the United States was licensing to Japan for a mere $500,000 per plane.

The Kearns geometry expanded to twelve senators co-signing a letter to President Bush. "Prestowitz's article did that." Bingaman and Helms topped the list of signatures on the two-page missive. Other signers were Danforth and Byrd, both long involved with the deal. Albert Gore, Jr., then the junior senator from Tennessee, signed midway on the list, in the sixth slot.

Senator Alan Dixon, another of the twelve co-signers, was about to throw himself full force into the debate. In a separate letter to Senator Bingaman that same day, he made a personal appeal: "Certainly, Jeff, if you decide to hold hearings on the FS-X, I will support you in any way I can."

There was another factor that drove Kearns to push for the senatorial letter to President Bush. In a matter of hours, Japanese Prime Minister Noboru Takeshita would be visiting the President. As Kearns recalls: "Takeshita was coming on Thursday or Friday night to meet with the President. We knew from people inside the government that the administration was going to try and seal the deal as a gift from Bush to Takeshita. We had to find a way to stop that."

The senatorial letter to the President was designed to kill that initiative. It put the President on notice that Congress was watching: "We realize that during the upcoming visit of Prime Minister Takeshita," the twelve senators wrote, "there will be intense pressure from the Japanese, and perhaps from those within DoD and State who negotiated the FS-X deal, to give the full commitment of the President to the program."

Endorsing the FS-X during the Takeshita visit would make a neat end run around any obstacles Kearns might have thrown in the path of the Chrysan-themum Club during the Baker hearings. "I had some people who I knew inside the bureaucracy scout around," Kearns said. "I told them to get hold of the briefing book that is being submitted to the White House by State, be-cause I'm certain there will be a gift in there to Takeshita, and it's going to be the FS-X."

What turned up in the talking points and briefing papers that were being prepared by the State Department was a copy of the President's proposed farewell remarks to the Japanese Prime Minister. Such comments are often written in advance of visits. To the horror of Kearns and his confederates, the language of the remarks constituted a virtual endorsement of the deal. The well-polished speech contained this paragraph:

"We noted with satisfaction the agreement on the co-development of a new fighter aircraft for the Japanese Air Self-Defense Force. This agreement will strengthen Japan's ability to defend itself and at the same time result in significant participation by U.S. industry and flowback to the United States of the latest technology. This agreement, the first military co-development program between the world's two most technologically advanced nations, should serve as a prototype for even closer collaboration between the United States and Japan."

Copies of the speech with the alarming paragraph were hastily faxed all over official Washington. If Bush were allowed to utter those words to Takeshita on February 3, it would represent the President's personal commitment to the program. That would surely doom serious opposition. A President typically has a hundred-day holiday with Congress and with the media— his honeymoon, as it is known—when his initiatives carry great power. With a presidential endorsement, the Republicans would pull together and the FS-X would succumb in a minor partisan debate, a turf war between Commerce and the DoD. The deal between the United States and Japan would be done, finally.

Clearly worried, Kearns sought out the help of Ed McGaffigan, Senator Bingaman's lead staffer on the FS-X. Just weeks before, McGaffigan was ready to give up on the FS-X. "Maybe our bosses would write a letter to the President," he told Kearns. That was the most they could hope for.

As it turned out, Kearns not only got the letter from McGaffigan's boss; he also had a chance to stop the deal, assuming the President did not accidentally hand it over to Takeshita. Now that the President was warned formally and in writing, McGaffigan urged Bingaman to invest still more political capital by intervening personally.

On the same day that the letter from the twelve senators arrived on Bush's desk, Senator Bingaman placed a telephone call to a friend, the new President's National Security Adviser, Brent Scowcroft. The two men knew each other from programs they had participated in at the Center for Strategic and International Studies, a leading Washington think tank specializing in security matters.

Bingaman adopted a cautionary tone with Scowcroft, who was the President's most trusted adviser. He warned Scowcroft that the FS-X was about to blow up in the face of the new administration. This was not a good deal, Bingaman said. He blamed the Pentagon's failure to consider the economic impact of the FS-X on the nation's industrial base. He warned that the Japanese would try to "railroad" the President into an agreement during the Prime Minister's stay. He urged that there was still time to make a "deliberate decision" on the deal.

Scowcroft said he had not heard of the FS-X until now. Though he was grateful for the news, he did not say that he would bring the matter up with the President. No commitments. But he was grateful for the warning shot. He thanked Bingaman.

At the State Department, Assistant Secretary for Intelligence and Research, Morton I. Abramowitz, wanted to know what the implications would be if the FS-X came under review by the new administration. What would be the reaction in Japan? Abramowitz wanted the new Secretary of State, James Baker, to know that there were differing perspectives on the matter, beyond what the Bureau of East Asian and Pacific Affairs was broadcasting. "There were people telling the Secretary that he had to sign off on the FS-X deal, period, or U.S.-Japan relations would fail," Abramowitz said. "I didn't feel that way."

Abramowitz ordered a memo prepared evaluating the Japanese response to a possible FS-X delay. He gave the job to a young man who had long contact with the deal and had spent three months at the Mutual Defense Assistance Office at the U.S. Embassy in Tokyo. This was none other than the peripatetic Presidential Management Intern, Craig Richardson, protégé of Kevin Kearns.

Richardson was at home nursing the flu when Abramowitz telephoned with the assignment. Even though Richardson felt ill, he also felt exceedingly fortunate. The timing of the Abramowitz call could not have been better, with the Takeshita visit just hours away. Now *he* was being asked to evaluate whether the Japanese would accept a delay! This was inviting the fox in to decorate the chicken coop. Richardson arrived at the office the next morning memo in hand.

Abramowitz had not told Richardson who had requested the analysis or where it was going, but Richardson took the liberty to craft the memo in his own way. "I assumed I was writing the memo for Baker," Richardson said. "I drafted it to the Secretary from Mort Abramowitz. My name went on the draft line."

His aim, Richardson said, was to delay the FS-X deal in the hope that a review by Congress or by the administration might kill it. Certainly it would postpone any commitment the President might make to Takeshita. "I will not shy away from the fact that this was not an intelligence piece." He explained: "There is a strong ethic in the intelligence bureau of not getting into policy, of presenting neutrally the info that comes in and analyzing it neutrally. I was not doing that. I was not being objective. I was politically driven. I was not being neutral."

Typically, memos from Intelligence and Research are not vetted by the Bureau of East Asian and Pacific Affairs, as are other memos. That is standard operating procedure. Richardson clearly thought this was his chance to appeal directly to the Secretary.

"I wanted to kill the deal, and I think I was right in doing so. I will not claim neutrality, however. I really wanted to stop the deal. So I wrote a two-page memo, basically saying, 'Look, the Japanese are acquainted with our foreign military sales system. They know there are delays. They had delays of their own. They can hardly complain.'

"Finally, I wrote that there are some real problems that we need to work out or we risk a greater conflagration, and so on . . . Then, as was the style of Mort, who liked memos with this gimmick, the last paragraph was the bottom line. I said, 'The Japanese will accept a three- to six-month delay without it seriously damaging our relationship.'"

Abramowitz does not dispute what happened next, although he said his recollections were vague. He said he discussed the memo with Richardson and hurriedly signed off on it, setting it aside on his desk, at which point he left to attend to another matter.

At that point, according to Richardson, a close friend of his in Abramowitz's office saw the memo on the desk with the signature on it and serendipitously placed it into the system to be circulated *directly* to the Secretary of State.

While memos from Intelligence and Research normally are not vetted because they are intended as objective and neutral appraisals, there are exceptions. A memo can be reviewed by the Asia bureau, which is what Abramowitz said he intended for Richardson's memo. In fact, Abramowitz had intended for Michael Armacost, the man in charge of notifying Congress on behalf of the State Department about the FS-X, to have a look at the memo before going any further and advising the Secretary. Instead, the memo went straight from Craig Richardson's typewriter to Secretary Baker's in-box.

Richardson flatly denies having rigged the events leading to Baker's special delivery. "I did not—I mean to tell you the truth, full disclosure. I know it looks bad. One of my dearest friends [in the office] looked at it, saw that Mort had signed off on it, and put it in the system. I had nothing to do with it. Honest to God."

Abramowitz said that he was quickly apprised of the problem and immediately notified his counterpart in the Bureau of East Asian and Pacific Affairs, Gaston Sigur, who was furious. "It caused a lot of heartache," Abramowitz said of the memo. "But nevertheless . . . and maybe in retrospect one could argue it wasn't worth it. I don't know."

Sigur and Armacost were the front-runners for the ambassadorship to Japan. Much of the credit for adjusting the Reagan administration's focus in its Pacific policy away from China and toward Japan was owed to Sigur. In that sense, he had raised Japan's profile immensely in Washington.

Sigur was a man much in the Mansfield-Reischauer mold, a charter member of the Chrysanthemum Club. He often warned that if Japan was pushed too hard on issues of trade, the United States risked driving it into the Communist camp. "There are some who would argue that trade is all that counts in our relations with Japan," he said. "I don't subscribe to that, and the Reagan administration did not subscribe to that. In our view we had a very broad and deep relationship with Japan. The world was evolving and so forth, the U.S.-Japan relationship was going to become more and more important, because of Japan's great economic power. This was a relationship that had to be nurtured."

In the days after Baker made his commitment to Helms during the confirmation hearings, Gaston Sigur was assigned to prepare a report on the FS-X for the Secretary. "Baker became very much interested in this," Sigur said.

As Assistant Secretary for East Asian and Pacific Affairs, Sigur's charge was Japan. A memo such as the one written by Richardson should have come from his office. The matter of judging how Japan would react to a postponement of the program was for Sigur to decide, not Abramowitz and certainly not his Presidential Management Intern, Craig Richardson.

When Sigur arrived in Baker's office to brief him about the FS-X and other Pacific Rim issues, he found that the Secretary had seen the Richardson memo and had already spoken to the President about it. Baker had ordered an interagency review to begin. No decision had been made on whether there would be a postponement, but a three- to six-month delay was to be considered.

"I knew nothing about it," Sigur said of the Richardson memo. "I was asked neither to agree nor to disagree about what was in that memo. I didn't like it. I'll put it that way."

This posed a serious problem for Sigur. "My own view was that the agreement had been negotiated, signed; all that had to be done was simply to look at it for a couple of weeks and then say, well, it was done under the previous administration and we abide by that decision. And that's it."

On Tuesday, January 31, Sigur held a meeting at the State Department in Room 6210. Specialists from the Commerce Department, Energy, Defense, Treasury, the National Security Council, the U.S. Trade Representative, and the Office of Science and Technology Policy, which is the President's science adviser, attended. Sigur announced a new policy directive, placing the Policy Coordinating Committee of the NSC in charge of the FS-X review. He warned of the March 31 deadline set by the Japanese budgeting process. If that was missed the deal could fall through.

Two days later, on Thursday, February 2, 1989, the day before Takeshita was to meet with the President, Sigur called a second meeting at the State Department. Now he was clearly worried about time eroding the deal. With the same departments and agencies present at this second meeting, Sigur argued for a judicious *and* expeditious review. Then he declared his unequivocal position: The State Department, he said, would support the current agreement as it stood.

Eugene K. Lawson, the Deputy Under Secretary for International Affairs in the Labor Department, told Sigur he was worried about the technology and had doubts about the agreement. A career bureaucrat, Lawson had once worked in the Commerce Department as a Deputy Assistant Secretary for East Asia and the Pacific. He knew Japan and had dealt with Japanese negotiators. Handsome, with the relaxed confidence of the privileged, he hammered at the problems in the deal like a man defending his homestead. He told Sigur that the MOU went way beyond anything that the government agencies had been told about the technology that was to be given to the Japanese.

Lawson had been well briefed by the aerospace industry representatives on the technology. They told him that a lot of the technology used to build this fighter plane could also be readily transferred to commercial aviation. "My bottom view was that I didn't want to be flying to Japan in a Japanese-built airplane," he said.

Lawson was backed in his presentation by the Energy Department. The technologies the United States might get back from Japan were old news in the United States, they argued. What was there to be gained from the deal?

Central Intelligence Agency reports showed there had been no technological breakthroughs in Japan that the United States needed. Lawson, who saw the report, thought it had been "well researched and had the ring of truth." The CIA said there were loopholes in the contract that might allow Japan not to perform as the United States anticipated. The agency's major concern was that the United States was giving away technology in a prime export industry to one of the nation's toughest competitors. Most important, the CIA disagreed with Secretary Carlucci's presumption that the F-16 was all weapon and no plowshare. The CIA report concluded that the technology transfer *would help* Japan's commercial aviation prospects.

The Commerce Department did not believe that catching up to the United States in aviation would be a simple matter for Japan. The man directly responsible for America's international trade in 1989, Under Secretary of Commerce J. Michael Farren, viewed Japanese ambitions against the model of Europe's headlong race with Airbus. As he recalled, "We had done extensive studies into Europe's subsidies. For them to catch up with the huge U.S. lead, they would have to spend $15 to $20 billion." This was by any measure a staggering investment, commensurate only with national defense or the overriding importance of becoming a player in this key industry.

Farren believed that the only reason American companies such as McDonnell Douglas and Boeing had survived in the commercial airline business was because they had already made that massive investment, having sunk their $20 billion in capital slowly over the forty years since the end of World War

II. Thus, the big "systems integrators," as the Boeings and McDonnell Douglases were called, were able to take their profits at the margins, the greatest part of their debt already behind them. "So long as all they had to do was to make incremental improvements in their planes, they could survive," Farren said. New iterations, upgrades on the same basic technology, were all that separated Boeing's first commercial success, the 707, and the great jumbos that dominated the skies.

But what would happen if the aircraft industry had to move to a new level of technology? What if the market demanded a new generation of aircraft? No more could McDonnell Douglas and Boeing live off old sunk capital. "We figured that when that happened, the United States and the Europeans would have to rethink their financial universe," Farren said, "and the Japanese, with their huge surplus of dollars, would be in a position to become pivotal players."

What the Japanese had to do in order to position themselves, Commerce believed, was to gain the know-how to do "systems integration," the incomprehensibly complex art of designing and manufacturing an economically efficient flying machine. "The Japanese arrived at the same analysis as the Europeans with regard to catching up with the United States," Farren said, "and decided against a Japanese version of the Airbus program. They made a conscious choice not to follow the European model." Instead, they would build up their industry by acting as junior partners to U.S. firms and wait patiently until the world moved into a new generation of passenger aircraft. Then they would play leapfrog.

This was the game Farren wanted to thwart. "If the Japanese learned how to do systems integration, then the need on their part to stay with the United States as a junior partner would diminish. They would be in a much tougher position to negotiate with us."

What was being planned by the world's aircraft manufacturers was an entirely new generation of aircraft: a hypersonic transport referred to as the "Orient Express," able to fly from Washington to Tokyo in three hours. Since the costs associated with the plane would be huge, the likelihood was that it would be the product of an international consortium, whose members were already jockeying for position.

"In a deal like that," said Farren, "Japan's bargaining position would change dramatically if they had made the leap to systems integration. If their technology base was below that, the chances were that they would have to maintain their junior partner status with the United States. We wanted our corporations to be in the strongest possible bargaining position with the Japanese when that time came."

Herein lay the danger of the FS-X deal. "We saw FS-X running the risk of giving Japan enormous new capabilities in systems integration. The plane—

even though it was a fighter jet and vastly different from a commercial aircraft —would be a window onto building a sophisticated supersonic aircraft. They would learn systems integration.

"That's what we wanted to frustrate, an independent Japan with systems integration capabilities. We wanted to keep them from gaining a new level of technology through the FS-X deal, so that our firms would be in a better position to compete for the next great leap in aircraft that was coming in ten or fifteen years."

Speaking for Mosbacher, Deputy Under Secretary Joan McEntee said her boss not only wanted a review of the MOU; he also said that Japan should buy these planes off the shelf, right off the Pentagon's showroom floor.

With pressure mounting in favor of a long review, Glenn Rudd, the man who negotiated the FS-X deal for the Pentagon, warned that a delay could kill the entire program. Delay and cancellation, he said ominously, could be one and the same thing.

Traveling with Prime Minister Takeshita to the meeting with Bush on Friday morning, February 3, 1989, was Seiki Nishihiro, the godfather of the defense agency, and the man closest to Richard Armitage, the last American left from the Reagan team that had initiated the FS-X. Months before, Auer had left to teach at Vanderbilt, and years before, Gregg Rubinstein had retired to private consulting. The Bush transition was taking its toll on the rest, as they switched jobs or lost jobs.

The continuity of the previous decade had come undone, and Nishihiro felt very much alone and unfamiliar with the new regime. He was a man who had grown up with the U.S.-Japan Mutual Security Treaty and based his career on its principles. He had promoted the idea of closer U.S.-Japan relations to a reluctant nation. He had fostered the security relationship. Soon he would retire, and what would he be remembered for, the man who was said to be the symbol of the new Japanese defense forces? What would be Nishihiro's legacy—the humiliation of his government over the FS-X? "The FS-X will be a monument to the failure of co-development," he would later say.

The bad news for Nishihiro was that at this point in the unsettling transition period, Armitage's influence was also on the wane. The close connection that he enjoyed with Weinberger had not been the same under Carlucci. Now, until Tower was through with his confirmation—and there was some doubt he might emerge at all—Armitage was without leverage. To complicate matters, Armitage was on his way out of the Defense Department and on his way to the State Department. Within a week, his nomination as Assistant Secretary of State for East Asian and Pacific Affairs was to take place. Nishihiro was without strong allies on the American side.

Prime Minister Noboru Takeshita held three hours of talks with the President and announced to the press at the farewell ceremonies that he and Bush were on a first-name basis, just like their predecessors, Ron and Yasu. Standing in the sickly warm January sun on the White House lawn, temperatures rising into the humid seventies, Takeshita looked stiff, like a puppet, with features perfect and so tiny.

Kearns was not at the White House gathering, but he was acutely aware of what was taking place. Indeed, he had seen the early version of the President's speech, in which he handed Takeshita the keys to the FS-X. This would be Bush's last chance to invoke the deal. If he was going to give it away, he would do it now, in the Rose Garden, during the farewell.

Early reports were that nothing as delicate as the FS-X had been openly discussed between the two heads of state, although Secretary Baker supposedly hinted to Sosuke Uno, his Japanese Foreign Ministry counterpart, that Congress might prove to be a problem. Takeshita himself was apprised of the situation by the National Security Council. There was no indication of whether Bush had given the Prime Minister any private assurances.

The President seemed to be enjoying the springlike Washington weather. Here he was doing what he did best: foreign policy. He would be the foreign policy President. As one of his first acts in the White House, he greeted a head of state, one to whom the United States wrote $93.5 *billion* in checks for imports each year.

Bush told Takeshita, "We respect one another. We need one another."

Takeshita put the best face on his talks. The meeting marked, he said, "a new start for U.S.-Japan cooperation."

When the ceremonies concluded, no mention had been made of the FS-X. The fateful paragraph in the first draft of the President's remarks had been deleted. No words were spoken by the President about the deal. No promises were made that couldn't be undone. Even the New York *Times* took notice of that the next day.

What had happened? Gaston Sigur briefed reporters after the meeting. He explained that the administration was "taking an intergovernmental look at this and seeing how we are going to proceed."

The opponents of the FS-X, Kearns and company, had gotten their delay. The question now was how long a delay they had succeeded in winning.

It had been Sigur's plan to railroad the FS-X through in the farewell speech to Takeshita by the President. But Kearns's intelligence effort rooted out the suspect language. The Senate had weighed in with messages to the President, by direct letter and by telephone calls to his top aides. In effect, Sigur was conceding defeat, for now. But he still had options, notably pushing to get the President to conclude the deal at the funeral of the Japanese Emperor, to be held at the end of February, less than three weeks away.

Fired up over the article written by Clyde Prestowitz in the Sunday Outlook section, the press pursued Takeshita about the fighter program. The Washington *Post* held an on-the-record breakfast for the Prime Minister. Asked if he thought the plane would ever fly, Takeshita said through a translator, "I'm convinced the agreement will be implemented," but he added that "the Bush administration could cause problems for us" if its review process went beyond the March 31 budget deadline faced by the Japan Defense Agency. Takeshita was indicating that Japan would not be pushed around.

Later, at the National Press Club, Takeshita held a forty-minute news conference to conclude his stay in the capital. Once again reporters raised the FS-X issue. The Prime Minister told them the agreement was the result of a long and difficult negotiation and that he expected the work to begin on schedule.

Seiki Nishihiro stayed grimly on in Washington after Takeshita left, holding talks with the State Department and the Pentagon. A news article that ran on the Kyodo wire quoted a senior Japan Defense Agency official visiting in Washington as saying that he was fearful that the United States was about to launch a full-scale review of the FS-X. The source, most likely Nishihiro himself, made plain that this could kill the deal.

"We are taking a wait-and-see attitude," the source said, but he condemned the idea of a review process. Though professing optimism, he already seemed to be examining his alternatives. "I don't think the deal will collapse," he concluded, *"but if it does we will simply continue to use the present fighter planes such as the F-15 and F-4"* (emphasis added).

Nishihiro had never been happy with the FS-X deal, but he had been willing to go along with the United States purely out of respect. But now developments in Washington bordered on the dishonorable. Japan had bargained in good faith with the U.S. government, and it had signed agreements between the U.S. ambassador to Japan and the foreign minister, making the deal official. Was the United States now backing out? Takeshita had set March 31, 1989, for the review process to be completed. Nishihiro began to plot Japan's way out of the FS-X deal.

21

The President's Best Friend

"I told the Japanese, 'You know we've been comrades-in-arms.' I went through all of that. But I said, 'If that's what you decide, to turn to the Europeans over this FS-X business, then you better get someone else to defend you.'"
—ROBERT A. MOSBACHER, Secretary of Commerce

LIKE HIS BEST FRIEND, George Bush, Secretary of Commerce Robert A. Mosbacher set off for the oil fields of Texas after World War II, a swashbuckling young Gatsby. There he founded the Mosbacher Energy Co., and $200 million later he reached a post in the Bush cabinet. Mosbacher was another of the President's Houston friends, along with James Baker and John Tower. Indeed, *The Wall Street Journal* noted that the four men shared zip codes.

Mosbacher made his big hit nationally by supporting Republicans. Between 1979 and 1988, he and his wife, Georgette, recorded personal contributions of $284,282 to Republican political campaigns and programs. Millions and millions more came from his fund raising. *Barron's*, Dow Jones's weekly business journal, called him a "straightforward Chamber of Commerce Republican." That is, he funded his way to high office, beginning at the county level working for Richard Nixon's Texas drive in 1968. From there he went on to become national finance chairman for Ford. He staked his own failed Senate race in 1984 and served as national finance chairman for Bush in 1980 and 1988. The only presidential campaign that did not appear in his confirmation record was Nixon's illegal manipulation of the 1972 election. This he appears to have sidestepped more from propriety than from guilt. He is not one of the villains who appear in *All the President's Men*.

More than anything perhaps, Robert Adam Mosbacher was an oilman, member of the All American Wildcatters Association (founder), American Association of Petroleum Landman (former president), American Petroleum Institute (board member), Independent Petroleum Association of America, International Association of Drilling Contractors, Mid-Continent Oil and Gas Association (former chairman), National Petroleum Council (former chairman), and Natural Gas Supply Association.

On January 31, 1989, Mosbacher assumed one of the least prominent posts in the President's cabinet. The Commerce Department was a boring backwater and a bureaucratic snake pit. It was that fat kid on the lean tough blocks of Pennsylvania Avenue. By and large, its staffers were paid some of the lowest wages in the capital, and thus the office did not attract the best and brightest minds.

This is what Mosbacher inherited. As *The Wall Street Journal* put it: ". . . in most administrations, the commerce secretaries have been figureheads, bit players to the secretaries of state, defense and treasury . . ." This was a patronage job pure and simple, a place where all the Bush loyalists finally settled, which would prove to be of crucial importance to the FS-X deal.

Mosbacher did not accept that role for himself. He dreamed big. There was a picture of Herbert Hoover above the fireplace in his monumental two-story office, and he explained to one and all who came to visit him, including his friend the President, that Hoover had made his way to the White House through the doors of this very office.

The Commerce Secretary was a man of great ambition. A *Time* magazine cover story once described Mosbacher's other very powerful friend and neighbor, Jim Baker, as "a gentleman who hates to lose." Autographing a copy of that issue for Mosbacher, the Secretary of State wrote: "To Bob, who hates to lose even more."

Mosbacher planned his takeoff around the FS-X. He crammed for it. Over six weeks he studied and toiled over the Pentagon's jargon, and by the time the fight for the President's attention was underway, he spoke their tech-speak. In small groups he could be formidable, although in large groups and with the press he could appear fumbling. He wore a pair of hearing aids, which sometimes made it difficult for him to gauge reactions. Up close, however, Mosbacher could be personable, a charmer who was also accomplished. Texas was his personal theme; Manhattan was his true aerie; Washington promised to be his oyster.

Mosbacher's friendship with Baker had a crushing effect on the Chrysanthemum Club at the State Department. Instead of rushing forward to protect an agreement crafted in part by the Tokyo embassy, Baker deferred to Mosbacher's single-minded determination that the FS-X be reviewed before it got presidential approval. The pragmatic Baker would have gained little by opposing Mosbacher, and he would have incurred the wrath of Jesse Helms and the Foreign Relations Committee. Getting off on the wrong foot with Congress was the last thing the pragmatic Baker wanted.

The FS-X had no advocate before President Bush, not even at the Pentagon. As Secretary of Defense, John Tower would have had the power to put the matter to rest with his friend the President. But Tower's confirmation was in flames.

Paul Weyrich, the one-man conservative bandwagon, testified at the confirmation that Tower was a drunk and a womanizer. Weyrich was chairman of Coalitions for America, a hub of right-wing religious activism. "Where there is smoke there is fire," he told the senators. "The smoke surrounding the nominee's personal life seems rather intense. I have made enough personal observation of this man, here in Washington, to have serious reservations about his moral character."

Questioned by the committee, Weyrich elaborated: "I have encountered the nominee in a condition—lack of sobriety—as well as with women to whom he was not married. I recognized the senator's wife because, you know, I worked here in the Senate for eleven years."

Mosbacher knew an advantage when he saw it. With Tower elbowed out by circumstance and Baker neutralized, the Commerce Department found itself in a unique situation, in the pole position in the President's cabinet. The Secretary exploited every advantage.

For much of the fall, Commerce's Japan counselor, Maureen Smith, had been organizing other cabinet departments in anticipation of a new administration. By the time she joined with other department officials in briefing Mosbacher, a coalition had formed among her and her allies in other departments: Energy, Labor, Treasury, the U.S. Trade Representative, along with the Office of Science and Technology Policy, and NASA. If this were a poker hand, Mosbacher held a full house. Only Treasury, which leaned toward supporting the Pentagon's position, posed a problem. They, however, were neutralized by Mosbacher's closest aide, Assistant Secretary Wayne Berman. "They didn't want to play because they had some horse trading they wanted to do with Commerce," Berman said. "I kept telling Treasury that if they got involved in this, they would get nothing but aggravation."

Commerce had another key advantage, Berman recalled. "We had one thing that Defense and Treasury and some parts of the White House didn't have: We had all the Bush loyalists, and George Bush knew that." Berman, incidentally, was the best friend of Bill Triplett on Jesse Helms's staff of the Foreign Relations Committee.

Finally, Mosbacher was part of an administration that wanted to distinguish itself from its charismatic predecessor. Soon after the elections in November 1988, Bush announced that there would be a sweeping policy review by the administration. The new President, who had promised a "kinder and gentler America," tried to distance himself from Reagan's robber baron past. "We're going to take whatever time is necessary for a thorough review and analysis on initiatives," Bush said. "Then [we'll] come out with our own strategic objectives . . ."

The timing and luck that had made Mosbacher rich, now made him powerful. He was charmed. Everything seemed to come together for him, and for his lowly Commerce Department. They were redefining policy and in the process making their presence felt in the highest echelons of government.

Mosbacher dazzled his staff. Instead of playing the party boy from Texas as everyone had expected, he worked long hours and showed up at his desk on Saturdays. He told Maureen Smith that he pursued the FS-X program "because he felt it belonged in his portfolio." This was rousing talk for the backwater bureaucrats. Whereas the Pentagon had struggled powerfully against linking trade and defense, Mosbacher was now taking Commerce a step beyond: linking security to the national economy. Consolidated around the principle of economic security, the department was asserting itself as never before.

Mosbacher's aide Wayne Berman deftly framed the debate for the press. Commerce and its allies appeared to be the carriers of righteousness and truth, all things American. The Defense Department emerged in these stories as backward-thinking Neanderthals, trading precious technology for the sorry promises of former foes. Clearly stated was that the Japanese were more dangerous to America than the Soviets. This was the new Cold War. The effect of Berman's press leaks was to galvanize opinion on Capitol Hill, which had a direct and measurable impact on the President. Mosbacher thus became the fulcrum on which the coming FS-X debate would hinge.

The plan to stop Mosbacher's charge emerged the Monday after the Takeshita visit, February 6, 1989. The counterattack was led by the youthful Karl Jackson, a bright-eyed Berkeley academic and a former aide to the head of the Little State Department at the Pentagon, Richard Armitage. Jackson was the NSC staffer charged with Japan issues, although his background was Indonesian studies. "When I started out I didn't know Japan from a turnip," he said. A vigorous and personable man, Jackson aimed to get an FS-X agreement on the President's agenda by the time Bush set out for Hirohito's funeral in Tokyo, a visit slotted for February 24, 1989, three weeks away.

Jackson's friendliness and easy manner concealed a lashing and nearly ruthless determination. He was a creature of Armitage, and a strong backer of the deal. Indeed, he had saved the FS-X agreement at the eleventh hour when a dispute arose over which nation would produce the plane's wings. The Japanese had balked about allowing General Dynamics to fabricate the experimental wings at its Texas plant. Jackson forged a compromise which assured equal work for the U.S. contractor and won his stripes as a tough-minded negotiator. Now he was bent on extending his success by wrapping up a final agreement at the Hirohito funeral.

Jackson referred to himself as "the wing man" because of his last-minute, last-ditch victory in the MOU talks. As he recalled: "At a really critical moment of the negotiation over the wing box, I was sitting on the opposite side of the table from Yamamoto"—Japan's chief negotiator—"and at a certain point the guy sitting next to him got up to go off to the john, and I got up from my position and went over and sat down next to Yamamoto, on his side of the table, and we worked up a draft copy, and I said let's work this out, and that broke the sort of physical cast of the room. It shattered the universes and broke open the negotiation, and we arrived at an agreement."

That Monday, February 6, Jackson sent by fax a list of twenty-five questions to the six agencies and departments backing the Commerce Secretary. Jackson set a Thursday deadline for their responses and called for an interagency meeting of the policy coordinating committee of the National Security Council for that Friday, to settle the matter once and for all. Jackson was playing his two-minute offense.

The plan was to use the answers from Jackson's questionnaire as background for a recommendation to the President from the NSC in support of the deal. This was a bit of bureaucratic legerdemain, and a bald attempt to steal a march on Commerce.

In response, someone in the Commerce camp leaked Jackson's ploy to the New York *Times*, which ran an unbylined story about it two days later. In the vaguest of terms, the paper quoted "Administration officials," who said "Secretary James A. Baker III would use those reports [faxed by Jackson] to help decide whether to advise President Bush to grant a 60-day delay on the fighter project that has been requested by several Senators."

Clyde Prestowitz confirmed in his book *Trading Places* that Jackson's queries aroused the ire of Mosbacher's coalition; some agencies were upset because they received Jackson's questions before they had received copies of the MOU. "Moreover, the questions seemed to the Commerce team to be slanted in such way as to lead to a conclusion in favor of the deal," he wrote. Jackson's attempt to railroad his opponents also drew fire because Jackson had been a negotiator on the FS-X deal when he was still in the Pentagon. Jackson was the man who told Maureen Smith that the FS-X agreement was locked away in a safe, and that he didn't know the combination. What objective analysis could he bring to the report?

The next day the proponents of the FS-X program fired off another shot at Mosbacher's crew. On the day before Jackson's deadline, a reply to Prestowitz's attack on the FS-X in the *Post* appeared on the paper's Op-Ed page, written by former Secretary of Defense Frank Carlucci. Entitled "The FS-X Project Is No Handout to Japan," the article had been drafted for Carlucci by Jim Auer's replacement in the Pentagon, Torkel Patterson.

The rebuttal stated flatly, "All of these arguments [offered by Prestowitz against the FS-X program] are factually wrong and analytically flawed. They reflect an image of Japanese negotiators as supermen and an equally unhealthy view that assumes America cannot hold its own at the negotiating table."

He staked out the government's public position on the deal: "By working together with Japan on a true co-development project, U.S. government and industry will have ready access to valuable Japanese technology that would otherwise be unavailable." This was the very same technology that the lead U.S. negotiator on the deal, Glenn Rudd, stated was superfluous. But, then, that was when the DoD was trying to sell the co-development idea to Japan. This time, the administration was trying to sell it to the U.S. public.

Said Carlucci, ". . . there are no technological spin-offs from the F-16 that Japan could apply to the wide-bodied commercial aircraft industry." This was a rather dismissive swipe at an important debate that rumbled forward with the flap over the FS-X. For one, it limited the argument to wide-body aircraft. The actual controversy was over the boost the FS-X would give to the commercial aviation industry *in general.* Though it was true that wide-body jumbo jets like the Boeing 747 had little in common structurally with mosquito-sized fighters, the comparison was too limited. By learning the inner workings of the F-16, Japanese engineers would be gaining rich insights into new approaches to airframe design, materials, engineering processes, production methods, testing, aerodynamics. The list was endless. That Japan was in the aviation business at all had everything to do with the co-production programs it enjoyed with the United States that preceded the FS-X. That relationship, that transmission of knowledge, could only be strengthened by increasing the level of cooperation from co-production to co-development.

The Op-Ed by Carlucci had a muted effect, for within hours Mosbacher's allies in Congress counterattacked. Illinois Democrat Alan Dixon prepared a sense-of-the-Senate resolution calling for a full sixty-day review of the FS-X deal. Resolution 61, as it was known, was co-sponsored by a formidably bipartisan roll call of twenty-one senators on February 9, 1989.

The resolution had been rushed forward by Senate staffers fearful that Karl Jackson's NSC initiative might work. A "Dear Colleague" letter written that Wednesday February 8, 1989, from Randy Ferryman, a staffer for Senator Dixon, said: "[The senator] intends to introduce [the resolution] before the mid-February break. It is important that this Resolution is submitted soon, because, according to *Defense News* and Commerce Department officials, a final decision from the administration on the FS-X may occur soon, possibly as early as Friday." This was Jackson's drop-dead date.

In a handwritten postscript, Ferryman said: "I just learned there may be a pro forma session only tomorrow. This constricts time-lines even more. Sorry to pressure you, but your immediate attention would be greatly appreciated!"

Deadline day, Friday, February 10, 1989, began with an unusual telephone call. The Secretary of State, James A. Baker, telephoned Senator Alan J. Dixon and asked him not to introduce Resolution 61 until after the recess for President's Day, which would have required Dixon to wait until *after* the President's return from Hirohito's funeral, when it might have been too late to stop Karl Jackson.

Baker's real concerns in the FS-X matter lay with Congress. Said Torkel Patterson of the Pentagon, "The way Baker operates is purely out of concern for Congress, with how Congress will react."

According to Prestowitz's account in *Trading Places*, Dixon at first agreed to Baker's request, but then had second thoughts. He "later called back [to Baker] to say that there were already twenty-one co-sponsors, and that the pressure was too great for him to delay." Peter Ennis of *Tokyo Business Today* reported that Dixon first consulted with Jesse Helms before deciding on his next move. Helms told Dixon to reject Baker's plea. The resolution was submitted that day.

Baker now knew firsthand the depth of congressional opposition. Not even a direct appeal from the Secretary of State—a rarity—on a mere resolution such as this could stem the rush toward a confrontation between the 101st Congress and the spanking-new administration.

The National Security Council is composed of three subgroups. There is the Principles Committee, made up of the President, the Vice President, the Secretaries of State and Defense, the National Security Adviser, the Director of the CIA, the Chairman of the Joint Chiefs of Staff. This is where the great decisions get made and presidential policy is implemented.

The second level in the organization is the Deputy's Council, which is a mirror of the upper council, but made up of the number two and number three representatives in each department: the State Department's Under Secretary for Political Affairs, the Deputy Director of the CIA, Vice Chairman of the Joint Chiefs of Staff. This is where the NSC's work is managed.

The third group is the Policy Coordinating Committee (PCC), which is organized into functional areas—international economics, intelligence, etc.— and regional areas—Europe, the Soviet Union, Japan, etc. Staffed by people on the assistant secretary level (equivalent in rank to an ambassador, presidential appointments all, confirmed by the Senate), it identifies and develops policy issues. A flexible committee, it can be cloned into different configurations depending on the need. This is where the NSC's work actually gets done, and this was where the showdown took place on Friday, February 10, over the FS-X.

William Clark, Gaston Sigur's deputy, chaired the meeting. Maureen Smith was also there, along with John Richards for the Commerce Department. Prestowitz described the meeting in his book as a "donnybrook, breaking at several points into a shouting match."

Clark was still fuming over the memo Craig Richardson wrote that landed directly on Secretary Baker's desk. Indeed, he had tackled Richardson so hard over the affair that Richardson was considering an administrative complaint against him.

The Pentagon was represented this day by Glenn Rudd, whose presentations fell flat. One representative recalled Rudd saying that Japan's Ministry of International Trade and Industry was not involved in the deal. While the comment was not surprising—Rudd was a contracting agent, not a Japan expert—the comment was regarded as dangerously uninformed.

"He was not smooth," Maureen Smith remembers of Rudd, "and he seemed defensive about the program." Prestowitz reports that Rudd admitted that he had not read the licensing agreements reached between the two contractors, Mitsubishi Heavy Industries and General Dynamics, that was signed just a month earlier in January 1989. This statement could have been more DoD stonewalling. On the other hand, less than thirty days had elapsed since the signing. Prestowitz and company, however, interpreted it as an example of Pentagon negligence.

The meeting was a victory for the Commerce Department camp because the review was not concluded as Jackson had planned. Instead, it was elevated within the NSC to the highest level of discussion below the President, the Deputy's Council. A second meeting was set for the following Wednesday.

That weekend, the Sunday New York *Times* condemned the FS-X deal on its editorial page, with a title that echoed both Prestowitz and Carlucci: "The Pentagon's Handout to Japan." It took direct aim at Bush's impending trip to Hirohito's funeral: "Mr. Bush is starting off on the wrong foot," the *Times* warned archly. The paper called on Japan to buy U.S. aircraft from the Pentagon and not try to build one on its own.

"So why does Japan insist on a deal that apparently makes no military or commercial sense for either partner?" the *Times* editorial asked. "Because it seeks to build its own civil aviation industry. The general experience of developing and making fighter planes would surely help that ambition, even if little of the technology were directly transferable to civilian aircraft."

The *Times* recognized a fundamental flaw in the arguments of Secretary Carlucci and the Pentagon. Co-production had always been conceived as a way to help a national ally *offset* the extraordinarily high cost of purchasing modern-day fighters. This was a commercial reality that was bound inextricably into the notions of a common defense. But Japan was not a struggling economy dependent on *offsets* to purchase weapons. As the editorial put it: "American allies, including Japan, have often co-produced American planes in the past. But the United States hasn't run a $55 billion trade deficit with any of its partners before."

Brent Scowcroft was as close to the President as anyone—Mosbacher, Baker, Tower. A former fighter pilot and air force general, Scowcroft was known for hard work and steadiness. He was a pragmatic man who was to become one of Bush's closest advisers. Scowcroft stood out in favor of the FS-X and was the strongest weapon in the fight to keep the FS-X alive. That gave the council the initiative and counterbalanced Mosbacher's forces.

In the end, the issue came down to a dogfight between Scowcroft and Mosbacher in the President's office. Though Baker was also there, according to John Richards of the Commerce Department, high noon pit Bush's most trusted adviser against Bush's best friend.

The meeting was held on Sunday, according to Mosbacher, in the President's private third-floor office. Scowcroft was still pushing for the NSC report based on the twenty-five questions sent out by Karl Jackson.

Mosbacher recalls that he was utterly determined that the deal would be reviewed. Though he acknowledges that he knew a lot more about oil than aerospace, he was primed for the meeting. Mosbacher argued that the Defense Authorization Act, which went into effect before the MOU for the FS-X was signed, required a Commerce Department review. He complained about the DoD's stonewalling on the MOU. He recited a litany of concerns about technology, from doubts about Japan's ability to produce a co-cured wing to questions about the quality of its phased array radar. Indeed, he recalls the President interrupting him at one point during his discourse and laughingly asking him, "Bob, where the hell did you get all this?"

Mosbacher's sincerity cannot be doubted. He knew the political lay of the land. He had been briefed. He understood the significance of the maneuvers Jackson was engaged in at the NSC. He told the President that if the Pentagon was put in charge of the study—that is, if the Jackson report emerged—the Commerce Department would produce a separate report of its own.

"I probably was a little heated," Mosbacher recalled. "I was trying to make points that were in my view absolutely essential to make. In government you don't always get those clear-cut positions."

Mosbacher was only arguing for time. "You took a little chance that they might walk. But what was the alternative, to roll over for them and give away your technology?"

As much as Bush was impressed with Mosbacher's passion, he was also concerned about the deep divisions appearing within his administration. Bush pushed for a compromise. While accepting the broad interagency review demanded by both Commerce and Congress, Bush sought to limit the deliberation to thirty days. That meant no commitment to Japan during the Hirohito funeral, but it allowed enough time for the administration to act by Japan's March 31 budget deadline.

22

Japanic

"I had my game face on, yeah. I thought Ishihara was wrong, and I thought it was time to tell him that the Japanese have been one-way players. They had been all take and no give, and as far as I was concerned, we weren't going to have that anymore."
—ROBERT MOSBACHER on discussions he held with Japanese politician Shintaro Ishihara

THE RIOT that broke out on Capitol Hill over the FS-X rocked the Japanese. The government, the press, the public, all had assumed that the United States had gotten its way on the co-development scheme, and at Tokyo's expense. The consensus reading of events was that Japan should have been fuming about the FS-X deal.

"We thought this deal favored the United States," said a senior Japanese diplomat in Washington. "Japanese taxpayers were paying for it, and the United States would gain new technology for free." The embassy official, who arrived at Dulles for a three-year Washington stint on January 15, 1989, had not expected a blowup over the deal.

"We thought there might be a hearing or two," the diplomat said. "Toshiba Machine was still around, and we were on the lookout for the next problem. But we did not think it would be the FS-X."

In fact, the Foreign Ministry had overlooked an early warning sign of their trials yet to come. Lost in the hubbub over Takeshita's visit and Hirohito's burial was a vicious incident involving the Japanese press and the Senate Foreign Relations Committee's Bill Triplett.

On Thursday, February 2, 1989, Hiroshi Kanashige, the bureau chief of Jiji, Japan's number two wire service in Washington, wrote a story timed for the visit of Prime Minister Takeshita. His article was based on two documents leaked to Jiji from the Foreign Relations Committee. One document savaged U.S.-Japan relations, the other tore up the FS-X deal. The language of the reports rang of jingoism and anti-Japan bias. Kanashige's wire story focused heavily on the tone.

One leaked document was dated December 29, 1988, and said, "Subject: The Impact of Japan's Economic Invasion of the U.S." The word "invasion" leaped out from the page. The names of the author and the recipient were scratched out on both documents.

The memo warned that the United States was fighting a "two-front global war. One conflict is being fought against the Soviet's military. The second, and more important, conflict is an economic and technological struggle being waged against the U.S. mainly by the Japanese, but with the assistance of the Asian NICs [newly industrialized countries]."

Interestingly, the author of this document did not foresee the changes that were about to overwhelm the crumbling Soviet empire: ". . . we are not winning the conflict with the Soviets. Statis [sic] is the order of the day here and no quick end to the conflict is in sight." This, despite *glasnost* and *perestroika*.

Kanashige underlined and circled the next passage. "Most U.S. policy makers do not look at the economic battle going on with Japan as a conflict involving vital national security interests. In actuality, the survyival [sic] of the U.S. and the world order as we know it are at stake." The melodramatic tone redounded from paragraph to paragraph, ending on a note of self-righteousness. The misspellings indicate that this document was still fairly new and had not been carefully edited. Another possibility is that the essay/memo was not aimed at a wider circulation, but was an intra-office think piece or backgrounder.

The five-page single-spaced essay concluded, "Like a good mercantile colony, [America's] functions will be (as it already is to a certain extent) to provide Japan with raw materials and to consume its industrial output. . . .

"To give up now without a fight in the face of the Japanese economic and technological onslaught would mean we are too mired in our own greed and hyper-individualism to be worthy of our precious heritage of liberty."

The second document was circulated more widely to Senate staffers. This one focused squarely on the FS-X. No date appears, although its contents suggest it was also written in December 1988, before the company-to-company agreements between Mitsubishi and General Dynamics were signed.

All references to authorship were again blacked out by Magic Marker and made gray by generations of photocopying. Indications are, from the memo's tone, subject matter (Japan), and typeface, that the same author was at work again. The four-page single-spaced memo was headlined: "U.S. Continues

Capitulation to Joint Development Program of Japan's New Fighter Aircraft, the FS-X." Kanashige encircled the word "Japan" in the title.

The memo starts out coolly and objectively, providing a synopsis of events in a terse narrative. Its arguments, however, were sharp. "[The Japanese] do not buy a product overseas if they can make a version of it at home, even if that version is inferior to the foreign product and even if it were running a trade surplus with another country."

The author writes about the fracas over the wing work. His familiarity with the arcana of the deal reveals an intimate knowledge of past and present developments. "In December, the Japan Defense Agency sent a special emissary with this proposal: that [U.S.] build none of the original six sets of wings but that we would be allowed to build a seventh, extra set. This set would not be fully tested and would not fly on any of the prototypes. DoD and GD's [General Dynamics] position was that GD needed to build at least half or more of the six wing sets in order to make sure that the technology was fully understood and fully mastered. Thus the Japanese proposal was rejected. Word came back from Japan that the head Japanese government FS-X official was furious with his special emissary and with DoD, and that he was threatening to cancel the program if the U.S. did not agree to this proposal."

The story Kanashige put together on the memos did not run immediately. He wanted to time it carefully, pegging it to the Takeshita visit. The story, which was widely picked up by the Japanese press, broke in Tokyo as the Prime Minister was landing at Andrews Air Force Base, according to Kanashige.

The next morning, at seven o'clock Washington time, February 3, Kanashige was abruptly awakened by a call from his office at the National Press Building. He was told that William Triplett, Senator Helms's lead staffer and Kevin Kearns's Capitol Hill mentor, had telephoned demanding that Kanashige come to his office immediately.

Kanashige would not be bullied, but agreed to meet with Triplett after lunch at the committee's fifth-floor offices in the Hart Office Building. A dashing man of medium height in his middle forties, Kanashige had spent much of his adult life posted as an international correspondent. His wife was American. Unlike most Japanese reporters, he did not wear the customary uniform—dark suit and white starched shirt. He preferred sport jackets and well-cut pleated slacks. He sported a Hemingway-sized mustache and spoke good English.

Kanashige took time to arrange a lunch with his committee source and discuss his strategy for handling the raging Triplett. They dined practically beneath Helms's office window, at the Monocle, a Hill watering hole frequented by Senate staffers. Kanashige agreed with his source that he would not return the original documents, but would offer photocopies to Triplett for authentication. Under no circumstances would he reveal his source.

"Triplett was furious," Kanashige recalled. "He demanded to know if I had taken the papers from one of the tables. He accused me of stealing them from the committee." Triplett's office, which is crammed with bookcases, piled with reports and stacked with studies, oversized folders everywhere spilling official-looking papers, seemed an unlikely place to be able to locate a document, let alone steal it.

What unhinged Triplett as much as the documents was that he had learned of the leak from the Japanese Embassy, which had called him that morning to confirm what was being reported in the Tokyo press.

Triplett demanded the documents back that day. They were the private musings of the committee, he said, and he dismissed the writings as the work of an unimportant intern. The two-hour meeting with Triplett, which Kanashige said deteriorated into a "shouting match," ended on a threat. Triplett told the Japanese bureau chief that he would use his leverage at the State Department to have him deported if he did not return the documents and confess the name of his source.

The shaken Kanashige countered with a dare. If Triplett did anything to him or his staff, he would go to the Washington *Post*. The matter ended with a draw.

Bill Triplett did not answer faxed queries or return direct telephone calls on the matter. Kevin Kearns, who was an obvious suspect as the author, said he did not want to be associated with the memo.

In the end, the uproar was contained, but the anger it signified was not. The ringingly anti-Japanese memos and Triplett's fierce reaction augured the explosion that lay in store for the incipient fighter program.

The Harris organization, one of the nation's leading political forecasters, did a poll for *Business Week* in 1989 in which 63 percent of the Japanese public said they had little or no admiration or fondness for the American people.

The depth of the resentment emerged more clearly and more dramatically in Tokyo within days of the Jiji disclosure (but not as a result of it), when two national figures, one of them a popular and attractive politician and the other a glamorous leading industrialist, co-authored a book entitled *The Japan That Can Say No.*

The industrialist was Akio Morita, the chairman of the Sony Corporation. His co-author was less well known to Americans. The colorful Shintaro Ishihara had few Western equivalents. He was a complex composite of a man with interests ranging from literature to the politics of power. He was an accomplished and successful author who was a major player in the parliament. Tall for his generation of Japanese, Ishihara was the silver fox of the Diet. If a middlebrow Hemingway were crossed with a sexy version of Georgia Republican congressman Newt Gingrich, something of an Ishihara might emerge.

Ishihara had written a string of best-sellers beginning in 1955. His first novel, entitled *Season of the Sun*, won the Akutagawa Prize, the Japanese literary equivalent of the Pulitzer Prize. The book was often compared with *The Sun Also Rises*.

An iconoclast, Ishihara favored European-style double-breasted herringbone suits. He would slouch in his chair during meetings, in characteristically un-Japanese fashion. Handsome as a shark, he was part flaneur, part provocateur. In public opinion poll after public opinion poll in Japan, the former transportation minister was rated the nation's number two most popular political figure. In 1968, when he first ran for public office, he got the largest number of votes of any candidate in the nationwide election. In 1989, he was one of three men mentioned as the next Prime Minister.

The book that Ishihara and Morita published would eventually sell more than a million copies worldwide because of the controversy it inspired. What piqued Washington's interest were the alarming and incendiary opinions of Ishihara. The Pentagon's elite research and development arm, the Defense Advanced Research Projects Agency, ordered that the Morita-Ishihara book be translated into English, with copies to be circulated within the security community.

Inevitably news leaked to the press of the existence of the text, and within a short time the book was being pirated, becoming more sought after on Capitol Hill than a Tom Clancy best-seller.

In the Pentagon's edition, Morita chided the United States, but Ishihara threw down the challenge. The novelist turned politician, zeroing in on the FS-X, wrote: "When the Pentagon saw the FS-X blueprints they panicked. The design is fantastic. No other fighter around will be able to hold a candle to the [Japanese] aircraft.

"The FS-X has a vertical stabilizer located approximately beneath the pilot's seat. Shaped like a shark's fin, it enables the aircraft to change altitude, nose direction, pitch, and roll without changing its flight pattern. An analogy would be to an automobile that can turn 360 degrees in either direction without moving forward or backward. It is a brilliant concept. American engineers might have thought of it, too, but [Mitsubishi Heavy Industries] was ready to build the aircraft."

Ishihara embroidered on the affront the FS-X represented to America: "To the Department of Defense, [the FS-X] was like a replay of the early stage of the Pacific War, when the Zero fighter dominated the skies. U.S. admirals had assumed the Imperial navy had nothing to match their aircraft, but the Zero proved far superior. Now, Japan was building another menacing weapon."

The belligerence of Ishihara was far worse for the company it kept. Having his friend Akio Morita as co-author gave credence to Ishihara's snarlings. Cheek to cheek, the duo gave evidence that Japan's economic juggernaut had a powerful and aggressive political component. Competition in the global market was tough enough, but when governments joined in, the game turned sinister. With key U.S. high-tech industries up for sale to Japanese companies, powerful elements in the Pentagon were worried. Did the duo of Morita and Ishihara represent the face of renewed Japanese imperialism? Was Japan trying to milk the United States like a colony?

The forty-five-year-old Ishihara was closely studied. While his flamboyant style appealed to the nationalistic side of the Japanese electorate, his popularity ran deeper than that. He was taken seriously and was well regarded in Japan. A player in national politics, he was considered to be one of three bright young men then heading toward the Prime Minister's post. (The others were Ryutaro Hashimoto and Ichiro Ozawa.) Ishihara's name had been a household word in Japan since *Season of the Sun* was published. He had a future as Japan's Ronald Reagan, and in many ways expressed the same bellicose view of the world.

Ishihara and his younger brother were lionized. The movie made from Ishihara's first book starred his younger brother, a man the Japanese compared to James Dean. The Ishiharas were symbols of youthful alienation. When the younger Ishihara died of cancer in 1987, "Japan mourned as if the entire nation had lost a member of the family," wrote Harvard Japan expert Ezra F. Vogel in the foreword to the Japanese authorized version of *The Japan That Can Say No*. "As a national public mourning, it was rivaled in the United States perhaps only by the public reaction to the death of John F. Kennedy or Robert Kennedy. In Japan, only the death of the Emperor received more public attention."

When Ishihara published an authorized English version of his book in 1991, he referred to the Pentagon translation as a "vile, error-filled pirate translation." By and large, however, the pirate edition was actually similar in many respects and in some cases nearly identical to the authorized version, particularly Ishihara's comments on the FS-X.

The chief difference between the two versions of Ishihara's book was the absence of co-author Akio Morita. The chairman of Sony declined to participate in the English version. Perhaps this was because the pirated Pentagon copy of his book appeared just as he was engaged in a controversial buyout of Columbia Pictures.

Japan's anger over the FS-X was matched by its grief over the loss of its Emperor. On January 7, 1989, the Imperial symbol of a long era of Japanese history closed his watery eyes for the last time. The death of Emperor Hirohito at age eighty-seven marked an end to a man once revered as a god. For sixty-two years, he had reigned as the symbol of his nation. With his passing a new age was truly upon Japan, as symbolized by the advent of new Japanese power embodied in the FS-X and by the coronation of a new Emperor for this new age.

On a cold, rainy day in February, Hirohito's 990-pound coffin was hoisted 99 feet up a hillside to be entombed, a process taking three hours. Artifacts too sacred for the common gaze accompanied the square black palanquin bearing Hirohito's remains. Five hundred foreign dignitaries, among them President Bush and Secretary Baker, attended the funeral along with 10,000 invited guests.

The solemnities quickly gave way to negotiations with the anxious Japanese over the FS-X. With the President expecting a report by March 15 from the interagency panel reviewing the FS-X, Baker decided while riding on Air Force One to try to settle the matter during a meeting with his Japanese counterpart, Sosuke Uno.

According to the Prestowitz account of these events, Baker sought concessions—clarifications, really—on the issues of workshare and a guarantee for the United States of a role in the future development of the plane. Prestowitz says Baker assumed this would be a simple matter of adjusting already negotiated language. "Baker obviously hoped to dispose of the issue quickly and smoothly by being able to report back to the Senate that he had gotten such a commitment while in Tokyo."

In fact, Baker had chosen to present Uno with one of the most contentious issues of the whole negotiating process. The language in the final agreement was vague on both issues because neither side could agree. The deal would have fallen through if the matter had been pressed.

"Uno sharply rejected the request," Prestowitz writes, angering Baker.

The Japanese later tried to explain Uno's blustery reaction. As they saw it, Baker had not used the standard State Department bureaucracy in dealing with the FS-X, but kept his own counsel. As a result, the Japanese side received no early warning signal of Baker's intention to discuss the FS-X. Uno's spirited reply was more surprise than pique, they explained. The foreign minister was startled and "reacted very negatively on the spot, seeing this (correctly) as an attempt to reopen the FS-X" agreement.

Though the Japanese wrote the outburst off as a misunderstanding, the damage had been done. Baker hardened his position. His demand that 40 percent of the work on the FS-X be performed in the United States became an absolute condition for the agreement to go forward.

This was a moment that needed to be glimpsed in its totality in order to appreciate the chaos it prefigured. In Tokyo, the Emperor was dead, the new Prime Minister was reeling from a stock-for-influence scandal, the foreign minister had just insulted the U.S. Secretary of State, the chairman of Sony had just published a book with a very popular Japanese politician who threatened to cut off computer chips to the United States if it didn't show more respect for Japan, and the worst was yet to come: Congress had called for hearings on the FS-X.

23

A Consumer Revolt

"By far the most startling thing was when we accused Japan of cheating. I was as dumbfounded as the Japanese. Clyde called to talk with me about that the week before he wrote that article in the Post. *I said, 'Clyde, you're smoking dope.'"*
—JIM AUER on his reaction to the hearings on the FS-X

A S AIR FORCE ONE gunned its engines and rolled down the runway at Andrews Air Force Base on its way to Tokyo with Bush and Baker on board, the House prepared to gavel to order the battle for the FS-X. Democrat Jim Florio chaired the opening hearing. An ex-Marine and a former Golden Gloves boxer, Florio was a man who fought his way into Congress by taking on and then defeating the corrupt political machine that ran South Jersey. His cold and handsome face bore a crease below his left eye, damaged in the prize ring. He wore his watch on the inside of his wrist. His Brooklyn-toughs pompadour, streaked gray, was muted by his neat, crisp conservative attire.

Held in the dignified comity of the Rayburn House Office Building across the street from the Capitol, the hearing was called to order at 9:33 A.M. on Thursday, February 23, 1989. Its agenda was plain from the name of the subcommittee: Commerce, Consumer Protection, and Competitiveness. Few other deliberative bodies in Congress wore their institutional biases so plainly above their doorposts. The subcommittee was a virtual totem to latter-day liberalism, a forum for the workingman. It protected his right to acquire goods, ensured that those goods would not injure him and that they would be Made in the U.S.A., presumably by union labor. In other words, this was where Congress watched over the link between workers and consumers. Jim Florio had made a reputation for himself by taking on Big Business.

The FS-X was a jobs issue for Florio. The Garden State he represented before Congress was attractive to high-tech business ventures. Electronics and information were emerging as the state's next high frontier. And Florio worried that the Pentagon dispensed technological advantage through deals like this one, to the detriment of his constituents. Florio was one of those in Congress who saw the nation's security rooted in its economic strength.

A year earlier, Florio and J. James Exon, the senior senator from Nebraska, co-authored a key provision in the 1988 trade bill that granted the President the authority to block foreign "acquisitions, mergers or takeovers" of business considered to be essential to national security. The much cited "Exon-Florio National Security Test" was driven in large part by the proposed acquisition of Fairchild Semiconductor by Japan's Fujitsu Ltd. During the 1980s, foreign interests spent $257 billion acquiring 5,194 U.S. businesses, many of them promising high-tech ventures. As Florio saw it, the FS-X was a part of that same corrosive process.

Seven people sat at the witness table before Florio's subcommittee. Two were like bookends, on opposing corners of the FS-X debate. There was James E. Auer, the man who created the FS-X project, and Clyde V. Prestowitz, the man who created the uproar over the FS-X. Florio left little doubt where he stood. With a flair for the dramatic, he began: "I would like to welcome everybody to this morning's hearing on an innocent-sounding proposal that could be troubling as far our long-range national security interests are concerned."

He continued: "Today, President Bush is in Japan paying his respects on the death of the former Emperor. That is something that he should do. But making massive amounts of sophisticated aircraft technology available to Japan or anyone else is something that quite possibly the President should not do."

Florio's argument had an inexorable logic. "We know that U.S. aircraft manufacturers are the world leaders and have technology that Japan lacks. We also know . . . that [Japan] intend[s] to become our competitor."

He wondered: "Are we shortening the time it would take to make Japan a world-class competitor of ours in the area of aircraft sales?

"[Such] questions are even more timely because our own Defense Department is warning that the United States is falling behind in many electronic and informational technology areas that are crucial to national security."

As Bruce Gwinn, the soft-spoken Florio aide who organized the panel, said, "FS-X wasn't shoes. It wasn't wheat. It was the U.S. aerospace industry. This FS-X deal expedited Japan's progress as a competitor. That's what worried us. Where's the benefit in it for us as a country in terms of competitive position?"

Florio was especially concerned about the new terms of this agreement, particularly the idea of co-development. He wanted to know what it meant. Like a competitor in a game of Jeopardy!, Clyde Prestowitz leapt to respond. Co-production, Prestowitz said, "is a matter of taking a knockdown kit and putting it back together." That was an oversimplification but it would do. It made the point. "Co-development means that we would jointly with Japan . . . do the design and development work in tandem, and that means the key aspects of aircraft engineering." This raised what Prestowitz thought was the central question at hand: To what extent was the United States pledged to share its technology with Japan?

Prestowitz was a powerful and provocative speaker. Through Kearns, Prestowitz had learned the inner workings of the FS-X deal, which he now turned against the Pentagon. "The idea of co-development arose not as a result of any comprehensive review or any study within the administration. It was a proposal that came out of the Defense Department and to some extent the State Department. There was never an interagency task force put together to study what co-development meant. There was never a consultation with private industry, with academia. It was an idea that came up very quickly and was proposed essentially as a political solution."

Prestowitz offered an anecdote about how President Reagan set the example on such matters. "In 1985, President Reagan made a [televised] speech in which he said that he had created a strike force to seek out and smite down unfair trade activity . . . When I heard it, I turned to my wife and said, 'You know, this is really funny, 240 million Americans think that the President, with all the power and resources of Washington at his fingertips, has carefully studied this issue and has appointed this strike force and that this strike force is going to handle unfair trade.'

"The fact of the matter was, there was no strike force. Nobody had ever heard tell of it. Two days later, I was called into Secretary of Commerce Baldrige's office, and the Secretary said to me, 'Clyde, did you hear the President's speech?' I said yes. He said, 'We need a strike force.'

"There was no strike force. It wasn't thought out. And the same is true here in this co-development proposal. It wasn't carefully thought out. It wasn't spec'd; it wasn't assessed. Nobody sat down to think about, what does it mean? What are the implications? What are we going to get? What are we going to give?"

Prestowitz noted that even as these hearings were underway, the President's cabinet was undertaking a review of the FS-X agreement. A report was expected in less than two weeks, at which time the President would decide the fate of the program. That worried him. "The Commerce Department is being asked to come up to speed in three weeks on a negotiation from which they were frozen out for three years . . .

"I'm also concerned because the results of the review are supposed to be fed into the National Security Council. Well, the fellow who will be handling this on the [NSC] is also the guy who was the . . . negotiator on the FS-X deal." Prestowitz was referring to Karl Jackson, who was attempting to railroad the FS-X through the council.

Now Prestowitz took direct aim at the attitudes that produced disastrous deals between the United States and Japan. "At one point in the course of negotiation," he said, "one of the American officials made the statement that his job was to mediate between the two governments . . . That concerns me . . . because I think the job of American negotiators should be to represent American interests, and when an American negotiator says that his job is to mediate, that's cause for great concern."

The accusation was backed by another witness, Frank J. Gaffney, Jr., the lead negotiator with Japan over Star Wars, President Reagan's plan to defend the world from intercontinental ballistic missiles. "Individuals in the U.S. government were often more forceful advocates of the Japanese position than their counterparts from Japan," Gaffney said.

Such comments were a direct attack on the policymaking of the Chrysanthemum Club. And while the slap was at the State Department, it was Jim Auer, returned from teaching at Vanderbilt to testify on behalf of the FS-X deal, who said "ouch."

"I was in the Defense Department what Mr. Prestowitz would call a mediator between the United States and Japan. He is certainly entitled to his position, but I would just like to add my opinion that for the 100 percent of the time that I was at the Defense Department I represented the interests of the United States rather than Japan."

Auer did not do a good job defending the deal before the committee, although he said all the right things and touched on all the important points. He simply was not convincing. At times he sounded caviling: "[Gerald Sullivan] was not a lieutenant colonel," as Prestowitz had mistakenly referred to him, "he was a career civilian engineer." At other times, he sounded fatuous: "Everybody wants to design a new aircraft. You aren't a man until you designed your own new aircraft."

Auer never testified before Congress when he was in government, although he wrote testimony for Weinberger and Carlucci. He was before the Florio subcommittee because the administration had put a gag order on its staff until a clear position emerged from the review that was underway.

At times, Auer's testimony seemed to bend facts and stretch credulity. He ducked the term "co-development" and referred to the FS-X as "an enhanced F-16," and argued that the FS-X "might be even better than the F-16 as it exists today because of state-of-the-art Japanese technology." No one believed the Japanese had successfully developed any major fighter technology that was state-of-the-art or surpassed current U.S. designs.

Elsewhere in his testimony, Auer professed the belief that "the [Japan] Defense Agency did not have a preconception" about whether it would buy a foreign plane off the shelf, retrofit a plane already in their defense inventory, or engage in domestic development: Japan's hoary three options. Auer was by himself in that opinion. In fact, Gregg Rubinstein, who helped conceive the notion of co-development with Auer, says there was never any doubt about Japan's intentions. "We always considered foreign purchase and licensed development to be straw men. The JDA's interest was in domestic development."

Worst of all, Auer sounded like an apologist for Japan. "I find it really surprising," he told the subcommittee, "that after the Japanese did what I believe they honestly thought was what we wanted them to do, there is now criticism that their true motive is to, in fact, advance their civilian aviation industry."

Coming from as careful a student of Japan as Auer, these comments rang false. More than 80 percent of all Japanese aircraft-related production work is funded by the defense agency. That Japan made no secret about its intentions in aerospace was common knowledge. Weeks before Auer's testimony, an interview with the president of Mitsubishi Heavy Industries in the widely read *Japan Economic Journal* drew this comment: "The role of acting as a prime contractor will be a great boon to [Mitsubishi]. Furthermore, *the technology we will develop and accumulate during the project will be instrumental in developing next-generation planes,* such as hypersonic and supersonic transports" (emphasis added). These were patently commercial applications.

The CIA produced a paper on March 3, 1989, for the interagency study group meeting within the National Security Council. According to *Trading Places:* "It concluded that the FS-X deal would significantly enhance Japan's ability to develop military aircraft on its own and to become an important competitor to U.S. industry in commercial aircraft." While Auer had been out of government for nine months, and may not have had access to the CIA report, he was the Pentagon's institutional memory on the FS-X. Surely he had seen similar analyses over the years. Had he merely dismissed them?

Defiant in his brief for Japan, Auer challenged the subcommittee: "If, in fact, that's what we think they're going to do [to use the FS-X to develop their commercial aviation industry], then I don't think we should co-develop this aircraft with them." Auer had no doubt that Japan's intentions were completely honorable, seeking to safeguard its national security. However, he ignored the fact that Japan's chief defense negotiator was home-based at the

Ministry of International Trade and Industry, an organization dedicated for thirty years to the dream of creating a Japanese aerospace industry.

As a young man embarking on his career in the navy, Auer had learned the power of positive reinforcement. Interested in psychology, he used this positive approach in his capacity as the Defense Department's point man on U.S.-Japan security issues. The successes he achieved spoke for themselves. During Auer's watch, Japan embarked on its greatest military buildup since the end of World War II. Auer pointed out to the subcommittee that Japan had as many warplanes defending the homeland as the United States. Although this omitted the key strategic fact that the United States stationed thousands of aircraft overseas, where it hoped to stall an attack before it reached the United States.

How much had the Japanese buildup over the 1980s actually achieved? There was less there than met the eye. Auer liked to point to Prime Minister Suzuki's 1981 commitment to defend Japan's sea lanes as a sign of Japan's commitment to Pacific security. Eight years later, the pledge had hardly been implemented. As well, Auer advertised that Prime Minister Nakasone's signature on a joint communiqué at the 1983 Williamsburg summit meant he had joined Japan's fate to the Western alliance. In reality, faced with a test of that resolve during the Iran-Iraq war, Japan left Americans to risk their lives in defense of Japanese imported oil.

Auer was so bent on maintaining a positive attitude about Japan that he sometimes sounded like a Pollyanna. He told the subcommittee that Japan had bought the AEGIS air defense system off the shelf, but he ignored the fact that they refused to buy the U.S.-made destroyers that went with AEGIS, accepting the disingenuous Japanese argument that U.S.-made ships are too big for their smaller Japanese crews. As a civilian in the Defense Department who knew Auer put it: "Fuck Jim Auer. He didn't think the Japanese would do anything wrong. Auer was the other side of the pendulum from Prestowitz. There wasn't enough we could do for the Japanese."

Auer was a Big Picture policymaker. He saw the world as the office of the Secretary of Defense saw it, as illustrated by the Mercator projection maps of the world so evident in Pentagon offices. America is depicted as the middle country on the wall map. The Soviet Union appears large, enveloping, its westernmost borders thrust into Europe and its easternmost borders probing the waters of the Pacific toward California. The menacing Soviet state appears on both sides of the map, as if it stretched all the way around the world to grasp crablike at little America. The effect of this was to see the United States surrounded and nearly in the clutches of its enemy, the Evil Empire.

The Japan that Auer depicted with unvarnished surety was a nation that put its defense concerns at the same level as the United States, which is to say, above all else. Auer believed that Japan and the United States were the same in this matter. Because Japan was a capitalist society, the Big Picture view assumed it had the same economic system as the United States. That because Japan was a democracy, it shared the same political system.

Arguably neither was true. Japanese capitalism was based on a system of corporate trusts that had been outlawed in the United States at the beginning of the twentieth century. In Japan, the relationship between business and government was far more intimate than in the United States, with the exception of defense contractors such as McDonnell Douglas and General Dynamics.

Japan's democratic institutions did not embrace a pluralistic party system that waged elections over ideas. The principle of one man, one vote was not a Japanese principle. The parliament was little more than a rubber stamp for the will of the powerful and unelected ministries from which national policy sprang. The Prime Minister was seldom more than a figurehead enjoying a two-year stint at the top.

Auer was the product of a particular era of postwar U.S.-Japan relations. As he put it: "I'm a victim of my old Edwin Reischauer training. I believe that Japan and the United States are tremendously different in language, culture, tradition, and yet we are both democracies. Reischauer said he was frequently wrong on estimating how much the United States and Japan could do together. He always found himself revising his estimates in even a more optimistic direction."

That's what Auer now did for the subcommittee. He assured them that Japan's intentions were good. Because of the FS-X, he said, advanced Japanese technology would flow to the United States, without cost if it was derived from U.S. products and for a licensing fee if the technology was uniquely Japanese. "We would not get either of these options, obviously," he said, "if Japan developed its own fighter and would have no requirement to share its technology with the United States."

This promise, too, offered far less than Auer advertised. Not only had the United States given little credence to the technology Auer now dangled before the committee, but the assertion ignored the fact that the United States had negotiated technology flow-back agreement after technology flow-back agreement with Japan and had practically nothing to show for it. After eight years, a mere three transfers from Japan to the United States had taken place under the 1983 agreements, on which the FS-X was based. Still, Auer boasted of these agreements to show Japan's commitment to the United States, as he boasted of the 1,000-mile sea lanes and the long-forgotten Williamsburg summit.

The investigative arm of Congress, the General Accounting Office, rounded out the day's testimony. They too took aim at Auer. "The United States enters into co-production arrangements primarily for defense and foreign policy reasons," said Joseph E. Kelly, director of the agency's security and international relations department. "At the time of our review [the Ministry of International Trade and Industry] stated that technological developments of those civil and military aircraft mutually supplement and complement each other because development and manufacturing techniques of both are closely related . . ."

As he began his testimony, Kelly introduced Davi D'Agostino, the Karen Allen look-alike who conducted the office's first exposé on U.S.-Japan co-production programs seven years earlier. Kelly zeroed in on Auer. He said that the stewards of U.S.-Japan defense relations had given "inadequate attention . . . to the economic implication of these transactions [such as the FS-X]."

This had been D'Agostino's recommendation in the first report: Consider U.S. economic interests before selling off prized technology. Defense Department officials, Auer chief among them, had ignored those findings, even ridiculed them. Now D'Agostino listened intently as Kelly told the subcommittee, "Japan's Ministry of International Trade and Industry, which is known as MITI, played an important role in the F-15 and other co-production programs. MITI set policies for both military and civil aircraft production in Japan."

Kelly had seen Japan's plans. Its goals were no secret. "At the time of our work, because Japan accounted for 10 percent of the world's Gross National Product, MITI believed that Japan's 3 percent or 4 percent share of the world's aircraft sales indicated the relative weakness of its industry." Plans were to triple their output relative to current GNP.

Frank Gaffney, the Star Wars negotiator, who professed deep misgivings about the FS-X deal, managed to get in the last word, ending the hearing on an ominous note. "I am advised that there are places [in the company-to-company agreements] in which things are committed to take place, to be transferred and so on that are not provided for in the overall government-to-government agreement."

Gaffney feared that technology was about to fall through the cracks between the two agreements with Japan on the FS-X. He also worried about more practical matters, such as the vague language that blurred the meaning of each individual document.

Aviation Week & Space Technology, the highly regarded industry publication, seemed to quote directly from a critical section of the classified government-to-government contract in its February 20, 1989, issue: " 'Japan agrees to provide U.S. industry with a share of production work based on its experiences in the development phase and the easiness of the operation and maintenance of the aircraft in Japan.' " This paragraph supposedly guaranteed the

U.S. contractor who helped develop the plane a decent share in the final and lucrative production phase of the FS-X, assuming it was produced at all.

The article continues: "A General Dynamics official acknowledged the wording is imprecise. 'But it's understood,' he said, 'that General Dynamics will gain a share of the production contract, comparable to the about 35 to 45 percent it will have in the development phase.'"

Florio's subcommittee was worried that wishful thinking and individuals' words were being substituted for hard-nosed business practices, such as getting the deal in writing. What happens if the people who made the commitment on the Japanese side all got different jobs? How could the United States verify its bargain? The Pentagon seemed to be defining terms with deliberate obscurity in order to keep the agreement from falling apart on the specifics. The actual knotty problems that were glossed over by the slippery language would have to be dealt with later, as they came up. The difficulty was that the Pentagon, by its own acknowledgment, was not very good at implementing accords. It didn't follow through. As far as the Pentagon was concerned, it didn't have to. What was the Japanese military compared with that of the United States? What was Dondi compared to Sergeant York?

24

Dirty Dancing

"They walked from the agreement, and that's when we went ballistic."
—JOAN MCENTEE, Deputy Under Secretary of Commerce

THE MOU turned out to be as controversial as Gaffney had warned. When the Commerce Department's leading technical expert got to examine the document, he turned up forty-four items deemed security risks, too sensitive to trade off to Japan. "The way the agreement read, it was like we were going to teach them how to build the fighter," said Secretary Mosbacher's choice to work out the technology exchange with the Pentagon, Tom Barksdale.

The very first instruction Mosbacher gave Barksdale was that everything in the deal was up for grabs but for one essential: "He told me that I was not to kill the deal. He said that the first time I briefed him on the technology at stake here," said Barksdale.

Mosbacher's policy had been formed by his general counsel, Wendell Willkie II, grandson of the industrialist who stiffly challenged Franklin D. Roosevelt in the 1940 elections. Willkie argued that the likelihood of stopping the deal was slim. By trying to stop it, the department would be casting itself in a losing position. Willkie proposed compromising backward, telling the President that this was a bad deal, but one that could be fixed.

As Mosbacher's chief aide, Wayne Berman, recalled: "Mosbacher believed in the idea of technology sharing, but he thought it should be a two-way street. He didn't like that fact that there were four lanes of technology flowing to Japan, with one unpaved shoulder heading back to the United States."

Barksdale got the message and set out to find a technology compromise. A former English major, Barksdale learned his engineering on the job. Before the FS-X, he had spent four years as the acting division director of the Commerce Department's NATO mission. Tall, slim, Barksdale was a fastidious man who had an eye for detail. He collected Japanese netsuke, the intricately carved miniatures depicting the court, mythical beasts, erotica.

By and large, Barksdale held the Commerce Department, where he worked, in disdain. He spoke of it as if it were an immense underfunded generator of red tape and internecine intrigue. By comparison, he held the Defense Department in great esteem. Indeed, Barksdale seemed to be more comfortable around the air force than the Bureau of Export Administration, where he worked.

"I told the Pentagon people that my father had been Inspector General in the air force at one time," said Barksdale of his opening meetings with the DoD. "I told them that I understood that they were not trying to destroy the defense industrial base with this deal," as some in his department believed. Barksdale, unlike anyone else on the Commerce side, trusted the Pentagon's basic approach to foreign military sales. When the Pentagon told him they were not giving away the family jewels, he listened to them.

"At the time I first reviewed the agreement," said Barksdale, "the technology transfer analysis had not been done," which was why he thought it was a dangerous giveaway. "The implication of the agreement was that it was going to be this very deep sharing of technology. But as I watched the technology transfer analysis develop within the air force, they proved to be very tough."

Barksdale's bonhomie was reciprocated by the DoD. Work proceeded so quickly that in just over three weeks only two of the forty-four original problems raised by Commerce remained to be negotiated. "Both of those cases involved source codes," said Barksdale.

Saying that the only problem was source codes was like saying that the only problem was the whole deal. The FS-X flew on these source codes, these computer instructions. It used them for attack, for defense, for takeoffs, and for landings. They were the soul of the machine.

Source codes, however mysterious, almost magical-sounding the name may be, were actually rather straightforward instructions. Source codes were the programmer's logic, his algorithms, his reasons for doing what he did. The word "source" in "source code" referred to the actual program written in that language. As opposed to the object code, or the machine language into which the source code was complied for the computer to digest. Whereas the object code was a featureless terrain of binary numbers—01 10 11 00 01— source codes were understandable. They were the language the computer was programmed in. Thus, anyone literate in a particular programming language who looked over the source codes would learn how to create or re-create a similar program. He would know how the program worked, and *why* it was designed to work that way.

In the case of the F-16, on which the FS-X would be based, having access to its source codes enabled a programmer to understand how the plane performed its mission, why it performed it in such a way. Which, incidentally, was the whole idea behind the co-development program as the Japanese understood it. The one advantage of working with the United States, as they saw it, would be to learn the process of building an F-16, so they could build an FS-X. They fully expected to get access to those source codes. To a person—Kurihara, Nishihiro, air chief Hitoshi Omura—all expected those codes.

Source codes were everything, the keys to the kingdom. They made the formidable F-16 the leading-edge fighter it was, one of the most agile, lethal all-weather day-night attack/interceptors in the West, as close as the world had come to a true multi-role warplane. A pilot could load programs into his F-16 as he would load them into his personal computer. Indeed, a pilot used the equivalent of a floppy disk to change the F-16's mission from flight to flight.

In the F-16, a pilot did not pull a mechanical trigger to fire his cannons, he toggled an enter key. Every part of the plane worked through its computers. The pilot's life as well as his mission were utterly dependent on the airplane's source code.

The first F-16 produced in the early 1970s flew with 50 processing chips, similar to those used in desktop computers, and 125,000 lines of software code. The F-16 scheduled to become the FS-X was far more complex, employing 300 processors and 230,000 lines of code, each line representing an instruction to the computer. The DoD did not know how much it spent a year on such software; estimates ranged from $24 to $32 billion *annually*, 8 to 11 percent of its total budget. The idea that such hard-won technological riches would be transferred in the FS-X deal rankled the Commerce alliance.

Said one Department of Energy consultant, "When you have a program's source code, you know all the secrets of how it works. All the logic is captured in the source code." The F-16's code was written in a 1960s-vintage programming language known as JOVIAL, which stood for Jules Own Vision of an Algorithmic Language. The result was that parts of the code could not be broken off and classified secret, allowing it to be transferred without giving away key data. "You either gave them all the code or nothing."

The two source code sticking points left between Commerce and the DoD were at the heart of the F-16's two main computers. One, the digital flight control computer, was the newest system to be incorporated into the airplane. In effect, it turned the F-16 into a Nintendo toy. Instead of the pilot moving a mechanical stick that actuated the plane's hydraulic systems, he wrapped his hand around a foam grip that remained almost stationary. Hand pressure on the stick was transformed into electrical impulses. A computer instantly assimilated those inputs and executed the optimum configuration of the plane's control surfaces for the maneuver. Flaps, rudder, stabilizers, elevators, ailerons were orchestrated automatically, far more precisely and efficiently than any idiosyncratic human pilot could hope to do.

So advanced was this system that the first production model F-16 C/D Block 40 using a digital fly-by-wire flight control computer did not enter the air force's inventory until one month after the FS-X agreement was signed.

The fly-by-wire system was a special security risk because it had direct commercial applications. The European Airbus Industries consortium employed the first commercial fly-by-wire system in 1984 on the A320. Though the F-16 was far more complex, the systems were analogous. Fly-by-wire appeared to be the future of aircraft control.

The other source code problem plaguing Commerce and the DoD was in the mission control computer. This computer and its software represented an extraordinarily up-to-date leap in the air combat arts, although it had little use in the commercial sector. Sam Sevier, the curmudgeonly keeper of the air force's source codes, realized that without the mission control computer's software the plane would be seriously degraded as a weapon. "There wouldn't be an FS-X program if we couldn't give them the source codes on the mission control computer," Sevier stated flatly.

There was an obvious and commonsense reason for this. The mission computer represented the sum of the air force's knowledge of air combat: how best to approach an enemy target; how to deliver a particular type of weapon on that target; how to respond to different threats. This was the sort of information that came from combat experience, in Korea, over the skies of Hanoi, in the Middle East, day after day in the cat-and-mouse game of Cold War confrontation. The Japanese, who had never flown a jet fighter in anger, could not know the final deadly tactics of air-to-air combat.

Over the weekend of March 4 and 5, the Commerce Department concluded what it thought was a final agreement with the DoD. Commerce seemed to win its points. The DoD would nail the Japanese down on workshare. No more vague language. Commerce would have a role overseeing the agreement as it progressed. Where the two sides had differences, they were expressed in the report to the National Security Council. That was Monday.

The following morning, Barksdale phoned his allies to say that the hard-won agreement they had secured over the weekend had collapsed. Armitage had reached in and killed the compromise. There was a meeting scheduled that afternoon at the Commerce Department with Defense to go over new terms.

The first thing Commerce discovered at the noon meeting was that Admiral Tim Wright, the Defense Department's chief interagency negotiator—the man with whom they had reached agreement just days before—had been replaced. Admiral Wright, they later learned, objected to the decision to overturn the agreement he had negotiated and recognized that he could no longer bargain in good faith. The problem, according to Stuart Auerbach of the Washington *Post,* was the DoD's refusal to limit technology flow and to ensure a role for Commerce in monitoring arms agreements.

Armitage now appointed Robert Costello to replace Wright. But as an observer in the science adviser's office put it: "Armitage's brand was on everything, even though he was nowhere to be found."

Costello was a surrogate. He was also a good choice to send to Commerce. Charming, robust, sympathetic, Costello was a champion of U.S. manufacturing. He feared for the future of the nation's industrial base, and worried that it was being eroded by shortsighted policy. There seemed to be much common ground between him and Commerce. He was an advocate for closer links between defense and trade. He recognized that Japanese commercial practices were undermining America's manufacturing capability. Costello had even testified before Jeff Bingaman's subcommittee in May 1988 in favor of increasing the role of Commerce in the MOU process.

The peacemaker, Costello, quickly found himself playing the raging partisan. "My feeling was that they didn't know what they were talking about," he said, referring to the Commerce officials. "I'd been in avionics, electronics, aircraft, composite structures, computer systems. I didn't see that same kind of talent sitting across the table from me. I saw lawyers and clerks."

The focus of Costello's wrath, according to Commerce representatives at the meeting, was Joan McEntee, the Deputy Under Secretary for Export Administration. Her office controlled policy on licensing high-tech commercial exports, to the tune of $71 billion in overseas orders. The nation's industrial base was her domain. She had led Commerce through its negotiations with the DoD, and now Costello turned on her.

Commerce seethed. McEntee had been the spark plug of their negotiating process and had the confidence of Mosbacher. J. Michael Farren, the under secretary in charge of all trade issues, stomped out of the meeting and into the office of Secretary Mosbacher. Said a source close to Farren and McEntee, "Mosbacher told Farren, 'My people don't get treated that way.' He was very serious. He told Farren that he wanted the DoD people to leave the building. And while I wouldn't say Farren threw them out, he certainly hastened their departure."

What trust and rapport was left between the two departments was completely shattered the next day. Craig Richardson, the Presidential Management Intern who had dedicated himself to helping Kevin Kearns kill the FS-X deal, received word from a friend on the NSC that the Pentagon had begun circulating its own set of proposals to be submitted to the National Security Council that Friday, the day of the final meeting. After weeks of agreement that there would be only one paper, the DoD was through kowtowing to Commerce.

The DoD paper was a complete departure from anything that had been negotiated between the two agencies. It cut out restrictions on technology; it eliminated Commerce oversight of technology transfer; it slashed the clarifying language Commerce had called for, such as definitions of derived and nonderived technologies and production workshare. Finally, it demanded a role for the DoD in the export licensing process as a quid pro quo for Commerce's participation in any future MOU talks held by Defense.

The Pentagon report did toss a bone to Commerce by calling for a committee to be formed within thirty days to consider a role for them. The paper had already reached Deputy National Security Adviser Robert Gates when Commerce got word of it through Craig Richardson. Once the DoD proposal was exposed, it became an embarrassment to the DoD, an attempted bureaucratic stab in the back that ended in a pratfall. McEntee would have her revenge.

Friday, just after the noon hour, Joan McEntee reached her limit. The Commerce Department's chief negotiator was staring at a six o'clock NSC deadline, and the Pentagon was still trying to roll back the agreement they had struck over the last weekend. The deadline for Commerce and the DoD to reach terms had already been put back from three o'clock, and now the six o'clock NSC deadline was in jeopardy.

By her own description, McEntee was "no wilting violet." With her straight blond hair and edgy blue eyes, she was at once alluring and tough. McEntee knew the power of theatrics, and by now the DoD saw her as a master of political intrigue. She had seen to it that in talks with the DoD all the top meetings were held at Commerce, on her turf.

In her middle thirties, she wore bright primary-colored business suits, the kind wealthy Washington women in power wore, accented by large earrings, oversized buttons, and a signature scarf. She was a graduate of Marymount and an attorney. A scarab-sized emerald flashed on her right ring finger.

McEntee saw the FS-X as a historic opportunity to expand the influence of her bureau *and* the department. Not often did an issue arise on which reputations could be made. The FS-X was one.

But did that reduce the matter of the FS-X to a mere turf battle, as the DoD argued, a pissing contest over the separation of powers? The Pentagon wouldn't see it any other way. Looking out over the not so wide Potomac, the military saw the Pennsylvania Avenue crowd as a bunch of empire-building bureaucrats. As Tim Tyler made plain, at the same time Commerce was caviling over the FS-X, they were rubber-stamping the sale of wide-body technology direct from Boeing to Mitsubishi. Such a double standard could have only one purpose: Commerce aimed to crowd in on the Pentagon's turf.

The turf-war charge might have had credence if it was only Congress yapping after the FS-X. The reality was that the DoD was nearly isolated on this one. The preponderance of opinion in government supported Commerce. Virtually every single economic agency in government that examined the FS-X deal expressed doubts about its terms. Many were agencies that had little contest with the DoD over this or any other issue. From the National Aeronautics and Space Administration to the obscure Office of Science and Technology Policy, otherwise benign and quiescent pencil pushers were red-faced with outrage.

At the center of this opposition was a group of people who characterized themselves at various times as "the Mob" or "the Mafia." The more senior of them could be recognized as the Black Ships Society. These were career officials in trade and technical posts throughout the government who questioned the motives and tactics of Japanese capitalism. These people, in NASA, the Office of Science and Technology Policy, Energy, Treasury, Commerce, the U.S. Trade Representative, Customs, were not aiming to score on the Pentagon. They were not in this for turf. The FS-X had grown into a cause.

Half-eaten sandwiches punctuated the large meeting-room table, Commerce on one side, Defense on the other. They were almost two hours into their third meeting that week with yet another DoD representative. At that rate, McEntee figured, they would never make it to the final NSC showdown, which was to convene in two hours. The likelihood that this was the DoD's plan was real.

Those closest to McEntee on the issue were Deborah Wince, of the Office of Science and Technology Policy, and Maureen Smith, of the Commerce Department's International Trade Administration. Both attended the meeting on the Commerce side of the table. The Japanese press referred to McEntee & Company as "the three bleached blondes." As Smith saw the meeting developing, the DoD was pushing McEntee, playing a game of brinkmanship. If this meeting fell apart, the NSC would probably take the matter into its own hands and neither Defense nor Commerce would be able to control events.

The DoD delegation now facing McEntee was led by Robert C. McCormack, Deputy Under Secretary for Industrial and International Programs.

McCormack's strategy was to drag Commerce back over the same issues they had settled on the previous weekend. At issue was whether Commerce should have a role on the technical steering committee, made up of American and Japanese representatives, who would oversee the development of the FS-X. This committee was crucial, because it had jurisdiction over the implementation of all the contracts.

McCormack was speaking, once again making the point that Commerce did not have expertise in defense trade and had to accept a more limited role. He was going along quietly when, suddenly, McEntee would hear no more. She exploded, according to one witness. Slamming her hands on the desk and springing to her feet, she snapped, "I'll be damned if I will sit here with my delegation and listen to this crap." Her voice became a growl. "I'm sick and tired of going over and over these same points again and again. We don't even know that you or anybody else from the DoD has the authority to negotiate. What's the point?"

A stunned McCormack attempted to give her assurances that his delegation spoke for the Defense Department, but McEntee cut him off. "I want my delegation to get up right now. We're going to recess and discuss whether the time has come for us to walk out of these negotiations and take the matter directly to the President." That put a chill in the DoD. The code was plain: "Directly to the President" meant Robert Mosbacher, George Bush's chief fund raiser for the last decade. The man responsible for paying for Bush's election campaign.

McEntee stormed out of the room.

As the door was shut behind her, she was heard to say in a loud and contemptuous voice, "We're not going to be jerked around on this anymore." John Richards of the Commerce Department, a twenty-four-year veteran of the trade wars, followed McEntee numbly from the room. He thought he saw the blood draining from McCormack's face as he left.

Next door, in an office not far from where the negotiations were taking place, McEntee broke into laughter. At first Richards did not get it, but in a moment he realized that McEntee, too, knew how to play at brinkmanship. She smiled at her delegation and said softly, "Let's see how they manage that."

McCormack had to understand that if Commerce balked now, the whole FS-X deal could go with it. Japan's March 31 deadline was just three weeks away, which meant that the deal could fall apart at either end. With little more than an hour remaining until the NSC meeting, a collapse would give Mosbacher a chance to take his complaints directly to the President.

As it happened, the Pentagon was in a particularly weakened position vis-à-vis its Commerce counterparts. That day, by a 53–47 vote, the Senate had rejected President Bush's nomination of John G. Tower to be Secretary of Defense. The DoD had no one to represent them before the President with the clout of a Mosbacher. As Maureen Smith put it: "They had no juice." When at last McEntee led her delegation back into the room, McCormack dropped any pretenses. We'll accept the single report, he said.

25

Air Force Won

"After more than a decade of negotiations, attempting to bring balance to our trade relations, the annual deficit with Japan stands at $55 billion, and is, once again, growing, despite the sharp fall in the value of the dollar since September 1985."
—JEFF BINGAMAN, FS-X hearings, March 10, 1989

THE PRESSURE from Congress was unmistakable. On the same day that McEntee was dueling with the DoD and the showdown meeting before the National Security Council was scheduled, the influential Senate Armed Services Committee called a hearing on the FS-X. Once again, Auer and Prestowitz, the alpha and omega of the FS-X, would bracket the issue.

Just as important was the timing. Originally, the hearing had been scheduled for the day before, Thursday, but the Republicans fought it off. Malcolm Wallop, the senior senator from Wyoming—a man rated 0 by the liberal American Civil Liberties Union and 100 by the right-wing American Conservative Union—was seething.

This was Wallop's debut performance as ranking minority member, and he threw his support fervently behind the administration. Fearing that Jeff Bingaman, chairman of the Armed Services Subcommittee on Defense Industry and Technology, was using strong-arm tactics by calling the hearing, he immediately set about laying down markers. "Let me begin by saying that I regret that the first hearing for 1989 for this committee . . . is taking place over my objections." The committee's motives were plain, Wallop said. "Holding a hearing at this time for the express purpose of influencing an interagency review that is taking place at the request of Congress is, I think, a sign of bad faith."

Wallop was correct in charging that the subcommittee was trying to muscle the interagency process. Robert C. Byrd, the former Majority Leader and one of the most powerful men in the chamber, debated with his staff over the timing of the hearings. He had in his possession the government-to-government agreement, and the Japanese Embassy had been lobbying his staff with promises of confidential information. They indicated, for example, that Japan might offer to buy (expensive) battle-management aircraft, known as AWACS, to coax Congress to accept the FS-X deal. But Byrd's staff saw the situation shifting from day to day, and felt the hearings would have substantial impact.

Certainly Bingaman was aware of the NSC meeting and the issues at stake. That morning, a Washington *Post* article had caught his eye because it spelled out the problem at hand. As he told Frank Carlucci, the former Secretary of Defense, who was testifying before Bingaman's subcommittee: "The article states that the Pentagon has balked at participation by a civilian agency in a military contract." The DoD did not want to give Commerce a role in MOU negotiations. This was a topic close to Bingaman's heart, and one he had been fighting for for years. Indeed, he had it written into law, in the Defense Authorization Act.

Carlucci, who was Secretary when the final FS-X agreements were signed, offered terms to Bingaman by way of reply. "I said there was no problem with their participation in an interagency forum," he told Bingaman, "provided their mission is carefully defined. If they are going to be there with a veto on national security matters, then I would object most strongly." A few moments later, he added, "Quite frankly, after thirty years of experience in government, Mr. Chairman, the more people you add to the process, the more constipated it becomes."

Lines were being drawn. While Prestowitz and Auer did not go at each other as they had before the House subcommittee, each became a separate target for partisan committee members. When Clyde Prestowitz testified, he was confronted by an angry Senator Wallop, who challenged the former Commerce Department official's sources. During Prestowitz's oral testimony, he had suggested that the committee could learn more about the FS-X by reading what the Japanese press was saying. Wallop snarled, "I would suggest that if you read the Japanese press, you would get about as much accurate information as you would if you read the American press and read articles by Mr. Clyde Prestowitz, who has not read the MOU. Is that a correct statement?"

In reply to Wallop's request that he engage in self-incrimination,

Prestowitz stammered, "Well, the MOU, as you know, is a classified document."

Snapped Wallop, "So that most of your opinion on it is based on hearsay?" Attacking Prestowitz's analysis of how much work the United States would get as a result of the agreement, Wallop said bluntly, "I must point out to you that you are simply wrong on this point. That is not what is in the agreement. It is classified. But I would simply, for the record, say that it is there—"

Prestowitz, who was not one to be easily cowed, tried to cut in. "Well, if you would allow me to respond." Wallop talked right over him.

When Prestowitz got his turn, he was angry but controlled. "If I am wrong I am happy to be wrong . . . The initial MOU was followed by an exchange of letters between the two governments, which took place on January 10, 1989. Up until that time, there had not been agreement on how the MOU was going to be—"

Now Wallop jumped in. "Could I ask you not to filibuster my time and just make your point, please."

Prestowitz attacked the side letters to the MOU, which superseded the main agreement. Those terms limited U.S. participation to 40 percent of the $1.2 billion development budget, about $440 million. This meant, Prestowitz argued, that if costs rose above the budgeted figure—and experience suggested it surely would, by two or three times—the United States would be limited to the same $440 million, which would no longer be 40 percent, but closer to 10 or 20 percent.

Wallop would not hear this. "Let me assure you on this instance," he said, "that is not what is contained." He did not say if he had read the side letters, or understood their significance as used by Japan in its negotiations with the United States.

When Wallop's time ran out, Senator Byrd came to Prestowitz's defense, plugging his book *Trading Places*. "I recommend that everyone interested in the general subject matter read this book," he said. As Wallop had taken on Prestowitz, Byrd now took on Auer, obliquely at first, in a reference to Japan bashing: "I don't think anyone wants to engage in Japan bashing. I certainly do not. I admire the Japanese . . . If there is any bashing to do, perhaps we ought to turn our sights on some of our negotiators who, from time to time, have apparently not been very good at defending our interests."

Byrd probed Auer on what sort of deal the United States was getting on the spare parts for the FS-X. "After all, isn't the spare parts tail of any weapons system, particularly aircraft, a very substantial part of the lifetime cost of that system?"

Auer tried to wriggle out. "I don't know, sir. I was not in defense sales in any of the time I was in the Pentagon."

Byrd did not let him off. "Well, I gathered from listening to your testimony that you had pretty expert knowledge of this agreement." After a brief cross-examination, in which Auer acknowledged the financial importance of spare parts but maintained that he knew nothing about them, Byrd turned to Bingaman. "I suppose [Auer] thinks this is a good agreement . . . It seems to me that we ought to know something about the spare parts."

Byrd was immediately followed by Democrat Carl Levin, the junior senator from Michigan, a state reeling from the Japanese onslaught in autos. Levin continued after Auer. Noting that Japan does not manufacture fighters but has always refused to buy them off the shelf from U.S. manufacturers. Levin asked, "Is that a protectionist policy?"

"I don't know if that word is accurate," Auer replied.

"Now isn't this FS-X deal clearly an example of protectionist policy on their part?" Levin demanded.

"I think [both the United States and Japan] are capable of protectionism, yes."

"Is that a protectionist policy on *their* part?" Levin's voice rose.

"Well—"

"Is that word not able to come out of our mouths when we apply it to them?" There was laughter in the hearing room.

"All right, sir. Japan can act in a protectionist manner."

The concession wasn't enough for Levin. "Are they acting in a protectionist manner here?"

Auer just could not bring himself to say that Japan was engaged in protectionism over the FS-X. "They are certainly going in accordance with their policy," he said, provoking more laughter. "They are a sovereign nation."

Senator Byrd piped in, "You made a good try, Senator."

Levin now had a full head of steam and the crowd behind him. "Oh, I'm doing better than just a 'try.' I think the failure to answer that question cleanly and straightforwardly says more about our problem than anything else."

Byrd agreed. "Absolutely."

"If we cannot even call a protectionist act by this name, and we are incapable of doing that, then we have a deep problem."

Byrd seemed to be enjoying himself. "[Auer] ought to read Mr. Prestowitz's book, if he has not already done so."

Wallop was silent as Auer's bad run of questioners continued with the junior senator from New York, Republican Alfonse D'Amato. He went right for Auer. "I think it's an absolute mockery when we have people who come before us and testify with glee that the United States actually enjoys a $1 billion [defense trade] surplus with the Japanese . . . We're supposed to get up and say gee, what a fantastic thing, how wonderful."

D'Amato, who had the accent and manner of a street tough, did not let up.

"We take Japanese cars, electronic equipment . . . because they can produce them better and more effectively. But when we produce the best of some other product, we are supposed to be apologetic for it, and we're supposed to say we will go into these phony co-production agreements. That is exactly what this is, a phony agreement."

Auer's morning ground on and on.

That evening, the National Security Council gathered to discuss the month-long review ordered by the President. Deputy Under Secretary McCormack's last-minute acceptance of McEntee's ultimatum set the edgy tone for the evening.

The sign outside the White House situation room said "Conference in Session." It shone brightly in the dimly lit hall, like the signs in broadcasting studios that announce when a program is on the air. Admittance here to the President's underground vineyard is on a need-for-access basis. No press. No visitors down here. Photos of the place show a modest interior decorated like a mid-level executive meeting room. A large curtain covers one wall, concealing a projection screen. The floors are carpeted. Ceilings are acoustic. Sound would be dead in such a place, treble and bass sponged from the air, robbing expression from the voice.

From this basement, America ponders its fate in the world. The minute-by-minute monitoring of the globe goes on night and day. Across the hall is a meeting room, where events are debated. Just at the entrance to the conference room, there is a low Parsons table stacked with china and lined with silverware for coffee and tea steeping in urns.

The meeting held that rainy Friday evening in March was formal and followed procedure. The atmosphere was tense. Joan McEntee once again faced Bob Costello, who had been asked to leave a meeting that Wednesday held at Commerce. Another McEntee antagonist, Karl Jackson, from the National Security Council, was also there. He recalls once having told McEntee "to go jump in a lake" over the FS-X.

Robert M. Gates, the Deputy National Security Adviser, chaired. Calm, professional, he let each party present its views, going around the room. Deputies from the cabinet and advisory agencies sat four by four at the table, Gates at the head. He set out the issues before them: the implications of technology transfer, trade with Japan, concerns for the U.S. industrial base, the role of the Commerce Department in the FS-X deal.

"The central focus was, should they recommend to the President that he proceed under the present terms, or that he modify them to make them more acceptable?" said a witness to the meeting. That meant clarifying how much work the United States would get on the deal and narrowing the terms under which technology would be transferred. There was also the matter of technical packages, the software source codes. Should the NSC recommend to the President that they be withheld? Would that risk the whole program? Was it worth it?

"There were two fears," said the witness. "First was that the Japanese might back out. That was probably a red herring. The second fear was more real, however. That concerned the political reaction in Japan. There was a substantial outcry in the Diet, where they thought we were jerking them around on a done deal. What repercussions might come from a new U.S. demand, *after* the deal had been signed," was less clear.

The meeting began with the State Department, led by Robert M. Kimmitt. A West Pointer with a degree in engineering, he earned three Bronze Stars for valor in Vietnam. At age forty-one, he was about to be confirmed as the number three man in the State Department, Under Secretary for Political Affairs. He replaced Michael H. Armacost, who had won the battle with Gaston Sigur to become ambassador to Japan. In press circles, Kimmitt had a reputation for being Jim Baker's eyes and ears, and though the Secretary had deferred on the FS-X in favor of his friend Robert Mosbacher, his deputy now joined a vigorous defense of the Pentagon's deal.

U.S.-Japan relations would be jeopardized for years to come if the FS-X did not go forward, Kimmitt warned. Key projects, such as Star Wars, might be threatened. In return for sharing twenty-year-old F-16 technology, we will gain access to some of Japan's latest developments in electronics and composite materials. Reneging on the deal now had the potential to set a low-water mark in U.S.-Japan relations in the postwar era.

Kimmitt got a quick response from Eugene Lawson, the Deputy Under Secretary of Labor for International Affairs. "Don't you think, Bob," he recalls saying, "that we would be a lot better off and that the Japanese would respect us a lot more if we showed them that we are serious about our economic security needs and stopped this deal?" Lawson leaned heavily for evidence on the recent CIA study that discounted Japanese technology claims, concluding that Japan had little to offer the United States. "That means that we just got the worst deal possible," Lawson said, thumping the table. "We're giving away the crown jewels and what are we getting in return?"

Deborah Wince, from the Office of Science and Technology Policy, which advises the President on science issues, helped bring Lawson on board the FS-X issue. She backed him now, telling the deputies that the FS-X represented another "one-way street of technology flow to Japan. I can't think of a single instance where we have gotten a significant technology coming from Japan to the United States," she said.

When the Pentagon was heard from, Robert Costello argued that no sensitive technologies were being given away. The programming language, the source codes everyone referred to, was old hat, "obsolete." The United States no longer used the same programming language, called JOVIAL, and now used ADA, a more powerful high-level software tool. The rest of the technology was nothing that we had not already shared with ten other nations in the course of co-producing the F-16. On the other hand, Japan had new technologies that we would be interested in, he said. And for the first time, Japan would be flowing important new technology back to the United States under this agreement.

Costello also proffered an olive branch. He said he agreed that Commerce should have a role in trade issues. He believed defense and trade did have links. But, he emphasized, the expertise, the talent, the experience with military technology is in the Pentagon. Besides, he said, Commerce and the DoD did not have great differences, except in the case of the source codes for the mission computer and the flight control computer.

Costello felt that those codes should be allowed to go to Japan because without them it might not be possible to successfully develop the plane. The object here wasn't to weaken Japan; the whole point was to strengthen it. Be assured, he said, we can protect sensitive technologies.

If anything, the meeting grew more tense as it went along, and the differences between Commerce and the Pentagon seemed to grow. More than an hour had passed with both sides reciting sharp reservations—Commerce about the agreement, and the DoD about Commerce, particularly the degree to which the economic agencies might influence future deals. Precedents were at stake here, and both sides remained firmly entrenched in their individual certainty that they had the best prescription for dealing with Japan.

This was what made the meeting extraordinary. As one of the aides to a deputy from an economic agency put it: "Not only was it unbelievable that Commerce had come this far, but that people were speaking their minds. Usually the DoD dominates moments like this and the State Department backs them. Agencies like Commerce just put their tails between their legs and do as they're told." That was not happening now before the NSC. Commerce was not holding back, it was holding forth. "It was one of the most extraordinary things I had ever seen in government."

The actual presentations were short, but there were many speakers and more comments. As the evening progressed toward an eight o'clock adjournment for dinner, the room began to feel smaller and smaller. The heavy conference table took up most of the available space. There was little room to move back comfortably. A row of advisers lined the walls just in back of the deputies. The room appeared as cramped as an English bed-sitter. The air was a close mix of cigarette fumes, aftershave, and perfume.

Presentations went around the room, from left to right, person by person, and the sense of expectation grew as Joan McEntee's turn to speak neared.

Though officially she represented Commerce, she also spoke for other economic agencies.

McEntee led the insurgents. Week after week now, she had fought battles with the Pentagon. The last five days had been like a knife fight. Just hours before, she had played a game of chicken with the DoD, bluffed, and won. She was marked; it was all on her. If she slipped, it would be a long and embarrassing drop from the dizzying heights Commerce had unexpectedly reached.

McEntee was known as a quick study, someone who could take a briefing on a complex problem and unravel the issue in a conference room as if she had been managing it herself. At the same time, it cannot be said that she had a deep appreciation for issues. The politics of government captured her imagination; the intricacies she left to others. The grand strategies came from above, the work from below. In between was where McEntee made her mark, in the my-face-in-your-face of cutting a deal.

This could just as easily be McEntee's meeting to lose, however. She was hot-tempered. She could be theatrical. She did not have experience before the NSC, and her presentation was crucial. The pressure was on her. For it had all come down to this, this meeting and this speech. If McEntee won, she could say she beat the DoD. She had set precedent. Maybe she had changed for the better the way the United States and Japan did business.

I want to thank everyone for your comments, she began, immediately setting a tone of collegiality. Instead of confronting Costello over the paper that had made its way into Gates's office, she rose above the fray by clinging to reason. She did not try to argue, for instance, that developing advanced fighters would set Japan up in the commercial aviation business. She acknowledged that developing wide-body jumbo jets was different from turning out dartlike warplanes.

Instead, McEntee made the point that aviation was too important an export to be viewed strictly in security terms. Or even in terms of companies like General Dynamics and Boeing, which supported the deal. They were airframers, systems integrators. The ones who stood to lose most in the deal were the thousands of small subcontracting companies that live off the giant systems integrators. This was the industrial base everyone in the room agreed had to be protected. Too much went into fighters in the way of electronics, for instance, that had uses in civilian aircraft. The flight control computer, for example, had commercial spin-offs, and Japan excelled at manufacturing electronics.

By not attacking the DoD, she disarmed them. At one point during her gracious opening remarks, Bob Costello broke in: "I wish I had said something like that." McEntee took the moral high ground. Within the NSC, the paper Armitage had circulated after killing the agreement with Commerce was seen as an act of bad faith.

Gates concluded what some saw as an inconclusive meeting and others saw as a big win for Commerce, by promising in an official way that he would play the honest broker. There was never an indication or suggestion that he did otherwise. As people left the room, Gates stood by the door shaking hands. McEntee and her delegation were the last out. Gates, who would soon go on to become the Director of the Central Intelligence Agency, smiled at her. McEntee recalls that Gates shook her hand when he said, "You blew them away."

The Washington *Post* reported on Monday about what it described as "an unusual Friday night meeting" at the National Security Council. According to the story: "The Commerce Department won significant changes in [the FS-X] deal and gained a role in monitoring the two-way flow of technology under it." Major differences remained within the administration over the source codes for the computers, and the fear was that Congress would kill the deal if the source codes went to Japan. The expectation that emerged was that Bush would allow the deal to go through but would apply a "significant limit" to technology flow.

A showdown meeting with the President was expected the next day. In fact, a confused administration would delay the decision until Wednesday, March 15, 1989.

Bush managed the FS-X well, even though he was up against a deadline and circumstances were stacked against him. March 30 loomed large because of Japan's budget requirements and the word "budget" was enough to inflict fear into the heart of any public official. That was just sixteen days away, barely more than two weeks. Making matters worse, the FS-X was not Bush's problem. The FS-X was a product of the Reagan years, the other guy's watch. Bush had gotten stuck doing damage control.

The President managed this delicate fight rationally, by compromise and orderly retreat. For all that, when he finally took his stand, Bush barely escaped with the deal.

The new administration had gotten off to a slow start. The presidential nomination process had been sluggish; confirmation had been slower still. Bush had even lost out on one major appointment: John Tower to Defense. By any measure, the FS-X was giving the new administration fits. Whereas its expertise was supposed to lie in foreign affairs, it appeared to be fumbling the effort at damage control. Ironically, no matter what decision Bush finally would have taken—to accept the agreement on its face, to kill it, or to hike up the middle of the road and review it—he would still have been scrambling around at the eleventh hour for those few undecided votes on the Senate floor to support it. The FS-X came with all sorts of problems.

Bush had never seen a situation where the cabinet was so torn. The scene was extraordinary. Bob Mosbacher had latched on to the FS-X like a cause. The Tower thing had exploded right in the middle of it all. The U.S. Trade Representative opposed the deal along with his science adviser. And the press seemed to have an inside view of every new development. What else was left?

Now, with a new Defense Secretary coming in, Dick Cheney, Bush was required to make some sort of gesture. Bush could not sack the incoming Cheney for a big loss by ignoring him in favor of Mosbacher. That would be a fine how-do-you-do. The man had hardly found his way into his new office, and the President was handing him and his department a vote of no confidence.

Cheney liked to tell a story about his first visit to the White House after the Bush appointment. He had been chief of staff under President Ford, but got lost on his way through the White House basement. "I remember that I was on my way to my first FS-X meeting. I couldn't find the meeting room." His initiation proved portentous.

The President's choices were few. He could notify Congress under the Arms Export Control Act and risk their reaction for the next thirty days. There had already been two hearings; no doubt there would be more. Making changes in the deal would satisfy Commerce, particularly if they were given an oversight role. But there would be an opposite effect on Japan. Reopening a negotiation less than six months after an agreement had been signed was, while not unprecedented, the wrong way for a new administration to introduce itself to Tokyo.

Bush managed these conflicts with a staff that had not yet had the opportunity to become fully acquainted. Advisers were jockeying for position. John Sununu, for example, the President's chief of staff, had a confrontation with General Larry Welch, the air force's man in charge of the FS-X. Welch claimed that the fighter represented twenty-year-old technology. Sununu would have none of that. He snapped, "We've been spending millions every year to upgrade that plane; if it is only old technology what have you been doing with the money?"

In the end, the pleadings before the President on March 15 ended inconclusively. In the days after the meeting, the President met with experts on the disputed technology. Said one presidential adviser about the exercise, "I thought at the time that it was just plain awful; it showed an absolute failure of the government that the President had to make a decision about source code versus object code. You could just hear yourself say, 'And which, sir, do you think we should give the Japanese?'"

The pressure was on Bush, and he took a welcome planned trip to Houston and Colorado on Thursday and Friday, March 16 and 17. George Bush was going home for the first time as President of the United States. He would be joined by his best pals, both members of his cabinet, for a hero's welcome. The flight was as happy as the moment was heady. Accompanying him on the plane were his FS-X briefing reports, FS-X position papers, and his old friend Bob Mosbacher. Mosbacher acknowledges the trip on Air Force One to Houston, but he demurs when questioned about it. "You know, I've never admitted that to anybody. I don't know whether now that he's [Bush] left office whether it's time to or not. I always have said, and I may have even heard him say this, that, you know, whatever I said to the President in private was private."

Mosbacher's chief aide, Wayne Berman, recalls, "George Bush had campaigned as a free trader. His theme was that free trade and tough negotiation will win the battle for competitive supremacy with Japan. Dukakis had called for an industrial policy. Now that he was President, Bush had to show that he was a tough negotiator. When Bob Mosbacher went up front in Air Force One to talk with the President, he made clear that reviewing the FS-X deal was the sort of tough stance the President should be taking. Coming from the President's best friend, a man who had only George Bush's best interests at heart, the argument made great sense. By the time Bush had returned to Washington, he had made up his mind on the FS-X."

26

The Mountain
and the Mouse

"Japan will benefit more than the U.S. from technology swapped under an agreement to jointly develop the FS-X jet fighter, U.S. Commerce Secretary Robert Mosbacher said yesterday [in Tokyo]."
—*Investor's Daily*, September 15, 1989, five months after Mosbacher endorsed the agreement

O N SATURDAY, MARCH 18, 1989, Karl Jackson got a phone message telling him that the President had made up his mind on the FS-X. The President was calling for a renegotiation of the agreement. Though he was supporting the broad terms of the deal, he wanted tightening and clarification. No public announcement had been made as yet; nor had the Japanese been notified.

The news of the President's decision did not come as a complete surprise to the man who administered the interagency process at the National Security Council. The Washington *Post* had been reporting for some time that the President was going to reopen talks on the agreement.

The plan now, Jackson was told, was for the Japanese ambassador to be called to the White House on Monday, March 20, to receive an aide-mémoire, a diplomatic memo which offered the new U.S. terms. The President would call on Japan to formally agree to a 40 percent U.S. workshare when the plane went into production. Also, no source codes for the flight control computer would be transferred. In addition, definitions for technology transfer agreements would have to be narrowed. Engine technologies would be restricted as well.

This represented a big loss for the Defense Department and a big win for the Commerce Department, which the President had also rewarded with a place alongside the DoD on the steering committee that would oversee FS-X development. Commerce was also to receive a role in future MOU negotiations. Essentially that was what the original report hammered out by McEntee had called for.

Jackson was worried about the Japanese reaction. The situation was already tense enough in Tokyo. The government was about to fall, brought down by an influence-peddling scandal. The United States was about to name Japan as an unfair trader under the 1988 Omnibus Trade Bill. Now a signed agreement for Japan's next-generation fighter jet was being second-guessed by the President of the United States.

One of the first things Jackson did was to call the director for national security affairs in the North American bureau of the embassy of Japan, Ryozo Kato. A first-rate diplomat and a natural fit with Washington, the handsome and debonair Kato had responsibility for the security side of the embassy's political section, which administered the FS-X deal. A distinguished and personable man, Kato (who was no relation to the former defense minister) spoke fluent English.

Jackson drove to Kato's Bethesda home for a meeting. He was acting on his own in the decision to inform Kato. Great nations do not like to be surprised by their close allies. However, this was unusual and violated an important rule. In Washington, you never preempt your boss's initiative. "As soon as I found out that we were going to seek clarification on those three points," Jackson says, "I went out to Ryozo's house in Bethesda, which is quite near mine, and told him what the situation was. And we agreed that we would do our level best on both sides to work this out."

Kato was neither surprised nor shocked at Jackson's message, although he was said to have warned the NSC staffer that the situation had the potential for disaster.

There's nothing we can do, Jackson was said to have replied. It's coming.

Jackson also informed Torkel Patterson at the Pentagon. Patterson, who had replaced Jim Auer at the International Security Agency, also paid a visit to Kato, arriving late Sunday evening, after ten. Together, the two men tried to develop a strategy for portraying the upcoming negotiations to their respective governments. Said a former Defense Department source with close access to the embassy of Japan, "Kato was trying to figure out what he was going to tell the Japanese government, so they wouldn't get too pissed off." These meetings went on for the next three weeks, as they tried to manage reaction.

The pressure was on. On Saturday the New York *Times* once again editorialized against the FS-X, calling for an end to the program: "Japan's trade deficit with the U.S. is a painful $50 billion a year and getting no better. The

F-16 is a high-quality product at an unmatchable price. Why wouldn't Japan seize such a chance to help itself and its chief ally and trading partner?" The editorial concluded that "Mr. Bush's best course would be to cancel the FS-X deal . . ."

Clyde Prestowitz reports that when the official word that the United States was calling for renegotiation went out to the Japanese Embassy, and the ambassador, Nobuo Matsunaga, was asked to come to the State Department to get an aide-mémoire on the FS-X from Secretary Baker, he declined, saying that he needed time to prepare.

Tokyo was in an uproar, and the FS-X was the least of it. The scandal sweeping Japan's Diet was downing high-ranking politicians throughout the ruling Liberal Democratic Party. The Prime Minister was on the verge of resigning over illegal campaign contributions, and his popularity nosed over and crashed, falling to just 3 percent.

Matsunaga finally received instructions and met with Baker on Monday. He was said to have been deeply distressed during the meeting, perspiring. If a deal such as this one fell through on his watch, a long and successful career could lose steam if not direction. At the State Department, Matsunaga faced four new cabinet members—Baker, Mosbacher, Cheney, and Scowcroft. The ambassador reportedly entreated Baker not to let this review process go further, imploring that the Secretary not impose onerous conditions on the agreement.

The Wall Street Journal reported that the cabinet officers were there as a show of solidarity by the U.S. government designed for Matsunaga's consumption. "We wanted to let [the Japanese] know they couldn't play one agency against another," the daily said, quoting a State Department aide.

The President went public with his decision the next day, Tuesday, but showed deference for Japanese anger over what they saw as a breach of agreement. The President promised that the deal would go forward, although he expected "certain clarifications" from Japan, on which he did not elaborate. "We've pretty much finished our deliberation here inside the administration," Bush told reporters.

In Tokyo reaction was uniform in its outrage. On Wednesday, in a blunt statement to the Japanese press, issued immediately after a meeting of the cabinet, the current defense chief, Kichiro Tazawa, called on the United States to "respect" the agreement. A Japanese official told the New York *Times,* "In the short term this particular issue will be solved. But in the longer term, it will leave a very serious scar . . ." A Japanese reporter waxed biblical for the *Asian Wall Street Journal:* "The first piece of fruit has been harvested from the deal, but it isn't really fruitful. It's like the piece Eve gave Adam." A rumor even circulated that Japan had gone shopping in Israel for an alternative to the U.S. deal.

On Thursday, presidential spokesman Marlin Fitzwater seemed to back off the administration's hard line. He said, "The President still has to make the basic decisions." In fact, by now, the United States was deeply concerned about Japanese reaction, and by not discussing terms Bush was keeping his options open. A high-ranking Japanese delegation was expected within hours at the State Department, and negotiations were about to begin.

Seiki Nishihiro's JAL flight touched down at Dulles Airport on schedule Thursday evening. The man many called the most important figure at the Japan Defense Agency was considered a friend of Washington. Now he was making an emergency house call, his second visit to the capital in six weeks.

The last time Nishihiro was in the capital, during the Takeshita visit, he warned in news reports that a lengthy review of the FS-X deal could doom it. Now Japan's March 31, 1989, deadline had shrunk to a bare week. The dreaded review by the new administration had come to pass. Nishihiro was the man on the spot.

"I got a call for help from Ambassador Matsunaga telling me what was taking place and asking me to come to Washington to try to salvage the matter," recalled Nishihiro. "My feelings were very strong. I wanted to quit the deal. Say, let's just forget it.

"This was an idea that I put before Prime Minister Takeshita. I told him that I did not want to make this trip to the United States if I did not have the freedom of choice to put an end to this.

"Takeshita would not agree, but a compromise was reached. I would make clear from the outset that it was Japan's wish to quit the deal, but that we would be open to negotiations." Nishihiro also reportedly carried a letter from the Prime Minister to Bush, but its contents were never disclosed.

In Washington that Thursday, March 23, Nishihiro held what he described as a "low-level briefing" with William Clark, Acting Assistant Secretary of State for the East Asian and Pacific Affairs. Clark had worked closely with Karl Jackson to try to bring the FS-X through the Bush transition. "I told Mr. Clark," said Nishihiro, " 'The Congress now is saying that they might not approve the agreement such as it is. Why not let them do so, if it will finish the whole deal?' "

Clark reacted with "stunned silence," recalled Nishihiro. Clark finally replied that that would be in neither nation's best interest to let the deal collapse. It could pose serious political problems for the new administration. There was no choice but to find a way through Congress. They had to go forward. "And so I understood that to bring down the whole deal was not possible," said Nishihiro.

A U.S. observer at the talks describes a very different view of the proceedings. "Before the meeting gets started Clark gets a call from Baker. Baker tells Clark, 'You're not to give anything away.' Clark goes into the meeting and just doesn't even give Nishihiro the simplest give on anything. Nishihiro was trying to be very reasonable, trying to enter into a negotiation. Clark's just saying No. No. No. No. No."

Over the next day or two, Nishihiro met with the FS-X principals in the Bush cabinet—Baker from State, Mosbacher from Commerce, Scowcroft from the National Security Council, and Dick Cheney, the Secretary of Defense. Baker had been designated by Bush to negotiate with Nishihiro, which was certainly an uneven matchup, at least officially. Meetings were held at the State Department.

This time, Nishihiro did not bring up the threat to kill the deal. "I had come to understand from Mr. Clark that this would cause serious problems for the new administration. However, I believe that Mr. Clark gave Mr. Baker my message." Nishihiro was rankled that the U.S. players who had been responsible for the FS-X—Weinberger, Armitage, Auer—were not available for consultations.

Once, when Richard Armitage had a direct line to Caspar Weinberger, Armitage and Nishihiro made quite a pair: two samurai, one tried in battle and the other who had grown up on war. Now Armitage was keeping a low profile, hoping for a job running the army or the navy. He was of little help to Nishihiro, who faced a whole new administration of strangers, none of whom shared a history with him or sympathy with the FS-X predicament.

"I told Mr. Baker that the Japanese side had no intention of changing the agreement," Nishihiro recalled. "If the U.S. side wants to break the agreement, that is not my business. We will not take the initiative."

Nishihiro argued against making a commitment on how much work the United States would get if the plane went into production. "Production depends on development. It would not be appropriate to decide that now." Nishihiro did not think U.S. companies would stick with the deal. "We are only going to produce a hundred fighters. Why would American companies want to produce parts for so few planes?" Nishihiro had a point: There was no economy of scale to keep U.S. producers involved.

In fact, Nishihiro was willing to concede 35 percent of the work to the United States in the production phase. But Baker, employing arguments crafted by Karl Jackson of the NSC, pushed for 40 percent, contending that the sale of 130 F-16s directly from General Dynamics to Japan would bring in $3 billion over the life of the program. But the co-development of 130 planes would bring in over $200 million more to General Dynamics, $3.2 billion over the life of the program. (The argument ignored the cost of the support package that went along with the direct off-the-shelf sale of an aircraft, which was valued at as much as three times the cost of the planes, a potential gain of $9 billion in this case.

Nishihiro's thoughts drifted to mountain climbing. "If you are about to make an ascent and already your team is bickering and having problems, the chances are that you will not make it to the top."

Auer's surrogate at the Defense Department, Torkel Patterson, thought that Nishihiro was ill treated by his U.S. hosts. "Nishihiro was there trying to make the deal work," said Patterson, "and he went up there and he was treated . . ." His voice trailed off. "There was totally no sense about Japanese sensitivities to this. Really terrible."

Nishihiro hung on in Washington for seven days. Originally, plans were for him to leave Saturday, after three days. But he stayed until March 29, just before the budget deadline set by the Ministry of Finance.

The end was bitter for Nishihiro. Not only was the United States going to strong-arm Japan to reopen a signed government agreement, but Japan was going to be forced into a humiliating proof that its budget deadline was a sham and that it could be postponed. Kyodo News Service reported on the day Nishihiro arrived back in Tokyo that the defense agency had signed its 10.7 billion yen ($80.4 million) contract with Mitsubishi for the FS-X. The budget deadline simply had vanished.

Clyde Prestowitz had predicted such an outcome three weeks earlier in congressional testimony, which bolstered the credibility of his arguments. As he presciently told Senator Bingaman's subcommittee on March 10: "Japan does not have to get this into its budget by March 31. I negotiated on telecommunications four years ago, and at that time we were told that we had to complete those negotiations by March 31 because it had to go to the Diet and get into the budget. In fact, we did not conclude the negotiation until May 31, and it went through fine."

Though negotiations lasted long enough to make Ryozo Kato "upset in the stomach," a settlement between the two governments actually came quickly, just twenty-nine days from the time Seiki Nishihiro arrived back in Tokyo. Much of it hinged on a midnight telephone call to Robert M. Kimmitt, who, as the number three man in the State Department, was handling the FS-X, from Wayne Berman, Mosbacher's right hand at Commerce. "I called Kimmitt and said your boss just called my boss wanting to know what we really want in this. He's got a three-point plan on the FS-X." Berman laid out Commerce's position. "We don't want computer source codes going out, we don't want certain engine technologies transferred, and we want flow-back. I told him, 'I don't want to make your job any harder. So if you get us these things from the Japanese, we will not only stand by you in the interagency process, we will sell this to the Hill and make it win.' "

Of course, there had been protests in Japan over these terms. Former defense chief Yuko Kurihara thought that the United States "changed the

spirit of co-development. The United States grew more selfish." The popular
Shintaro Ishihara presented a petition in the Diet calling on the Prime Minister to scrap the deal. But that was largely a matter of show. More serious was
that defense chief Tazawa followed through on his earlier remarks and canceled a planned visit to the United States. So there was posturing, and anger
was plain, but the Japanese agreed.

In reality, however, Tokyo was in no position to quibble, let alone quarrel.
The Takeshita government was disintegrating. On April 24, the Prime Minister submitted his resignation. (The Tokyo stock market rose more than 400
points on the news.) His former secretary of thirty years, Ihei Aoki, fifty-
eight, committed suicide. The cumulative weight of successive scandals took
their toll on Japan's bargaining position: the Toshiba affair, the Recruit scandal.

Yet for all Japan's vulnerabilities, for all the fierce opposition in the U.S.
government, the terms of the final agreement still included technologies crucial to boosting Japan's aviation industry. These were the very tools Kevin
Kearns and Clyde Prestowitz considered so prejudicial to America's economic
security: computer methods, systems integration, the last twenty years of
aviation know-how.

On close examination, the United States clearly was not asking for major
concessions from its Japanese allies. A total of five paragraphs and three
subparagraphs polished off the Bush administration's concerns. This had
been the big dance around what became a rather small fire. The entire agreement, signed on April 28, 1989, consisted of just three pages: a single-page
single-spaced letter from Ambassador Nobuo Matsunaga to Secretary Baker;
a single-page single-spaced letter from Baker to Matsunaga; and a one-page
double-spaced "oral exchange."

This was it, the final terms. On these few words turned some $10 billion in
gleaming national treasure, decades of accumulated engineering wisdom, the
secrets of advanced design, the security of the West and the Pacific Rim. Here
was presumably the next ten to fifteen years of U.S.-Japan defense relations.
How many jobs were won and lost in these two signatures? What number of
small businesses and multinational corporations risked their futures and their
shareholders' fortunes for these carefully typed sentences? Was the future of
America's greatest industry finally up for grabs?

The Matsunaga letter began: "With respect to the FS-X development program, I wish to make the following *clarifications* in response to U.S. *inquiries*"
(emphasis added). He did not speak of terms or demands, but rather "inquiries" and "clarifications." The ambassador went on to say that Japan promised the United States 40 percent "value" of the total production work. No
mention was made about the quality of this work, whether it would be high-
tech labor or whether the United States would end up bending metal. The

ambassador also agreed that there would be a technical steering committee. Here was a role for Commerce, if the United States saw fit. As for the airplane's radar, electronic countermeasures, navigation system, and mission computer, those would be considered nonderived technologies, which would be available to the United States if Japanese firms were willing to license them. All other technologies derived from FS-X development would be available to the United States free of charge. There was nothing in the terse memo about software source codes.

Baker accepted the note and offered his own clarifications: ". . . the [Japan Defense Agency] should be assured that under the terms of the FS-X MOU Japan will receive access to the source codes necessary to develop the *mission control computer*" (emphasis added). He left open the question of the source codes for the commercially applicable flight control computer. "With the clarifications provided in this exchange of letters, we will move forward to notify the Congress of the United States in accordance with our requirements."

In the oral exchange that accompanied the letters, Japan said it "wishes to confirm that software will be made accessible to Japan as much as possible . . ." The United States replied, "[We] will make the required software accessible to Japan to the maximum extent consistent with [our] disclosure process . . ." Even after the agreement was reached with Japan, Nishihiro believed that Japan would receive the source codes for the F-16, including the flight control computer.

The Defense Department claims this is the language under which access to the commercially valuable source codes for the fly-by-wire system would be denied to Japan. "The fact is, the United States never gives away its source code," said Tim Tyler. The fact was, the DoD was giving away source code to the mission control computer.

Commerce and company were forced to settle for this explanation. They had only the assurance of the DoD that it was never their intention to transfer these codes. Though the latter is hard to prove, the Pentagon insists it declined to allow Japan access to the commercially applicable codes.

At 4:55 that same afternoon, Bush made a statement to the press and announced that he was submitting the FS-X to Congress for review. "We weighed this matter from the standpoint of trade, of our industrial growth, and technology transfer, as well as strategic and foreign policy considerations." The statement was significant because it implied that Bush had forged a very clear link between trade and defense, in direct contravention of the Reagan administration, which had created the FS-X deal. In spite of this, the United States still planned to hand over technologies which the Japanese themselves considered vital additions to their aviation industry.

The President went on to say, "We did have several initial concerns about the agreement, but I want to assure you that sensitive source codes for the aircraft's computer will be strictly controlled . . ." This gave the weight of a presidential pledge that the Pentagon would retain the key software language. At 4:57 the President concluded his remarks.

A few minutes later, in a press conference, the issue of the flight control computer was addressed. "That is new to the F-16s," said an unnamed administration official. "The airplanes with those computers just came out last December. We think the technology is new. We did not release the software codes . . ."

Reaction to the final agreement was mixed in Washington. The Washington *Post* reported the next day that, predictably, "Senator Jesse Helms (R-N.C.), a strong opponent of the original deal, called the revised agreement 'a disappointment' because 'the administration appears to have given in on many points.' "

But Senator Jeff Bingaman, who had long been skeptical of the Pentagon's push for co-development, was wait-and-see but still upbeat in his press release. "If my concerns on the production workshare and technology transfer have been adequately addressed, I hope to be in a position to support the new agreement."

The Dallas *Morning News* reported that General Dynamics officials did not hold out much hope for additional jobs for the economically strapped Dallas–Fort Worth area, where the F-16 was built. Company officials were quoted as saying the additional work would "stabilize" the current workforce. No new jobs were forecast. Nor did the company offer much solace to the 4,500 subcontractors on the F-16 program. Many would be cut out of the FS-X by Japanese suppliers, who were guaranteed more than 60 percent of the work on the plane.

Clyde Prestowitz, in an article in the Chicago *Tribune*, aptly described the Bush administration's efforts: "The FS-X mountain has labored and brought forth a mouse."

On Monday, May 1, the President made it official. He sent notification to Jim Wright, Speaker of the House, and to Claiborne Pell of Rhode Island, chairman of the Foreign Relations Committee, that the United States was going to move along with the FS-X deal. The one-page notice from the State Department's legislative affairs office looked like boilerplate: "Pursuant to section 36(d) of the Arms Export Control Act . . ."

Signed by Assistant Secretary of State Janet G. Mullins, the cover letter was submitted along with a one-page enclosure, MC-9-89, the formal notification. It itemized the particulars of the agreement but gave no details: "*Authorized Sales Territory:* Japan." "*Foreign Country in Which Manufacturing Will Take Place:* Japan." The notification estimated the value of the deal at $350 million, not including the engines, which, it said, "may be the subject of a separate notification at a later date."

Now Congress had thirty days to pass a joint resolution opposing the agreement. This was the moment opponents of co-development had been awaiting for two years, since March 5, 1987, when Senator John Danforth wrote to Secretary of Defense Weinberger ridiculing Japan's requirements for the FS-X as "glorified non-tariff barriers."

On Capitol Hill, Kevin Kearns was about to make his last stand. He had become the coordinator on the issue, a reality check against the Pentagon's inflated claims, and the in-house authority on the deal. His forces were organized and mobilized. As his mentor Bill Triplett put it: "I was the chief executive officer and Kevin was the chief operating officer."

The one thing that stood in Kearns's way was compromise. Already a key opponent of the deal had fallen. Mosbacher was on board the deal. By accepting the President's terms for "clarification," the President's best friend, Commerce Secretary Mosbacher, eliminated crucial opposition from within the cabinet and exerted a powerful tug toward the center.

What sway Mosbacher's new choice would hold over congressional opinion was uncertain, but one important ally, Jeff Bingaman, had already shown some optimism for the President's efforts. What is more, the junior senator from New Mexico tended to migrate toward the middle ground in search of solutions, rather than confrontation. Kearns could no longer count on him.

Kearns, however, knew there was powerful bipartisan support in both the House and the Senate for doing away with the FS-X. The day the President notified Congress of the deal, Democrat Alan Dixon introduced Senate Joint Resolution 113 to stop the FS-X deal. The next day, California Democrat Mel Levine introduced House Joint Resolution 254, which would also have killed the program. Republicans Al D'Amato of New York and Jesse Helms of North Carolina were active and aggressive in their opposition, full of passionate intensity. To date, Congress had held five hearings on the FS-X, voted 97–0 back in 1987 to call on Japan to buy F-16s instead of building the FS-X, wrote the issue into committee reports in 1988, and enacted legislation that same year. Though these were largely just gestures, hand waving and hand wringing, they were not to be dismissed. To that extent Kevin Kearns had the FS-X right where he wanted it. This was his moment.

27

The Center Holds

"We're starting to get concerned because we were hearing reports coming out that the administration is really going to try to push this thing."
—CHARLES SMITH, legislative assistant to Democrat Alan J. Dixon, senior senator from Illinois

ALMOST TWO MONTHS to the day since his Subcommittee on Defense Industry and Technology first held a hearing on the FS-X, Jeff Bingaman gaveled the room to order at 9:34 A.M. Tuesday, May 9, 1989. Six days had passed since the President notified Congress that he was going forward with the FS-X. Now attention was riveted on the hearing. The number of senators attending this meeting was more than double that of the first. Staff size burgeoned from sixteen to twenty-six. The number of TV cameras tripled. Still photographers arrayed themselves in the semicircle at the foot of the dais, snapping their strobes in syncopation at the motionless witnesses.

In a matter of moments, Kevin Kearns would have his anxieties about the direction Senator Bingaman was taking on the fighter answered, if not satisfied. Not only would Bingaman give some indication of his official reaction to the Bush review, but Missouri's John Danforth would offer testimony as well. They had been the two water carriers on the issue, and they would now serve as bellwethers on congressional intentions.

"When I convened the first hearing," Bingaman told the audience in the crowded auditorium in the marmoreal Russell Office Building, "I said I had strong reservations about the agreement. . . .

"Now, after almost three months of hard work, it appears that President Bush has made major improvements in the agreement."

Bingaman stopped short, however, of an outright endorsement of the Bush compromise, saying that concerns remained. "One of the purposes of today's hearing is to learn more about the improvements from the administration." He ended up praising the administration's handling of the Commerce Department's role in the affair. "I want to commend President Bush for adopting the spirit and letter of this law in the interagency FS-X review that he directed.

"The result is an obviously stronger and more reciprocal agreement." The procedure followed precisely what he had written into the Defense Authorization Act of 1989. This process had been Bingaman's mission, creating a province for Commerce in the oversight of defense sales. In many ways the FS-X had been a vehicle to force this change, not a cause in and of itself. More than a year before, he had set in motion the process with his subcommittee's report on the Defense Authorization Act, specifically citing the FS-X. The strategy had worked, and the FS-X had become a test case. Bingaman was now saying that the President had passed the test. That bode well for Bush.

When Danforth's turn came, he underlined the same points. "It seems to me that one of the most important considerations before us is who is going to be responsible for negotiating memoranda of understanding with Japan or any other country," Danforth said.

The President's findings clearly represented a remedy to what both Danforth and Bingaman saw as the fatal flaw in the FS-X deal: the narrow security focus the Pentagon took in its arms sales agreements. Assuming Commerce created the staff and developed the expertise to make a significant contribution in the future, they would be able to leverage the DoD into a better negotiating position, in much the same way as Japan's Ministry of International Trade and Industry provided a counterweight to the defense agency's ambitions.

But that did not mean that Danforth was entirely happy with the deal. "It was absolutely clear and it was a matter of public record that the government of Japan intended to set itself up in the aerospace industry and despite that clear statement, no agency, no department of our executive branch with any responsibility for looking out for the competitive future of our country, had any role whatsoever to play in negotiating this arrangement."

However, Danforth seemed prepared to get off the fence, though reluctantly. Speaking of the administration's efforts, he told the committee, "My own feeling with respect to this particular transaction is that it is a little bit late. I think that Congress is going to end up agreeing to it . . . I think that to the credit of Bob Mosbacher in particular . . . they were able to reopen the details of the transaction. They were able to improve the situation, at least somewhat, and my own view is that it is a little late to pull the rug out from under them."

Kearns winced.

The next day, May 11, 1989, Bingaman was scheduled to testify at a hearing before the Senate Foreign Relations Committee, where Kearns worked under Jesse Helms and Bill Triplett. This hearing represented the principal stepping-stone in the legislative process set off by Senator Alan Dixon's decision to file a resolution disapproving of the President's notification. The committee's job was to decide whether to recommend that resolution to the full Senate.

When Bingaman's turn came to testify before the committee, he immediately signaled his new course. "I oppose . . . the resolution of disapproval," he said. No waffling there. "I think that on balance we need to go forward. The resolution of disapproval would essentially say that in the circumstances we find ourselves, we would rather stand on the sidelines and watch the Japanese develop this plane on their own or in alliance with our European allies, we would rather watch that happen than participate." This represented a major defection for the Kearns forces: first Danforth, now Bingaman.

Ed McGaffigan, Bingaman's senior staffer on the FS-X, recalled the evolution of Bingaman's position. "Kevin believed no agreement was a good agreement on this. I think my boss and I were of the school that there has to be an agreement that is a good agreement. This is not beyond the reach of man. The best agreement was to buy off the shelf. We all agreed on that, but we were more willing to accept the world as it was."

The outcome of the hearing, however, was ordained even before Bingaman's declaration, largely because of the committee's own predispositions. Despite the likes of Jesse Helms, the committee was considered an extension of the State Department, its annex on the Hill. Most members of the committee liked to think of themselves as part of the same priesthood to which members of the foreign service belong. The Chrysanthemum Club had a chapter on the Foreign Relations Committee, along with the Arabists and the Sovietologists. Jesse Helms referred to this as the "fascination of the Foreign Relations Committee."

That relationship is what Senator Dixon's chief aide on the FS-X issue, Charlie Smith, explained to Kearns. He did not think that the committee would report his boss's resolution of disapproval to the Senate favorably. Basically, he and Kearns were now fighting a rearguard action in what was developing into a symbolic and closely fought battle.

As a result of the President's interagency process and the determined efforts of Congress, the FS-X had become less and less a weapons deal and more and more a symbol of industrial leadership, national wealth, enterprise, and technological superiority. These were the measures of power in a maturing global economy. As much as anything, the plight of the Soviet Union proved that there was no military power apart from an efficient industrial base.

The impulse toward compromise created by the President's review split opponents of the FS-X between those who thought they had made the best of a bad deal—Bingaman and Danforth—and those who thought that the only way to improve the deal was to crush it—Helms, Dixon, D'Amato.

As evidence of the ripening acrimony, the transcript of the committee's proceedings was never published. Apart from two closed sessions of the House Select Intelligence Committee, Foreign Relations alone did not publish the text of its deliberations. NEXIS, the news and information service, carried it, and the committee did make it available on some vague preferential basis. But parts have been lost to memory.

What took place during the afternoon session is anybody's guess. This decision to forgo publication appeared to be more spiteful than nefarious, although the effect was to make the historic record less available. The fact that little of significance was added that day to the FS-X debate does not lessen the rancorous message in burying the proceedings.

As Bingaman and Danforth drew off in an opposing direction, Kevin Kearns relied increasingly on Senator Dixon's staffer Charlie Smith for support. He became essential to Kearns's efforts, because Kearns desperately needed the voice and vote from the *majority* side of Armed Services Committee, the "Dems" as Kearns called them. This was crucial. With Dixon and Helms, the FS-X issue could still be couched in bipartisan terms. The focus would be fixed upon Japan, not the institutional rivalries of the executive or the narrower self-interest of the elected.

Smith had been impressed with Kearns from the first, when they met at a Pentagon briefing on the FS-X. "Kevin had expertise from the other side, from the Pentagon side, and he knew what was going on over in Japan," Smith said.

Overweight, overworked, Smith was a chain-smoking policy entrepreneur who spoke with a Chicago twang. He was without illusions, and was deft in the art of the leak and the trial balloon. He was bred to business and politics: his father served Illinois as its assistant attorney general; his Ph.D. mom taught business at the University of Illinois. Smith learned the security trade from five years of active duty in army intelligence and ten years in the reserves.

Politics was most of all a sporting event for Smith. To him, a vote on the Senate floor was to be tallied like points at a Redskins game. So competitive was he that he would offer spreads on the outcomes of certain votes. He took legislative issues personally. Once, Tim Tyler, who had been Glenn Rudd's day-to-day operator on the FS-X negotiations, bumped into Smith at a cocktail party sponsored by defense contractors.

Smith recalled that Tyler asked him what he thought was going to happen in Congress on the Japanese fighter. "I think we're gonna try to stop the agreement," Smith told him.

With typical self-confidence, Tyler told Smith he could never stop the agreement—it was just too good a deal.

"No, Tim," Smith said. "*You're* wrong. This one really smells." But Smith had little reason to be so sanguine.

Pressures were applied on Smith and Senator Dixon directly by General Dynamics. "I remember one day when the chairman of the board of the Material Services Corporation, which was the majority stockholder in General Dynamics, phoned Dixon," Smith said. "He told my boss that this is really a good deal for GD and blah, blah, blah. Dixon basically said to him, 'Lester, I'm with you a lot of times on a lot of programs and I'd be with you if you were selling F-16s to Japan. But I'm not with you on this one.'"

Lester was Lester Crown, the scion of the prodigiously wealthy and influential Crown family, which called Chicago, Alan Dixon's political base, their hometown. "Dixon was determined to see this through," Smith said, even at the potentially high cost of alienating the Crowns by taking the lead on a deal that would cut $3 billion from General Dynamics' bottom line over the decade.

With all his savvy, however, Smith was not able to predict the outcome of the committee vote, which was held the next day, May 11, 1989. In the morning, the committee devoted a closed-door hearing to discussions about Libya's Rabta Gas Plant, in which Mitsubishi Heavy had allegedly been involved in supplying manufacturing equipment. In the afternoon, the committee at last voted.

"It was a surprise," said Smith of the outcome. He had not expected so close a vote, even though he came up on the short end 9–8. Indeed, the narrow margin of victory was a disconcerting surprise for some. State Department staffers there to monitor the measure were stunned. At most, they thought there might be four in favor of the resolution, not double that and just one short of passage. Though the FS-X had survived its first real test, the close vote was alarming, because the committee was generally so pro-State Department.

As Helms later explained to his colleagues in the Senate: "The resolution of disapproval was defeated by a one-vote margin, nine to eight, with two senators *courageously not being present to vote*" (emphasis added). The disdain dripping from the remark was aimed at conservative Republican Gordon

Humphrey. The senior senator from New Hampshire had been lobbied hard by the administration. Humphrey's governor had been John Sununu, who now controlled the front door to the President's office as Bush's chief of staff. Sununu was not a man to cross, and Humphrey thought it wise not to show up for the vote.

South Dakota's Larry Pressler was another story. Helms thought he had him in his pocket. An opponent of the FS-X deal, Pressler would ultimately oppose the President on the FS-X. But here, in committee, the focus was just too bright, the outcome too demonstrable. In the full Senate, he became safe among the many voices opposing the FS-X.

If Helms was disdainful of his two putative conservative allies, he was contemptuous of the committee's witnesses—Defense Secretary Cheney, Commerce Secretary Mosbacher, and the troubleshooting deputy of the State Department, Lawrence Eagleburger. Helms explained before the Senate that listening to their testimony, "I was reminded of something I learned back in high school . . . When promulgating your esoteric cogitations or articulating your superficial sentimentalities, beware of platitudinous ponderosities."

The cabinet officers testified as they had nearly two weeks before, when they appeared ensemble before the House Foreign Affairs Committee. Eagleburger, for example, repeated to the Senate what he told the House: "[The] review was undertaken with great care. There was no rush to judgment. The review underscored a need for certain clarifications from the Japanese side, clarifications which we obtained as a consequence of protracted negotiations." In fact, the President wanted an answer from his interagency group in just twenty-three days, counting weekends, from February 15 to March 10, 1989. Eight more days passed before Karl Jackson got the President's final decision. From there it was just a month reaching a settlement with the Japanese.

Though the committee voted to report Dixon's resolution negatively to the full Senate, committee chairman Pell did Dixon a big favor by allowing him to manage the matter during the debate before the full Senate. This put Dixon in charge, in effect offsetting the committee's decision not to support the deal. As a grateful Dixon made plain before the Senate: "I think we come to this floor *unburdened* of the committee process."

Dixon immediately sought to defuse the recommendation of the committee, which in some circumstances might have had a powerful effect on the position taken by the full Senate. "Many times . . . the committee function is paramount. Not so here," asserted Dixon. "The vote was exceedingly close." Two members abstained. "And those two members had the power to change the result." He might have added that the influence of the committee had deteriorated badly over the years in the eyes of the Senate, diminished by its hoary vision, the dotage of its chair, and its complicity with Foggy Bottom.

In a prescient memo written on May 3, 1989, Senator Robert Byrd's staffer on security issues, Dick D'Amato, foresaw that Bingaman would agree with the President's findings, noting that the new terms were not without appeal. D'Amato told Byrd that the President had succeeded in making two changes that could not be described as cosmetic. He liked the fact, for one, that the additional side letters to the government-to-government contract guaranteed that there would be a second MOU before the FS-X went into production. The clear enunciation of America's expectation about access to Japanese technology also marked an advance, he thought.

D'Amato was disappointed, however, at the equivocating word "approximately" used to describe the percentage of U.S. workshare in the production phase. After all the brouhaha over the terms of the FS-X deal, the efforts at delineation and definition, the use of the word "approximately" seemed feckless.

Even so, D'Amato thought the President had gained the upper hand, and that Dixon's resolution of disapproval was doomed. This did not mean, however, that he thought that Congress should roll over. There was a powerful and angry movement against the FS-X in the House, led by Californian Mel Levine, who represented the pace setting Santa Monica area. And certainly Byrd was aware of the mood in the Senate.

The idea D'Amato came up with to put Congress's own spin on the FS-X deal was an exercise in legislative elegance. Turning the entire concept of the Arms Export Control Act upside down, he suggested to Byrd that they find a way to sponsor a resolution of *approval,* a prerogative that did not exist under the act.

What D'Amato did not foresee was that as debate moved toward its climax on Tuesday, May 16, 1989, *support for Dixon was building,* and, if anything, the resolution of approval he had concocted undermined Senator Dixon's efforts to kill the FS-X outright. In other words, Byrd's inventive response to FS-X gave senators an alternative to the more divisive and dramatic resolution of disapproval.

Charlie Smith thought that the whole debate would come down to a vote or two, just as it had in committee. This time, however, Smith expected to win, and he pinned his hopes on Lloyd Bentsen, the Democrat who chaired the prestigious Finance Committee. Bentsen strongly wanted to hold Japan to a standard of fair play, and seemed weary of unkept promises and bad faith deals. "A few weeks ago," he began in his statement before the full Senate, "Masaaki Kurokawa, who is the chairman of Nomura Securities," one of the largest brokerage firms in the world, "came up with an interesting way he thought he could solve the American trade deficit."

Kurokawa proposed weakening the dollar by more than a third against the yen.

Bentsen wondered what the United States would have to do in return for the immense evaluation of Japan's currency. After all, this raised the cost of Japanese products on the American market. Kurokawa lightheartedly suggested one solution might be to give Japan the state of California.

Bentsen told the Senate, "There are those who already think Japan *owns* California."

This was vintage Bentsen, and Charlie Smith had visions of covering his bets. The Texan continued, casting a cold eye on Japan's trade record: "They are absolutely determined to have market dominance. How did they react to the reduction of the value of the dollar? They dropped their prices and dumped products in the United States." Whereas America's trade gap with Europe narrowed and then disappeared in the wake of the devalued dollar, little happened in the case of Japan.

Bentsen was on a roll. "Japan means to dominate any sector of the economy that is at the high end, calling for top research, top salaries, and long-term top profits." The conclusion that the FS-X would allow them to do the same in aerospace was just a half-step of logic away.

"I do not know a better example of their recalcitrance," Bentsen continued, "than the FS-X." This was what Smith was waiting to hear. The fall of the FS-X was at hand. "If we had the deal to do over," Bentsen said, "I would not accept the terms of what has been accomplished." But to Smith's surprise, Bentsen suddenly came to a far different conclusion than the one he had expected: ". . . under the circumstances and with the assurances now specified in black and white, I am not going to oppose this co-development and co-production plan.

"I have listened to my good friend the senator from Illinois [Alan Dixon] . . . But my concern is that the horse is out of the barn. It has gone too far. We cannot put it back together."

Charlie Smith was disconsolate. "The thing that hurt us really was Bentsen's speech. You listen to that whole speech and you think he's on our side and it's like the last sentence, he says, 'But I'm still going to vote against Dixon.' There were a lot of members who believed in putting an end to the FS-X deal, but they thought with Byrd in the background, they could vote against us and still come out all right."

Another blow was struck by Bill Bradley. The senior senator from New Jersey, a business-oriented liberal and former professional basketball star who had the last word before the final vote. Dixon had tried to elbow him out of the way, knowing that Bradley was the one Democrat who was no ally. Dixon, who ran the debate, spoke up, "I have no problem with [Bradley's] eight minutes . . . [but] if we are going to accommodate the senator from

New Jersey," then he had a list of people he thought should also receive time to talk.

Dixon knew that Bradley was widely perceived as a rational, dispassionate, and intelligent purveyor of senatorial power, whose opinions were well regarded. Dixon also knew that Bradley opposed his amendment. But there was little he could do.

Bradley favored the deal and attacked the idea that Japan would buy F-16s off the shelf. The Japanese, he said, "would not be purchasing an F-16 until 1995 or 1996." That was why they were developing the FS-X now, so that it would be ready then. "Co-development of the FS-X meant jobs now, not in 1995."

The senator from New Jersey said he was worried about political conditions in Japan. He feared that the FS-X would destabilize an already dangerous situation. "The entire [Japanese] cabinet has resigned; they are in a state of flux, different from any time since the late 1950s. This kind of disapproval on an issue of such high visibility in Japan at this critical time in their political process will have unpredictable results."

Bradley's view of Japanese politics came through a man known as the "Sam Nunn of Japan," Motoo Shiina. The fifty-four-year-old Shiina controlled the defense caucus in Japan's parliament. The scion of a powerful Japanese political family, he had his own personal lobbying office in Washington. This was unusual, and it was unprecedented for a foreign legislator to hope to influence the internal politics of another sovereign nation. The office, which held seminars and social affairs, later closed when Shiina's representative in the capital, Craig J. Spence, came under suspicion for influence peddling.

Spence ended up tainting Shiina. The Washington *Times* revealed, among other improprieties in Spence's past, that a house bought by Spence with Shiina's funds was bugged. It quoted William Harbin, a former U.S. foreign service official who worked with Spence, as saying that "he pretty much blackmailed a Japanese client" with the electronic information he collected.

Said an observer of the Bradley-Shiina relationship, "Shiina and Bradley had regular meetings. In 1988, they worked together to coordinate what they would say about COCOM and the FS-X." COCOM was the acronym for the Coordinating Committee for Multilateral Export Controls, the international security organization which guarded against the flow of technology to the Soviets. COCOM had been the agency that broke open the Toshiba affair, the selling of Japanese machine tools to the Soviet Union to silence its submarines. "Shiina delivered Bradley on the FS-X."

Indeed, Bradley, who was a Democrat, joined with Richard Lugar, who managed the FS-X debate on behalf of the administration, to organize FS-X briefings for the Senate in favor of the deal. Obviously Bradley thought this was an important issue, as he dramatically and portentously told the Senate at the close of his testimony. "This is a vote about the future of the U.S.-Japan relationship and the prospect for prosperity and democracy in our world."

When at last the vote was held, 47 senators backed Dixon and 52 opposed him. Just three senators saved the FS-X from the resolution of disapproval. But the Bush victory lasted less than a moment. Immediately after the vote was entered into the record, North Dakota's junior senator, Kent Conrad, who was the presiding officer, announced that "under the previous order of the Senate, the Byrd Amendment is now before us."

This was what Byrd and his staffer Dick D'Amato had planned for in that prescient memo written at the beginning of the month. Byrd was the Senate's resident genius in the parliamentary process. The thirty-year veteran had rummaged through the Senate rules to cobble together this neat legislative backstop. Instead of focusing on the current agreement, which the Arms Export Control Act required, the Senate gadfly focused on the *future* agreement, the MOU that would be required when and if the FS-X graduated from the current *development* phase and got slotted for *production*.

Byrd's resolution of approval cut off transfer to Japan of secret engine technologies in the future agreement. The second no-no was transfer by Japan of "FS-X aircraft or technology to third parties." This prohibition aimed at hobbling Japan's ability to sell FS-X spin-offs in the commercial aviation export market.

Three other, softer measures laid out the "sense of the Senate." Though not binding, the language was a sure measure of the legislators' expectations of the President. One such benchmark called on the United States to get 40 percent of the work when the plane went into production. As it presently stood, the United States was to get "approximately" that amount. As Byrd put it: "[Japan] and we do not agree on the definition of the word 'open,' so perhaps we do not agree on the word 'approximately.'"

The senator also called for continual congressional scrutiny of the fighter program through the investigative arm of Congress, the General Accounting Office. Finally, Byrd's amendment contained a provision for binding the Commerce Department's role to any future high-tech weapons agreement, such as this one.

Deputy Secretary of State Lawrence S. Eagleburger had written to Minority Leader Robert Dole denouncing the Byrd tactic. "As you know, a resolution of approval is not procedurally required for notification submitted pursuant to section 36 of the [Arms Export Control Act]." Dole had the letter read into the record and told the Senate that the Byrd resolution now before them was "the third bite of the apple." The first was when the FS-X came up during the Reagan administration, the second occurred in the Bush administration, and the third in the debate over the resolution of disapproval. Later

Dole added: ". . . the Byrd amendment is simply another bite of the apple." For good measure, he solidified his argument a third time. "This is really the third bite at the apple, not the second but the third." Actually, it was the *fourth* bite, since the original resolution had already been defeated.

In the one-hour debate that followed the introduction of the Byrd amendment, the Senate seemed galvanized. Even Dixon shifted gears and threw his support behind Byrd. "By passing this legislation, the Congress will send the strongest possible message about the fact that this entire [agreement], done in the dark, mostly flawed, was against the best interests of the United States of America," Dixon declared.

Other senators stood to support Byrd. "I have been appalled by our government's lack of understanding about the negotiating process with Japan," said Democrat Jay Rockefeller of West Virginia.

". . . fundamentally flawed . . . based on a faulty premise," said Senator Joseph Biden of Delaware of the deal.

Senator Lugar, who worked closely with Bill Bradley on the FS-X, spoke for the administration, attacking the measure as an "intrusion upon the negotiating powers of the President."

Lugar explained that the amendment "comes after the fact of the Senate's action which affirms the agreement the President [endorsed]."

Despite Lugar's best efforts, Senate sentiment was plain. The vote on the Byrd amendment was an overwhelming message to the President, who was expected to veto any measure that emerged from Congress. The 72–27 vote in favor of Byrd represented a clear two-thirds majority, enough for a veto override.

Senator Dole was worried. He confronted the sponsor of the resolution of disapproval, Alan Dixon, as he was leaving the Senate floor. "I should have let your resolution pass," Dole told him, "and kept Byrd from getting through." As Dixon staffer Charlie Smith explained: "Byrd wouldn't have had the chance to substitute his amendment if my boss's resolution had passed." A Dixon amendment would not have garnered such large support, because it was more extreme. Thus, the big numbers wouldn't be available for a veto override. Said Smith, "Because Byrd got seventy-two votes, Dole was worried about having to change the minds of six senators in order to save the President from an override."

Kevin Kearns had not lost yet.

28

Power Shift

"To avoid a presidential defeat guerrilla warfare would have been something that Dole would have relished."
—Statement from the Democratic Policy Committee

THE FS-X IMBROGLIO rose hydra-headed before the Bush administration. Cut off when the Senate voted down Dixon's resolution of disapproval, the controversy was instantaneously reborn as a resolution of approval. A new version of the Senate-passed measure then appeared in the House of Representatives, which had been negotiating a resolution of disapproval of its own. In the end, three amendments sprouted out of House efforts on the successful Senate resolution, all of which had the potential to destroy the FS-X deal, and one of which was sure to survive and go to conference, at the least.

The administration shifted strategy. Unable to convince Congress of its cause, it tried to nullify its powers. As the Republican side argued in the Committee on Foreign Affairs report on the FS-X, "Proponents of [Senate Joint Resolution 113] are really saying 'we cannot win under the rules so we're going to change them.' . . . If a procedure becomes unworkable, we should consider changing the procedure, but not on an *ad hoc* basis. To do otherwise would undermine the ability of this or any administration to reach conclusive agreements with foreign governments."

In other words, for the President's supporters, the issue wasn't the FS-X but a Congress that was overstepping its powers. Instead of focusing on the deal and its merits, Bush tried to shift the debate to a constitutional struggle between the executive and the legislative: a turf battle. The fear was that if the

resolution was adopted, it would force the President into a humiliating renegotiation.

On May 18, 1989, Secretary Baker wrote imploringly in a one-page letter
to the Foreign Affairs Committee's ranking minority member, William S.
Broomfield of Michigan: "This resolution jeopardizes the FS-X program
with Japan, establishes an unacceptable precedent infringing on the President's constitutional authority with respect to the conduct of negotiations
with foreign powers, and impermissibly would require the President to conduct executive branch deliberations according to legislative fiat." He closed
by warning: "Passage [of any resolution] can only create unnecessary tensions
between the two branches and would serve no useful purpose."

Stephen Solarz of New York City, cocky and smart, part rabbi, part lawyer,
street-wise, one of the most powerful foreign affairs voices in the House,
squared off with Broomfield over the matter when the amendments went to
markup on May 23, 1989.

Broomfield started it. "I would like to ask you what I think is the $64
question. Why the heck is the Majority Leadership so determined to have a
vote on this when the Senate has already taken action on the Byrd resolution?" He cited Baker's letter and said, "*Any* resolution [passed by the House]
amending the Byrd resolution would still be vetoed. Now what advantage is
there in adopting such a resolution? The deal has been made. It does not
make a darn bit of difference what we do."

Solarz understood the Bush strategy and tried to avert a turf war. He
argued that the reason for a House vote was the overwhelming message of the
Senate vote. "[The Byrd amendment] passed by over a three-to-one margin
. . . This was not some partisan maneuver in the Senate, rammed through
by a Democratic majority over the squeals and opposition of the Republican
minority. It had strong support on both sides of the aisle."

He pounded on that answer for a moment before Talmudically handing
back to Broomfield his $64 question. "And let me say to my very good friend
from Michigan, for whom I really do have the greatest respect, that I might
ask another question. Why is the administration so determined to veto anything we do regardless of its substantive merit? You know what it reminds me
of? It reminds me of a conversation a former President frequently quoted by
Republicans these days, Franklin Delano Roosevelt, had with some of his
aides midway through his administration. He said, 'Boys, send me some bills I
can veto so I can send Congress a message who's boss.' "

Solarz argued convincingly that he did not want to see the deal renegoti-
ated or jeopardized. In fact, he said, he thought the FS-X would be good for
U.S. business: that it brought jobs and new technology; that it kept Japan
from developing the FS-X on its own.

Solarz claimed that the purpose of the amendment was to give the administration greater bargaining leverage when the production MOU was negotiated. Why was that so difficult for the President to understand? he wondered. "I think the President appears to have low interest in the substance of what we are doing," Solarz said. "He seems intent on trying to drive home a point that he can veto legislation. Well, we have our responsibilities, too."

The administration would have none of this. Testifying before the committee was the Acting Assistant Secretary of State for East Asian and Pacific Affairs, William Clark, who had conducted the brutal negotiations with Japan's Seiki Nishihiro. He told Solarz in his testimony that any further discussion of the FS-X with Japan would be an act of bad faith.

"Now even the substitute offered by the gentleman from New York puts additional requirements on the production phase," said Clark. "These are not negotiated. They go beyond where we stand now. We would have to go back in good faith to the Japanese because this is a position of the Congress, and say that these requirements have been put on by a body to which we must resubmit the production MOU and it has to be considered."

Solarz tried to defend his position, but he was cut off by committee chairman Dante Fascell of Florida. "I want to follow up on Mr. Clark's rationale," the chairman said. "First of all, the co-development memorandum has already been agreed to and that is the end of that."

"That is right, sir," Clark responded.

The man who represented Miami and the Florida Keys was a strong chairman with a reputation for bipartisan leadership. With his square, avuncular face and amiable manner, his inviting persona hid a wily intellect. Emulating the sports fishermen he represented in his district, Fascell was reeling Clark in. "Now, you are talking about having to go back with respect to the co-production memorandum which has not yet been agreed to."

"That is right," Clark said again.

Fascell jerked in Clark's line. "Are you saying that the language in this amendment would require you to go back to the Japanese to discuss a memorandum of understanding that you will not be discussing for five years?"

Clark tried to fight him off. "No, that is not quite right, sir."

"You are going to do it right away?" The chairman grinned at this meeting of the absurd and the ridiculous, having gotten his hook well into Clark's argument.

The situation in Japan deteriorated day by day. The nation was essentially rudderless and, if the State Department was a credible witness, near panic. Takeshita was within hours of quitting; Nakasone stood in disgrace before the Diet; the finance minister during the FS-X negotiations, Kiichi Miyazawa, the leader of former defense chief Kurihara's political faction, a man in line to become Prime Minister, was humiliated by his role in the growing influence-peddling scandal sweeping Tokyo.

The FS-X was only part of this larger problem. Japan's luck was about to run out with the United States on trade. Its huge yearly surpluses and fierce attacks on the American market had taken their toll on Washington's patience. Japan was about to be named an unfair trading partner by the U.S. Trade Representative. On top of it, there were calls for a new round of talks known as the Structural Impediments Initiative, aimed at opening Japan's closed markets.

The Chrysanthemum Club was delirious with fears for U.S.-Japan relations. The New York *Times* revealed that the U.S. Embassy in Tokyo was desperately calling home, warning of the dire consequences of America's policies for that most precious relationship. Back in Washington, Torkel Patterson in the Pentagon and Karl Jackson at the National Security Council paid close attention to their Japanese counterparts, worrying with them, strategizing with them.

The House of Representatives was defiantly oblivious to it all. In the two-hour debate on what to do about the FS-X it held on June 7, 1989, sentiments were unvarnished and raw. Representative James Traficant, Jr., was a Democrat from Ohio representing a region that lost out when Japan smelted off the U.S. steel industry in the 1960s. "After World War II we allowed the Japanese to come in and take pictures and photographs of our steel mills and factories," Traficant told the representatives. "We were not satisfied with that. We gave them blueprints to take back so they could build up their economy, and they did. They have the factories today and we have the photographs. We have unemployment, we have home foreclosure." Traficant, whom *The Almanac of American Politics 1992* labeled "one of Congress's most flamboyant protectionists," had never been more eloquent.

The House, which more closely reflects the views of the American people than any other part of government, was like a county fair. Men from small towns stood to deliberate on great themes: The FS-X and the future of the American worker. The FS-X and the security of the Pacific. The FS-X and the failure of America to compete in the global marketplace. The FS-X and the threat to aerospace, America's greatest export.

Representatives such as Traficant and Helen Bentley (who had wielded a sledgehammer against a tape recorder on the Capitol lawn to protest the Toshiba affair) fired the debate, but the House brain trust guided it. Richard Gephardt, Solarz, and Mel Levine crewed the House's defense of congressional authority. Their counterattack was based on speed. The idea was to avoid having to take the House's efforts—whatever they turned out to be—to a conference committee to square their terms with the Senate.

A push developed in the Rules Committee to set aside the Solarz amendment, in an effort to seize the initiative from Bush. A new amendment was offered by Terry Bruce of Illinois, which was essentially a photocopy of the Byrd amendment. The tactic eliminated a need for a conference committee, an exercise that would eat up precious days, perhaps weeks, laming the effort to sustain Congress's authority over the deal.

"This way we are taking the same identical language and we are sending it right to the White House," said the veteran Joe Moakley, a Boston Democrat and chairman of the Rules Committee, who moved the Bruce amendment into the forefront of the House debate.

Time was of the essence. The House had to act to keep the administration from delaying the measure and then vetoing it. The summer recess was little more than eight weeks away, and Congress would not reconvene until September. That would give the Bush partisans time to round up the votes needed to sustain an inevitable veto.

The big obstacle was an amendment by conservative Republican Gerald Solomon of New York, which functioned much as the Dixon resolution had in the Senate: an outright vote to kill the deal. Though the congressman acknowledged that such a resolution would carry no substantive weight, Solomon thought it represented a bold and worthwhile reminder to the President of congressional displeasure.

The amendment drew almost frenzied support, with 320 voting in favor of it and only 98 opposing it; 15 members did not vote. The reason for the amendment's overwhelming support was that it symbolized a "safe" vote. The opportunity was there to take a stand against Japan without having to explain it to the voters back home. The vote represented a moot point, however. The Senate had already defeated Dixon, and no resolution could be sent to the President without Senate support.

There was the additional argument that the Solarz and Solomon amendments, if carried, would lead to a protracted battle with the Senate. That would give the administration more time to glean support on the Hill. The House decided that the surest way to reach the President was to avoid a conference committee debate. Most important, the Rules Committee set the vote up in such a way that if the Bruce amendment carried it would take precedence over both Solomon and Solarz.

This is precisely what happened. The Bruce amendment enjoyed a substantial majority, 262–155. Though the numbers did not add up to the necessary two-thirds majority (short by 27 votes) to override a presidential veto, they were within arm-twisting distance. Also, because the amendment had originated in the Senate, any override was up to them. Though there was another roll call to recommit the Solomon amendment of disapproval, it failed. The net effect of the strategy was to place the House shoulder to shoulder with the Senate, in what became known as the Byrd-Bruce amendment.

President Bush was in trouble. The administration had only one option tactically: It had to stall. Stall Bush did. He succeeded in slowing down the process by almost two full months, from June 7, 1989, to July 31, 54 days, before issuing that long-promised veto.

Though it was a "curiosity," as one congressional expert characterized it, that nearly two months should elapse between the time the Byrd-Bruce amendment emerged from the House until it was delivered to the White House, it was understandable. There was the rush, for example, to clear legislation that begins each year in Congress after May. Appropriations measures typically clog committee schedules and must be available for the President's signature by September.

The House had done its job, passed an amendment that mirrored the Senate version and avoided the additional complications of a conference committee. At the same time, they did this in a big hurry, much to their credit. The House expected that the Senate would also act immediately to send the measure to the President.

That did not happen, however. Time ticked away, day by day, but the Senate did not act. The man making the decisions was George J. Mitchell of Maine, the Senate Majority Leader. And this turned out to be a bow to the Republicans.

"The GOP wanted this delayed. They wanted until September, and they were in a position to make life pretty difficult if they didn't get what they wanted," said a Senate staffer. In other words, if the Majority Leader did not give the Minority Leader, Robert Dole of Kansas, what he wanted, Dole would take it. He had the tools, the tactics, the rank, and the expertise to defend the President with all manner of legislative glue.

Nothing would have been gained if Mitchell opposed him, Mitchell partisans argue, except the chance to override a presidential veto. On the other hand, a congressional victory on an issue of such symbolic importance as Japan would have stood as a landmark. It would have exploded in Tokyo. Loud and clear, it would have said that tougher trade measures were in tow: The hundred-headed beast of Capitol Hill was terrorizing the White House. The good old days were over.

That's what Robert Byrd wanted. In private, he called on the Majority Leader to use the privilege of a veto situation and bring the issue immediately before the Senate for a vote. The concept of "privilege" meant that the bill could be brought before the chamber to which it was sent at any time. Consultation with the majority and minority floor leaders wasn't necessary, although it was the usual practice. And even beyond privilege, "it is the usual but not invariable rule that a bill returned with the President's objections, must be voted on at once . . ." The Democrats clearly had the opportunity to override the President. All it took was initiative. That was up to Mitchell.

With the votes available in the Senate, there was every reason to confront the President and have the confidence that a veto override was possible, Byrd believed. This was particularly true after the resounding votes on both measures in each house of Congress. As a well-informed Senate staffer put it: "If you're within one or two votes of an override, the President will always win, but this was more like six or seven votes, and that's hard to do overnight."

If it were done overnight.

Clearly the Majority Leader had the window of opportunity. There were two full months remaining on the congressional schedule before the recess. Precedent was on Mitchell's side; there was also the matter of privilege; a quick vote was expected. Waiting could be self-defeating, because it played into the President's strategy of delay.

Byrd tried almost daily to have the vote called before the Senate, but to no avail. "If Byrd had been the Majority Leader," said one staffer, "he would have called for an immediate vote. [Byrd's staff] never understood Mitchell's delay," he said. "He had the votes to override the President."

The reason Mitchell hesitated was Robert Dole. The Minority Leader was not only a tremendous power in the Senate, a man of great moral authority; he was also a ruthless enemy. Ignoring his powers was an invitation to filibuster, scheduling delays, the galling processes of legislative friction. A rule of thumb in Congress is that the Minority Leader's powers always increase around the recess. "If a Majority Leader wants to pick an issue and make it a hobbyhorse and hold up the entire Senate by working late, delaying the recess, he can affect things on the margins," said an expert from Mitchell's Democratic Policy Committee. The senator from Maine did not play that way.

Mitchell was a very different man from his immediate predecessor, Robert Byrd, less confrontational and more compromising, less secretive and more accommodating. Whereas Byrd was domineering, Mitchell was even-tempered. Byrd read Machiavelli; Mitchell had been a federal judge. "There are those who would like more hellfire and damnation [from Mitchell], but that's not in his nature," said Senator Lloyd Bentsen of Texas.

And not everyone thought Byrd could have lived up to his own bravado. "Byrd might have won, but he would have had to endure enormous anger and animosity from his own folks who resented the delay, and enormous anger from the Republicans, who wanted more time, and the President, who wanted more time. One could reasonably wonder whether a prudent Majority Leader would take on that fight even if it's winnable."

Another staffer who asked not to be identified put it this way: "Mitchell was new, feeling his way around. He wanted to run a smooth operation. He's trying to be accommodating. I agree that if Byrd had been Majority Leader the President would have faced an override immediately."

Said the Democratic Policy Committee source, "Mitchell didn't agonize over this." The calculation was simple and direct. Beating George Bush or beating the Republicans in an override would never be easy. Done sooner rather than later was no guarantee that it would be done better. "The Republicans always came together to support the President in the end. They may have disagreed along the way, but they would not override his veto."

The veto was finally returned on a Monday. The next Friday, August 4, was the beginning of the congressional recess, and summer vacation lasted until September 12. If someone in the Bush administration had strategized and tallied the delay, as they surely did, they would have recognized that they would have nearly 100 days to let the Senate chill on the FS-X, including 44 distracting days of vacation before the confrontation on the override.

As it turned out, the administration would need every one of those 100 days to keep its cause alive. For when the veto did finally arrive, it sounded a clarion call to congressional confrontation. As one legislative participant put it: "The President's message pissed a lot of senators off."

Bush, who had so successfully managed to stall the matter, now attempted to turn it on its head. As he wrote to the Senate: "The [Congress's] resolution is neither necessary to protect the interest of the United States, nor consistent with long-standing requirements of the Arms Export Control Act. Further, the resolution contains binding provisions that unconstitutionally infringe on the powers of the Executive."

Here, in writing, was the administration's strategy. "In the conduct of negotiations with foreign governments, it is imperative that the United States speak with one voice. The Constitution provides that one voice is the President's. While of course the Congress has the authority under the Constitution to regulate commerce with foreign nations, it may not use that authority to intrude into areas entrusted by the Constitution exclusively to the Executive." What had been a policy matter had now become a constitutional issue.

At times, the President's veto message sounded almost cranky. "I cannot accept binding provisions like those in S. J. Res. 113 that would tie my hands . . ."

Bush focused special attention on the section of the Byrd amendment that called for the General Accounting Office to play honest broker. "It would require the GAO, for example, to track within the Japanese aerospace industry applications of technology involved in the development of the FS-X, including technology developed solely by Japan. Such a role, tantamount to intelligence gathering, is inappropriate for [Congress]."

The President's archrival on the FS-X was now the sponsor of the House-Senate legislation, Senator Robert Byrd—formal, brilliant, elaborately chivalrous—a man who loved a legislative dogfight. As powerful as anyone in the Senate, certainly a fitting rival for Senator Dole, Byrd had stepped down in

January after twelve years as Majority Leader to become the man in charge of the powerful Appropriations Committee, which doled out money for the discretionary portion of the federal budget; the money, for example, that went to NASA or Amtrak. This was where the pork met the barrel.

Byrd was also President Pro Tempore of the Senate, the man fourth in line in the presidential succession, and number two in charge of managing the Senate. As Helen Dewar of the Washington *Post* put it: "With one hand on the gavel and the other on [Congress's] purse strings . . . Byrd concedes that [Vice President] Quayle would be within his rights to preside at length, including critical moments in legislative deliberations, but warns that he would be ill advised to do so.

" 'It would be rather awkward for him to do it and, I think, unpolitic and unwise in the long run,' said Byrd. 'It would not augur well for bipartisanship for the President's program.' "

The legerdemain employed by the President in his veto message displeased the imperious senator, who was a staunch defender of Congress's overseas powers. Byrd was no less convinced that he could beat the President even now, after Mitchell had sat on his amendment for nearly two months. Just the same, there was little time for delay. If Mitchell was going to act, he had to act fast, for that Friday was the last day before the recess.

But Mitchell disregarded the eager Byrd and chose discretion over valor. He figured that the Republicans would circle their wagons and protect their President from an override. This was, after all, the first formative months of the new administration, and a big loss now would be especially painful. Mitchell reasoned that if he waited until September, and Dole still could not sustain the President's veto, then he owed the Minority Leader nothing. Two months had already passed and the President was still a long six votes away. Would another month or so make the difference? Mitchell took the percentage shot. At least by waiting, he was assured that Dole would not gum up the last legislative days before recess.

29

A Single Vote

"In the end, instead of arguing over reasonable differences, they ended up fighting over symbols."
—Congressional staffer

TIME TOOK ITS TOLL on override efforts in one important way at least. Kevin Kearns was no longer on the Hill. By September, he was back at the State Department. He had helped to strengthen the Byrd amendment, but he was no longer there for the day-to-day fight.

The recess was a worry to Kearns and to his former ally Charlie Smith. There was a sense of letdown. Too much time had elapsed, though Smith was still confident enough to place a bet with administration staffers that the Senate would override the President. "I figured we had two or three votes to spare," he said, handicapping his odds.

To carry the day, Bush would have to lobby hard at a difficult task. He had to turn seven senators, but since he would lose some votes along the way to the Democrats, who were also hard at work, Bush would have to swing at least ten senators to give the administration the secure victory it needed. That was a tall order. Bush lobbied personally, as did high-ranking members of the administration.

The going was not always easy. Robert Kimmitt, the number three man in the State Department, telephoned Senator Bingaman's office trying to get him to change his vote. Bingaman, a longtime opponent of the FS-X deal, had switched to oppose the Dixon resolution of disapproval and might be flexible on the veto, the administration reasoned. Kimmitt assured the senator that the administration had acted on all of the concerns that Bingaman had addressed in his hearings, in his correspondence with the White House, in testimony. Everything that was in the Byrd amendment has been committed to by the administration, Kimmitt told him. Bingaman's office replied tartly that the senator was not going to be the one to bail them out.

The Democrats mounted a formidable and methodical offensive of their own, led by Danforth and Byrd, a powerful bipartisan duo paired off against Dole and Lugar. The debate posed a symmetry of strengths, with Byrd and Dole competing on wiliness and experience, and Danforth and Lugar on passion and righteous conviction.

The Byrd supporters kept up a steady drumbeat. On July 11, the senator from West Virginia engineered a "Dear Colleague" letter, calling on the membership to support S. J. Res. 113. "We believe the resolution adopted by both the House and the Senate is a necessary measure to guarantee continued American technological competitiveness in aerospace," it said.

Three days later, Byrd received a study he requested from the American Law Division of the Congressional Research Service, the bipartisan public policy analysis arm of the legislative branch. Byrd was testing the President's constitutional hold over the Congress on arms sales. The CRS told Byrd that the President's line of attack was becoming a "commonplace" argument in favor of increased executive privilege. It said, "The tendency of Presidential advisers to wave one of his titles, be it Commander in Chief or sole organ of foreign relations, is an old tactic."

The CRS analysis quoted Chief Justice John Marshall: " 'What is power? It is the power to regulate; that is to prescribe the rule by which commerce is to be governed. This power, like all others vested in Congress, is complete in itself, may be exercised to its utmost extent, and acknowledges no limitations . . . The power of commerce with foreign nations . . . is vested in Congress as absolutely as it would be in a single government . . .' "

On July 19, the House wrote the President hoping to fend off a veto fight: "Quality jobs that provide good wages and promise a decent future are always important. Through S. J. Res. 113, we seek to ensure that the FS-X agreement actually translates into new opportunities for employment for American workers. We owe it to our workers to settle for nothing less." It concluded gravely: "America's future is at stake." The letter contained a weighty and impressive four pages of signatures, seventy-nine in all.

On July 31, when the President announced his veto, Byrd's supporters continued to press the issue through the media. Danforth issued a release declaring that he would vote to override the President. On August 3, just one day before the infamous recess commenced, Danforth fired off another release announcing the Senate's passage of language institutionalizing the role of the Commerce Department in overseas arms sales.

Again, two weeks later, Danforth put out another release in the form of an essay, an incipient Op-Ed piece. Expressing his concern about America's high-tech future, he noted, "When Congress returns to work in September, we will make a decision that is highly significant . . ." The issue was the FS-X.

The day before the override debate, Byrd initiated another "Dear Colleague" letter, signed by eight senators and accompanied by a two-page single-spaced memo written by Senator Danforth. "The principal issue is no longer the language of the legislation itself," the letter said. "Instead, the administration now contends that the FS-X resolution amounts to an unconstitutional infringement on Executive branch prerogatives."

The Danforth memo argued three points. Congress, for one, had the authority to restrict technology transfer. He cited the case of high-tech early-warning aircraft denied to the Saudis. Calling the issue into question was "gratuitous" on the part of the President, he charged. The second point seemed obvious: that what the President was vetoing was a mere resolution, a sense of what Congress *wanted.* Congress's desire was no small thing, but, still, the President was overreacting. Danforth called the veto message "an exceedingly confrontational, non-constructive act by the President." Finally, the memo argued, specifying a role for Commerce was standard operating procedure for Congress, that in fact it had a long history in such matters. Citing an instance in 1962, he wrote, "Congress provided that 'The President shall establish an interagency organization' to assist in the trade policymaking process." The FS-X implemented those ambitions.

This was an anguishing process for Danforth, as he struggled to explain in the course of the override debate. "I am behind the President. I consider myself one of his staunchest supporters, and I have been especially behind him in matters relating to the prerogatives of the presidency.

"I have written Op-Ed pieces. I have made speeches on the floor of the Senate. I believe I have been one of his strongest advocates."

On the day of the debate, Danforth wore a dark blue suit, a blue shirt with a button-down collar, and a green tie with a white paisley print. With his steely gray hair and his Hieronymus Bosch nose, the set of his square, noble chin bespoke the gravity of the moment. He chopped at the air when he gestured and punched key words passionately. He was indignant.

"I did not *pick* this fight. I did not *want* this fight. I did *everything* I could think of to *avoid* this fight. I called up the chief of staff, Mr. Sununu, and I called up Roger Porter [the President's domestic policy adviser]. I asked them if there was any way we could have ways to finesse this whole situation."

This was more than bully-pulpit oratory. Danforth addressed the Senate in personal terms, confiding his actions. "I *asked* for a meeting with the President. I *went* to the White House. I presented him with a memo *explaining* our position." The memo cited above. "I did not want a *confrontation.*" Emphasis landed heavily upon each word. "It is not *our* side of this argument that is asking for a confrontation between the White House and the Congress."

Danforth named the culprit in the matter: the President's White House lawyer, C. Boyden Gray, personal counsel to George Bush since 1981, when he became Vice President. Gray had concocted this position on executive privilege. The pugnacity was his, and Danforth didn't like Gray's tactic one bit. "It is viewed as some sort of *test,*" Danforth said, cleaving his views with his hacking hand gestures, "but it is *not* a test to preserve *existing* presidential power. It is a test which would contract existing *congressional* power. It is a statement by the administration that the Congress should simply *get out of the way* in trade matters; that even a sense-of-the-Senate resolution *is too much* for Congress . . . that we should just get out of the way"—his voice was breathy with contempt—"that it is *not our business.*"

Danforth and Boyden Gray made an interesting pair in this confrontation. Both were heirs to the wealthiest of American families. Whereas Danforth had grown up in the gospel of Ralston Purina, Gray grew up in the southern comfort of Reynolds tobacco. Along with the late distinguished Senator John H. Heinz III, whose family provided America's ketchup supply, and Jay Rockefeller, these men represented the bedrock of Washington wealth.

Boyden Gray, aged forty-six, was the archetypal white Anglo-Saxon Protestant. George Bush's father, senator from Connecticut, played golf with Boyden Gray's father, President Eisenhower's National Security Adviser. " 'Boyden's father was what you might call one of "The Wise Men" of that generation,' says Lloyd Cutler, former White House counsel to President Jimmy Carter and Boyden Gray's mentor at Wilmer, Cutler & Pickering," a Washington law firm. " 'He was a citizen-statesman who followed the tradition of Cincinnatus . . . Boyden is in that mold of citizen-statesman.' "

Gray was a very tall man at six feet six inches, with a reedy frame. His eyebrows, bushy as caterpillars, were his signature. He had been seen around Washington with large holes in the soles of his expensive shoes. Where Jack Danforth had God, Boyden Gray had eccentricity. He drove a methanol car because methanol was his cause. Quick to judge others, he exposed John Sununu's travel extravagances and James Baker's investment interests, at the same moment he kept a seat on the board of his family's $500 million communications company, Summit Communications, Inc., and served George Bush at the Old Executive Office Building.

On the day of the override debate, the burden of representing Boyden Gray's argument was left to Richard Lugar. During the debate, Lugar gamely slogged through Gray's logic, trying to flesh it out. For an interminable forty-seven minutes he rambled through a monologue that ricocheted and meandered and looped back. Lugar's efforts to put a realistic spin on Boyden

Gray's vision of the Constitution left him long-winded and damned by another man's cause.

There was an attempt at openness, however. Addressing the presiding officer, Lugar said, "Mr. President, to be very candid, during the debate on the FS-X, sentiment on the floor in my judgment was ambivalent. There was a strong voice of reason which said: As members of the U.S. Senate, we are concerned about the Japanese trading relationship. We are deeply troubled by the huge deficits we have with Japan." This, like much else in his speech, went nowhere.

Echoing Dole, the Minority Leader, Lugar spoke of Congress taking "bites of the apple." He said he feared that if the administration gave Congress this bite, they would "sort of nibble away at this." He thought he spied a devil in the details. "We affirmed that the deal ought to occur," when the Senate voted down Dixon's resolution of disapproval. "What we did after that in my judgment has been mischievous in that we had attempted to undo what we had done and to claim that we had really not undone a thing . . ." Lugar seemed tired.

So did the rest of the Senate. Alan Dixon, who had continued to oppose the FS-X deal even after his resolution failed in the Foreign Relations Committee, tried to fend off the unfolding politics of party unity. "There is no way . . . that this deal will ever add up to a plus for the United States," he said again.

Charlie Smith sat to the senator's left as he spoke. Smith felt like a man about to lose a bet. Dixon enunciated the opposition's theme as crafted by John Danforth. The senator from Illinois had the passion but lacked Danforth's spontaneity. "This senator has not sought a fight with the administration. I have not been interested in tying the administration's hands. I have been concerned about the impact this agreement will have on the future of our aerospace industry . . ." Charlie Smith looked owlish as he turned his gaze upward toward his boss. His only hope was that Dixon could land a knockout blow.

Robert Byrd, the man who had shepherded the issue since 1987 and had now succeeded Dixon as its champion on the Hill, knew what Charlie Smith knew. When Byrd rose to speak before the final vote, the energy seemed gone from him. He had no fight. The man with the flair for the dramatic adopted the monotone of surrender. Instead of setting the microphone aside, to allow himself to speechify and grow expansive, drawing the great chamber against his breast, he grasped the pill-bottle-sized black microphone in one hand and looked down at the lectern and read from his notes. The brief speech recapitulated in two hundred words the old arguments.

As the last minutes of debate moved toward the appointed vote at 5:15 P.M., Robert Dole, the Minority Leader, acknowledged what they all knew at this late hour. "I do not think we change any votes at this point," he said, turning his head and shoulders as he surveyed the Senate floor. "It is going to be very close," he declared. He seemed relaxed, as if savoring the moment. His impeccably tailored gray suit made him look especially handsome, his bronze features set off by a sharp red tie and wing-collared white shirt.

Dole found it impossible not to take the opportunity to scramble the eggs of the Democrats. "I wanted to renew this call for bipartisanship," he said almost mockingly. "We hear a lot about it, read a lot about it; we do not see too much of it, particularly coming from that side." He couldn't even pronounce the word "Democrat."

"We welcome every little crumb we get," he continued. "But this is very important. This is President Bush's first veto." Dole's blade always seemed sharp and at the ready. He was an icy Senate professional, and he knew how to count votes as well as how to collect them. His use of this last little turn of phrase—"This is President Bush's first veto"—was a stroke of genius. By invoking the President's honor, he did more to educate the Senate in presidential prerogatives than Lugar's forty-seven-minute expedition through Boyden Gray's tortured logic. Dole said it best: Let's not embarrass a Republican President before a Democratic Senate by voting to override this bill. Instinctively, Dole's epiphany drove the party to gather around its embattled leader. The final vote thus had nothing to do with the virtues or the failures of the FS-X deal. It was about standing up for George Bush.

This became clear as the roll was called. The Republicans rallied behind the President. Among them was Warren Rudman, the junior senator from New Hampshire. Rudman was no fan of Boyden Gray. In fact he had once told the Washington *Post* that "the counsel's constitutional views were 'more appropriate to 17th-century monarchy' than to modern times." As with Gordon Humphrey, who angered Jesse Helms by abstaining from voting on the Dixon amendment in the Foreign Relations Committee, the influence upon these senators of their former governor, John Sununu, could not be overlooked.

Senator Charles Grassley was another Republican who had voted for the Dixon resolution to disapprove of the FS-X deal but changed his mind to support President Bush. Back in the May 11, 1989, debate, Grassley made plain his misgivings. From what he learned in briefings, he said, Japan didn't have much technology to offer. Particularly, he was concerned about the term "approximately 40 percent." What did it mean? "We do not know. . . . I began my statement a few minutes ago by saying that there is no clear evidence that the agreement is either blatantly good or bad. However, Mr. President, I will conclude by saying that everything I have learned to date has not convinced me that it is *fair*. And that in my estimation is the bottom line . . . The point is . . . we are looking at a great big deep black hole."

When the time came around to vote the override, nothing had changed about the FS-X agreement except Grassley. Now he felt that the Senate was playing politics, and according to a spokesman, he would not involve himself by toying with U.S. foreign policy. He switched his "bottom line" convictions to vote with the party.

Pete Domenici, Jeff Bingaman's significant other from New Mexico, was well regarded in Republican ranks. Obviously he shared constituencies with Bingaman, a longtime opponent of the FS-X. When push came to shove, Republican Domenici proved demonstrably tougher on the FS-X deal than Democrat Bingaman, who talked a good fight. Domenici had supported Dixon's resolution to kill the agreement. Bingaman, of course, in what was a dramatic reversal, had not. Now, however, the issue was "the President's first veto," as Senator Dole had so well put it, and Domenici closed ranks and voted with the President.

Altogether 33 of 42 Republican senators voted to sustain the President, one short of the votes Bush needed to beat back Byrd's charge. Bush was perilously close to a major defeat, but for one vote. As it turned out, that did not come from Republicans switching sides and supporting their President. It came from Bill Bradley.

The senator did not seem to care that this policy issue had now been perverted into a partisan affair, a Republican loyalty test. There was a principle to uphold for Bradley, even though principles had been cast aside in the debate. Bradley turned out to be more loyal to his friends in Japan than to his friends from New Jersey. After all, it was Jim Florio who held the first hearing on the FS-X, fearing the impact the FS-X would have on jobs in the Garden State.

Thus it all came down to that one bare vote, and one lone Democrat who sided with the Republicans. The ringing oratory was over, and the Senate went back to work. What had come to an end was a decade of struggle over a Japanese plan to build an airplane. Over that time, America's perception of Japan and Japan's perception of itself so changed that this airplane grew into an international issue. This was a win for the President, although it did not represent an actual victory for Bush.

For nine months the FS-X had haunted George Bush's White House. In the end, he had barely escaped with his authority intact. From late January until nearly Halloween, it had been in the papers nearly every day. The doubts, the charges, the angry accusations had turned the fighter deal into a touchstone and a case study, a talisman on which to hang the steady decline of the U.S. manufacturing base.

Indeed, after the FS-X the White House went into retreat on Japan issues, taking cover under the shibboleths of free trade, choosing axioms over reason, believing that the invisible hand of the marketplace would eradicate shuttered markets and unfair traders far better than an up-to-date policy on Japan. Bush did not again openly revisit the Japan problem until the last days of his four-year term. Then he embarrassed himself by becoming ill and throwing up on the Prime Minister's leg. Of course, the Prime Minister was now Kiichi Miyazawa, the leader of the faction of defense chiefs Kurihara and Kato, the former finance minister who opposed the costly F/A-18, and who just two years before was disgraced in a stock-for-influence scandal.

In the area of the Senate just below the presiding officer's bench, known as "the well," Senator Dole finally caught up with Alan Dixon, confronting him once again, as he had months before, when the Byrd amendment was carried. Then, Dole was kicking himself because he had allowed Byrd to outposition him. Now, the Minority Leader was bragging about his political acumen. He told Dixon that if he needed them, he had enough votes in his back pocket, in reserve, to sustain the President. The President, he told Dixon, was not going to lose this one.

Charlie Smith, who was standing nearby, overheard the exchange and fished his wallet from the pocket of his trousers. He opened the billfold and took out a five-dollar bill. He picked out another. He had remembered to bring enough money to cover his bets.

30

The Test of Time

"We are pledged to seeing the success of the FS-X."
—Ichiro Ogawa, director of the FS-X program, Mitsubishi Heavy Industries

YOU COULD ONLY SAY of that July day in 1992 that it was bright. That was its nearest virtue. The sun was not directly visible through the thin, humid layer of rainy-season clouds, but its diffused glare made the ticking heat still more intolerable. The merciless sky seemed sealed shut.

That made it a hot day for a Big Day in Nagoya, in the industrial district just north of the city, where the municipal airport's taxiways funneled into the narrow roadways of the Komaki South plant of Mitsubishi Heavy Industries.

This was once Zero territory, the deltalike flatlands near the great port, where the legendary fighter was manufactured, its cannons licensed from the Swiss and its instruments licensed from America's Bendix Company, much like the FS-X. The region saw punishing B-29 raids beginning in 1944. But in the lean, scrimping years that followed, before there was a Japan Defense Agency, there was Komaki South. Its corporate name and three diamonds trademark had been obliterated by a General MacArthur edict in January 1950, but it quickly and defiantly reconstituted itself, beginning here, when the occupation ended in 1952.

Komaki South represented one-third of Mitsubishi's aviation business outside of Tokyo. The Oye plant to the south was an engineering, manufacturing, and research center. Oye West, across the harbor, produced parts for Boeing. At Komaki, Mitsubishi's finished products were rolled out for their maiden flights. Six aircraft hangars were boxed around the rectangular site. Hangar 4 was the scene for the day's ceremonies.

Reporters covering events that steamy afternoon drove past a corporate amusement park, complete with a tall, inviting water slide that stood at the plant's entryway. Salarymen in fluttering white short-sleeved shirts could be seen practicing golf shots on the rooftop of the main office during the lunch break. Low-flying F-1s, looking deceptively slim and sleek, scored the air. Great cape-winged F-15s were parked in the open areas between hangars, as were the bulbous-nosed Phantoms, dangerous machines painted dull gray.

The oily smell of jet fuels coated the humid air, but inside Hangar 4 the shady atmosphere gave off the fine, peppery smell of a wood shop, green and pithy. There were no coping saws inside the shedlike space, however, no hammers, nails, chisels, no glue pots, and certainly no shavings on the glossy off-white concrete. Freshly painted and buffed to a metallic shine, the floor was a mirror of the gray sky, as well as a stage for the introduction of the mosquito-shaped full-scale model of the FS-X.

At last.

The star of the day's ceremonies, a wooden mock-up whittled to aerodynamic perfection, almost gold in color, like an idol, sat for the first time on public view, the lustrous blue-green bubble of its clear plastic canopy cocked open. The general in charge of the fighter program, Kiyoshi Matsumiya, a sincere and compact man with a curling black pompadour, stood with Mitsubishi dignitaries and introduced the new plane. "This will be the Zero fighter of the modern era," he declared, inadvertently stirring the nagging concerns of some by openly conferring praise on an age preferably forgotten. The point, however, was pride, and not in militarism. As the general later put it: "pride in the technological achievement of those two eras."

The wooden bird at the general's back was purely representational, but it was striking nonetheless as an anachronism: one of the world's most advanced fighters made from birch and pine and a Japanese version of Elmer's glue. This was an eighteenth-century carver's craft testing the design tolerances of a twenty-first-century weapon. Even its teardrop-shaped bombs were made of wood, its sleek external tanks, its pencil-thin heat-seeking missiles, all wood. This golden bird belonged on a desktop, not poised at the flight line.

There were those there that day who thought that was how the FS-X would end up someday, a toy that never went into production. General Matsumiya denied that. "The development team works very well together," he said. Though the program has been set back two years, the new schedule was working. "The mock-up was on time. Drawings have gone out to subcontractors. The engineering teams are working well together. We have three hundred and thirty people at Nagoya, almost seventy from General Dynamics."

The general expected the crucial and controversial production MOU to be signed by June 1994, but he did not make this important detail official.

What General Matsumiya and everyone else invariably acknowledged in their comments about the program was that the FS-X had been born in ambivalence. Rarely was it praised. Perhaps the only person who seemed pleased with the program was Jim Auer, who had pushed it so vigorously as an emblem of U.S.-Japan cooperation. Seiki Nishihiro, the don of the defense agency, who forged the compromise for Japan, had predicted that "the FS-X will become a monument to the failure of co-development." Even the general seemed driven less by conviction than by devotion to duty. Certainly that was true of the father of the FS-X, Ryozo Tsutsui, who, when he spoke of the program, seemed to grow rigid and blank, like a soldier forced to salute the enemy flag in surrender.

Still, the FS-X had passed the test of time. Though there were egregious cost overruns, the largest in the history of the defense agency, funding appeared stable. The Soviet threat was gone, but Japan could readily point to other dangers lurking in China and North Korea. The need for new fighters had not disappeared, and the aging F-1s would still have to be replaced by the end of the decade.

Even the investigative arm of Congress, the General Accounting Office, which had always taken a hard-nosed view of the program, seemed satisfied, for the most part. Restricted technologies weren't leaking out. Their most recent report said, "Sensitive F-16 software and design data were being withheld. Further, the U.S. government release policy has been stringently implemented to protect critical F-16 technologies." On the negative side, the GAO found that Japanese technology still wasn't readily flowing to the United States. "[The FS-X] agreement . . . has not succeeded in promoting a significant number of transfers of military technology."

Coincidentally, Mitsubishi Electric seemed to contradict those findings by traveling to Washington to conduct a one-day symposium on its vaunted radar system for the FS-X. The gathering was neatly timed to the rollout of the mock-up in Nagoya, occurring just three days later, like a one-two punch. Whereas the ceremony in Japan was designed to be a tale of budding cooperation, the visit to Washington was intended to show Japan's openness.

Mitsubishi Electric's symbolism was as bold as it was plain. The meeting, instead of being held in the Pentagon, was held at the Commerce Department, dispelling the perception of conflict between the two cabinet offices. As if for effect, Joan McEntee, whom the Japanese once characterized as being one of "the three bleached blondes" who opposed the FS-X, was there to welcome the audience and present opening remarks. John Richards, one of McEntee's closest allies in the battle with the Pentagon, closed the meetings. Representatives from Boeing were there, McDonnell Douglas, Fairchild,

Westinghouse, all the four-star members of the electronics division of the military-industrial complex.

Despite the fanfare, no one was predicting that the FS-X program would succeed. Opinion on the future of the fighter was evenly divided. The conventional wisdom was that Japan would build a prototype to test its design efforts. Beyond that was anybody's guess. Perhaps the Japanese did not know themselves.

Several days after the FS-X mock-up was unveiled in Nagoya, Mitsubishi engineers, in their signature blue ball caps, stood around in the shade of Hangar 4 and discussed the program. In the background was the golden mock-up of the FS-X, looking every bit the perfect model of its predecessor, the U.S.-designed F-16. Kuniichi Kanda, team leader of the engineering group, said he was encouraged by the increasing progress being made on the program, pointing to the production drawings which were nearly complete and would paper the way to the first prototype aircraft.

Graying but still youthful at age fifty-three, Kanda began working on FS-X development for Mitsubishi in 1979. At that time, he dreamed of an all-Japanese fighter, a Heisei Zero—that is, a Zero for the generation represented by the new Emperor. Now, he gestured toward the mock-up with pride, and ticked off its key Japanese components. "The co-cured wing was everything we hoped it would be," he said, although it was still in the testing phase and a full-scale wing had yet to be produced. The radar was going well. The mission control computer was advancing.

Professional, passionless, Kanda had no doubts about Mitsubishi's ability to produce the fighter. Indeed, he remained a staunch believer in domestic development. He claimed to have learned little from working on the F-16 that he didn't already know, which was surprising. "We learned that wiring and components could be put closer together without their interfering. So this was a more compact fighter than our domestic design."

Kanda fully appreciated the irony of his point. So much had been made of what Japan would get in this deal: technology that had cost U.S. taxpayers some $7 billion to develop; the keys to unlocking the mysteries of modern commercial aviation; the secrets of systems integration. And here was a leading engineer yawning at what he had learned. He was unequivocating. Nothing that he had seen so far indicated that Japan could not have built its own fighter.

Partly this was bravado, which was clear from the comparison of the original drawings of the F-16/FS-X with the mock-up that was finally rolled out in Nagoya. In the artist's conception, the FS-X was depicted barreling wing over wing into a fiery sunset, its distinctive canards raked downward against red billowing clouds. Gone now were those canards, symbols of the Japanization of the FS-X, the single feature that distinguished it from its antecedent F-16. These were the shark fins novelist-politician Shintaro Ishihara called "a brilliant concept."

Though the United States had experimented with canards, and McDonnell Douglas employed them in a version of its Super Hornet Plus, the joke was that the best place for the little winglets was on the other guy's plane. This had been the Pentagon's final assessment of the technology and its best advice to Mitsubishi. While no one taunted Japanese aerospace engineers with I-told-you-sos when they dropped the canards, the Pentagon gloated. As Mitsubishi's Kanda had come to understand: "Canards add weight and drag to the aircraft, and they are useful only for short periods during certain maneuvers. By switching modes, a pilot can achieve the same effect without sacrificing payload or performance."

The much touted radar also appeared oversold. Japanese engineers at Mitsubishi's high-profile presentation in Washington were reportedly stunned at U.S. advances. A meeting between Mitsubishi Electric and Texas Instruments revealed just how far ahead the United States was in the critical area of size. The Japanese had proposed building a "dragonfly's eye" phased array radar using 800 tiny scanning modules. The United States envisioned using more than 1,000, each a separate radar antenna.

In the briefing, which occurred some time after the Mitsubishi Electric symposium, photos of the U.S. radar modules were provided. The Japanese who inspected the pictures were shocked at the dimensions of the module. A coin was used in the photos to depict the unit's relative size. Taking a quarter from his pocket, the Japanese radar expert marveled at the comparison.

"The coin in the picture is not a quarter," the American engineer volunteered. "It's a *dime*."

The Japanese manufacturers clearly had their limits. In the case of the source codes, they had succeeded only in confirming the Pentagon's worst fears. Japan Aviation Electronics Industry, Ltd., half owned by the NEC Corporation, had been caught selling air-to-air missile parts to Iran in violation of Japan's military export laws and the weapons embargo imposed by the United States. Gyroscopes and guidance systems manufactured under U.S. license were also sold to warring Iran.

The NEC-owned company had responsibility for two key FS-X contracts, one for the prototype inertial guidance system and the other for the crucial and controversial software for the flight control computer. The latter was the main stumbling block in the congressional uproar over the FS-X. At best, writing this all-important software would be stubbornly difficult. As it was, the company was penalized by being barred from participating in the FS-X or any other U.S.-related program for months, causing a program-bending delay that reverberated through the defense industry.

Kanda claimed that the episode had not been as serious as some said. "At the math level, the development of the software source code is complete," he said. "Now we have to build the equipment and make the two work together." This was something of an understatement. Building the equipment and making it work together was the whole problem. U.S. officials believed the obstacles Japan faced were far greater than they were admitting.

To imply, as Kanda did, that he had learned little from the F-16 smacks of pique and bitterness. Why wouldn't an airplane manufacturer be delighted to get a document-by-document, plan-by-plan view of its competitor's best airplane? If the F-16 was twenty-year-old technology, it also represented twenty years of refinement and advancement.

What Kanda was trying to say harked back to the old argument over domestic development. By insisting that he had learned nothing from the FS-X, he was boasting that Japan *already* had the keys to the aerospace kingdom, a full set. Through decades of work with the best fighter and aircraft manufacturers in the world—Boeing, McDonnell Douglas, Lockheed—Japanese industry had been well inculcated in the art and science of aircraft building. Design was the culmination of that process, which is where the FS-X came in.

Through programs such as the FS-X, the Pentagon had built the foundations for Japan's commercial aviation industry. The FS-X and its predecessors created the infrastructure—the factories, the tools, the jobs for aerospace engineers—that put Japan in business. Companies such as General Dynamics may have professed that fighter technology did not hold the key to success in commercial aviation, but *GD did not build passenger planes.* Mitsubishi, however, did, right there on the same assembly line with its fighters. Those engineers and technicians whose jobs depended on U.S. defense programs were there forging parts for Boeing's commercial wide-bodies.

As Jim Auer was busily trying to build up Japan's defense in the 1980s, he was unwittingly abetting the demise of America's industrial base. Yet this is what the nation had called for. If Congress was in concert with the administration on any one point with regard to Japan, it was that Tokyo owed it to Washington to share more of its defense burden. In other words, more jet fighters from the United States, more AWACSs, more Patriots, more AEGIS, more cooperation, more, more, more. Which is precisely what Auer did in the FS-X. He steered between Japan's desire for a homemade defense and Capitol Hill's call for Japan to pay for its own protection.

Yet this proved to be a very narrow view of events; and for all his ability, Auer had a perspective limited by the Pentagon's portholes. As an issue, Japan was as large and no larger than Jim Auer's desk. There was a lack of counterpoint because the Pentagon's view was to the Atlantic. The Pacific was secondary. In terms of staff alone, the Pentagon assigned four times the personnel to NATO duties. Indeed, Japan's reluctant defense efforts were matched only by the Pentagon's own low priorities, as evidenced by the lack of staff. Auer often complained of this.

There is no excuse, however, for the State Department. Their job was to bring the very sort of perspective that Auer lacked. The embassy in Tokyo had an economic section, although it was badly understaffed. It contributed even less to policy, acting more like an annex to the Chamber of Commerce. This was Mike Mansfield's fault. The State Department was still living in the 1950s, fearful that Japan might slip into the Communist camp, as Foggy Bottom's point man on Japan, Gaston Sigur, had warned. The embassy saw as its job the maintenance of the U.S.-Japan relationship. While that may have been a justifiable objective for America's interests in Asia, it was allowed to become a sacred cow. As State saw it, the national interest had this *larger* national interest called the U.S.-Japan relationship. It was never the other way around.

Perpetuating this diplomatic fallacy was the Chrysanthemum Club, a self-selecting clique in the State Department whose mission was to beg the question of U.S.-Japan relations. Looking at Tokyo through a microscope, they mistook certain parts for the whole story, the larger story, which was that U.S. policy was perpetuating Japanese mercantilism.

The brouhaha over the FS-X did little to change matters. If anything, the situation grew worse. Sergeant York is alive and well and reveling in the fall of the Soviet Union and the quick high-tech dispatch of nasty Saddam Hussein. Though the apologists for the FS-X will praise the results of technology sharing, the large fact remains that, despite repeated calls, the Pentagon has not developed an organizational response to this dangerous shortcoming. The DoD appears no more serious about fostering technology flow from Japan than it was before the FS-X.

Largely as a result of the FS-X, the Commerce Department was charged with riding herd on the Pentagon on high-technology weapons sales. The GAO, in its most recent public report on the FS-X, praised Commerce and the DoD for their efforts at cooperation. John Richards, of the Bureau of Export Administration, who participated in the steering committee that oversaw the FS-X and cleared MOUs under the Defense Authorization Act of 1989, said he was pleased with the Pentagon's efforts. The Pentagon returns the bouquet.

In reality, rumors abound that the Bureau of Export Administration, which Richards runs, is a mere rubber stamp for the DoD; that MOUs, instead of being scrutinized and vetted, were being approved by telephone. The plausibility of these rumors arises from the fact that neither the Pentagon nor Commerce has sufficient staff or sufficient budgets to do the job properly. Homage to the industrial base is a buzzword but not a priority. The wishy-washy language of the Defense Authorization Act, which gives Commerce a role in such military sales, provides no mandate. The attitudes and institutional framework that resulted in the FS-X deal have been little changed.

Looking at the wooden mock-up of the FS-X, an observer has to marvel at the exquisite craftsmanship that produced the swooping curves, the realistic weapons ports, and the intricate electronics pods. There is a meticulousness about the model, a devotion to detail that is emblematic of Japanese manufacturing prowess. Without rhapsodizing about the Japanese spirit imbued in the mock-up, what is clear is that its makers were boundlessly capable and relentlessly painstaking. In this wooden model, and in the presentation that hot day in Nagoya, there is a combination of ingenuity and determination that can only result in success.

Already, Japan poses a substantial competitive threat to U.S. components makers. That challenge will only grow as a result of the FS-X program. Aerospace is simply too rich and too promising a kingdom for Japan to ignore. Though, for now, Mitsubishi, Fuji, and Kawasaki have confined their broad aims to components, subsystems, electronics, and instrumentation, these are the guts of a modern flying machine. And though the whole is greater than the sum of its parts, that's what Japan expects to take away from the FS-X program, that synergy, known as systems integration.

Once, McDonnell Douglas and General Dynamics and Boeing were the preeminent prime contractors of the fighter world. Now, for the first time, an American company is subcontracting in that same exclusive arena. Determining whether this represents a trend or a chance drift merely requires a quick glance backward along the graph depicting Japan's marketing successes. In industry after industry, with rare exceptions, Japanese manufacturers have set goals and met them. Though Europe's Airbus Industries consortium poses the more immediate threat to U.S. systems integrators like Boeing and McDonnell Douglas, Japan stands to profit on both continents. Perhaps when the Big Two or Three airframe companies have killed each other off, Japan will have to create an industry of its own to make use of all the parts it has manufactured.

The United States has put Japan in a position where it can bide its time. In the years after World War II, when Tokyo set about winning market share, the United States set about winning the Cold War. In the end, both nations reached their goals. To achieve its aim, the United States employed an industrial policy toward Japan known in Washington as defense industrial cooperation. During the Korean War, that policy as much as the endeavors of MITI saved Toyota Motor Corp. from extinction. In fostering the stability of Japan against the onslaught of Communism, the United States created a ruthless economic competitor.

That was the message in the FS-X mock-up: U.S. support.

Curiously, in the charm and enchantment created by the wooden airplane, the metal contraption holding it together got overlooked. There were bluish metal jacks bracing the nose and center fuselage; a transom with a crane and turnbuckles attached to steel cords hoisting up the wing and tail sections. The plane's wooden landing gear couldn't bear the weight. Such underpinnings are essential at this stage of development. Indeed, without them, there would be no model and no FS-X.

Notes

Prologue: February 24, 1989

p. x "in separate residences": Karel van Wolferen, *The Enigma of Japanese Power: People and Politics in a Stateless Nation* (New York: Alfred A. Knopf, 1989).

p. x "to study at Oxford": Rich Miller, "Japan Begins to Pay Last Respects to Hirohito," Far East Reuters General News, January 7, 1989.

p. xi "turn flat, almost like a compass needle": For description of performance, as the Japanese saw it: Shintaro Ishihara, *The Japan That Can Say No: Why Japan Will Be First Among Equals* (New York: Simon & Schuster, 1991), p. 46; also, for comparison of actual performance, as the United States saw it: Congressional Research Service report of FS-X capabilities, p. 19.

Introduction

p. xiii "Every company employing . . . unethical and unfair": Jacob Goodwin, *Brotherhood of Arms: General Dynamics and the Business of Defending America* (New York: Times Books, 1985), pp. 58–59.

p. xiii "hotels, instruments, and business services": Data prepared by the Aerospace Industries Association for the Congressional Economic Leadership Institute, October 10, 1991.

p. xiii "Along the Pacific Rim": Aerospace Research Center Facts and Perspectives, June 1990, p. 5.

p. xiv "nearly 35,000 jobs were created": Testimony of Mark E. Gebicke, director, NASA issues, before the House Government Operations Subcommittee on Government Activities and Transportation, p. 2.

p. xiv "employed 698,700 people": Aerospace Facts and Figures, AIA, 1989–90, pp. 136–51.

p. xiv "The $180 billion invested . . . built by one company": Richard J. Samuels and Benjamin C. Whipple, *Defense Production and Industrial Development: The Case of Japanese Aircraft*, MIT-Japan Program, September 1988, p. 27, note 3. Also interviews with Richard Samuels.

p. xiv "In 1990 . . . in state revenues": Polly Lane, "Boeing Cut," Seattle *Times*, February 18, 1993, p. A1.

p. xiv "Southern California . . . by 1995": Los Angeles County Aerospace Task Force, reported in the Los Angeles *Times*, March 17, 1992, p. 1, Pt. A.

p. xiv "Airbus Industries . . . 30 percent to 15": Lester Thurow, *Head to Head: The Coming Economic Battle Among Japan, Europe and America* (New York: Warner Books, 1993), p. 35.

p. xiv "more cancellations than orders": Amy Harmon, "McDonnell Will Lay Off Another 4,000," Los Angeles *Times*, January 23, 1993, p. 1D.

p. xiv "In 1983 . . . it was ¹/₁₅": David B. Friedman and Richard Samuels, *How to Succeed Without Really Flying*, MIT-Japan Program, January 1992, pp. 19–20.

p. xv "In the 1980s . . . a stunning $358.8 billion": U.S. International Trade Commission, *International Economic Review*, March 1991, pp. 63–65.

1. Rebuilding the Future: 1980

Most of the reporting for this section was done in Japan through Japanese sources speaking on and off the record. During these interviews, I received the clear impression that Japan was embarked on launching a new Zero, although this was not to be stated publicly. Much of the material on Laboratory Three comes from visits to the Technical Research and Development Institute and from interviews with former director general Tsutsui and defense agency staff.

p. 3 "the Imperial Army's center for research and development activities": Letter from Ryozo Tsutsui, August 20, 1992.

p. 4 "In the first brutal years . . . the American disease, VD": Edwin Seidensticker, *Tokyo Rising: The City Since the Great Earthquake* (New York: Alfred A. Knopf, 1990), pp. 253–54.

p. 4 "it scrimped along . . . about $518 million per year": Technical Research and Development Institute report of 1990 budget.

p. 5 "F-1, introduced into service in 1977": Samuels and Whipple, *Defense Production and Industrial Development*, pp. 14–15. Also interviews with Richard Samuels.

p. 5 "80 planes were finally built": Ibid.

p. 5 "Fully 85 percent": *Industrial Policy: Case Studies in the Japanese Experience*, GAO/id83-11, October 20, 1982, appendix III, p. 35.

p. 6 "The top JDA man": Ibid., p. 7.

p. 6 "government subsidies for jet engine development": Ibid., p. 1.

p. 6 " 'You aren't a man' ": Interview with James E. Auer.

p. 7 "fifty-two-year-old Ryozo Tsutsui": Tsutsui was never actually assigned to Laboratory Three, but he viewed it as his charge. During this time, his title was Director of Research and Development Planning, Equipment Bureau.

p. 7 " 'important and intimate institute for me' ": Letter dated September 6, 1993, in answer to the author's queries.

p. 8 "After years of painstakingly": Samuels and Whipple, *Defense Production and Industrial Development*, p. 29, note 20.

p. 8 "the nation built 70 percent of the F-15": Michael J. Green, *Kokusanka: FS-X and Japan's Search for Autonomous Defense Production*, MIT-Japan Program, September 1990, table 4, p. 60. Also interviews with Rhinehart Drifte.

p. 8 "sealed black boxes, representing 40 percent": Ibid., p. 17. Also interviews with Ken Yoshiyama of Mitsubishi.

p. 9 "an umbrella was necessary": Interviews with James E. Auer.

2. Zero-Sum Game

p. 12 "The 'gentlemen of Mitsubishi' . . . without this spirit?" Yasuo Mishima, John P. McKay, ed., *Industrial Development and the Social Fabric*, vol. 11, *The Mitsubishi: Its Challenge and Strategy* (Greenwich, Conn.: Jai Press, 1989), p. xxix.

p. 12 "The company made . . . at Tokyo's disposal": Ibid., pp. 21–25.

pp. 12–13 "Iwasaki saw the American presence . . . unable to compete": Ibid., p. xxix.

p. 13 "Beginning in 1916 . . . round trips to their targets": Ibid., pp. 21–25. Also Jim Rearden, *Cracking the Zero Mystery* (Harrisburg, Pa.: Stackpole Books, 1990); Jiro Horikoshi, *Eagles of Mitsubishi* (Seattle: University of Washington Press, 1992); and *A Brief History of Mitsubishi* (Mitsubishi Corp., 1992).

p. 13 "The plane's chief engineer": *Air & Space Magazine*, February–March 1990, pp. 28–38.

p. 13 "the infamous Zero": Rearden, *Cracking the Zero Mystery*, pp. 13, 14.

p. 13 "As was customary . . . into operation in 1940": *Air & Space Magazine*, February–March 1990, p. 34.

p. 14 "They declared the plane an 'aerodynamic impossibility' ": Rearden, *Cracking the Zero Mystery*, p. 17.

p. 14 "it lost a mere 40 knots of forward airspeed in the process": Ibid., p. 21.

p. 14 "a knockoff from a Western design": Ibid.

p. 14 "Not even the vaunted British Spitfire": Ibid., p. 24.

p. 14 " 'Never dogfight with a Zero' ": *Air & Space Magazine*, February–March 1990, p. 35.

p. 14 " 'most faithfully executed' ": Rearden, *Cracking the Zero Mystery*, p. 95.

p. 15 "From Toray's tennis racket": Interview with Takashi Obata.

p. 16 "take off in less than 230 feet into a 30-mile-per-hour headwind": Rearden, *Cracking the Zero Mystery*, p. 21.

3. Congress Stirs

pp. 19–20 "The trade deficit . . . in 1978": "How a Humbled Nation Revived," Los Angeles *Times*, August 7, 1985, p. 16.

p. 20 "to more than $16 billion in 1981": U.S. International Trade Commission, *International Economic Review*, March 1991, pp. 63–65.

p. 20 "Its budget grew to $440 million a year": Dana Priest, "GAO Analysts Often End Up Caught in the Middle of Political Fray," Washington *Post*, April 29, 1992, p. A21.

p. 20 "Nearly one-quarter of the agency's": Morton Mintz, "GAO Auditing Defense Firms for Nearly 20 Years, the Agency Kept Hands Off," Washington *Post*, October 6, 1985, p. 1.

p. 20 "Whether the GAO cast doubts . . . test results": Morton Mintz, "Fresh Doubt Cast by GAO on New Missile," Washington *Post*, May 11, 1983, p. 1.

p. 20 "in the strategic stockpile": Cass Peterson, "Military Footwear Supplies Fall Short. GAO Reports Pentagon Stockpiles of Shoes and Boots Won't Fit Needs," Washington *Post*, February 8, 1985, p. 17.

p. 21 *"the build-up of capital industries"*: General Accounting Office, "U.S. Military Co-production Programs Assist Japan in Developing Its Civil Aircraft Industry," March 18, 1982, p. i.

p. 21 "quality-control procedures": Ibid.

p. 21 "even closely resembling that of the United States": Interview with Dr. Stephen Bryen.

p. 21 "the U.S.-designed F-86 Starfighter": Samuels and Whipple, *Defense Production and Industrial Development.*

p. 22 "the GAO's key findings . . . it instigates": General Accounting Office, "U.S. Military Co-production Programs Assist Japan in Developing Its Civil Aircraft Industry," pp. i–iv.

p. 22 " 'can be mutually anticipated' ": Ibid., p. 11.

p. 22 "instrumentation, and propulsion": Ibid., p. 15.

p. 23 " 'We were paid to put them in business' ": Ibid., p. 12.

p. 23 " 'industrial and labor interests' ": Ibid., p. iv.

p. 25 " 'provided they're all the same' ": Anthony Sampson, *The Arms Bazaar: From Lebanon to Lockheed* (New York: Viking, 1977), p. 113.

p. 25 "the sale of licenses": Ibid., p. 112.

p. 26 " *'Aircraft production represents an integration of these new technologies'* ": General Accounting Office, "U.S. Military Co-production Programs Assist Japan in Developing Its Civil Aircraft Industry," March 18, 1982, p. 13.

4. The Little State Department in the Pentagon

p. 28 "Thirteen thousand laborers . . . seven minutes apart": Pentagon tour and tour literature.

p. 28 "Old now . . . up to two hours each": Washington *Post.*

p. 29 "A retired navy commander . . . remembered him saying": Interview with James E. Auer.

pp. 29–30 "From 1971 to 1973 . . . Auer emphasized the great savings this allowed the U.S. military": Interview with James E. Auer.

p. 30 "He got his job . . . Chairman of the Joint Chiefs of Staff in the Reagan administration": Speech by James E. Auer before the Japan America Society, June 22, 1989, Los Angeles.

pp. 30–31 "A graduate of the Naval Academy . . . in the heart of Southeast Asia's darkness": Interview with Richard Armitage.

p. 31 "Armitage's weekly routine . . . talk about the week": Interview with Torkel Patterson.

p. 31 "He was Japan's most influential advocate": Interview with Michael J. Green, professor of Japanese studies, Foreign Policy Institute, Johns Hopkins School of Advanced International Studies.

p. 32 "Auer was modest . . . 'I don't know' ": Interview with James E. Auer.

p. 34 "Leery of technical matters . . . circumspect Caspar Weinberger": Interview with Koichi Kato.

p. 34 "who figured that with the FS-X still . . . 'forward with domestic development?' ": Interview with Caspar Weinberger.

pp. 35–36 "In August 1985 . . . had any other choice in the matter": Interviews with James E. Auer and Takeshi Isayama.

5. American Desires

pp. 38–39 "The cable he produced . . . 'Co-production-plus' was how he saw it": Interviews with Gregg Rubinstein.

p. 39 "The Emperor was the symbol . . . succeeded his father": Edwin P. Hoyt, *Japan's War: The Great Pacific Conflict* (New York: McGraw-Hill, 1986), p. 15.

p. 40 "Rubinstein's proposal for the FS-X . . . no matter what name was finally attached to the process": Interviews with Gregg Rubinstein.

p. 41 "The word for ally . . . between a nation's representatives": Caspar Weinberger, *Fighting for Peace: Seven Critical Years in the Pentagon* (New York: Warner Books, 1990), p. 228.

pp. 41–42 "In Europe, the United States maintained . . . signified a time of transition": Interviews with Gregg Rubinstein.

p. 42 "half the price of developing the FS-X": In a letter to President Reagan from the House Energy and Commerce Subcommittee on Oversight and Investigations dated April 22, 1987, chairman John D. Dingell wrote: The Pentagon has found that "Japan pays 2.2 times the amount to co-produce equipment that could be bought from U.S. contractors." Japan paid $626 million to build fifty-eight F-4s that could have been purchased in toto from the United States for $279 million.

pp. 42–43 "Washington reacted positively . . . Buy American": Interview with John Scott.

p. 43 " 'The Department of State . . . because of this issue' ": Michael J. Green, "Alliance Politics and Technonationalism: Japan Policy-Making on FS-X," a paper delivered to the U.S.-Japan Economic Agenda at the Gaston Sigur Center, Elliot School of International Affairs at George Washington University, June 8, 1993.

p. 43 " 'no-pressure pressure' ": Clyde V. Prestowitz, *Trading Places: How We Are Giving Our Future to Japan and How to Reclaim It*, 2nd ed. (New York: Basic Books, 1989), p. 17.

p. 44 "Originally aimed at . . . real business was transacted after hours": Interviews with Gregg Rubinstein.

p. 44 "The January 1986 convocation . . . the U.S.-Japan Mutual Security Treaty of 1960": "Guidelines for U.S.-Japan Defense Cooperation," reprinted in *The Defense of Japan 1986*, Japan Defense Agency, pp. 87–89.

p. 44 "Richard Armitage . . . $147.2 billion five-year defense budget": Shinji Otsuki, "Battle over the FS-X Fighter: Who Won?," *Japan Quarterly*, April–June 1988, p. 139.

p. 44 "pressures building in Congress": Masaru Kohno, "Japanese Defense Policy Making: The FS-X Selection, 1985–1987," *Asian Survey*, May 1989, p. 462.

p. 44 "A self-contained man": Interviews with Seiki Nishihiro and Katsuhisa Yamada.

p. 44 "Popular and well regarded": Muneyuki Kaai, "Geography of Personnel Veins in Bureaucratic World, Central Government Ministries & Agencies," *Kankai*, October 1987. U.S. Embassy translation.

p. 46 " 'Yes, [there is the choice of joint development] but is that not also a form of domestic development?' ": Quoted by Michael J. Green in "Alliance Politics and Technonationalism" from the *Mainichi Shimbun*, March 13, 1986.

p. 46 " 'they could not really build the plane' ": Interviews with Seiki Nishihiro.

p. 46 "the U.S. side returned": Andrew J. Button, *Cooperation in the Development of the*

FS-X: An Analysis of the Decision Process, Industrial College of the Armed Forces, p. 8.

6. An Airport Theory of Nations

pp. 48–50 Interviews with Kevin Kearns, direct personal observations, wide discussions with various sources.

pp. 50–51 "Kearns brought a different set of experiences . . . the whole Japanese military establishment": Interviews with Kevin Kearns, Craig Richardson, and Gregg Rubinstein.

p. 52 "Weinberger was quoted": Kohno, "Japanese Defense Policy Making," p. 462.

p. 52 "The key, Weinberger emphasized": Prestowitz, *Trading Places,* 2nd ed., pp. 21–22.

pp. 51–55 The story of the May 1986 Pentagon meeting came through interviews with James E. Auer, Gregg Rubinstein, Kevin Kearns, Ryozo Tsutsui, Hitoshi Omura, and Seiki Nishihiro; Andrew Button's *Cooperation in the Development of the FS-X;* letters from Senator Danforth to Caspar Weinberger, and *Trading Places* by Clyde Prestowitz. Freedom of Information Act requests were denied.

p. 55 "In a case study of Mitsubishi's role": Michael W. Chinworth, *Industry and Government in Japanese Defense Procurment: The Case of the Patriot Missile System,* MIT-Japan Program, April 1989, p. 48.

7. The Sound of One Shoe Dropping

p. 57 "Prices were out of hand": Clyde C. Haberman, "Embassies Face Hard Times in Costly Tokyo," New York *Times,* August 16, 1987.

p. 57 "The land encompassing the Imperial Palace": Interview with Masuro Yoshi-tomi, director general, Economic Planning Agency.

p. 59 "Japan's telephone company . . . a monumental quirk in the law": Interviews with Clyde Prestowitz.

p. 59 "$123.3 billion trade deficit, $36.8 billion of which resulted from trade with Japan": U.S. International Trade Commission, *International Economic Review,* March 1991, pp. 63–65.

p. 59 "a prodigious $46.6 billion": Ibid.

p. 59 "But as issues of the deficit . . . or the Lenin tomb": This and other similar characterizations from interviews with embassy sources who worked at the embassy and often with Mansfield.

p. 59 " 'as many people say' ": Washington *Post,* January 1989.

p. 61 "the man who held the post": Kohno, "Japanese Defense Policy Making," p. 463.

p. 61 "lost out to a change in administrations": Weinberger, p. 236.

p. 62 "A one-day September meeting . . . 'anything we like' ": Japan Economic Newswire, September 3, 1986. Source: Department of Defense, Ministry of Foreign Affairs.

p. 62 " 'A military aircraft industry is something they could have done very easily' ": Interview with Caspar Weinberger.

p. 63 "Although less than . . . symbolism": Kohno, "Japanese Defense Policy Making," p. 463. Also James E. Auer, "Japan's Defense Policy," *Current History,* April 1988, p. 181, note 15.

p. 63 "The not surprising explanation . . . more time-consuming than expected": Button, *Cooperation in the Development of the FS-X*, p. 14.

pp. 63–65 The October 1986 meeting was reported through interviews with Kevin Kearns, General Dynamics and McDonnell Douglas officials, the Mutual Defense Assistance Office staff; *Trading Places* by Clyde Prestowitz.

p. 66 "A meeting was scheduled at the Pentagon in December": Button, *Cooperation*, p. 16.

8. A D-Day in December

The account of the December 1986 Pentagon meeting came from interviews with Kevin Kearns, James E. Auer, Phil Gast, Tim Tyler, Glenn Rudd, Andrew Button, Walter Dziedzic, Gregg Rubinstein, Ryozo Tsutsui, Seiki Nishihiro, Takeshi Isayama, General Takao, Yukio Okamoto, representatives of Nissho Iwai and Mitsubishi, Hideo Kimura, and Masuro Honda. Also Andrew Button's *Cooperation in the Development of the FS-X* and *Trading Places* by Clyde Prestowitz.

p. 67 "Just a year earlier . . . 'with less demanding technology' ": Samuels and Whipple, *Defense Production and Industrial Development*, p. 20. Also Green, "Alliance Politics and Technonationalism."

p. 68 " 'From the standpoint . . . matter of principle' ": Green, *Kokusanka*, p. 25.

p. 68 "Each year the government of Japan bought . . . Great Britain, France, and Italy combined": Senate Armed Services Subcommittee on Defense Industry and Technology, "Implications of the FS-X Aircraft Agreement Between the United States and Japan," March 10, 1989, p. 4.

p. 68 "$56 billion trade deficit with Japan": U.S. International Trade Commission, *International Economic Review*, March 1991, pp. 63–65.

p. 71 "$81.9 billion worth of imports it sold in the American marketplace": Ibid.

pp. 74–75 "Back home, Tsutsui reported . . . U.S. technical staff who endorsed Japan's presentation": This point was made by Tsutsui during an interview on June 24, 1992. Some days after this talk, Mr. Tsutsui took the initiative to telephone me at my office to make certain that his answer had been clear.

9. Sounding the Alarm

pp. 76–77 The *Rashomon*-like interplay of events became clear in interviews with the principals: Kearns, his interpreter Roy Aka, James E. Auer, Ryozo Tsutsui, and Seiki Nishihiro.

p. 77 "Kearns understood this to mean . . . the new fighter": Prestowitz, *Trading Places*, 2nd ed., p. 25.

p. 77 Aka, who was in his seventies when interviewed, had no recollection of this meeting, but he thought it was possible Kearns met Nishihiro. Aka considered Nishihiro to be his friend. They frequently golfed together.

p. 77 "A creature of the defense agency": Button, *Cooperation in the Development of the FS-X*, p. 18.

p. 78 Interview with Yasuhiro Nakasone.

p. 78 "Weinberger's reply was . . . 'which Japan must decide' ": James E. Auer, "The U.S.-Japan FS-X Agreement: Cooperation or Confrontation in High Technology," *Business in the Contemporary World*, Summer 1990. This article, which originally appeared in Japan's well-regarded intellectual monthly *Chuon Koron*, was written in response to Clyde Prestowitz's portrayal of the FS-X deal in the paperback edition of *Trading Places.*

p. 78 "The United States did . . . aircraft like the F-1": "U.S. Desires Joint Development of the FS-X, Omura Says," Japan Economic Newswire, March 5, 1987.

p. 79 "Nakasone shot back . . . 'Japan's tax system reform' ": Eric Margolis, "Japan Fret: Big Threat, Tiny Army," Los Angeles *Times*, April 3, 1987, Opinion, p. 2.

p. 79 "Trojan Horse": Susan and Martin Tolchin, *Buying into America* (New York: Berkley Books, 1989), p. 11.

pp. 80–82 Numerous attempts to interview Chris LaFleur about this matter were declined both by LaFleur himself and by the State Department. Many of the sources in this section asked to speak on background only.

p. 83 "Danforth's formal three-page letter": Letter obtained through the Freedom of Information Act.

p. 83 "With his coarse gray locks . . . Ralston Purina": Michael Barone and Grant Ujifusa, *The Almanac of American Politics 1992* (Washington, D.C.: National Journal), p. 700.

p. 83 " 'Good morning, Your Grace' ": Lloyd Grove, "John Danforth's Noble Callings. The Minister and Senator: Born to Privilege, Champion of Thomas and the Civil Rights Act," Washington *Post*, October 7, 1991, Style, p. 1.

pp. 85–86 Confrontation between Kevin Kearns and Desaix Anderson from interviews with Kearns. Although Mr. Anderson replied to a letter about these matters, he declined to comment.

10. Dondi at the Boei-cho

pp. 89–93 The section on the Sullivan mission, as it was known, was drawn from interviews with Kevin Kearns, Gerald Sullivan, Ryozo Tsutsui, and Seiki Nishihiro. Notes made by Arthur Alexander, a Rand Corporation analyst, and the president of the Japan Economic Institute, provided additional perspective, as did Clyde Prestowitz's *Trading Places.*

p. 92 "The other technology that . . . compound eye of an insect": Martin and Susan Tolchin, *Selling Our Security: The Erosion of America's Assets* (New York: Alfred A. Knopf, 1992), p. 74.

11. The Silence of the Subs

This chapter was based on extensive interviews with Hideo Kimura and his counterparts in Tokyo. James E. Auer was also interviewed, as well as Dr. Stephen Bryen. Richard Armitage failed to acknowledge written requests to discuss the matter.

p. 99 "Three times the Japanese . . . Toshiba Corporation": Debora L. Spar, "U.S. Trade Policy and Security Export Controls: The Toshiba-Kongsberg Affair," *Iron Triangles and Revolving Doors* (New York: Praeger, 1991).

p. 99 "Though Defense Secretary Weinberger . . . called Toshiba executives in for questioning": Sam Jameson, "Shock Waves from Toshiba-Soviet Deal Still Rattle Japan," Los Angeles *Times*, August 11, 1987, Business, p. 1.

p. 99 "Indeed, nothing happened in Japan . . . and 50 of their deputies": Spar, "U.S. Trade Policy," p. 120.

p. 99 "In Tokyo, punishment was swift, if light . . . Kazuo Iimura, resigned": John

Burgess, "Japan Fines Firms over Soviet Sales; Computer Tools Said to Help Subs," Washington *Post*, May 16, 1987, p. A17.

p. 99 "Prime Minister Nakasone labeled Toshiba's . . . 'an unforgettable criminal act' ": Jameson, "Shock Waves from Toshiba-Soviet Deal."

pp. 99–100 "The chairman of the giant Mitsui trading firm . . . to make better detection devices": Ibid.

p. 100 "In July 1987, eight congressmen . . . Toshiba tape recorder on the Capitol grounds": Robert A. Rosenblatt, "How 'Swat Team' of Toshiba Lobbyists Took on Congress—and Won," Washington *Post*, May 1, 1988, Financial, p. 1.

p. 100 "a potential cost to the company of $2.5 billion a year": Editorial, "The Toshiba Affair," Los Angeles *Times*, July 16, 1987, Metro, p. 4.

p. 101 "In April, he told Japan's largest daily . . . subs were much quieter since the Toshiba incident": Jameson, "Shock Waves from Toshiba-Soviet Deal." Also interviews with Mikio Haruna, then Washington bureau chief of the Kyodo News Service.

12. June 1987: The Power Play

p. 105 "Caspar Weinberger unexpectedly announced . . . by Japan's Prime Minister, Nakasone": Kohno, "Japan Defense Policy Making," p. 466.

p. 105 "If Nishihiro had indeed embraced Ryozo Tsutsui's position": Interviews with Kevin Kearns

p. 105 "Thus even though Armitage": Interviews with James E. Auer.

pp. 105–6 "Nishihiro arrived in Washington personally opposed . . . or serious problems would arise": Interviews with Seiki Nishihiro.

p. 106 "Jim Auer . . . not for himself": Interview with James E. Auer.

p. 107 "This was what Nishihiro's boss, Yuko Kurihara, wanted": Interview with Yuko Kurihara.

p. 107 "But such a concept . . . not cost-effective": Button, *Cooperation in the Development of the FS-X*, p. 22.

p. 107 "F-15 Eagle, the F-15E Strike Eagle, a plane so advanced . . . in the U.S. military": Interviews with Gerald R. Sullivan and Clyde Prestowitz.

pp. 107–8 "Weinberger characterized U.S. losses . . . he promised": Weinberger, *Fighting for Peace*, p. 242. Also interviews with Caspar Weinberger, Koichi Kato, Yuko Kurihara, and Yasuhiro Nakasone.

p. 108 "at a chic $3,846 per night" Exchange rate: 130Y/$; as quoted in *The Wall Street Journal*.

pp. 108–9 "When Weinberger entered the elegant reception room . . . *and* the Reds that night": Interviews with Caspar Weinberger and Yuko Kurihara.

p. 109 " 'went right to the heart of the U.S.-Japan relationship' ": Prestowitz, *Trading Places*, 2nd ed., p. 29.

p. 109 " 'Japanese government leaders . . . build its own defense capability' ": Japan Economic Newswire, May 28, 1987.

p. 109 "the Ministry of Foreign Affairs . . . Japan's limited commitment to mutual security": Interviews with Yukio Okamoto.

p. 110 "Until the Toshiba affair . . . in the push for co-development": Interviews with Michael Green.

p. 110 "the area in which . . . subsystems, components, materials": Dr. Julie Fox Gorte, Sr. Assoc., Office of Science and Technology Policy, testifying before the

House Committee on Government Operations Subcommittee on Government Activities and Transportation, March 18, 1992.

p. 110 "which are considered the 'backbone' of the industry": "Competitive Profile of the Aerospace Industry," *Gaining New Ground*, The Competitiveness Council, 1991.

p. 111 " 'the FS-X program should employ the best technologies of both nations' ": Interviews with Kevin Kearns.

13. A Beauty Contest

pp. 113–15 The announcement section was re-created through interviews with Seiki Nishihiro, Yuko Kurihara, Richard Armitage, and James E. Auer. Also *Fighting for Peace* by Caspar Weinberger and *Trading Places* by Clyde Prestowitz.

p. 115 "The number two man in Tokyo . . . where the ambassador had his offices": Interview with Walter Dziedzic.

p. 115 "The embattled Kearns . . . 'technology was the weapon' ": Interviews with Kevin Kearns.

p. 115 LaFleur declined to comment.

pp. 116–17 "By the time Richardson . . . sash of Japanese influence that girdled the American Embassy": Interviews with Craig Richardson.

p. 117 "In preparation for the October selection of a U.S. . . . the skies, the soaring F-15": Interview with Andrew Button.

pp. 118–22 "Craig Richardson remembered": Based on interviews with Craig Richardson, Walter Dziedzic, Kevin Kearns, Andrew Button, Tim Tyler, and Glenn Rudd.

14. Kurihara's Choice

The materials for this chapter came from extensive interviews with officials of Nissho Iwai, Mitsubishi Corp., Mitsubishi Heavy Industries, General Dynamics (including David Wheaton, Charles Anderson, Vernon Lee, Joseph Jopeline, and Rich Mann), McDonnell Douglas (including Tom Gunn and Donald McDonald), Yuko Kurihara, Seiki Nishihiro, Hitoshi Omura, Hideo Kimura, Pentagon officials in Tokyo and Washington, MITI officials, officers of the Air-Self Defense Forces, and numerous experts on the Japanese military.

p. 127 Interview with Jack Simon, Office of Science and Technology Policy.

p. 127 "What is more, they acted . . . FS-X Joint Study Team," Button, *Cooperation in the Development of the FS-X*, p. 18.

p. 127 Interview with Joseph Jopeline.

p. 129 "In fact, the Private": Green, *Kokusanka*, p. 44.

p. 129 "created by Kurihara's JDA": Button, *Cooperation*, p. 18.

p. 129 *"recommended that September that the defense agency adopt the F-18"*: "Japanese Aircraft Makers Agree on FS-X Plan with McDonnell Douglas," Japan Economic Newswire, September 11, 1987, Dialog File 611, Accession No. 0047322.

p. 129 "In Kurihara's three . . . would be ignored": Interview with Yuko Kurihara.

p. 130 "Mitsubishi Corp. was . . . high-level security clearance": Mitsubishi promotional literature.

p. 130 "The three diamonds of . . . stock is held by members of the *keiretsu*": *Business Week*, September 24, 1990, p. 99.

p. 130 "In addition to cross-ownership . . . astounding 10 percent of Japan's GNP": William J. Holstein, *The Japanese Power Game* (New York: Scribners, 1990), p. 202.

p. 131 " 'The hugeness of the money' ": Ibid., p. 146.

p. 132 "It was a pity": Interview with Seiki Nishihiro.

15. Mutiny in a Hot Tub

Virtually all the materials in this chapter came from direct back-and-forth interviews on the phone, in person, and on location with Clyde Prestowitz in Potomac, Maryland, and Washington, D.C., and Craig Richardson in Pomona, California.

p. 138 "In 1986 America's trade balance in high-tech goods . . . for the first time ever": Robert Reich, *The Atlantic*, May 1987.

p. 138 "would go to 55 percent in the next five years": Ibid.

p. 139 "Prestowitz knew a good story . . . 'watching the Roman Empire crumble,' he said": Interview with Clyde Prestowitz.

p. 139 " 'Not only was I . . . in the United States' ": Prestowitz, *Trading Places*, 1st ed., p. 13.

p. 140 " 'One reason was . . . that might be desired' ": Ibid., p. 301.

p. 140 "Unlike most academics writing . . . top echelons of the Commerce Department": Interview with Ron Morse.

p. 141 "Prestowitz was a lifelong Republican . . . of his post": Interviews with Clyde Prestowitz.

p. 141 " 'Japan basher,' a term of accusation . . . by insinuation and innuendo": John Judis, *Columbia Journalism Review*, November–December 1992, p. 39.

p. 141 "The phrase quickly became . . . 'proposes remedies that are extreme' ": Interview with Hobart Rowen.

p. 142 "The idea central to . . . had served it well": *U.S. News & World Report*, May 7, 1990.

16. A Coup for Congress

pp. 143–44 "The momentum for the mutiny . . . a mission: the FS-X": Interviews with Kevin Kearns.

p. 144 "In March 1988, while . . . Kearns returned from Tokyo": Interviews with Kevin Kearns and Edward McGaffigan.

pp. 144–48 "The disappointed Kearns . . . we were bluffing too": Interviews with Kevin Kearns and William Triplett.

p. 146 "H. William Tanaka . . . 120,000 other Americans of Japanese descent": *Business Tokyo*, November 1988, p. 22.

p. 146 "When the new Bush administration . . . turned the job down": *Nekkei Weekly*, October 26, 1992.

p. 146 " 'the man in soft shoes' ": *Business Tokyo*, November 1988, p. 21.

p. 146 "testified before Congress more than a hundred times on U.S.-Japan trade issues": *Nekkei Weekly*, October 26, 1992.

p. 146 "His clients were": *Washington Representatives, 1989* (Washington, D.C.: Columbia Books).

p. 148 " 'The committee therefore . . . the Department of Commerce' ": Report to accompany S 2355, The National Defense Authorization Act for the Fiscal Year 1989.

p. 148 " 'license fee in return' ": The DoD certainly was aware of the committee's report. In a summer 1989 issue of *The DISAM Journal* (Defense Institute of Security and Assistance Management, a Pentagon think tank), Defense Secretary Richard Cheney wrote: "The Senate Armed Services Committee, in its May 1988 report on the FY89 defense authorization bill, agreed that this alternative co-development based on an existing U.S. aircraft was the most workable approach at that point." Of course, the Secretary's citation completely mischaracterized the sense of the committee's report.

p. 149 "This was a crucial point for Japan . . . were also considered *nonderived*": JEI Report, Number 9B, March 2, 1990, p. 11.

17. The Sound of One Hand Washing the Other

p. 153 " 'It is desirable to . . . on consumer technologies' ": "Defense Technologies Seen as Arena for U.S.-Japan Cooperation, Competition," *Nikkan Kogyo Shimbun*, November 29, 1988.

p. 154 "Rudd wanted a steering committee . . . back to the United States": Interview with Glenn Rudd.

pp. 154–55 "Whereas Rudd approached defense cooperation . . . can proceed from there": A Pentagon source.

p. 155 "Rudd declared that before . . . produce the plane on their own": Button, *Cooperation in the Development of the FS-X*, pp. 26–27.

p. 155 "On the very day . . . Technical Research and Development Institute": Interview with Ryozo Tsutsui.

pp. 156–58 "tensions continued to mount in Japan . . . 'ham in the sandwich' ": Interview with Hideo Kimura.

18. The Grandfather Clause

p. 161 "Richardson had told Prestowitz of Rudd's reaction": Interview with Craig Richardson.

p. 161 " 'Although [General] Brown fell . . . to get smarter' ": Prestowitz, *Trading Places*, 2nd ed., p. 36.

p. 162 " 'We, as a government . . . a global economic market' ": Senate Armed Services Subcommittee on Defense Industry and Technology, "Department of Defense Authorization for Appropriations for Fiscal Year 1989," March 29, 1988, p. 189.

p. 162 "the acquisitions side of . . . the government of Japan": Interview with Glenn Rudd.

pp. 162–63 "In a paper Tyler circulated privately . . . interests of national security' ": Essays provided by Tim Tyler.

p. 163 " 'We had to struggle internally to be put on the FS-X team . . . no role for the DTSA on technology transfers' ": Interview with Dr. Stephen Bryen.

p. 163 "In January 1988 . . . may not be much left for our defense industries' ": Prestowitz, *Trading Places*, 2nd ed., p. 37.

pp. 163–64 "As Auer later wrote . . . need to protect sensitive technology' ": Auer, "The U.S.-Japan FS-X Agreement: Cooperation or Confrontation in High Technology," p. 109.

p. 164 "The final agreement called for 130 to 170 planes": "FS-X Risk Assessment," June 19, 1988, p. 19. Obtained under the Freedom of Information Act.

p. 165 "Homegrown Japanese technologies developed . . . assuming Japanese contractors were willing": General Dynamics in-house newsletter.

p. 165 "while publicly proclaiming steadfastness on the issue": In an April 14, 1989, Op-Ed piece in the New York *Times*, Prestowitz raised the issue of the FS-X side letters: "Side letters aren't worth the paper they're written on. . . . In practice a secret side letter . . . is simply a clever way to paper over differences and to appear to make concessions without actually making them."

p. 165 "The text of the MOU . . . Licensed Technology Assistance Agreement": The contents of the actual secret agreement are based upon material gleaned from a variety of publications. Japanese policy requires that such agreements as MOUs and LTAAs be kept secret, and though the MOU was said to have been leaked to the press during the FS-X debate, the author was never able to obtain a copy, if, indeed, copies existed outside of the DoD. From the manner in which Prestowitz described the MOU and from his later testimony before Congress, he clearly appeared to have had contact with the document, though he denied this.

p. 166 "Armacost, who managed . . . regional bureaus": New York *Times*, January 5, 1993, p. A11.

p. 168 "edging toward a disreputable $57,766,631,255 in 1987": U.S. International Trade Commission, *International Economic Review*, March 1991, pp. 63–65.

pp. 168–69 "She continued: 'Someone' . . . 'they can stonewall a legitimate request, they're dead wrong' ": Interviews with Maureen Smith and Karl Jackson.

p. 170 "Still, Tyler arrived at Richards's . . . the skirmish escalated into general warfare": Interviews with John Richards, Joan McEntee, Tim Tyler, Brad Botwin, and Tom Barksdale.

19. The Baker Gambit

p. 171 "On January 10, 1989 . . . Japan's Prime Minister": "Takeshita Likely to Visit U.S. Early Next Month," Reuters, January 10, 1989, Dialog File 111, Accession No. 07239787.

pp. 171–72 "In early January 1989, Kearns . . . 'a rather severe disappointment' ": Interview with Kevin Kearns.

p. 172 "Back in the offices of the Foreign Relations Committee . . . 'the Baker hearing' ": Interviews with Kevin Kearns and William Triplett.

pp. 172–73 "Secretary of State George Shultz . . . impose his own people on the department": Hedrick Smith, *The Power Game: How Washington Works* (New York: Random House, 1988), p. 68.

p. 173 "As Baker said the day before": All quotes from the hearing are from the Senate Committee on Foreign Relations, "Nomination of James A. Baker III of Texas to be Secretary of State," January 17–18, 1989.

p. 175 " 'your husband and your dad' ": On March 2, 1989, a letter signed by three senators was sent to Baker, telling him that the State Department had been hampering the General Accounting Office's investigation into the FS-X. The senators wanted Baker to get things moving. The letter, which was sent under the letterhead of the Foreign Relations Committee, interestingly enough, was signed by Jeff Bingaman, Alan J. Dixon, and "Jesse," just "Jesse," which is all the North Carolina senator needed to say to remind the Secretary of the understanding, born this day, at Baker's confirmation hearing.

pp. 175–77 "Jesse Helms stood in the hallway . . . Nirenberg's pen and the other on the clock": Interviews with Kevin Kearns, William Triplett, and Darryl Nirenberg.

p. 179 "Some days later . . . these technologies to our industrial base": Senate Committee on Commerce, Science, and Transportation, "Nomination of Robert A. Mosbacher to be Secretary of Commerce," January 24, 1989, p. 131.

pp. 179–80 "The next day, when Tower . . . I would tend to have some apprehensions about": Senate Committee on Armed Services, "Nomination of John G. Tower to be Secretary of Defense," January 25, 1989, p. 59.

p. 180 "Two days after that . . . variety of areas across government": Senate Committee on Finance, "Nomination of Carla Anderson Hills to be U.S. Trade Representative," January 27, 1989, p. 15.

20. A Shot Across the Bow

p. 183 " 'As a result, Japanese Prime Minister . . . notify Congress of the deal' ": Edward Lachica and Steve Yoder, *The Wall Street Journal*, January 31, 1989, p. 15.

p. 183 "The senatorial letter": Dated January 31, 1989.

p. 187 "On Tuesday, January 31 . . . the deal could fall through": From the logbooks of one of the participants.

p. 191 "Prime Minister Noboru Takeshita . . . Ron and Yasu": Japan Economic Newswire, February 2, 1989.

p. 191 "wrote $93.5 *billion* in checks for imports each year": U.S. International Trade Commission, *International Economic Review*, March 1991, pp. 63–65.

p. 191 "Bush told Takeshita . . . are going to proceed": Clyde H. Farnsworth, "Bush and Takeshita Explore Problem-Solving," New York *Times*, February 2, 1989, p. 5.

p. 192 "The Washington *Post* held an on-the-record breakfast . . . faced by the Japan Defense Agency": Dan Oberdorfer, "Japanese Prime Minister Confident of U.S. Approval of Warplane Deal," Washington *Post*, February 4, 1989, p. A22.

p. 192 "Later, at the National Press Club . . . the work to begin on schedule": "Takeshita Rules Out a Larger Military Role for Japan," Kyodo News Service, February 3, 1989, Dialog File 612, Accession No. 0579815.

21. The President's Best Friend

p. 193 "There he founded . . . in the Bush cabinet": "Nomination of Robert A. Mosbacher to be Secretary of Commerce," pp. 6–12.

p. 193 *"The Wall Street Journal* noted": "Bob Mosbacher Wields Rare Degree of Power for a Commerce Chief," *The Wall Street Journal*, September 1, 1989, p. 1.

p. 193 *"Barron's* . . . called him": Thomas G. Dolan, *Barron's*, May 14, 1990, p. 22.

p. 194 "Robert Adam Mosbacher was an oilman . . . Natural Gas Supply Association": "Nomination of Robert A. Mosbacher to be Secretary of Commerce," pp. 6–12.

p. 194 " 'in most administrations . . . defense and treasury' ": "Bob Mosbacher Wields Rare Degree of Power," p. 1.

p. 194 "There was a picture of Herbert Hoover . . . two-story office": Clyde H.

Farnsworth, "Mosbacher Pessimistic on Steel Pact," New York *Times*, February 15, 1989, p. 1.

p. 194 "he explained to one and all . . . the doors of this very office": "Bob Mosbacher Wields Rare Degree of Power," p. 1.

p. 194 "A *Time* magazine cover story . . . 'To Bob, who hates to lose even more' ": Stuart Auerbach, Washington *Post*, April 28, 1989, p. 23.

p. 195 "Paul Weyrich, the one-man conservative bandwagon . . . I worked here in the Senate for eleven years": Senate Committee on Armed Services, "Nomination of John G. Tower to be Secretary of Defense," pp. 240–51.

p. 196 " 'We're going to take whatever time . . . our own strategic objectives' ": John Prados, *Keepers of the Keys: A History of the National Security Council from Truman to Bush* (New York: William Morrow, 1991), p. 548.

p. 197 "That Monday, February 6 . . . a list of twenty-five questions": Peter Ennis, *Tokyo Business Today*, October 1989, p. 25.

p. 198 "Illinois Democrat Alan Dixon . . . twenty-one senators on February 9, 1989": Richard Grimmet, "Japanese FS-X Fighter Controversy," Congressional Research Service, Report for Congress, June 20, 1990.

p. 200 "William Clark, Gaston Sigur's deputy . . . of Pentagon negligence": Accounts of this meeting from interviews with Maureen Smith, John Richards, and Joan McEntee.

p. 200 "The meeting was a victory . . . set for the following Wednesday": Elaine Sciolino, New York *Times*, February 15, 1989, p. 3.

p. 201 "Mosbacher recalls . . . 'Bob, where the hell did you get all this?' ": Interview with Robert A. Mosbacher.

22. Japanic

pp. 203–6 "On Thursday, February 2, 1989 . . . did not want to be associated with the memo": Interviews with Hiroshi Kanashige, Ron Morse, and Kevin Kearns.

p. 207 Interview with Shintaro Ishihara.

p. 207 "An iconoclast, Ishihara . . . candidate in the nationwide election": Ishihara, *The Japan That Can Say No*, p. 8.

p. 207 "Inevitably news leaked . . . best-seller": According to Pete Williams, DoD press conference, January 18, 1990.

p. 208 "Ishihara and his younger brother . . . were symbols of youthful alienation": Ishihara, *The Japan That Can Say No*, p. 8.

p. 209 "On a cold, rainy day . . . along with 10,000 invited guests": Los Angeles *Times*, February 24, 1989, p. 18; *Time*, February 23, 1989.

p. 209 "Baker decided while riding on Air Force One . . . Sosuke Uno": Ennis, *Tokyo Business Today*, October 1989, p. 25.

p. 209 " 'Baker obviously hoped . . . while in Tokyo' ": Prestowitz, *Trading Places*, 2nd ed., p. 49.

p. 209 " 'The foreign minister was . . . 'to reopen the FS-X' agreement": "Wuthering Flights," *Tokyo Insider*, No. 34, April 20, 1989, p. 5.

23. A Consumer Revolt

p. 212 "A year earlier, Florio and J. James Exon . . . essential to national security": "Foreign Investment: The Exon-Florio National Security Test," Congressional Research Service, Report for Congress, September 26, 1990.

p. 212 "The much cited 'Exon-Florio National Security Test' . . . promising high-tech ventures": Ibid.

p. 212 "Seven people sat at the witness . . . 'are crucial to national security' ": Energy and Commerce Subcommittee on Commerce, Consumer Protection, and Competitiveness, "FS-X Co-development Project," February 23, 1989.

pp. 213–15 "Florio was especially concerned . . . 'their civilian aviation industry' ": Ibid.

p. 215 According to Prestowitz's *Trading Places*, a second CIA report concluded that killing the FS-X deal would entail steep diplomatic costs.

p. 215 "Defiant in his brief for Japan . . . 'this aircraft with them' ": Hearing of Subcommittee on Commerce, Consumer Protection, and Competitiveness.

p. 216 "Auer liked to point to Prime Minister Suzuki's 1981 . . . U.S.-made ships are too big for their smaller Japanese crews": Interviews with James E. Auer.

p. 216 "as illustrated by the Mercator projection . . . surrounded and nearly in the clutches of its enemy, the Evil Empire": Map image and metaphor, interview with Ellen Frost.

p. 217 "That's what Auer now did for the subcommittee . . . 'to share its technology with the United States' ": Hearing of Subcommittee on Commerce, Consumer Protection, and Competitiveness.

24. Dirty Dancing

pp. 220–21 "When the Commerce Department's leading technical expert . . . They were the soul of the machine": Interviews with Tom Barksdale.

p. 222 "$24 to $32 billion": General Accounting Office, "Embedded Computer Systems," July 1992, p. 1.

pp. 221–22 "Source codes, however mysterious . . . 'You either gave them all the code or nothing' ": Background interview, Department of Energy.

p. 223 "So advanced was this system . . . after the FS-X agreement was signed": Senate Armed Services Subcommittee on Defense Industry and Technology, "Implications of the FS-X Aircraft Agreement Between the United States and Japan," March 10, 1989.

p. 223 "The fly-by-wire system . . . in 1984 on the A320": *Aerospace America*, May 1991, p. 28.

p. 223 "The following morning, Barksdale . . . go over new terms": Interview with Tom Barksdale.

pp. 223–25 "Over the weekend of March 4 and 5 . . . McEntee would have her revenge": This section is based largely on interviews with Tom Barksdale, Robert Costello, Eugene Lawson, Joan McEntee, John Richards, and Maureen Smith.

p. 224 "The problem, according to Stuart Auerbach . . . in monitoring arms agreements": Stuart Auerbach, Washington *Post*, March 9, 1989, p. 33.

p. 224 "Her office controlled policy . . . The nation's industrial base was her domain": Commerce Department biography of Joan McEntee.

p. 224 "Farren, the under secretary in charge . . . 'certainly hastened their departure' ": Farren declined comment.

p. 225 "The DoD paper was a complete departure . . . in any future MOU talks held by Defense": Interviews with Joan McEntee.

pp. 226–28 "The DoD delegation now facing McEntee . . . We'll accept the single report, he said": Interviews with the meeting's participants.

25. Air Force Won

p. 229 "Malcolm Wallop, the senior senator from Wyoming . . . the American Conservative Union": *The Almanac of American Politics 1992*, p. 1367.

p. 229 "This was Wallop's debut performance . . . he immediately set about laying down markers": Interview with Judy Ansley, Wallop's legislative aide on the committee.

pp. 229–33 " 'Let me begin by saying that I regret' . . . Auer's morning ground on and on": Senate Armed Services Subcommittee on Defense Industry and Technology, "Implications of the FS-X Aircraft Agreement Between the United States and Japan."

p. 233 "The sign outside the White House situation room . . . tea steeping in urns": Prados, *Keepers of the Keys*, photo section.

pp. 233–37 "The meeting held that rainy Friday evening . . . 'You blew them away' ": Interviews with Robert Costello, Eugene Lawson, Joan McEntee, John Richards, Maureen Smith, and Deborah Wince-Smith.

p. 237 "A showdown meeting with the President was expected the next day": Stuart Auerbach, Washington *Post*, March 13, 1989, p. A24.

p. 238 " 'We've been spending millions . . . what have you been doing with the money?' ": Prestowitz, *Trading Places*, 2nd ed., p. 53.

p. 239 John Sununu declined to be interviewed.

p. 239 " 'You know, I've never admitted that to anybody' . . . made up his mind on FS-X": Interview with Robert A. Mosbacher.

26. The Mountain and the Mouse

pp. 240–41 "On Saturday, March 18, 1989, Karl Jackson . . . as they tried to manage reaction": Interviews with Ryozo Kato, Karl Jackson, and Torkel Patterson.

p. 242 " 'We've pretty much finished our deliberation here inside the administration,' Bush told reporters": Dallas *Morning News*, March 22, 1989.

p. 242 "On Wednesday, in a blunt statement . . . a meeting of the cabinet": Kyodo News Service, March 22, 1989, Dialog File 612, Accession No. 07125364.

p. 242 "the current defense chief, Kichiro Tazawa, called on the United States to "respect" the agreement": Kyodo News Service, March 22, 1989, Dialog File 612, Accession No. 0584080.

p. 243 "Nishihiro also reportedly . . . were never disclosed": "Nishihiro Arrives for FS-X Talks with U.S.," Japan Economic Newswire, March 23, 1989, Dialog File 649, Accession No. 07128260.

p. 243 Clark declined to comment.

pp. 243–45 "Seiki Nishihiro's JAL flight . . . 'the chances are that you will not make it to the top' ": Interviews with Seiki Nishihiro.

p. 244 "The argument ignored . . . $9 billion in this case": Senator Alan Dixon's figures used in the floor debate over Senate Joint Resolution 113, May 16, 1989.

p. 245 "Originally, plans were for him to leave Saturday, after three days": "Defense Vice Minister to Visit U.S. to Discuss FS-X," *Japan Economic News Wire*, March 22, 1989, Dialog File 649, Accession No. 07127280.

p. 246 "The popular Shintaro Ishihara presented a petition in the Diet calling on the Prime Minister to scrap the deal": *Asian Wall Street Journal*, April 3, 1989.

p. 249 "The next day . . . killed the program": Grimmet, "Japanese FS-X Fighter Controversy," p. 7.

27. The Center Holds

pp. 250–52 " 'When I convened the first hearing' . . . 'from under them' ": Senate Armed Services Subcommittee on Defense Industry and Technology, "Implications of the FS-X Aircraft Agreement Between the United States and Japan."

p. 252 " 'I oppose . . . happen than participate' ": Senate Foreign Relations Committee, "Proposed FS-X Co-development project with Japan," May 10, 1989.

p. 252 "Jesse Helms referred . . . 'fascination of the Foreign Relations Committee' ": Senate Foreign Relations Committee hearings on the FS-X.

p. 252 "That relationship is what Senator Dixon's chief aide . . . closely fought battle": Interviews with Charles Smith.

pp. 253–54 "Smith had been impressed with Kearns . . . He took legislative issues personally": Interviews with Charles Smith.

p. 254 The account of Smith's encounter with Tim Tyler was based on interviews with both subjects.

p. 254 "Mitsubishi Heavy had allegedly been involved in supplying manufacturing equipment": In a March 8, 1989, letter to President Bush, John D. Dingell, chairman of the Energy and Commerce Subcommittee on Oversight and Investigation, wrote: "We now learn the Central Intelligence Agency has just briefed the Senate Foreign Relations Committee that the Japanese played a significant role in the development, construction, and operation of the Libyan Chemical Gas Plant. General Dynamics' proposed partner in the FS-X agreement appears to be heavily involved in the construction, training, and providing of machinery, including technology, to the Libyans. Further, the subcommittee has been told that Toshiba is, once again, involved. Apparently the CIA has concluded that the Japanese knew exactly what the effort was intended for and provided assistance nonetheless."

A Freedom of Information Act request to the State Department turned up four documents, only two of which were provided. An appeal is pending for the other two documents. Of those made public, one was a February 28, 1989, article that appeared in the daily *Sankei*, one of Japan's largest newspapers. It reported that a West German engineer had given evidence that Japan Steel Works had contracted to build a missile factory in Libya. The chemical plant appeared to be a large forty-company West German operation. A dozen Japanese firms were involved in the steel plant. Conjecture was, from the dimensions of this plant, it was built "for the manufacture and shipment of missiles."

A second document, written in question-and-answer form, possibly as part of a State Department briefing (this is not clear), was dated May 25, 1989. "Question: What was the nature of Japanese firms' involvement in the Libyan [chemical weapons] plant at Rabta? Was Mitsubishi Heavy Industries involved? Answer: Since

August 1988, we have had a series of consultations with the Japanese government concerning the Libyan chemical weapons plant at Rabta.

"We have no information indicating Japanese firms were directly involved in the Libyan chemical weapons plant itself, although Japanese firms were involved in the co-located metal fabrication facility. . . . The Japanese government has informed us that, as of July 1988, Japanese firms ceased all involvement at Rabta."

Appeals to secure the two denied documents were rejected.

pp. 255–60 Direct quotes appear in the *Congressional Record* for this period. Memos and other documents cited were provided to the author through legislative sources. Also interviews with Charles Smith.

28. Power Shift

p. 262 "On May 18, 1989 . . . 'and would serve no useful purpose' ": House Foreign Affairs Committee, "United States-Japanese Security Cooperation and the FS-X Agreement," p. 265.

pp. 262–63 From House Armed Services Committee testimony, May 23, 1989.

p. 264 "Its huge yearly surpluses . . . Japan's closed markets": "SII Talks," JEI Report, June 10, 1989, p. 1.

p. 264 "The New York *Times* revealed that . . . most precious relationship": Robert Pear, "Embassy Asks Trade Caution; Cables from Tokyo Oppose Retaliation": New York *Times*, May 16, 1989, p. 1.

p. 264 "In the two-hour debate . . . 'we have home foreclosure' ": *Congressional Record*, June 7, 1989, p. 11151.

p. 265 "with 320 voting in favor of it and only 98 opposing it; 15 members did not vote": Grimmet, "Japanese FS-X Fighter Controversy," p. 12.

p. 266 "President Bush was in trouble": For a discussion of the actual debate, see ibid., pp. 11–12. A third amendment, which was essentially stillborn, was introduced by Congressman Solomon and recommitted immediately after the Bruce amendment passed. But it failed.

p. 266 " 'it is the usual . . . must be voted on at once' ": Edward F. Willet, Jr., *How Our Laws Are Made*, Law Division Counsel, U.S. House of Representatives, pp. 22–23, 44–45.

p. 267 " 'There are those . . . but that's not in his nature' ": Helen Dewar, "Byrd to Remain a Senate Power," Washington *Post*, May 15, 1989, p. A11.

29. A Single Vote

p. 271 Raymond J. Celada, American Law Division, Congressional Research Service, July 14, 1989.

p. 271 Senator Danforth wrote in a memo circulated among Senate staffers: "[S. J. Res. 113] provisions have ample precedent. If the powers of Congress under Article 1, Section 8 no longer include restricting the transfer of military technology, passing sense of the Congress resolutions, and providing a mechanism for the commercial interests of our country to be safeguarded, *then one must ask whether Congress has any remaining power to regulate foreign commerce*" (emphasis added).

p. 272 " 'I am behind the President . . . one of his strongest supporters' ": *Congressional Record*, September 13, 1989, p. 20283.

pp. 272–73 " 'I did not *pick* this fight . . . the White House and the Congress' ": Ibid.

p. 273 " 'It is viewed as some sort of *test* . . . that it is *not our business*": Ibid.

p. 273 "Boyden Gray, aged forty-six . . . Eisenhower's National Security Adviser": John E. Yang and Sharon LaFraniere, "Gray's Role Differs from Predecessors'. Counsel at Forefront on Domestic Policy," Washington *Post*, November 22, 1991, p. A14.

p. 273 " 'Boyden's father was . . . in that mold of citizen-statesman' ": Phil Mc-Combs, "The Distant Drum of C. Boyden Gray; the President's Friend and Ethics Czar, Pursuing His Causes & Clashing with Insiders," Washington *Post*, March 31, 1989, Style, p. D01.

p. 273 "Gray was a very tall man . . . at the Old Executive Office Building": Walter Pincus, "White House Counsel Gray to Put Assets in Blind Trust; Position with Family Firm to Be Given Up," Washington *Post*, February 7, 1989, p. A01.

p. 274 "Lugar said, 'Mr. President' . . . plus for the United States": *Congressional Record*, September 13, 1989, pp. 20241–84.

pp. 274–75 Interviews with Charles Smith. Also videotape of the debate from the Library of Congress. Also *Congressional Record*, September 13, 1989, pp. 20241–84.

pp. 275–76 Interviews with staffers of Senators Rudman, Domenici, Grassley, and Bradley.

p. 277 Interviews with Charles Smith.

30. The Test of Time

p. 278 "Its corporate name . . . ended in 1952": *Mitsubishi: A Short History*, by the Mitsubishi Group.

p. 279 " 'This will be the Zero fighter of the modern era' ": Michael Hirsch, Associated Press, published in the San Francisco *Chronicle*, June 6, 1992, Business, p. 1.

p. 279 " 'pride in the technological achievement of those two eras' ": Interview with General Matsumiya.

p. 280 " 'Sensitive F-16 software and design data . . . of transfers of military technology' ": General Accounting Office, "U.S.-Japan Co-development, Update of the FS-X Program," June 1992.

pp. 281–83 Interview with Kuniichi Kanda.

p. 282 "The NEC-owned company . . . flight control computer": *Defense News*, August 19, 1991, p. 4.

p. 283 "a full set": Virtually every successful Japanese aerospace program has had U.S. help. They are: Mitsubishi with Raytheon's Patriot missile, General Dynamics' FS-X, and McDonnell Douglas's F-4 and F-15. Kawasaki is building a research plant for its JEM module, to be part of the U.S.-led space station. Jet engine production is largely licensed from the United States. Plans for a hypersonic air transport go forward with the United States in mind. Japan's H-1 rocket booster is based on a U.S. design.

When Japanese companies are involved by themselves, there are funding problems or failures, as is the case with the H-2 domestic rocket booster, which is far behind schedule and has suffered a string of failures. A Japanese short-takeoff aircraft faces a bleak future due to funding shortfalls. Similarly, only a small Japanese design team has been assigned to the HOPE unmanned reusable space plane for the JEM module.

In almost every case in which Japanese programs are without U.S. partners, budgets are small. See Neil W. David, "Japan Broadens Its Aerospace Interests," *Aerospace America*, March 1989. Also Senator Jay Rockefeller: "Between 1951 and 1984, Japan spent $17 billion on 42,000 contracts for the importation of technology from abroad"; *Congressional Record*, March 7, 1989, p. S2210.

Index

Abe, Shintaro, 79
Abramowitz, Morton I., 185–86
ADA (software), 235
AEGIS-class destroyers, 34, 42, 157, 216, 283
Aerospace industry
  European, xiv, 6
  Japanese, xiv–xv
    competition in components by, 285
    co-production, 21–27, 50–51, 118, 126, 140
    FS-X as means to gain technology, xi–xii, 54, 94, 126, 153, 188, 198, 200, 215, 246, 283
    funds scattered in government budget, 26
    GAO report on, 21–27
    importance to Japan's economy, 6–7
    Laboratory Three, 3–7, 15, 27, 33, 67, 70, 75
    military and civilian production combined, 18–21, 26, 51, 89–90, 110, 123, 215, 218, 283
    as prime contractor of FS-X over U.S., 115–16
    systems integration needed by, 188–90, 246, 285
  U.S.
    economic importance of, xiii–xiv
    as high risk, xiv
    not to be viewed strictly in security terms, 236
    as "tar baby" to the Japanese, 8–9

Aihara, Hironori, 130
Aircraft Industrial Promotion Law (Japan), 19, 68
"Airport theory of nations," 49
Aka, Roy, 77
Akahata (newspaper), 30
Akihito (Emperor of Japan), x
Allen, Jodie, 182
Almanac of American Politics 1992, The, 19, 83, 264
Altman, Robert A., 136
American Honda Motor (company), 146
Anderson, Charles, 65, 118–19
Anderson, Desaix, 85–86, 88, 115
Angel, Robert, 141
Aoki, Ihei, 246
Apple computers, 23
Armacost, Michael H., 30, 166–67, 186, 234
Armitage, Richard L., 30–31, 36, 44–46, 61, 76, 77, 78, 88, 89, 98, 102–3, 106–7, 111, 114, 152, 161, 190, 196, 223–24, 237, 244
Arms Export Control Act, 166, 238, 256, 259, 268
Asian Wall Street Journal, 242
ATF (Advanced Tactical Fighter), 70, 93, 128
Atsugi (Japan), 101
Auer, James E., 27–33, 35–37, 43, 45, 46, 76, 88, 89, 95–97, 101–3, 106, 113, 114, 123, 135, 151, 198, 280, 283–84
  Congressional testimony by, 212, 214–18, 231–33

on FS-X's chances in Congress, 163–64
large and complex responsibility of, 95
in MOU negotiations, 152, 154, 156–58
at 1986 meeting with Tsutsui, 70–71, 73–75
retirement of, 150, 190, 244
in U.S.-Japanese naval cooperation, 157
Auerbach, Stuart, 100, 224
Australia, aerospace exports to, xiii
Aviation Week & Space Technology, 128, 218–19
AWACS airplane, 34, 42, 72, 230, 283
AX fighter, 128

B-29 (bomber), 278
Baker, James A., III, 171, 193, 194, 209, 273
  confirmation hearings for, 171–79
  FS-X and, 178, 185–88, 194–95, 197, 199, 201, 209, 234, 242–44, 246–47, 262
Baldrige, Malcolm, 213
Barksdale, Tom, 220–21, 223
Barron's, 193
Bendix Corp., 14, 278
Bentley, Helen, 100, 264
Bentsen, Lloyd, 256–57, 267
Berman, Wayne, 195, 196, 220, 245
Biden, Joseph, 177–78, 260
Bingaman, Jeff, 144, 148, 150, 161, 172, 179–80, 183, 184, 224, 229–30, 232, 248, 249–53, 256, 270, 276
Black boxes, 126
Black Ships Society, 167–68, 226
Boei-cho, 88, 90, 118. *See also* Japan Defense Agency (JDA)
Boeing Co., 128, 152, 280, 283
  jet transports of, xiv, 188–89, 198, 226
  recent problems of, xiv
Booz, Allen & Hamilton, xiv
Bowsher, Charles, 183
Bradley, Bill, 257–58, 260, 276
Broomfield, William S., 262
Brother International Corp., 146
Brown, Charles, 138, 161
Bruce, Terry, 265
Bryen, Stephen, 24, 103, 163
Bullet Train, brakes on, 21, 90
Bush, George, 31, 146, 167, 170
  as free trader, 239, 277
  FS-X and
    Byrd-Bruce Amendment vetoed, 266–77
    his decision, 237–43, 246–48, 251, 256
    senatorial letter, 183
    Takeshita visit, 183–84, 191–92

at Hirohito's funeral, ix, 192, 196–97, 199, 200, 202, 209, 212
  policy review of Reagan administration promised by, 195–96
Bush, Prescott (George Bush's father), 273
Bushido, 4, 14
Business Week, 142, 206
Button, Andrew J., 55, 69, 71–72, 117–18, 120–21, 125, 128, 137, 154, 161
Buy American, 24, 43
Byrd, Robert C., 62, 150, 183, 230–32, 256, 259–60, 262, 265–69, 271, 272, 274, 277

C. Itoh & Co., 99
Canards, 9–10, 16, 53–54, 91, 127, 281–82
Carlucci, Frank, 158–59, 188, 190, 198, 200, 214, 230
Carter, Jimmy, 273
Carter, Lynda, 135
Casey, Hugh Pat, 28
Casey, William J., 79
Cellular phones, 52, 84
Central Intelligence Agency (CIA), FS-X opposed by, 33, 188, 215, 234
Cheney, Dick, 238, 242, 244, 255
Chennault, Claire, 14
Chicago *Tribune*, 248
Chinworth, Michael, 143
Chrysanthemum Club, 59–61, 75, 79–80, 115, 151, 167, 183, 186, 194, 214, 252, 284
Clark, William, 200, 243–44, 263
Clifford, Clark M., 136
Clinton, Bill, trade deficit and, xv
Coalitions for America, 195
COCOM, 101, 258
Co-development, 38–47, 51, 55, 61, 63, 93–95, 105–6, 110–16, 140, 153, 169, 198, 258
  final agreement for, 114–15
  Prestowitz's definition of, 213
Cold War, x–xi, 285
  FS-X agreement as product of, 112
  Japanese-American relations and, xv, 32, 52, 94
  "new," 196
Columbia Pictures, 208
Commerce Department, U.S.
  in Bush's decision on FS-X, 240–41
  Defense Department's war with, 168–70, 223–28, 230, 235
  high-technology weapons sales overseen by, 284

and outflow of technologies, 162, 164
in review of bilateral MOU's, 148, 161–
    62, 284–85
review of FS-X MOU wanted, 188–90,
    195–96, 201–2, 213–14
unimportance of, 194
Communism. *See* Cold War; Soviet Union
Composites, xi, 9, 15, 64, 91–92, 129
Computer chips, Japanese, dumping of, 52,
    78–79
Congress, U.S.
    Central Hearing Facility of, 174
    hearings and votes on FS-X in, 249–77
    informing of, on FS-X, 166–67, 182, 238,
        247–49
    regulation of commerce vested in, 271
    See also House of Representatives; Senate
Congressional Research Service, 271
Conrad, Joseph, *Heart of Darkness*, 31
Conrad, Kent, 259
Consolidated Aircraft, xiii
Cooper, Gary, 87
Coppola, Francis Ford, *Apocalypse Now*, 31
Co-production, 21–27, 50–51, 118, 126, 140,
    154, 213, 217–18
Costello, Robert B., 161–62, 224, 233–36
Crowe, William J., Jr., 30
Crown, Lester, 254
Cutler, Lloyd, 273

D'Agostino, Davi M., 25–26, 218
Dallas *Morning News*, 248
D'Amato, Alphonse, 68, 150, 232–33, 249,
    253
D'Amato, Dick, 256, 259
Danforth, John, 81, 83–84, 105, 109, 114,
    142, 144, 145, 150, 179, 180, 183,
    249, 251, 253, 271–74
Defense Advanced Research Projects
    Agency, 207
Defense Authorization Act of 1989, 148,
    160–62, 164, 166, 169–70, 179, 201,
    230, 251, 284
Defense Department, U.S.
    co-production sought by, 61
    GAO and, 20, 25–27
    reason for fighter development by, 70
    Security Assistance Manual on royalty fees
        of, 155
    technology transfer by, 20–27
    war with Commerce Department by, 168–
        70, 223–28, 230, 235
    See also International Security Agency
        (ISA)

Defense News, 198
Defense Security Assistance Agency (DSAA),
    61, 69, 74, 116, 117, 149, 151, 162–
    63
Defense Technology Security Administration
    (DTSA), 24, 33
Democratic Socialist Party (Japan), 97
Department of Air Systems Development
    (Japan). *See* Laboratory Three
Derived technologies, 149
Detroit *News*, 98
Dewar, Helen, 269
Dixon, Alan J., 150, 183, 198, 199, 249, 250,
    252–54, 256–60, 265, 274, 277
Dole, Robert, 259–61, 266–69, 271, 274–77
Domenici, Pete, 276
Dondi (comic strip character), 87–88, 90,
    96, 219
Dual-use technology, 89–90, 140
Dukakis, Michael, 239
Dumping, 52, 78–79, 146–47
Dziedzic, Walter, 118

Eagleburger, Lawrence S., 255, 259
EFA (European Fighter Aircraft), 6
Eisenhower, Dwight D., 273
Electronics Industries Association of Japan,
    146
Energy Department, U.S., 188, 195
Ennis, Peter, 165, 199
European Airbus Industries, xiv, 19, 82, 188,
    189, 285
Exon, J. James, 212
Extra Super Duralumin, 15

F-1 (fighter), 5, 10, 32–33, 42, 43, 55, 70,
    279, 280
F-4 (fighter), 5, 126, 192
F-4J (fighter), 38, 42
F6F Hellcat (fighter), 14
F-15 (fighter), 5, 8, 9, 19, 21, 24–26, 55, 70,
    117, 125–26, 192, 279
F-15E (fighter), 107
F-16 (fighter), 6, 40, 51, 52, 55, 63–65, 91,
    93, 179–80, 198, 214, 234, 242, 244,
    248, 258, 280–83
    as model for FS-X, 117–19, 123–25, 128–
        29
    source codes for, 222–23, 234–35, 238,
        240, 245, 247–48
F-86 (fighter), 21, 90
F-104 (fighter), 64
F/A-18 fighter, 40, 51, 52, 55, 63, 91, 125–
    32

Fairchild Republic T-46A, 67–68
Fairchild Semiconductor (company), 58, 79, 212
Fallows, James, 141–42
Farren, J. Michael, 188–90, 224
Fascell, Dante, 263
Ferryman, Randy, 198–99
Fitzwater, Marlin, 243
Fleet, Reuben Hollis, xiii
Florio, James, subcommittee of, 211–19, 276
Flying Tigers, 14
Ford, Gerald, 193, 238
Ford, Henry, 25
France
   in Airbus Industries, xiv
   fighter program of, 6, 72
   Pentagon staff coverage of, 95
   U.S. co-production with, 21
FS-X (Fighter Support Experimental)
   Baker and, 178, 185–88, 194–95, 197, 199, 201, 209, 234, 242–44, 246–47, 262
   cost estimates for, 72–73, 77, 93, 104, 117, 280
   description of, xi
      active phased array radar, 9, 92, 149, 152, 280
      canards, 9–10, 16, 53–54, 91, 127, 281–82
      cockpit, 16, 91
      composites in wings, 9, 15, 91–92
      in Morita-Ishihara book, 207
      source codes, 221–23, 234–35, 238, 240, 245, 247–48
      stealth technology, 152
   engines for, 46, 71, 72, 127, 152, 240, 245, 259
   F-16 as model for, 117–19, 123–24
   Japanese consortium for, 77, 90–91, 129
   Japanese specs (mission requirements) for, 16, 53–55, 64, 90, 93
   Japan's policy for
      Air Staff Office opposition, 156
      co-development agreed upon, 114–15
      derived-technologies problem, 149, 247
      domestic development, 34–35, 37–38, 70, 77–78, 106–7, 110–11, 114, 126, 156
      Japanese character and, 54, 111, 165
      Japan's gain of aerospace technology, xi–xii, 54, 94, 126, 153, 188, 198, 200, 215, 246, 283
      selection of U.S. airframe, 115, 117–19, 123–32
      three original options, 35, 37, 215

JF-210 as early name for, 126
MOU on
   Bush's decision, 237–43, 246–48, 251, 256
   Congressional hearings and votes on, 249–77
   final text, 164–65
   final text as unclear, 209, 218–20, 223, 225
   government-to-government negotiations for, 148–60, 196–97
   informing of Congress, 166–67, 182, 238, 247–49
   refused to Maureen Smith, 168–69, 197
   signed by Mansfield, 164, 165
spare parts for, 231–32
Toshiba affair and, 99–100, 109–10
U.S. attitude to
   "best technologies of both nations," 111, 112
   by CIA, 33, 188, 215, 234
   co-development proposed, 38–47, 51, 55, 61, 63, 93–95, 105–6, 110–16, 198
   Danforth-Weinberger exchange, 83–85
   FS-X as test of Japanese allegiance, 109, 111–12
   1989 Congressional report, 148
   "no-pressure pressure" approach, 36, 43, 45
   originally not linked to trade, 52–53
   Pentagon policy, 34–36, 61–63
   Senate battle, 145–50, 161, 164, 198–99
   Sullivan mission, 88–95, 107, 111, 153
   U.S. Embassy's role in support, 82
   U.S. opposition, xi–xii, 73–75, 94, 115–22, 136–37, 140, 181–219, 246, 249
   wooden mock-up of, 279, 281, 285, 286
   workshare for, 121–22, 125, 155, 158–59, 165, 209, 223, 231, 240, 244, 246, 256, 259
   Zero compared to, 15–17, 279
Fuji Heavy Industries, 90, 129, 285
Fujitsu Ltd., 58, 79, 212

Gaffney, Frank J., Jr., 214, 218, 220
"Gang of Four" (foreign commentators), 141–42
Garn, Jake, 100
Gast, Phil, 74, 89
Gates, Robert M., 225, 233, 236, 237
General Accounting Office (GAO), 18, 126, 217, 259, 268
   "burden-sharing" studies of, 26

description of, 20
 letter on FS-X to, 182–83
 on progress of FS-X program, 280
 technology-transfer report of, 20–27
General Dynamics Corp., 52, 100, 285
 FS-X contract won by, 123–24, 127–32
 FS-X proposal of, 61, 63–65, 77, 82–83,
  114, 118–20
 lobbying in Congress by, 254
 Mitsubishi agreement signed by, 173, 179,
  200
 Nagoya representatives of, 279
 share of production contract by, 219
 in technology transfer to Japan, 165
General Electric Co., 52
Gephardt, Richard, 141, 264
Germany, in Airbus Industries, xiv
Gibbons, Sam M., 18–20, 24
Gore, Albert, Jr., 183
Grassley, Charles, 275–76
Gray, C. Boyden, 273–75
Great Britain
 in Airbus Industries, xiv
 Harrier fighter of, 6
 Pentagon staff coverage of, 95
 U.S. co-production with, 21
Green, Michael J., 91, 104
Gwinn, Bruce, 212

Haberman, Clyde C., 57
Hamilton Standard (company), 14
Harbin, William, 258
Harrier (fighter), 6
Harris organization, 206
Hashimoto, Ryutaro, 208
Hawaii defense talks, 43–44, 52, 76, 111
Heinz, John H., III, 273
Heisei (reign-period), x–xii, 17, 281
Helms, Jesse, xi, 144, 145, 147, 150, 167,
  172–79, 182, 183, 199, 248, 249,
  252–55, 275
Hickam Field (Hawaii), 139
Hills, Carla, 180
Hirohito (Emperor of Japan), death of, ix–xi,
  192, 208–10
Honda automobiles, 146
Hong Kong, aerospace exports to, xiii
Honolulu Star-Bulletin, 139
Hoover, Herbert, 194
Horikoshi, Jiro, 11, 13, 15–17
Hossho (Japanese general), 65
House of Representatives, U.S., FS-X
  hearings by, 211–19, 255
 See also Congress, U.S.

Hudson's press guide, 147
Hughes Aircraft (company), 51–52, 153
Hull, Cordell, 19
Humphrey, Gordon, 254–55, 275
Hunter, Duncan, 100

Ignatius, David, 181
Iimura, Kazuo, 99
Ikle, Fred C., 102, 103, 163
International Civil Aviation Organization,
  xiii
International Security Agency (ISA), 28–29
Investor's Daily, 240
Iran, Japanese sales to, 282
Iran-Iraq war, 108, 110, 216
Isayama, Takeshi, 35–36, 129
Ishihara, Shintaro, 203, 206–8, 282
Ishikawajima Harima (company), 90, 129
Israel, fighter program of, 35, 72, 127
Italy
 Pentagon staff coverage of, 95
 U.S. co-production with, 21
Iwasaki, Yataro, 12–13

Jackson, Karl, 168–69, 196–201, 214, 233,
  240–41, 244, 255, 264
Jagger, Mick, 108
Japan
 aerospace exports to, xiii
 airports in, 48–50, 52, 145
 defense exports forbidden by, 40, 282
 defense spending in
  1% limit on, 42, 52, 62, 63, 68
  for R&D, 4, 153
 discrediting of critics of, 141
 dumping by, 52, 78–79, 146–47
 "economic invasion" of U.S. by, 204
 Emperor system in, ix–xi, 58
 marriage networks in, 81
 military toughness in, 4–5
 1980s military buildup by, 216
 1985 elections in, 61
 political corruption in, 123, 131–32, 263–
  64
 political institutions of, 216–17
 rigged economic system of, 139–42
 strategic importance of, 32
 trustworthiness and efficiency in, 50
 U.S. construction firms excluded from,
  145
 U.S. military equipment purchased by,
  68–69
 U.S. opening of (1854), 12, 167
 U.S. postwar occupation of, 4, 7, 96, 278

war renounced by, 7
  See also MITI
Japan Aviation Electronics Industry, Ltd.,
    282
"Japan bashing," 141–42, 167, 231
Japan Defense Agency (JDA)
  Boei-cho headquarters of, 88, 90, 118
  directors of, 33–35, 61, 158, 242
  FS-X specs set up by, 16
  MITI and, 5–6
  Technical Research and Development
      Institute of, 3, 4, 33, 65, 69, 75, 155
  Yamamoto as negotiator for, 137–38
Japan Economic Institute, 141
Japan Economic Journal, 215
Japanese-American relations
  Auer's belief in, 29–30
  Hawaii defense talks on, 43–44, 52, 76,
      111
  Japan and U.S. not allies, 41
  Japan as Americentric, 41
  Japan named unfair trading partner, 264
  Mutual Defense Assistance Office (MDO),
      41–42, 47, 48, 51, 60–61, 76, 80, 116
  1989 shift in, ix, 209
  trade barriers, 52, 58–59, 83, 264
  trade-defense link in, xv, 68–69, 71, 73–74
  trade deficit
    aerospace industry and, xiii
    amount of, xv, 19–20, 52, 59, 73, 79,
        139, 168, 191, 201, 229, 241
    electronic defense systems and, 138
    Mansfield on, 59
    voluntary restraints on Japanese auto
        imports, 83
  Weinberger on FS-X and, 109
Japanese-Americans in World War II, 146
Japanese Automobile Manufacturers
    Association, 146
Japanese character
  Narita airport as indication of, 49–50
  reality and background in, 54, 111, 165
  trustworthiness and efficiency in, 50
Japanese Communist Party, 30
Japan Self-Defense Forces
  Air
    Air Staff Office opposition to FS-X,
        156–58
    fighter planes, 5, 8, 10
    U.S. disparagement of, 88, 157
  Maritime
    staff college of, 29
    U.S. Navy cooperation with, 157
  as third-largest military in world, 30

  See also Japan Defense Agency (JDA)
Japan Times, 52
Jennings, Peter, 182
JF-210 (early name of FS-X), 126
Jiji wire service, 203–6
Johnson, Chalmers, 142
Joint development. *See* Co-development
Jopeline, Joseph, 127–28
JOVIAL (programming language), 222, 235

Kanamori, Masao, 109
Kanashige, Hiroshi, 203–6
Kanda, Kuniichi, 281–83
Kato, Koichi, 33–35, 37, 44, 61, 132
Kato, Ryozo, 241, 245
Kawara, Tsutomu, 158–59
Kawasaki Heavy Industries, 55, 67, 90, 129,
    131, 285
Kearns, Kevin
  background of, 48–50, 143–44, 147
  protégé of, 116–17
  as State Department fellow in Senate,
      143–44, 147–50, 167, 169, 171–73,
      175–79, 182–84, 206, 249, 250, 252,
      253, 260, 270
  in Tokyo Embassy, 51, 53, 55–57, 59–61,
      63–65, 69, 73, 76–78, 80–82, 85–86,
      95, 105, 111, 136
    FS-X airframe negotiations, 113, 115–
        20, 122
Keiretsu, 130
Kelly, Joseph E., 218
Kennedy, John F., 139, 208
Kennedy, Paul, *The Rise and Fall of the Great
    Powers*, 138
Kennedy, Robert, 208
Kimmitt, Robert M., 234, 245, 270
Kimura, Hideo, 96–98, 100–103, 156–58
Kissinger, Henry, 108, 175
Korea, third-generation Japanese from, 115
Korean War, 285
Kubrick, Stanley, *Dr. Strangelove*, 118
Kurihara, Yuko, 61–63, 80, 83, 99, 105,
      107–14, 123, 125, 126, 129, 131, 132,
      157, 222, 245
Kurokawa, Masaaki, 256–57
Kyodo News Service, 158, 192, 245

L-1011 jet, 124
Laboratory Three (Japan), 3–7, 15, 27, 33,
      67, 70, 75
Labor Department, U.S., 188, 195
LaFleur, Chris, 80–82, 115, 145
Laird, Melvin, 29

Lavi (fighter), 35, 72
Lawson, Eugene K., 188, 234
Leonard, Sugar Ray, 135
Leonard, William N., 14
Levin, Carl, 232
Levine, Mel, 249, 256, 264
Liberal Democratic Party (Japan), 61–62, 97, 182, 242
Libya, Rabta Gas Plant in, 254
Licensed Technology Assistance Agreement (LTAA), 165
Lockheed Corp., 64, 81, 124, 128, 131, 283
Los Angeles *Times*, 102
Lugar, Richard, 258, 260, 271, 273–75

McCormack, Robert C., 226–27, 233
McDonnell Douglas Corp., xiv, 38, 52, 81, 128, 188–89, 280, 282, 283, 285
  fighters licensed in Japan by, 5, 19, 70
  FS-X proposal by, 61, 63–65, 77, 82–83, 114, 124–27, 129
McEntee, Joan, 190, 220, 224–28, 233, 235–37, 280
McGaffigan, Ed, 144, 148, 150, 163, 171, 184, 252
McGrory, Mary, 173–74
Managed trade, 121
Mansfield, Mike, 27, 30, 40, 44, 94, 164, 165, 284
  his vision of Japan, 58–59, 85
  retirement of, 149, 247
Marlette, Doug, 176
Marshall, John, 271
Marshall Plan, 25
Massachusetts Institute of Technology (MIT), 6, 55, 67
Massey, Joseph, 167
Material Services Corp., 254
Matsumiya, Kiyoshi, 279–80
Matsunaga, Nobuo, 242, 243, 246–47
Meiji Emperor, 39
Meiji Restoration, 12–13, 16–17, 44
Mid-Term Defense Estimate, 37
Midway, U.S.S., 29–30, 101, 157
Minebea Co., 146
Minesweeping, 108
Mirage (fighter), 6
Mitchell, George J., 266–69
MITI (Ministry of International Trade and Industry)
  aerospace industry targeted by, 5–6, 19, 35, 68, 80, 110
  F-16 opposed by, 125, 129
  importance of, in Japan's rise, 5

  both military and civil policies set by, 218
  side letter repudiated by, 165
  in Toshiba affair, 99, 110
Mitsubishi Bank, 129–30
Mitsubishi Corp., 129–32
Mitsubishi Electric (company), 55, 90, 92, 129, 280, 282
Mitsubishi group
  history of, 11–13
  Miyazawa and, 80–81
Mitsubishi Heavy Industries, xi, 55, 130, 254, 285
  in FS-X consortium, 77, 90–92, 109, 115–16, 125, 129, 132, 156–57, 215, 245
  Nagoya celebration, 278–80
  General Dynamics agreement signed by, 173, 179, 200
  pre-World War II military aircraft of, 13. *See also* Zero
  U.S. fighters built by, 5
Mitsui group, 15, 99, 130
Miyazawa, Kiichi, 61–62, 80–82, 93, 131–32, 263–64, 277
Moakley, Joe, 265
Mori, Shigehiro, 105
Morita, Akio, 206–8
Mosbacher, Georgette, 193
Mosbacher, Robert A., 170, 179, 190
  background of, 193–94
  FS-X and, 194–96, 201–2, 220, 224, 227–28, 234, 238–40, 242, 249, 251, 255
MOUs (memorandums of understanding), 23, 118, 121, 148, 154
  on FS-X
    Bush's decision, 237–43, 246–48, 251, 256
    Congressional hearings and votes on, 249–77
    final text, 164–65
    final text as unclear, 209, 218–20, 223, 225
    informing of Congress, 166–67, 182, 238, 247–49
    negotiations, 148–60, 196–97
    refused to Maureen Smith, 168–69, 197
    signed by Mansfield, 164, 165
    side letters to, 165, 231
Moynihan, Daniel Patrick, 83
Mullins, Janet G., 248
Mutual Defense Assistance Office (MDO), 39, 41–42, 47, 48, 51, 60–61, 76, 80, 116
Mutual Security Treaty (1960), 41, 44

Nagoya (Japan), 157, 278–80, 285
Nakasone, Yasuhiro, 34, 44, 52, 53, 61–63,
    68, 78, 79, 99–100, 105, 107–8, 113,
    131–32, 182, 216, 263
Narita airport (Tokyo), 49–50
NASA (National Aeronautics and Space
    Administration), 195, 226
National Press Club, 192
National Security Council (NSC)
    FS-X and, 197–201, 214, 215, 223, 225–
        27, 229, 230, 233–37
    subgroups of, 199–200
NATO (North Atlantic Treaty Organization)
    co-development with, 38–39
    U.S. co-production with, 21
NEC Corp., 282
Newsweek, 180
New York *Times*, 179, 191, 197, 200–201,
    241–42, 264
NEXIS, 253
Nicolson, Harold, 39
Nihon Keizai Shimbun, 10
Nippon Telegraph and Telephone
    (company), 59
Nirenberg, Darryl D., 176–78
Nishihiro, Seiki, 44–46, 65–67, 71, 73–74,
    76–77, 85, 88, 105–7, 113–15, 124,
    125, 131, 132, 152, 190, 192, 222,
    243–45, 263, 280
Nissho Iwai (company), 125, 129
Nixon, Richard M., 193
Nixon Doctrine, 29
Nokyo, 114
Nomura Securities, 256
Noriega, Manuel, 31
North, Oliver, 30
Northwest Airlines, 53
Nunn, Sam, 81

Office of Defense Policy, 28
Office of Science and Technology Policy,
    195, 226, 234
Ogawa, Ichiro, 278
Olmer, Lionel, 167, 168
Omnibus Trade Bill (1988), 241
Omura, Hitoshi, 78, 222
Osaka (Japan), 145
Oxford University, 108–9
Ozawa, Ichiro, 208

Pacific Mail Steamship Co., 12–13
Panavia consortium, 51, 77
Patriot missile, 55–56, 283
Patterson, Torkel, 198, 199, 241, 245, 264

Pearl Harbor attack (1941), 5
Pell, Claiborne, 174, 177, 248, 255
Pentagon
    construction of, 28
    See also Defense Department, U.S.
Pentagon Papers, The, 29
Perry, Matthew Calbraith, 12, 167
Plaza Accords (1985), 59
Policy Coordinating Committee (PCC),
    199–200
Political merchants *(seisbo)*, 12–13, 15, 17
Porter, Roger, 272
Potomac (Maryland), 135–36
Presidential Management Interns, 116
Pressler, Larry, 255
Prestowitz, Clyde V., Jr., 136–42, 167–69,
    211, 242, 246, 248
    background of, 136
    Congressional testimony by, 212–14, 230–
        31, 245
    Trading Places, 76, 135, 136, 141, 161,
        165, 197, 199, 200, 209, 215, 231
    Washington *Post* article of, 181–83, 192,
        197–98, 200
Program Analysis and Evaluation, 69
Programming, source codes in, 221–23,
    234–35, 238, 240, 245, 247–48

Quayle, Dan, 269

Radar, 8, 9, 52, 92, 149, 152, 280, 282
Rand Corp., 22
Rape, 4
Reagan, Ronald, xi, xv, 31, 32, 52, 62, 78,
    98
    free trade encouraged by, 121, 142, 168,
        213
Recruit Cosmos scandal, 132, 246
Refale program, 6
Reischauer, Edwin O., 40, 217
Reuters News Service, 171
Richards, John, 167, 169–70, 200, 201, 227,
    280, 284
Richardson, Craig, 116–20, 122, 136–38,
    150, 152, 161, 169, 185–86, 200, 224,
    225
River Falls (Maryland), 136
Rockefeller, Jay, 260
Roosevelt, Franklin Delano, 262
Rowen, Hobart, 141
Rubinstein, Gregg A., 23–27, 37–43, 46, 48,
    50–51, 53, 54, 60, 64, 112, 190, 215
Rudd, Glenn, 120–22, 138, 149, 151–55,
    159–61, 163, 190, 198, 200

background of, 151–52
Rudman, Warren, 275

Saddam Hussein, 284
Sampson, Anthony, 123
Samuels, Richard, 6, 110
Sanford, Terry, 177
Schwab, Susan, 145
Schwarzenegger, Arnold, 135
Scott, John D., 42
Scowcroft, Brent, 184, 201, 242, 244
Seattle (Washington), xiv
Security Consultative Group (SSC), 44, 52
Semiconductors, 58, 79, 137, 140, 212
Semiconductor Trade Agreement, side letter
    to, 165
Senate, U.S.
    Armed Services Committee, 144, 148,
        179–80, 229–33, 253
    Foreign Relations Committee
        as annex of State Department, 252
        Baker's confirmation hearing, 172–79
        Kearns as fellow with, 153–44, 147–50,
            167, 169, 171–73, 175–79, 182–84,
            206, 249, 250, 252, 253, 260, 270
        leaked documents, 203–6
        FS-X battle in, 145–50, 161, 164, 198–99
    See also Congress, U.S.
Sevier, Sam, 223
Shields, Brooke, x
Shiina, Moroo, 258
Showa (reign-period), x, xi
Shriver, R. Sargent, 135
Shultz, George, 172–73, 175
Side letters, 165, 231
Sigur, Gaston, 186–87, 191, 200, 234, 284
Smith, Charles, 250, 252–54, 256, 257, 260,
    270, 274, 277
Smith, Hedrick, 173
Smith, Maureen, 168, 195–97, 200, 226, 228
Smith, Michael B., 81–82, 145–46, 167
Solarz, Stephen, 262–65
Solomon, Gerald, 265
Sone, Eki, 96–97
Sony Corp., 206
Sophia University, 96
Source codes, 221–23, 234–35, 238, 240,
    245, 247–48
Soviet Union
    COCOM's role and, 101, 258
    as Evil Empire, 216
    Japan as more dangerous than, 196
    Japanese machine tools sold to (Toshiba

affair), 79, 96, 98–103, 107–10, 181,
    203, 246
    in leaked Senate document, 204
    submarines of, 98
    See also Cold War
Spain, in Airbus Industries, xiv
Sparr, Deborah, 102
Spence, Craig J., 258
"Spin-ons," 15
Standardization, co-production and, 25
Star Wars, 34, 42, 52, 62, 63, 68, 177–78,
    214, 218, 234
State Department, U.S.
    co-production authorized by, 23
    fellowships of, 143
    Helms's remarks about, 175
    narrow view toward Japan by, 284
    Richardson's criticism of, 116–17
Structural Impediments Initiative, 264
Submarines
    Soviet, 98, 101–2, 107
    U.S., 100
Sullivan, Gerald, 88–95, 107, 111, 153, 214
Sumitomo Metal Industries, 15
Summit Communications, Inc., 273
Sununu, John, 238, 255, 273, 275
Suzuki, Zenko, 216
Sweden, fighter program of, 72
Switzerland, fighter program of, 127
Systems integration, 189–90, 246, 285

T-4 trainer, 67–68, 73
T-46A trainer, 67–68
Tachikawa (Japan), 3–4
Taiwan, aerospace exports to, xiii
Takeshita, Noboru, 171, 182, 183–85, 190–
    92, 204, 205, 243, 246
Talmadge, Herman, 175
Tamura, Hajime, 99
Tamura, Hideaki, 156, 158
Tanaka, H. William, 146
Tanaka, Kakuei, 124, 131
Taylor, Maxwell, 139
Tazawa, Kichiro, 242, 246
Technology, derived and nonderived, 149,
    247
Technology transfer, 20–27
    Congressional authority to restrict, 272
    DTSA and, 162–63
    in FS-X agreement, 165, 217, 235
        Carlucci on, 198
        GAO on lack of flow-out to U.S., 280
        New York Times on, 200–201

1983 U.S.-Japanese agreement on, 154, 217
opposed by Labor and Energy, 188
in proposed airframe agreement, 119
two-way, 40–41, 140
Telecommunications, 59, 84, 168
Texas Instruments, Inc., 153, 282
Thailand, airport in, 50
Thompson, E. P., 109
Time magazine, ix, 194
Tokyo (Japan)
Hotel Okura in, 108
Narita airport in, 49–50
prices in, 57
U.S. Embassy in, 57–58, 115, 117, 284
See also Kearns, Kevin
Tokyo Business Today, 165, 199
Tokyo Marine and Fire Insurance, 131
Tokyo Shimbun, 43
Toray Industries, 9, 15
Tornado fighter, 51, 78
Toshiba affair, machine tools sold to Soviet in, 79, 96, 98–103, 107–10, 181, 203, 246
Tower, John G., 179–80, 190, 193, 195, 228, 237, 238
Toyota Motor Corp., 285
Trade Estimate Report, 83
Traficant, James, Jr., 264
Treasury Department, U.S., 195
Triplett, William, 144–48, 172, 176, 177, 195, 203, 205–6, 249
Truman, Harry, 58
Tsutsui, Ryozo, 3, 7–11, 15–17, 27, 33, 46, 53, 65–66, 91, 131, 280
in 1986 Pentagon meetings, 66–76, 88, 105, 149
promoted to director of TRDI, 155–56
Sullivan mission and, 92–93
Tyler, John Tim, 69, 72, 119–21, 152, 160–64, 169–70, 226, 247, 254

U.S. Trade Representative (USTR), 79, 81, 180, 195, 238
United States
defense R&D spending in, 4, 153
at end of Cold War, x–xi
inability to negotiate by, 120–21
Japanese insurance companies as a central bank of, 138
Japanese investments in, 79
1987 stock crash in, 138
short-term security vs. long-term production in, 138

See also Aerospace industry; Japanese-American relations
United Technologies Pratt & Whitney plant, 52
Uno, Sosuke, 165, 191, 209

Van Wolferen, Karel, 48, 81, 142
Versailles Treaty, 39
Vietnam War, 31, 139
Vining, Elizabeth, x
Vogel, Ezra F., 208
Vought 143 fighter, 14

Wako Koeki Co., 99
Wallop, Malcolm, 229–31
Wall Street Journal, The, 95, 182, 194, 242
Warsaw Pact, 25
Washington *Post*, 59, 100, 102, 137, 141, 179, 181–82, 192, 197–98, 206, 224, 230, 237, 240, 248, 269
Washington *Times*, 258
Weinberger, Caspar W., 28, 30–32, 36, 98, 99, 214
FS-X and, 74, 78, 103, 127
Kato's visit to, 33–35
Kurihara visit, 62–63
letters exchange with Danforth, 83–85
Weinberger's Tokyo visits, 52–53, 105, 107–12
resignation of, 158, 244
Welch, Larry, 238
Westinghouse Electric Corp., 51, 153, 281
Weyrich, Paul, 195
Wheaton, David, 64–65, 130
White House situation room, 233
Willkie, Wendell, II, 220
Wilmer, Cutler & Pickering, 273
Wince, Deborah, 226, 234
Workshare concept, 121–22, 125, 155, 158–59, 165, 209, 223, 231, 240, 244, 246, 256, 259
Wright, Jim, 248
Wright, Tim, 224

Yaita (admiral), 156–57
Yamamoto, Masaji, 137–38, 153–55, 197
Yeutter, Clayton K., 79, 82
Yokosuka (Japan), 29, 96, 97, 101
Yomiuri Shimbun, 101, 102
York, Alvin Cullum, 87–90, 219, 284

Zenith Electronics Corp., 101
Zero (fighter plane), xi, 5, 11, 13–15, 207, 278